Interviewing
strategy, techniques, and tactics

THE DORSEY SERIES IN SOCIOLOGY

Editor ROBIN M. WILLIAMS, JR. *Cornell University*

Interviewing

strategy, techniques, and tactics

RAYMOND L. GORDEN, Ph.D.

Professor in Cross-Cultural Research
Department of Sociology-Anthropology
Antioch College

1969

The Dorsey Press   Homewood, Illinois   60430
Irwin-Dorsey International   London, England   WC2H 9NJ
Irwin-Dorsey Limited   Georgetown, Ontario   L7G 4B3

First Printing, April, 1969

Second Printing, June, 1970

Third Printing, April, 1971

Fourth Printing, February, 1972

Fifth Printing, December, 1972

Sixth Printing, October, 1973

Seventh Printing, May, 1974

Library of Congress Catalog Card No. 69-19984

Printed in the United States of America

To Charlotte, Gregory, and Karen

Preface

This book presents a panorama of the basic processes often involved when one human being attempts to obtain valid and reliable information from another. The intent is to increase sensitivity to a broad spectrum of communication problems, to present a wide assortment of interviewing tools, and to introduce a frame of reference useful in bringing the tools to bear on these problems.

Although the title of this book does not include the word questionnaire, most of the concepts presented either suggest criteria for choosing between the interview and the questionnaire, or provide a guide to the development, construction, and testing of questionnaires. Chapter 2 includes a section on the relative values of the questionnaire versus the interview. In general, the questionnaire is viewed as an extension of the more basic method of interviewing.

We intentionally deal with the broad range of strategies, techniques, and tactics that should be considered in any interviewing project, even though the responsibility for this full range of problems is often not assumed by a person who bears the title of "interviewer." In this sense not all interviewing is done by interviewers, but may be done by research directors, supervisors, or consultants.

Only *planners* and *supervisors* of research will find all phases of this book directly relevant to them, since they assume responsibility for the total interviewing process. This group would include actual or potential research directors, supervisors of interviewers in large data-collection projects, the member of a small research team, the lone-wolf researcher, and serious students of the social sciences.

The *specialized interviewer* with responsibility for a more restricted portion of the total information-gathering process will find only certain portions of this book to be directly relevant. This group includes the interviewers hired by large-scale polling, market-research, and motivation-research organizations. Generally, these interviewers do not make any of the strategy decisions and have most of the techniques and tactics specified for them in advance.

There is, however, a larger number of people whose daily professional functions require them to interview even though they may not call themselves "interviewers." These *auxiliary interviewers* include teachers, counselors, nurses, doctors, clergy, social workers, law enforcement officers, and managers and supervisors in business and industry. The ideas presented in this book should assist this group since they need to build a high degree of autonomy and self-direction.

Of course, anyone responsible for training these auxiliary interviewers should be aware of the full spectrum of interviewing problems and tools in order to maximize the auxiliary interviewers' effectiveness within the limitations of a particular institutional framework. It is often considered unnecessary for these people to have any systematic training in interviewing since "they just talk to people and ask a few questions." We sincerely hope that our impression is correct that there is a growing realization of the value of some specific training to upgrade the skills and insights of these auxiliary interviewers.

Portions of this book are directly relevant to all types of interviewers, since there is a minimal core area in which all are required to make decisions and exercise skill and insights.

Other parts are indirectly relevant to all readers interested in interviewing, even though the ideas may deal with several phases and types of interviewing for which a particular reader may not be directly responsible. This indirectly relevant material may be useful in several ways. First, it can raise morale on large projects by giving the interviewer a keener appreciation of what goes into the strategy planning and the structuring of an excellent interview schedule and by showing him the vital importance of his particular responsibility to the success of the total project. Second, a more inclusive view facilitates communication among all the members of the research enterprise. Third, through increased insight into the real limitations placed upon interviewing within certain settings, the interviewer can avoid undue frustration from trying to achieve the impossible; he can make more valid interpretations of the results in view of these limitations, and suggest possible tactics and techniques to compensate for these restrictions. Finally, in some cases the interviewer will be led to discover that some of the traditionally accepted limitations are not functionally necessary and can be changed to improve the validity of the information received.

In the interests of maintaining a holistic overview of interviewing, we have omitted detailed treatments of some of the refinements and important housekeeping chores associated with some types of interviewing; but we feel that this loss is more than compensated by maintaining a broad perspective while ·demonstrating the practical relevance of the key concepts.

In mentioning the use of the tape recorder at several points throughout this book, we do not intend to give the impression that most interviewing should be done with a tape recorder. However, we do feel strongly that the tape recorder is of inestimable value in the process of learning to interview. Most of the examples given in this book would not have been possible if there had not been a wide variety of tape-recorded interviews.

This book is addressed to anyone who wants to share an attempt to specify and systematize those basic problems that have to be dealt with in a variety of interviewing projects and to present an array of strategies, techniques, and tactics for attacking these problems. In this broader sense we address all students of interviewing.

I gratefully acknowledge the inspiration and encouragement given along the way by John W. Bennet, Everett C. Hughes, David Riesman, and Everett Wilson. Stephen A. Richardson helped during the early formulation and criticism of the first rough draft. Outstanding among the several people who quietly labored on various stages of production was Rebecca Mellinger, who patiently read and corrected the prefinal draft. I am particularly indebted to my wife, Charlotte Gilson Gorden, who mercilessly, but diplomatically, cut hundreds of pages of rough draft, revised some of the author's stylistic peculiarities, read proof, and supervised the production of the final draft of the manuscript.

Among the groups of persons who had a vital place in the writer's experiences leading to the writing of this book should be mentioned the interviewers of the Disaster Study Team at the National Opinion Research Center, and the many interviewers who were subjected to the author's attempt to train and evaluate their performance for various organizations in Grand Forks, North Dakota; Chicago, Illinois; Dayton, Ohio; and Bogota, Colombia. The most important group has been the students at Antioch College, who over a period of six years showed a keen interest in learning to interview and in applying what they learned on their various jobs in the Cooperative Program. They helped demonstrate to the writer the practical effectiveness of a broad but systematic approach to interviewer training.

Yellow Springs, Ohio R. L. G.
March, 1969

Table of contents

1
The uses of interviewing

The demand for scientific approaches to human problems is growing rapidly. This demand results from the accelerating rate of social change coupled with the growing acceptance and success of applying the basic canons of scientific method to studies of human behavior.

This growing demand is reflected in more rigorous methodology. The cry "How do you know?" frequently enters discussions of both pure and applied studies of human behavior. In many studies this question is so central to the purpose and so uppermost in the consciousness of the investigators that no one need utter it aloud.

TRENDS IN INTERVIEWING

Accompanying this increasing consciousness of the need for greater validity and reliability in methodology is an increase in the methodological difficulty intrinsic to the types of problems being posed. For example, social anthropology has seen a shift from the description of external environment, artifacts and behavioral patterns to analysis of the subjective meaning of these for the members of the culture. Thus there has been increasing emphasis on values, world-view, beliefs, expectations, and socialization of the child.

In social psychology there has been a gradual shift in empirical

1

studies from observation of external forms of behavior, where high reliability is relatively easy to obtain, to more theoretically meaningful categories of human phenomena that tend to have greater predictive value but which present more difficult problems of data gathering.[1]

In sociology there has been an increasing shift of emphasis from the use of easily observable facts such as sex, race, and residential location to more meaningful but less obvious categories such as social distance, expectations, cognitive dissonance, attitude, definition of the situation, latent and operative values, channels of influence and decision making. There has also been a historical shift in emphasis from static descriptions of public opinion or social class, for example, to the more dynamic problems of the formation and function of public opinion and social stratification systems. There has also been a historical shift away from reliance on the use of data already collected for some official or practical purpose toward the collection of information more directly relevant to the theoretical or practical requirements of the specific problem at hand. These general trends in the basic behavioral sciences of social anthropology, social psychology and sociology are reflected in trends which follow in applied areas such as industrial relations, race relations, family relations, mental health, and education.

This increasing demand for methodological sophistication has two complementary facets. First is the data-analysis aspect which includes research design, theoretical models, sampling, statistical methods and electronic data processing. Although this phase of the answer to "How do you know?" is vital, it cannot be emphasized to the exclusion of the second aspect which concerns data-gathering methodology.

It is clear that no amount of refinement in data analysis can counteract the effects of faulty data-collection methods that provide raw information which is false, distorted, or incomplete. Nevertheless, there is still a tendency for the advances in data-gathering methodology to lag behind those in data analysis. This can be seen in the content of contemporary examinations on methodology for the doctorate degree in anthropology, sociology and psychology; these

1/ For example see Roger W. Heyns and Ronald Lippitt, "Systematic Observation Techniques," in Gardner Lindzey (ed.), *Handbook of Social Psychology*, Vol. I. (Cambridge: Addison-Wesley Publishing Co., 1954).

are mainly devoted to methods of analysis rather than collection of data. This same imbalance is seen in the title of the papers presented in the methodology section of professional meetings of social scientists.

Considerable effort has been made over the past two decades to improve data-gathering methods. There have been substantial advances in knowledge about interviewing based upon experimental studies. However, much of this has not yet been integrated into a general theoretical framework, nor has it been put into a form to be translated into applied skills in interviewing. Thus, along with the steady growth in the use of interviewing and the increased knowledge about the interviewing process, there appears to be a widening gap between what is known and what is applied in interviewing.

The writer's experience in consulting on data-gathering problems and in training interviewers has suggested several obstacles to closing this gap. First, there is an unfortunate tendency to consider data gathering as a lower status activity than data analysis or theorizing about the data. Second, large research organizations or consultants often discover that there is a demand for pseudoscientific "findings" that a client needs either to justify decisions already made or to transfer the blame for a decision to the "independent research organization." In either case, there is no need for data-gathering methods which probe deeply into social reality.

Another barrier to the actual application of the best data-gathering methods is the fact that it often costs more in time or money to collect valid data than it does to collect invalid data. Of course, this is a false economy if any real decisions are to be based on the data. This conflict between the realities of collecting valid information and the demands of economy can result in irrational behavior by otherwise intelligent people. For example, the writer was asked to design a study of certain aspects of a community to help decide future directions of the local public school system. An interesting dilemma developed when the consultant was told that the valid but more time-consuming methods could not be used because "the information must be in the hands of the Citizens' Committee on Curriculum and Physical Plant before February 15 so they can use it to make some important decisions before the meeting of the Finance Committee in March." In essence, the argument was that since the information was so vitally important, they had no time to be concerned with its accuracy.

A third and perhaps the most significant factor contributing to this lag between what is known and what is applied in interviewing is the shortage of qualified interviewers. Often a research organization or project is aware that the methods they are using are not the most desirable, but they are the best second choice in view of the short supply of well trained interviewers. If an organization were to devote its energies to convincing the client of the values of high quality interviewing, they might then only be embarrassed by not being able to find qualified personnel to do the interviewing or to train others to do it well.

This shortage of skilled interviewers is felt not only by research organizations hiring specialized interviewers, but also by institutions whose employees need interviewing as an auxiliary skill. It is impossible to estimate the social cost of ineffective interviewing when important decisions in practically all types of institutions depend at some point upon one human being obtaining valid information from another.

RELIABILITY AND VALIDITY

The central aim of any data-gathering methodology is to improve both the reliability and validity of the information obtained. By *reliability* we mean the degree to which a given observation or measurement could be repeated by an independent observer with the same result. By *validity* we mean the extent to which we are able to observe or measure that which we intend to observe or measure. To take either the reliability or validity of our observations for granted is to be innocent of any scientific sophistication. Yet, to assume that scientific knowledge cannot be advanced until we have arrived at perfect reliability and validity in all our observations is to stop all pioneer efforts as well as many highly advanced projects. We must be content with improving reliability and validity or with measuring shortcomings in each to avoid unwarranted generalizations or distorted interpretations of the information we receive and analyze.

We are all familiar with reliability and the lack of reliability in some types of observations. The same person making the same observation at different times may obtain a qualitative or quantitative difference in results. Different persons observing the same object at the same or different times may also obtain different results. The significance of a particular degree of reliability may be measured statistically and in terms of the amount of reliability demanded by the particular purpose we are trying to achieve.

The lack of perfect validity is more difficult to demonstrate, explain or measure than is the lack of perfect reliability. To understand the concept of validity is to realize that many observations are *indirect* in the sense that we cannot directly grasp and measure the object or variable in which we are interested; we must be content with defining some index, indicator, or indicant of the presence of the object we are observing.

In the social sciences there is a great variation in the directness of the observations we need to make. We sometimes make observations which are so direct that there is no problem in establishing the validity of the measurement. For example, we might simply count the number of people in a certain precinct who voted for a certain presidential candidate. This is a direct measurement of a socially significant act. But if we want to measure the strength of a person's attitude, we must use an indirect technique which depends upon the effect of a person's attitude upon his perception (as in a thematic perception test), upon his reasoning (as in a syllogistic reasoning test), upon his memory (as in an association test), or upon his verbal statements (as in a Guttman attitude scale). Insofar as all of these are indirect measures of the same attitude, they will correlate with each other.

Although reliability and validity can be clearly defined as distinct variables which do not necessarily come as a unit, they both depend upon and are influenced by four aspects in any act of observation. These aspects include the nature of the *object*, the nature or state of the *observer*, the *concepts* which guide the observation, and the *methods* used by the observer. Without presenting a general epistemological treatment of these aspects of knowing, let us simply demonstrate that in interviewing as a form of observation, all of these aspects come into play in posing problems of reliability and validity.

In interviewing, different *objects* of observation offer different problems of reliability and validity. As we have already pointed out, objects may vary in the degree of directness of the observation which must be used. Also, the object of observation may vary considerably in the degree or duration of its stability. For example, we may be interested in a stable phenomenon such as a person's public opinion on the desirability of monogamy, a less stable thing such as his preference for a presidential candidate, or something as fleeting as a person's thoughts which lead him to run from a theater building in panic.

The object may also vary in its complexity. For example, information on a family may vary from the number of children in a nuclear family to the pattern of mutual obligations felt between members of an extended family. All of these variations in the potential objects of investigation offer different problems in reliability and validity. Here, we intend no systematic classification of objects of observation. We merely wish to point out that in interviewing *the nature of the object to be observed* translates into *the type of information desired;* this is the starting point for any decisions about methods needed to maximize the relevance, validity and reliability of the data.

The nature or state of the *observer* in the interview has been demonstrated by many studies to be a source of both unreliability and invalidity. For example, the interviewer may have a strong emotional bias which distorts the results by actually affecting what the respondent will tell or withhold from the interviewer, by affecting the interviewer's interpretation of what is said, by distorting his memory of what is said, or by determining the selection of what to record. Furthermore, an interviewer completely free of internal biases of any kind may bias the responses because of the respondent's perception (right or wrong) of him and the subsequent relationship between interviewer and respondent. Obviously, these considerations would lower the validity of the information obtained and generally would lower the amount of agreement between observers.

The *concepts* brought to bear on the problem of the interview and the methods used by the interviewer can be conceived as vital links between the observer, the observed and the purpose of the observation. If the general purpose of the interview is unclear, the intent and meaning of specific questions will be ambiguous, and different interpretations of the same question will be made by different interviewers and respondents. The concepts need to be sharpened to perform several vital functions. They designate the general nature and purpose of the interview. They delineate between the relevant and the irrelevant question or answer. They define specific objects, categories or variables by providing operational indices for their identification. The validity can be low not only because the indices are so vague that they are not clearly connectable to the reality they intend to indicate, but also because it is possible to have beautifully clear concepts with precise operational indices which are still invalid if these indices do not in fact indicate or accurately reflect anything in reality. This may be the case where concepts are hastily constructed without being inductively derived from observation or where the premises from which they have been deduced with impeccable logic have not been inductively derived or verified. Concepts vary not only in their logical clarity and degree of empirical base but also in their level of abstraction which is the amount of inference needed to bridge the gap between the definition and the concrete observable indices. The more inference required, the greater the precautions needed to avoid error in either the inductive or deductive processes involved.

The *method* used in any particular interviewing problem should be conceived broadly to include anything that can be done to obtain information relevant to the problem at hand. This encompasses anything that influences the relationship between the concepts (including the purpose), the observer and the observed.

This whole book is an attempt to share experience, insight and ideas on increasing the validity and reliability of information gathered through interviewing. We will begin by showing the similarities and differences between interviewing and ordinary conversation so that the reader may retain some of the basic skills while discarding some of the limiting habits built up in his conversational experience. Then we relate basic styles of interviewing to the basic objectives of discovery and measurement. The conceptual heart of the book is a theoretical frame of reference defining eight major facilitators and eight major inhibitors of valid communication in the interview. The major portion of the book presents a variety of strategies, techniques, and tactics as tools at the interviewer's disposal to minimize the inhibitors and to maximize the facilitators of the flow of relevant and accurate information in the interview. Since we do not merely intend to discuss interviewing but also want to help improve interviewing, we have presented a procedure for developing the skills necessary to put the concepts into practice.

ILLUSTRATIVE INTERVIEWING PROBLEMS

Rather than rush on anxiously to the concepts and tools of interviewing, let us pause for a moment to observe some concrete examples of typical errors made in different interviewing situations.

These cases show that success in many different fields may depend upon one's ability to obtain complete and accurate information from another person. Much of the art of human relations lies in the skills of creative, sympathetic listening and artful probing beneath the usual superficial level of communication. To help break down the stereotype of the interviewer as a housewife who knocks on a random sample of doors to obtain responses on public opinion or buyer motivation, we offer the following examples of a range of interviewing situations in which the person asking the questions may or may not think of himself as an interviewer.

In each of these seven cases consider the purpose of the interview, its setting, the nature of the interviewer and the respondent, and then try to empathize with the respondent to determine when he might be unwilling or unable to give the information sought by the interviewer in view of the methods used. The discussions which follow each case are intentionally short and nontechnical since they are aimed at illustrating some of the typical problems in interviewing which transcend particular interviewing purposes and settings.

Situation 1. A settlement house social worker in the Puerto Rican area of New York City is collecting life histories of delinquents and pre-delinquents to determine how peer groups, parents and cultural conflict influence attitudes in the teenager, leading him to perform illegal acts. In the portion of the interview reported here the interviewer is probing the respondent's attitudes toward the New York police. The social worker is a 40-year-old man and the respondent is a 15-year-old Puerto Rican boy. The respondent can speak Spanish more fluently than English, but insists upon being interviewed in English although the social worker is fluent in Spanish.[2]

I: Manuel, you know I have been working here at Washington Center for years and I am interested in how so many in this area get in trouble with the law. I'm not interested in blaming anyone, but want to know how these situations develop from your point of view. Could you tell me how you first got into trouble with the police?

R: The first time was when we were fighting the gang on 129th street. The cops came and grabbed three of us and all the others got away.

I: What was the fight about?

R: This gang, the Eagles, were rumbling about us coming in on their territory, but it wasn't true. They said they were going to beat us up the next time they saw us. That was about two weeks before the big fight.

I: I see, and what were you doing in the meantime?

R: What else? We started packing some weapons to defend ourselves. I had a blackjack and a knife. I heard that one of the Eagles had a gun he made.

2/ The interviewer is designated by *"I"* and the respondent by *"R."*

I: Why didn't you call the police instead of trying to protect yourselves with knives?

R: The police would not believe us. They would just tell you to go along and peddle your papers. They are just a big bunch of crooks looking for an easy buck, besides how could they protect us, even if they were interested?

I: You don't feel that the police are interested in protecting you?

R: No!

I: Where did you get that idea?

R: I knew that all the time.

I: Did your pals in the gang tell you this?

R: I have always hated the cops for good reason.

I: Do your parents feel the same way about the police?

R: I don't know how they feel.

I: How long have you been in New York?

R: We left Puerto Rico in June, 1965, and came here.

I: You say that you have always disliked the police?

R: Yes, always!

I: Then you didn't get this idea about the police from your friends or from your family?

R: No.

I: I see, whose idea was it to start carrying knives?

At this point the interviewer shifts the discussion to how the gang member decides what kind of weapon to carry. The interview lasted over two hours and the above portion of the interview involves a basic communication problem which the interviewer seems to have no tactics for solving. This same problem recurred throughout the interview.

Discussion. If we remember that this interview is trying to determine the effect of peer groups, parents and cultural conflicts in forming attitudes leading to delinquency, it is clear that the interview was not successful. One of the basic attitudes often found in the delinquent is that the police are "crooks." There is hostility toward the police which is often reciprocated. Yet according to the delinquent's testimony, he had not obtained this attitude from anybody. To him it seemed to be a self-evident truth.

One basic problem here is that the interviewer assumes that the respondent will be conscious of the source of his attitudes; therefore, he asks for a direct report by the respondent. But the source of a person's attitudes is often unknown to the person himself. To obtain this information accurately it would be necessary for the interviewer to ask the respondent to begin with a detailed account of his attitude toward police in Puerto Rico. If "the Puerto Rican police were different," the interviewer could begin unraveling the respondent's experiences before his arrival in New York. He might discover when the delinquent had first heard about the New York police. To insure validity, the information should be a natural part of an account of the respondent's total ego-involved experience pattern. Thus, by encouraging the respondent to verbally re-live his first contacts with the New York police, relevant information might be obtained so that the interviewer, rather than the respondent, could judge the source of the attitude. Sometimes in such an interview the respondent himself becomes aware of the sources of his attitudes for the first time.

Situation 2. A social scientist has been hired as a consultant to study what effects a profit-sharing plan in a manufacturing company has upon morale in the plant. Some of the employees do not own stock, others own one share which was deducted from their first month's pay check, and others have purchased additional shares in response to company drives. Those with only one share have purchased it after they had indicated in their job application that they would like to participate in the profit-sharing plan to the extent of one share. Interviewers were assigned to interview a random sample of the 1600 workers in the plant. The interviewers were to discover how long each respondent had been employed at the plant and how much stock he owned. Then they asked him a series of questions to measure his morale level.

I: How long have you worked for Morris Johnson Co.?

R: It's been almost three years now.

I: Has it been nearer to three than two years?

R: Yes.

I: Have you purchased stock in the company to participate in the profit-sharing plan?

R: No.

I: Now, I have a series of questions here asking for your opinion of Morris Johnson Co. as a place to work.

R: Okay, let's hear them!

I: We assume that you will feel free to give your frank opinion on these questions. That is why the interviewing is being done by someone from the outside rather than by management or other plant personnel who might know you and have some axe to grind.

R: I don't care, I'd tell the boss how I feel. But I know what you mean. Some people are timid.

I: Right. . . .

The interviewer goes on to ask the ten morale questions which takes approximately a half hour since this respondent seems willing to volunteer full information. However, after the first 25 of 100 interviews were completed it was discovered that a basic communication barrier was operating and seriously distorting a portion of the information.

Discussion. Amazing as it seems, employees are often unable to report accurately whether or not they own stock in the company where they are employed. If the respondent owns only one share, deducted from his first paycheck three years ago, he may not recall the fact, particularly if the method of paying dividends is such that he is not clearly reminded of his stock ownership. A study by Moore, for example, showed that only 50% of the employees in a British company could accurately report whether or not they owned stock in the company.[3]

Situation 3. A high school teacher is interviewing the students of her home room class to obtain a health record. Since this is the freshman class, the school does not have any previous record. The state law requires vaccination for smallpox before entering elementary school. In addition, the health record must indicate when the child had any communicable diseases as well as when he had been immunized. The teacher interviews each student privately.

I: We must get a medical record of each student when he comes to Bryan High School. There are a few questions we need to ask. Have you missed any school in the last year because of illness?

R: No, except for a cough one time; I missed two days.

I: Uh huh. Have you ever been vaccinated for smallpox?

R: Yes, I guess everybody has!

I: Have you ever had chicken pox?

R: No.

I: Have you ever had whooping cough?

R: No.

I: Measles?

R: No.

I: Did you have a chest x-ray in the last year?

R: Yes!

I: Did you have a tuberculin test in the last year? That's where they put a little scratch on your arm and a little patch over it for a few days.

R: No.

I: Did you have all three of your polio shots?

3/ B. V. Moore, "The Interview in Industrial Research," *Social Forces,* Vol. 7 (1929), pp. 445-52.

R: Yes.

I: Has any of your family been in the mental hospital?

R: No.

I: Will you usually bring your lunch, eat in the school cafeteria, or go home for lunch?

R: I'll bring my lunch.

I: That's all, thank you.

In view of the techniques and tactics used for obtaining the medical history in this case, it is highly doubtful that the information is accurate enough to warrant the time expenditure.

Discussion. It is doubtful that the student's memory would be accurate enough to make such a superficial interview worthwhile. A more reliable respondent would be the child's mother. Additional information could be obtained from the family physician's records.

Situation 4. State police investigators found that the defendant's auto skidded a considerable distance before it crashed into a car entering the highway from a side road. The defendant is being sued and his lawyer is interviewing him to determine the exact nature of the accident and the legal and moral liability.

I: In order to prepare a defense, I must know exactly what happened in the accident! Were you exceeding the speed limit when it happened?

R: No.

I: Did you see the other car before it had entered the highway?

R: It came out very suddenly from this little side road, and there were trees along the shoulder of the road. He was a fool to pull out like that!

I: Did you hit the other car near the front or the rear?

R: Near the rear.

Although the client might be telling the truth, the whole truth and nothing but the truth, thus far the lawyer has unknowingly left the door open for falsification by the client.

Discussion. The lawyer should depend upon the State Police reports for an estimate of the car's speed. If it is clear that his client was exceeding the speed limit, the lawyer should indicate this to the respondent by saying:

The report by the State Police, based on the measurement of your skid marks, clearly indicates that you were exceeding the legal speed limit. Did you realize that at the time?

Or if the lawyer has not yet had an opportunity to see the police report, he might say:

I haven't seen the police report yet, but as you probably know, it is part of their routine investigation to measure the skid marks and determine quite accurately the speed of your car. How much were you exceeding the speed limit? It is quite important that I know this before talking to the police.

Once the client is allowed to make a defensive false statement, *rapport* may be damaged if the lawyer points out the client's falsification. Therefore, tactics should be used to *prevent* falsification.

Situation 5. A personnel manager in a large corporation with over 15,000 employees is doing an exit interview to determine why an employee is leaving the company after five years of service. Management wants to obtain information to reduce the turnover of employees.

I: As you know, we always talk to employees who are leaving because we are interested in knowing if there is anything in particular they dislike about the company policy or anything we could have done to make the employee more satisfied with her work here.

R: I see.

I: I believe you are going to work for Pacific Electric, is that right?

R: That's right.

I: I see that it is closer to where you live, isn't it?

R: Yes, it is about six miles closer.

I: Is there any particular reason why you are leaving Johnson Electric?

R: No, nothing in particular.

I: Is there anything which we could have done differently to make you more satisfied with the work here?

R: No, there's nothing you could have done. I have nothing against Johnson Electric.

I: What kind of work will you be doing with Pacific Electric?

R: I'll be wiring panels almost the same as those I do here.

I: Then you're not getting a promotion.

R: Oh, no!

I: What would you say is your main reason for leaving Johnson Electric?

R: Well, like I said, it is easier to work closer to home and Pacific Electric is six miles closer . . . so I will drive 12 miles less each day.

I: I see. Thank you very much, Mrs. Robin. Good luck to you and I hope you enjoy working for Pacific Electric.

Discussion. In this type of exit interview, the respondent tends to show deference to the interviewer who represents management. He may be inclined to withhold his gripes about Johnson Electric, rationalizing that it is "too late to do any good with my complaints."

The interviewer then unwittingly assists the respondent in evading his complaints and in rationalizing his move by pointing out that Pacific Electric is six miles closer to the respondent's home. Note that four questions later the interviewer obtains the answer which he had suggested earlier.

One possible solution to this problem is to have a person who does not represent the company conduct the exit interview. If this is impossible several techniques and tactics can help in overcoming this etiquette barrier. We will discuss these later.

Situation 6. The dermatologist for the Student Health Service at a large university is interviewing a graduate student. He wants to obtain a medical history which might explain the causes of a rash on the patient's right hand. The dermatologist suspects an allergy and is trying to narrow down the field of possible causal agents.

    I: How long have you been at the university?

    R: Five years. I'm working on my dissertation now.

    I: Do you spend time in dusty stacks in the library?

    R: Yes, I spend some time there each week.

    I: Are you worried about taking the Ph.D. exams?

    R: No ... I couldn't be worried about that because I have passed them all and have only my thesis to finish.

    I: When did you first notice the rash?

    R: I have had it several times before.

    I: When was that?

    R: When I first arrived in Chicago six years ago. Before I enrolled here I was a group worker at a settlement house.

    I: Did you have any medical treatment at that time?

    R: No, it just seemed to disappear for no reason that I was aware of.

    I: When did it disappear?

    R: I remember I had it in June just before I went to spend the summer in a small village in Mexico. After I was in the village for about two days it disappeared. When I went to Mexico City it returned. I came back to Chicago and still had it until I went on a field trip to rural Arkansas and it disappeared in a day or two. Then I returned to Chicago and the rash reappeared. That was last fall, in October, and I have had it in varying degrees since that time.

    I: I see. Every time you came back to Chicago the rash appeared. Now let's see how you write. Here is a pencil and paper, just show me how you hold the pencil when you write. (The patient writes something on the paper.) That's just as I suspected. See, the sides of your fingers constantly rub on the paper. If the paper is dusty you can work the dust into the epidermis and set up an irritation ... it might even be the paper fibers rather than the dust. I'll give you a prescription to apply each morning. ...

The above interview contains a problem typical in situations where the interviewer has high status. It was later discovered that the tentative diagnosis was wrong and could have been avoided if the physician had been a more skilled interviewer.

Discussion. The dermatologist seems to initially suspect that the rash results from some type of nervous tension. Then he relinquishes this hypothesis in favor of the possibility that it is an allergy to the dust found in libraries or on paper. After leaving the physician's office the patient reported, "That dermatologist is a poor diagnostician. He either didn't hear what I said, or he didn't believe me, or he can't think logically. This rash reappeared *not only* when I returned to my studies in Chicago, but also when I was on vacation in Mexico City. The one consistent pattern is that in rural areas it goes away and when I am back in a big city it returns."

Note that the patient did not point out the apparent diagnostic error to the dermatologist. People who enjoy high status must be particularly careful not to depend on correction from the respondent.

Situation 7. A guest's room in a large hotel in Detroit has been burglarized and the house detective is interviewing the cleaning maid in order to establish the time of the robbery.

I: Did you clean room 819 this morning?
R: Yes, I did.
I: Did you notice anything out of order when you went in?
R: No, sir, I don't think so. It looked just like it has the last three days since the same man has been there.
I: What time did you clean the room?
R: I don't know exactly.
I: Was it the first thing when you came on shift?
R: Oh, no! I came on at 6:30. It was later than that.
I: Was it as late as 10 a.m.?
R: I don't think so.
I: About 9?
R: That's about right. Yes, it was about 9 a.m.
I: Thank you—that's all.

In this case the detective has committed a common error in interviewing, making the accuracy of the information doubtful.

Discussion. In view of the probable difficulty in remembering the exact time she cleaned the room, the maid would be susceptible to the detective's loaded question "About 9 a.m.?" Also the higher social status of the interviewer tends to make the maid susceptible to the detective's suggestion. In a situation like this it would be particularly important to take time to stimulate the respondent's memory. A series of questions could lead up to the time the room was cleaned and help the maid find clues which would narrow down the time segment in which the burglary took place.

The seven episodes above contain typical examples of errors made in interviewing. The errors are not all obvious and the interviewer in each case is not particulary inept. In fact, there are many good points in each interview showing insight into the information-gathering process. In each of these cases, however, the interviewer is unaware that the situation contains social-psychological dimensions which tend to make the respondent either unable or unwilling to give accurate information. The following chapters discuss these dimensions and provide strategies, tactics and techniques for dealing with these barriers to communication.

2
Perspectives on interviewing

To the uninitiated, interviewing is "just talking to people." Perhaps this deceptively simple appearance helps to account for the historically recent advent of systematic attempts to analyze and experiment with the interaction between interviewer and respondent. Since the dawn of civilization, man's survival in organized groups has depended upon his ability to ask a question and get an answer. Even though a certain amount of confusion, distortion, incompleteness and outright lying has always occurred in this communication dyad, there was enough success to keep society functioning. Man became curious about himself and his society and even systematically collected data about human beings in the ancient world, but it is likely that more systematic analysis of this communication process has been done in the last 25 years than in the preceding centuries.

Rather than reporting, criticizing and synthesizing these sorts of studies, the writer will present his way of thinking about interviewing problems which has developed partly from his reading but mainly from his own direct experiences in doing, planning, and teaching interviewing. To provide a broader understanding of the complexities of interviewing, this chapter will deal with interviewing in five perspectives. First, interviewing is related to other basic methods of collecting information on human behavior such as *empathizing, participating* and *observing*. Second, we will show important similarities and differences between interviewing and ordinary conversation. Third, we will present some of the broad types of interviewing and show which of these will be the principal concern of this book. Fourth, the two basic functions of interviewing—discovery and measurement—will be described and related to styles of interviewing. Finally, we will show how the questionnaire is actually an extension of the interview method rather than a basically different mode of collecting data on human behavior. We will also discuss some of the advantages and disadvantages of the questionnaire in comparison with the interview. The panorama illustrates how interviewing fits into the larger endeavor of studying human behavior and how the interview as a basic tool is intertwined with others.

INTERVIEWING RELATED TO OTHER METHODS

In pointing out relationships between interviewing and other basic methods, we will first discuss the basic approaches separately. This does not imply, however, that they are actually used in a compartmentalized fashion. On the contrary *empathy, participation,* and *observation* are intertwined with the interviewing process.

These four methods are *basic* because they involve social skills used in varying degrees by all people. Furthermore, they underlie all other sources of data on human behavior such as that obtained by questionnaires, projective tests, case histories, official records, and census.

Empathy

The concept of empathy, under various names, is found in the literature of philosophy, anthropology, sociology and psychology. George Herbert Mead used the phrase "taking the role of the other," and Max Weber discussed what he called the "verstehende" method. Charles H. Cooley used the term "sympathetic introspection," while Freud and others speak of "empathy," "identification," and "rapport." Anthropologists have often dealt with the problem of understanding the meaning behind overt acts of people in a culture foreign to the observer. They might use the term "rapport," "insight," or "understanding." All of these concepts overlap in their meaning and involve to some extent what we mean by empathy. We define empathy as the process by which one person is able to imaginatively place himself in another's role and situation in order to understand the other's feelings, point of view, attitudes, and tendencies to act in a given situation. In essence, empathy is the ability to correctly answer the question, "How would I feel or act in the situation if I were in his place?"

Some reject this method as being too subjective. They argue that it is useless because it is based upon an *if* proposition which may be untrue. Others have too much faith in empathy and rely upon it in situations where it is not dependable. We prefer to turn away from the question, "Is it or is it not reliable?" to the more fruitful question, "Under what conditions is it valid or invalid?"

In general terms we can say that a person's ability to successfully empathize with another person in a situation depends upon:

a) the degree to which this person's knowledge of the other's situation is complete and accurate;

b) the extent to which this person has experienced the same situation, or the degree to which he can imaginatively construct such a situation from elements of several similar situations;

c) the degree to which this person accurately observes and remembers his own experiences.

Let us assume that one person's observation and inferences regarding the other's situation are complete and accurate. Then we can ask how the probable validity of empathic prediction varies with the probability that the observer has had an experience similar to the one observed. This probability generally corresponds to the degree of universality of the behavior to be predicted. We can think of all forms of behavior and experience as ranging on a continuum from the most to the least universal.

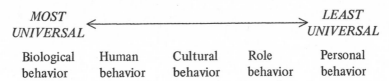

MOST UNIVERSAL				*LEAST UNIVERSAL*
Biological behavior	Human behavior	Cultural behavior	Role behavior	Personal behavior

Biological behavior includes those biological attributes which *all* members of the *homo sapiens* species share. For example all people are born, must eat and must eliminate waste material from the body. All people have sexual impulses, are startled by loud, unexpected noises, become fatigued and must finally die. These are all necessary aspects of man's biological nature, regardless of the amount or type of interaction with other human beings.

Human behavior signifies those characteristics of behavior which all human beings share as a result of interaction with other human beings. In contrast to biological behavior, which is inherited, human nature must be learned in social interaction. Therefore, characteristics of behavior such as the use of language, self-consciousness, conscience, and sentiments (such as love, hate, embarrassment, or the desire for recognition) are acquired, but are universal to mankind.

Cultural behavior encompasses those aspects of behavior which are common to a particular group of people, but which distinguish them from another group. This would include such aspects as the particular *content* of the conscience rather than the mere possession of a conscience. Similarly, culture determines the *particular* language spoken by a group as distinguished from the more general characteristic of having a language. It includes all the folkways, mores, values, ideologies, and attitudes which distinguish one group from another and which all members of each group normally hold in common.

Role behavior includes those actions which depend upon a particular *role* played within a culture group. Therefore, this aspect of behavior varies *within* a culture group, depending upon the role or combination of roles played by a person. A corollary to this is that the range of role behavior within a culture group depends upon the complexity of the social organization (role structure) in that group. The differences between the behavior of a father and a mother toward their child are essentially differences in role.

Personal behavior indicates those characteristics of behavior which may vary from person to person while playing the same role in the same culture. Here we are intentionally avoiding the concept of personality as the "total behavior pattern of an individual" sometimes used in anthropology, sociology and psychology, because our scheme is intended to bring into sharp focus the varying degrees of universality of behavior forms. Our definition includes such things as individual tastes, preferences, basic personality traits such as optimism or pessimism, and feelings of security or insecurity.

This scheme suggests that one person cannot empathize with all people in all situations with equal success. He will be limited by the degree of universality of the situation and by his own experience. Thus, if the behavior to be understood is at the biological or the human behavior level, the empathizer need not be from the same culture or have the same role in society as the person with whom he is empathizing. However, if the behavior is at the cultural or role level, the person attempting to empathize may fail miserably in the attempt unless he has participated in the same culture or the same role.

This is not to suggest that anyone can empathize with others at the biological or human behavior level. That has been proved untrue. But if the person attempting to empathize at this level is not successful, it is not for lack of common experience, but rather because he does not perceive the other person as being human in the same sense as himself. In other words, he does not appreciate the other's circumstances, or he is unaware of what his own reactions would be in the same circumstances.

Not only would we expect a person with a wider fund of experiences to empathize more successfully, but we would also expect a person who accurately observes and remembers his own behavior to have more success. We have all encountered individuals who have difficulty understanding or predicting the behavior of others mainly because they miscalculate how they themselves would behave under the same conditions.

Often, this type of person has difficulty empathizing because he tends to preserve his feeling of security by hiding, even from himself, any discrepancy between what he feels *should be* and what actually *is*. He may repress any memory of his own behavior unflattering to his self-image. Differences in this ability to see oneself objectively were dramatically demonstrated by respondents in studies of disaster-stricken communities. For example, one respondent would readily admit that he did not act in a heroic fashion but thought of his own physical safety first. Another person would feel compelled to explain the behavior of others as well as his own behavior in terms of heroism. In the eyes of such a person, the community emerged from chaos through a series of miracles. Frequently, upon closer examination, this type of respondent was found to have acted in a singularly self-centered fashion even after he was removed from physical danger. Thus, he was often genuinely disturbed and puzzled by the less than ideal forms of behavior brought to his attention.

A person's ability to empathize may be distorted by his tendency to see only the "good" aspect of reality. All human beings tend to do this to some extent, but there are wide variations in people's ability to see themselves or others objectively when what they see does not correspond with what they would like to see.

The following situations illustrate some of the values and limitations of empathy. Agreement will vary greatly, but the situations will demonstrate some of the strengths and weaknesses of the method.

Situation 1. Samu lived in the crescent-shaped clearing in the palm grove. His thatched hut was near the coral reef on the island of

Baikta. Although he was only 10 years old, he proudly assisted his father who, like most of the inhabitants of the island, was a fisherman. These pre-literate people had never seen a movie nor heard a radio. The island was a battleground between the Americans and the Japanese for about three days in 1945. These soldiers were the last foreigners on the island. The fastest transportation on the island was the dugout canoe with outrigger pontoons and no sails. Samu's father was proud of his skill in launching and paddling a canoe in the heavy surf when they went fishing each day. None of the islanders had been farther than Choru Island about 60 miles away.

Samu had never seen a white man until a boat arrived in the lagoon with the technical staff of the movie "Coral Sands." In Samu's words, "My father told me that they were not a war party like the last white men he had seen, but that they wanted to make a story which the white man called a 'movie.' They talked to my father and asked whether they could take me with them for several weeks to an island about 285 miles east of Baikta. No one lives on the island because no fruit trees grow there. They said that I was just the right size for the movie. One of them spoke our language, but it was difficult to understand his words. He told my father that if I would stay for six weeks or more he would give my father a new fishing net. That is something my father would like very much. They had no room for any of my relatives on their boat and they needed a boy just my size."

In this case what would the father's reaction be?

Discussion. If we look at this situation more abstractly, we see a father being asked to let his ten-year-old son leave home with strangers. They would be taking the boy to an uninhabited island almost five times as far away as any of his acquaintances had traveled in their lives. Furthermore, all but one could speak only a foreign language, and that one person showed only a crude knowledge of the native language and was difficult to understand. In effect, the father was being asked to entrust his son to strangers with no more compensation than the *promise* of a fishing net. The boy would be among strangers who spoke a foreign language and ate strange food. None of his relatives would be with him.

In the primitive culture, where kinship ties are extremely strong, a ten-year-old boy is an important asset in helping his father and his absence would upset the family's usual division of labor. Samu's people had never heard a radio, seen a movie, or read any books which might have given them knowledge beyond the traditional folklore of the tribe. Therefore, little motivation could be attached to appearing in a movie. Furthermore, it is improbable that the earlier battle between the Americans and Japanese would make the father remember Americans as kind, predictable people.

Considering these factors, we are almost certain that the father would refuse the offer. The ten anthropologists and sociologists who were consulted agreed unanimously.

Untrained interviewers gave various reasons for believing that Samu's father would accept the offer: "The father is proud of his son and would like to have him in a movie." "The father realized that these men were different from the other white men he had seen." "The father knew that the white men would not harm Samu." "The islanders would be honored that Samu was chosen." "The father would want to give Samu an opportunity that he himself had never had." "There's not enough information." "There's no information about this particular culture telling how they react to strangers."

The "reasons" above reflect two general types of errors: first, the failure to realize that there are certain conditions which, when viewed abstractly, become *universal* tendencies or forces; second, the tendency of an observer to *project* the values of his own culture and to assume that people in another culture have knowledge which they could not possibly have.

Situation 2. It seemed like any other Saturday afternoon when a typical farm family had one of its most unforgettable experiences. Mrs. Boswell, the farmer's wife, was in the country visiting a friend while her husband and seven-year-old daughter went to Judsonia, Arkansas, about five miles away. The husband dropped his daughter off at Aunt Emma's house as had been planned and then went to a friend's garage to help him repair a tractor. Aunt Emma lived three blocks north of the main highway, and the garage was an equal distance south of the highway on the same cross street. Later that afternoon, Mrs. Boswell heard a newscast reporting that a tornado had struck Judsonia, demolishing all its buildings. Unable to believe it, she asked her friend to drive her to Judsonia in the pickup truck. As they approached the town on the main highway, from almost a mile away they could see that the steel water tower had been crushed like a piece of tin foil. Mrs. Boswell became distraught and screamed, "Almighty God, what has happened?"

Assuming that they are equally accessible, would you expect Mrs. Boswell to go to her husband or her daughter first in this situation?

Discussion. One basic question here is, which dominates Mrs.

Boswell, her role as a mother or as a wife? Another question is, how will she define the situation regarding the relative threat to two members of her family?

We will assume that (*a*) the mother believes that both her husband and daughter are in mortal danger, (*b*) that both are equally accessible, and (*c*) that the equal access to each calls for a *choice* between the two alternatives.

Any general knowledge about the relationships in a rural family, in contrast to those in a suburban professional family would be relevant. Certainly, the mother would be more emotionally attached to a seven-year-old daughter than the father would be. Also, she is considered more directly responsible for the daughter than is the father. The usual assumption is that children are helpless and that "big strong men" can care for themselves. The rural community would consider it natural for the "mother instinct" to be manifested during an emergency.

The validity of this rationale has been affirmed in empirical studies of disasters. There is little evidence to compare the rural family's reaction in a disaster to that of an urban or suburban family. However, most of the studies done by the National Opinion Research Center of disasters in rural areas revealed a pattern of interaction during the crisis where the mother was first concerned for her children, particularly if they were young and female, and second for her husband. In contrast to this, the husband was usually concerned first with the welfare of his wife and later with that of the children, although this pattern is not so clear as the first.

Of course we must remember that the tendency to conform to such a pattern is only one social-psychological force and that there are other forces in the situation.

Disagreements with this pattern follow such lines of reasoning as: "It depends on the particular mother." "The mother would be more concerned with her husband because she is dependent, at least financially, upon him." "She has been attached to her husband longer than to her daughter." "It depends on Mrs. Boswell's previous experiences in disasters." "The daughter is in the care of relatives so there is nothing to worry about."

The solution to this problem depends mainly upon understanding the mother's position in the structure of the rural farm family considered as a subculture pattern. It might be argued that all American families as a common culture would share this pattern or that it would be universal to *homo sapiens* as a biological instinct or universal trait. Without evaluating either of these points of view, we say that their truth or falsity is logically irrelevant to the stated problem, because with either or both true, the answer to the problem would be the same. There is reason to suspect, however, that such a pattern is *not* universal to all families in disaster situations.

Situation 3. A friend has offered Bob, a student at college X, free transportation and lodging for a weekend of skiing. If they go, it will be impossible for Bob to return to campus in time to attend his Monday morning philosophy class. Although college regulations do not require obtaining permission to miss classes, Bob feels that he should find out from the professor how to make up anything he might miss in the Monday session. He goes to the professor's office and says:

Bob: Hello, Dr. Belden! Could I speak to you for a minute?
Dr. Belden: Surely.
Bob: I was just wondering if anything important will be going on in class on Monday?
Dr. Belden: Why do you ask?
Bob: (Enthusiastically) Well, to be frank, I have a chance to take a skiing trip this weekend, and I wanted to find out if I would be missing anything.

What is likely to be Dr. Belden's reaction in this situation?

Discussion. This situation is a matter of two points of view associated with two complementary roles in an institutional setting. In general, professors feel that they work hard to transform the raw material they find in freshmen into a more educated version of man. They usually do not enter a field unless they think it is important, and their egos are intimately involved with that field. Under these conditions, the student, who has been wondering if "anything important" would go on in class Monday, implies with his choice of words that there have been days when nothing important occurred.

Even though the professor responds with a civil "Why do you ask?" he certainly has not been flattered by the student's question. Nor is the student's answer gratifying. Instead of asking how he can make up what he will miss, he asks whether he will miss anything.

For these reasons, it seems that the professor would react with a negative feeling. This hypothesis has been substantiated by the responses of a small sample of college professors teaching where class attendance is not required. None of them reacted favorably. Two said they would have no special reaction, and the remaining 19 said they would react unfavorably.

Several typical reasons were offered by untrained observers who thought the professor would react positively: "The professor will probably be impressed by the student's interest in making up the work." "The student didn't have to make any excuses since permission to miss class is not required." "The professor would admire the student's honesty. After all he could have used the 'sick aunt' excuse."

These types of replies simply show an inability to empathize with the professor's role in the student-teacher relationship, and their complete identification with the student causes them to marvel at Bob's honesty.

Situation 4. Bob Cains and Roger Holden, 20 and 24 years old, were hiking in the Sierra Nevada mountains. They had driven as far up as the side road would take them and after packing their food and camping equipment into knapsacks, headed for the top of Donner Pass. They reached their objective the morning of the second day's hike. They decided to return by another trail in order to enjoy a variety of scenery, and they thought it would be worthwhile to take their time and explore interesting side trails. However, they took a wrong turn and became hopelessly lost. They had wandered for three days without food and had hiked about 35 miles when they accidentally stumbled upon a good trail. They followed it downhill for about seven miles, and came to a fork which was clearly marked. A sign pointing to the right said, "Kyber Creek—5 miles" and a sign to the left said "Camino Ranger Station—4 miles." (A ranger station is a place where U.S. Forest Rangers or Forest Guards live the year around.)

"We've gone around in a circle!" Bob observed. "Our car would be about one mile upstream from where this trail hits Kyber Creek, or about three miles by the highway downstream from the Ranger Station which is also on Kyber Creek."

"That's right," said Roger, scratching his head. "That means it is about six miles to our car if we take the trail to the right and about seven miles if we go by way of the Ranger Station. It's cold now but it won't be dark for three more hours."

"Okay, Roger," Bob replied. "Since it is downhill either way, and the trails are both good, we had better head for . . . ."

Assuming that Bob and Roger's assessment of the situation when making the decision is correct, which way would they go?

Discussion. This problem is a clear-cut example of behavior which would be universal to man, primarily because of the simple biological urges of hunger and fatigue. The crux of the problem is to determine which alternative would be chosen by a man who has been without food and has hiked 35 miles in three days. Will he hike four miles to the ranger station where he can obtain food and shelter? Or will he walk six miles to the car which he can drive to get food?

For anyone who has had a similar experience, there is little doubt of what they would do under the circumstances. The basic error made by people who predicted the wrong decision in this case was an overemphasis on the importance of getting to the car rather than to food. They failed to appreciate the significance of two miles under such conditions.

The ability to empathize is an integral part of the interviewing process. An interviewer who is incapable of empathizing with the respondent has little success. Differences between individual interviewers' abilities to empathize are more striking when the general style of interviewing is less structured and when the topic of the interview contains more ego-involved material for the respondent. This is true because the non-scheduled interview gives more freedom to the interviewer to select the content, form and sequence of questions. He is freer either to make more errors or to take advantage of opportunities not open to him if he were restricted by a highly scheduled interview.

It is the interviewer's ability to empathize which allows him to select techniques and tactics most appropriate to the circumstances. Without this basic skill, the interviewer who has learned several specific techniques, cannot use them effectively when faced with the respondent. He can only proceed either in a mechanical fashion, or in a way that satisfies his own ego. Neither course will produce best results.

Although empathic predictions are sometimes incorrect, the interviewer must constantly *try* to empathize in order to utilize his observations of himself and the respondent as a guide to effectively modifying his own behavior during the interview.

This possibility of error makes it necessary for him to treat his prediction of the respondent's behavior as a tentative hypothesis to be modified by subsequent observations. Thus, the interviewer, through the use of empathy and observation, is constantly revising his predictions of the respondent's behavior and adjusting his own behavior accordingly.

An interviewer also should be aware of his strengths and limitations in empathic observation in order to judge which types of interviews he can handle effectively. For example, a social worker whose background was anti-Catholic might have great difficulty empathizing with a Catholic's feeling on the socialist state or on contraception. Or a young sociology student doing a community study might find that his Protestant background interferes with his appreciation of an older Jewish woman's feelings about anti-Semitism in the community. A personnel interviewer in a large industry might not be able to empathize with the employee's untrusting attitude toward the company's in-service education program.

The individual researcher who will do most of his own interviewing must recognize his own limitations and either select his problem accordingly or, when necessary for a particular problem, use another interviewer. From the point of view of a director or supervisor of any large-scale research project, it is often more efficient to *select* interviewers with the best background experiences and personality characteristics for a project rather than to try to train people for increased empathic ability.

Participation

We define participation as acting in a situation where the pursuit of individual or group goals necessitates communication and reciprocal modification of activities between two or more persons.

Particularly in the literature of sociology and anthropology, we frequently find the term participant observation used to refer to a basic approach to studying human behavior. We shall deal with participation and observation separately and then show various ways they can be combined. For the moment, it is useful to think of a continuum with pure participation at one end and pure observation at the other. In between, there are various combinations of participant observation.

People who have participated in society for many years might still have little insight into human behavior because they were unable to observe themselves or others systematically while participating. However, their participation might have had constructive results for the group and have been a satisfying experience for the individual. The goals and results of this type of participation differ from those desired by the research participant.

Without considering the range of goals involved in all forms of participation, let us focus on the researcher's main goals. First, the researcher may participate in a given situation in order to observe his own reactions. He may analyze his own experiences introspectively while participating in the situation or retrospectively after leaving the situation.

Second, he may participate in a situation to gain a vantage point for observing others in the same situation. In this case the problem is to participate in a way that will minimize the distorting effect of the observer's presence. In some situations, where an observer role has not been institutionalized, the presence of the non-participant observer disrupts the scene more than the presence of an additional participant; in other situations, the opposite may be true.

Finally, the goal of the research-participator may be to manipulate variables in the situation which are relevant to his problem, taking care to manipulate only the intended variables without disturbing additional factors. (If he cannot avoid these accidental disturbances, he can correct his analysis by detecting them and accounting for their influence.) Of course, this manipulation usually involves the observation both of oneself and others.

These types of participation can increase the researcher's ability to empathize, since they provide him with practice in self-observation and build up his general backlog of social experience, thus opening up areas in common with new groups or categories of people. This method aided many early advances in the understanding of different cultural groups or socioeconomic groups.[1]

Observation

There is no useful socioscientific function of participation completely divorced from all forms of observation. Just as a person's ability to empathize is expanded by increasing his range of social participation, a person's ability to observe is also enhanced by his ability to empathize. For this reason, anthropologists point out that it is one thing to meticulously describe the costumes, music, and dance steps involved in a tribal ritual, but quite a different matter to understand the meaning of the ritual for the participants or its function in the social solidarity of that tribe.

This does not imply that successful observation depends merely upon successful participation and empathy. Scientific observations must be based upon accurate perception at the purely sensory level.

1/ For example, Nels Anderson, *The Hobo: The Sociology of the Homeless Man* (Chicago: University of Chicago Press, 1923); or William F. Whyte, *Street Corner Society: The Social Structure of an Italian Slum* (Chicago: University of Chicago Press, 1943).

Furthermore, they must be selected from among many possible observations with the help of a guiding theoretical framework, and must be subjected to logical inferences (both deductive and inductive).[2] However, this trinity of accurate perceptions, accurate inferences, and guiding theory must be involved in all scientific observation, whether in the physical, biological, or social sciences. Here we restrict ourselves to the methodological tools unique to the social sciences; thus, the emphasis on participation, empathy, and observation as they relate to interviewing.

INTERVIEWING COMPARED WITH ORDINARY CONVERSATION

Just as interviewing cannot be divorced from other methods of gaining understanding of human behavior, neither can it be separated from the basic skills of ordinary conversation. Any two-way conversation involves many of the same skills and insights needed for successful interviewing. The main difference is in the *central purpose* of interviewing as opposed to other forms of conversation.

There is a tendency for those faced with the problems of obtaining information on human behavior to vacillate between two views: that interviewing is just talking to people in a spontaneous sociable way or that it is a magical and mysterious formula which allows the interviewer to put away all of his common-sense knowledge, insight and intuition. People with the latter view tend to follow a single "technique" with a slavish rigidity. During the process of training interviewers in industrial, governmental, and educational settings, it is common to hear that "here, we use the ———— technique of interviewing." This blank is filled in with such words as "permissive," "non-directive," "focused," "understanding-listening," "supportive," "depth," "structured," "unstructured," "free wheeling," "subjective," "expressive," "spontaneous," "projective," "phenomenological," "indirect," "transactional," or "psychiatric." The remarkable thing is that the same technique is often used for divergent types of interviewing situations and at all points within a particular interview.

Experience in interviewing, training others to interview, and doing research on interviewing methods, shows that no single approach,

2/ Some of the more thoughtful treatments of the methods and limitations of participant observation with additional references to older treatments are given in the following items in the bibliography: Becker, Janes and Schwartz.

style, or technique of interviewing is adequate except within narrow limits. The interviewer should strive to increase his range of techniques and his ability to adapt flexibly to the purposes of the interview and the requirements of the specific situation.

The interviewer should realize the wide range of functions of ordinary conversation and how they relate to interviewing. If this is not done in a self-conscious way, the interviewer may be limited by habits acquired in previous forms of conversation, or be reluctant to use insights or skills learned previously, for fear that they are not "techniques" but merely "common sense."

Whenever two or more human beings are conversing, several social-psychological types of communication may prevail, one at a time or in combination. These types may be delineated according to their purpose.

Expression

One of the most common functions of conversation is the joy of self-expression. One or both of the conversationalists may be fulfilling the need to express ideas, feelings, attitudes or moods. One person may assume that the other is listening in fascination when in reality his expression is in response to his own thoughts which he is organizing for the next assault. This illusion of an audience is important to the person expressing himself. Such a conversation may be quite satisfying to both participants even though neither has the slightest idea of what the other has said. Of course there are times when one person's eagerness to express himself interferes with the other's opportunity to do the same.

This urge for spontaneous expression can be a vital asset in interviewing, provided that once it has been encouraged in the respondent, it can (*a*) then be directed by the interviewer toward the information-gathering objectives of the interview, and (*b*) the interviewer himself does not give way to the urge for self-expression.

One of the common errors made by the novice interviewer is to yield to the temptation to impress the respondent with his own knowledge of the subject of the interview. This form of expression runs the risk of threatening the respondent, who will then tend to guard his responses rather than expressing his thoughts and feelings frankly. It should not be inferred from this that it is always undesirable for the respondent to express ideas not directly relevant. On the contrary, it is often vital to the respondent's morale. Neither should it be assumed that any spontaneous expression of feeling by the interviewer is detrimental to the success of the interview. However, the interviewer must keep both his own and the respondent's urge to express within bounds by constantly asking himself, "How will this effect the completeness and accuracy of the information I seek?" This self-discipline distinguishes the interviewer from the conversationalist.

Persuasion

To a certain extent, the concepts of expression and of persuasion overlap in that both involve the expression of feelings and ideas. Expression includes only those cases where the speaker is not concerned with convincing the other person. He merely wants an opportunity to express his own ideas and feelings spontaneously. Persuasion is behavior which may or may not be spontaneous but which is essentially aimed at convincing the other person.

There are times when persuasive conversation is an integral part of the information-gathering process. In certain types of survey work one of the chief problems is to "sell" the potential respondent on the importance of the study, to persuade him that he is of vital interest, or that the information will be kept anonymous.

There are many situations in which an interviewer's urge to persuade the respondent may endanger the interview. In extreme cases, yielding to this urge has sent the interviewer to jail. For example, the sociology department in a graduate school was studying racial tensions in an area between an all-Negro and an all-white residential area. One of the graduate student interviewers felt strongly about the injustices of the violence against Negroes who moved into the white residential area. During interviews, he could not resist the temptation of admonishing the respondents for their social values and for their superstitions about race. Respondents began to react defensively and aggressively, and a rumor began to circulate that a "bunch of Communists" were going from house to house "stirring up trouble." One respondent then called the police, informing them that a Communist was molesting his wife, and the police took the interviewer to jail. This dramatically illustrates a situation in which the role of the information-gatherer and the role of reformer could not be mixed.

More frequently, the interviewer's urge to persuade results in gathering distorted information. Tape recorded interviews have provided the following examples: a minister could not resist the opportunity to "convert" disaster victims during the interview; a social worker could not separate her therapeutic function from giving the client advice; and an opinion pollster unconsciously and subtly influenced the respondent by the context and wording of the questions used. Only by the systematic analysis of tape recorded interviews can these subtle manifestations of the persuasive urge be demonstrated.

Therapy

In ordinary conversation with a friend, a person often expresses ideas and feelings to release emotional tension. This release is called catharsis and is encouraged by the psychiatrist or clinical psychologist in therapeutic interviews.

The permissive atmosphere and spontaneous give-and-take involved in certain types of social science interviews may also have a therapeutic effect on the respondent by fulfilling his need for catharsis. However, the interviewer should not delve into the respondent's inner conflicts if these conflicts are not connected to the information he seeks. In some cases, the respondent will feel resentful later if the interviewer has "allowed" him to talk of irrelevant matters in seeking catharsis. This is a particular danger when the attempt is unsuccessful and when the interviewer needs to establish a continuing relationship with the respondent or with some of his acquaintances.

There are many times when the information sought is closely related to the respondent's inner conflicts and tensions. This was frequently the case in interviews with disaster victims. Many times it was obvious to the interviewer that the respondent was suffering from guilt feelings about his behavior in the disaster. For example, a mayor of a small town felt guilty because he had been unable to direct the rescue operations and had become confused "just like anyone else." A mother felt guilty because she had let the tornado jerk her baby from her arms while her husband had kept the other child safely. And a husband felt guilty because, when the storm struck his house, he was talking with a waitress rather than eating supper at home with his wife.

In a study of industrial personnel, the interviewer might detect an employee's guilt feelings about stealing certain supplies from his employer. He might note that a management person feels guilty that he teaches honesty in his Sunday school class, but keeps two sets of records on production efficiency, sending the "fixed" set of records to the central office. He feels forced into dishonesty because an accurate record would compare him unfavorably with heads of other departments whose efficiency records are also "fixed." He cannot expose their deceit because he is also guilty.

The social scientist, primarily concerned with collecting valid information, sometimes finds it necessary to play a therapeutic role temporarily to get the desired information. Other times he feels a moral obligation to do what he can therapeutically if he is qualified to do so. More often, however, the interviewer finds that some therapy results without any special effort.

Often the sensitive interviewer is concerned with the ethics of dabbling in therapy while obtaining information. This cannot altogether be avoided. Anyone who speaks to another person giving sympathetic understanding or creating a permissive nonjudgmental atmosphere is likely to encourage cathartic release in the other person. This is true whether the two people involved in the conversation are just good friends or whether the conversation takes place in the confessional or on the psychoanalyst's couch. In trying to obtain valid information it is often necessary for the person studying human behavior to offer just such an atmosphere.

Ritual

Another common form of conversation might be called ritualistic. It is merely a form of verbal behavior which has no real significance other than to provide the security in interpersonal relations which comes with having certain forms of verbal behavior acceptable in all instances of a certain type of occasion. These empty forms may provide little real information. When a person says "Good morning!" he is not trying to persuade, nor does he give information which characterizes the particular morning. Occasionally, situations are confusing because a question is asked but the responding person does not know whether the question calls for objective information or for a ritualistic answer. For example, in the hospital when the nurse says, "How are you this morning?" the patient doesn't know whether to say, "I have a bad headache," or to say, "Fine, thanks, and how are you?"

In interviewing, we must learn to detect ritualistic answers by the respondent and also learn to avoid giving them ourselves. For example, a common error appears when the respondent says, "You know what I mean!" and the unwary interviewer unthinkingly responds as he would in an ordinary conversation with, "Uh huh," when he does not actually understand what the respondent has in mind. To obtain more accurate information, it would be much better to say, "I'm not sure I know exactly what you mean. Could you tell me a little more about it?"

In general, this ritualistic function of conversation has little use in gathering information. The interviewer must merely be aware of the danger of engaging in such ritualistic conversation and then confusing the results with valid information.

Information

A fifth function of conversation is to exchange information. Although the previous four functions have a peripheral place in the type of interview we are dealing with, the exchange of information is the *central* purpose of the interview. The word "exchange" reminds us that in the interview the flow of information must be two-way. Too frequently, an interviewer becomes so concerned with the information he wishes to obtain, and with interpreting what the respondent says, that he forgets to be equally concerned with communicating to the respondent the type of information he needs. He must also communicate the appropriate attitude toward the respondent and toward the information to motivate the respondent to continue to give relevant information.

The exchange of information is not found only in interviews. Two excavators discussing possible ways to avoid a cave-in, two scientists engaged in a discussion of a common problem, a teacher leading a discussion, or two criminals planning a bank robbery—all are participating in an exchange of information. Two characteristics often distinguish an interview from the other situations just mentioned. Often the problem about which the interviewer is seeking information is not equally important to the respondent, hence there might be certain motivational problems. Also interviewers often deal with a wide variety of types of people in obtaining a wide variety of types of information; because of this diversity, there may be an initial communication barrier between interviewer and respondent which does not exist between two people whose activities bring them into regular contact.

This lack of an equal stake in the problem and of a habitual channel of communication between the interviewer and respondent puts the burden of overcoming these barriers on the interviewer. He must translate the problem to a level of concreteness clearly understood by the respondent and learn the vocabulary familiar to the respondent. The interviewer must be sensitive to the important difference between the information he needs in conceptual terms and the concrete questions he asks in order to obtain the information. For example, it is hopeless for an anthropologist to try to explain to a tribesman that he would like his help in a structural-functional analysis of the kinship system of the tribe. It is equally difficult to explain to a disaster victim that you are interested in the process of progressive redefinition of the situation in the first few minutes of the crisis period and its relationship to adaptive behavior and psychosomatic illness during and after the crisis. Less obviously, it is expecting far too much to ask a college freshman, "Why did you come to this college rather than to some other one?"

In studies where the investigator will have many contacts with the respondent, it becomes more possible to build up a rational sharing relationship, even where the cultural backgrounds of the interviewer and the respondent may be quite different. For example, Whyte[3] found that his informants were becoming sophisticated in their observations and in the way they thought about them as a result of a process of progressive sharing and mutual education. However, in studies involving only one contact between the interviewer and respondent, rarely do we find a respondent with whom we can discuss the problem directly in common theoretical terms.

Many interviews may involve the functions of expression, persuasion, therapy, and even a minimum of ritual; but the interviewer must keep in mind that these four functions (whether they are found in the behavior of the interviewer or the respondent) must be subordinated to the main function of exchanging information. This does not mean that the interviewer should hesitate to use any mode or type of communication that aids in the free flow of relevant information.

Thus far we have shown some of the relationships between interviewing and other general methods of obtaining information about human behavior such as empathy, participation and observation. Also, we focused more closely on the relationship between various

3/ William F. Whyte, *Street Corner Society: The Social Structure of an Italian Slum* (Chicago: University of Chicago Press, 1943).

functions of conversation and the central function of the information-gathering interview. Now we will be concerned only with the information-gathering interview, looking at it from the point of view of its various forms.

DIMENSIONS OF INTERVIEWING STYLE

We are not attempting at this point to deal with all dimensions and styles of interviewing since we have already narrowed our concern to interviews in which the central purpose is to gather valid and relevant information. We will also assume that we are dealing with *overt* interviewing situations in which the respondent realizes that he is being interviewed. Within these two broad limitations of purpose and situation, the interviewing method may vary widely. The wide range of variation in interviewing style becomes apparent when a group of interviewers are given the same problem and are asked to get two or three tape recorded interviews. We find a wide variation in the *patterns* of each interview.

These differing patterns can be most efficiently described as combinations of basic dimensions of information-gathering behavior. General styles of interviewing can be defined in terms of two basic dimensions. The first dimension deals with the degree to which communication between the interviewer and respondent is specified and controlled by a prepared schedule.[4] The second deals with the amount of freedom which the interviewer allows the respondent in selecting topics and sequences of topics related to the objective of the interview. As will be shown, an interviewer can purposefully vary his behavior both in the dimension of *scheduling* and the dimension of *topic control*.

Scheduled and non-scheduled interviews

The completely non-scheduled interview is one in which the interviewer is guided only by a central purpose and must decide for himself the means. In contrast to this, the completely scheduled interview spells out the objectives in terms of specific questions

---

4/ In most interviewing literature "schedule" refers to a list of questions used by the interviewer, but not used directly by the respondent, in which case the schedule becomes a questionnaire. Interview schedules may vary considerably in the degree to which they specify details of context, question wording, sequence of topics, and forms of answers needed.

which must be asked in a fixed sequence, using specific words. It may also restrict the respondent by providing answer categories from which he is allowed to select. The schedule to a great extent restricts the techniques used by the interviewer and the form of information given by the respondent.

An interview may be scheduled in varying degrees depending on how many aspects are specified. A schedule may specify (*a*) the content of questions related to the central problem, (*b*) the exact wording of the question, (*c*) any context to be supplied with each question, (*d*) the sequence in which the questions are asked, and (*e*) the answer categories, if any, which are to be used. In the case of the completely scheduled interview, these decisions are made by the person who designs the interview schedule; in non-scheduled interviews, the interviewer himself makes these decisions. To illustrate control of interview style by a schedule, let us look at a completely non-scheduled interview, a moderately scheduled interview, and a highly scheduled interview, all concerned with the same interview topic.

Assume that we wish to discover types of conflict between parents and children and their relationship to juvenile crime. We interview a sample of children who are known to have committed no crimes and a group who have been known to commit several typical juvenile crimes.

THE NON-SCHEDULED INTERVIEW

> *Instructions to the interviewer:* Discover the kinds of conflicts that the child has had with the parents. Conflicts should include disagreements, tensions due to past, present or potential disagreements, outright arguments and physical conflicts. Be alert for as many categories and examples of conflicts and tensions as possible.

THE MODERATELY SCHEDULED INTERVIEW

> *Instructions to the interviewer:* Your task is to discover as many specific kinds of conflicts and tensions between child and parent as possible. The more *concrete* and detailed the account of each type of conflict the better. Although there are 12 areas of possible conflict which we want to explore (listed in question 3 below), you should not mention any area

THE MODERATELY SCHEDULED INTERVIEW (Continued)

until after you have asked the first two questions in the order indicated. The first question takes an indirect approach, giving you time to build up rapport with the respondent and to demonstrate a non-judgmental attitude toward teenagers who have conflicts with their parents.

1. What sorts of problems do teenagers have in getting along with their parents?

   (Possible probes: Do they always agree with their parents? Do any of your friends have "problem parents"? What other kinds of disagreements do they have?)

2. What sorts of disagreements do you have with your parents?

   (Possible probes: Do they cause you any problems? In what ways do they try to restrict you? Do you always agree with them on everything? Do they like the same things you do? Do they try to get you to do some things you don't like? Do they ever bore you? Make you mad? Do they understand you? etc.)

3. Have you ever had any disagreements with either of your parents over:
   a) Using the family car
   b) Friends of the same sex
   c) Dating
   d) School (homework, grades, activities).
   e) Religion (church, beliefs, etc.)
   f) Political views
   g) Working for pay outside the home
   h) Allowances
   i) Smoking
   j) Drinking
   k) Eating habits
   l) Household chores

THE HIGHLY SCHEDULED INTERVIEW

Interviewer's explanation to the teenage respondent: We are interested in the kinds of problems teenagers have with their parents. We need to know how many teenagers have which kinds of conflicts with their parents and whether they are just mild disagreements or serious fights. We have a checklist here of some of the kinds of things that happen. Would you think about your own situation and put a check to show which conflicts you, personally, have had and about how often they have happened. Be

THE HIGHLY SCHEDULED INTERVIEW (Continued)

---

sure to put a check in every row. If you have never had such a conflict then put the check in the first column where it says "never."
(Hand him the first card dealing with conflicts over the use of the automobile, saying "If you don't understand any of those things listed or have some other things you would like to mention about how you disagree with your parents over the automobile let me know and we'll talk about it.")

AUTOMOBILE	Never	Only Once	More than Once	Many Times
1. Wanting to learn to drive				
2. Getting a driver's license				
3. Wanting to use the family car				
4. What you use the car for				
5. The way you drive it				
6. Using it too much				
7. Keeping the car clean				
8. Putting gas or oil in the car				
9. Repairing the car				
10. Driving someone else's car				
11. Wanting to own a car				
12. The way you drive your own car				
13. What you use your car for				
14. Other				

(When the respondent finishes checking all rows, hand him card number 2, saying, "Here is a list of types of conflicts teenagers have with their parents over their friends of the same sex. Do the same with this as you did with the last list.")

The first of the three examples above does not provide any specific questions to be asked, but merely states the problem for the interviewer, leaving him with the choice of techniques. In the second example, specific questions related to the central problem are provided. The order of the three basic questions is indicated and some possible probes are suggested but not mandatory. Question 3 is followed by a guide of various areas of possible conflict which should be covered by the interviewer. However, neither the actual wording of the questions nor the answer categories are supplied. The third example shows how the information designated by question 3-*a* in the second example is obtained by completely scheduled interviewing in which not only the exact wording of the questions and their sequence is given, but the answers are also structured qualitatively and quantitatively.

As is implied in the examples above, an interview may be scheduled to a consistent degree throughout its total length, or certain portions of it may be more completely scheduled than others. The degree of scheduling of any portion of an interview depends upon the purpose to be achieved. This will be discussed in detail later. At the moment we will proceed to define the second dimension of style and relate both dimensions to the two basic objectives of information gathering.

Topic control

Just as the first dimension dealt with the degree to which the interviewer's behavior is determined by an outside source, the schedule, the second dimension deals with the degree to which the interviewer allows his behavior to be controlled by another outside source, the respondent.

Topic control is the extent to which the interviewer, controls the topic of discussion and so takes the initiative in directing the course of the interview. It is helpful to think of the area of discussion as having (*a*) a central focus and (*b*) a certain scope with the boundaries more or less defined. Thus, the amount of topic control exercised by the interviewer depends upon the extent to which he takes the initiative in either shifting the central focus of the discussion or changing the scope of the topic. At one extreme, the respondent leads while the interviewer merely listens and shows interest in anything he wishes to say, and at the other, the interviewer abruptly changes the central focus and scope of the discussion, even if he has to interrupt the respondent's trend of thought to do so.

With the two basic dimensions of interviewing style defined, let us now describe the two basic objectives of interviewing—discovery and measurement—in order to relate them to the dimensions of style.

BASIC OBJECTIVES OF INTERVIEWING

Discovery objectives

Discovery indicates gaining new consciousness of certain qualitative aspects of the problem. The problem is viewed broadly to include both substantive and methodological aspects of the interview. This will become clearer as the specific discovery functions are described.

Locating special informants. In many types of surveys and community studies where the informants are not all selected by random sampling, a rough-and-ready pilot study is done to locate a certain type of informant. Often there is no need to interview all informants of this class, but several must be located because they have had certain relevant experiences. In this case, the only reason for interviewing more than one is to obtain a more detailed account of the event and to cross-check the accuracy of the informant's observations.

In this type of situation, the interviewer, often a stranger in the community, does not know whether the person he first contacts is one or several steps removed from the type of person he needs to interview. The first informant may be the type of person he is trying to locate, know someone who is, or know someone who knows someone who is. He may or may not wish to help the interviewer find the type of person he seeks. An interviewer studying the conditions which contribute toward peaceful integration of public schools would probably have to do a long series of interviews leading him to the persons involved in bombing the local school board office.

Focusing of the problem. It is helpful to think of any study as involving four interrelated levels: first, focusing the problem; second, deciding upon definite types of information relevant to the problem; third, formulating specific questions to be asked in order to obtain relevant information; and fourth, deciding upon the strategy, techniques, and tactics to be used in obtaining answers to the questions. Often it becomes apparent in the early exploratory field work that the problem must be focused more clearly on some specific manifestation of the more general problem being studied.

For example, in a study of intergenerational conflict a few exploratory interviews indicated that most of the conflict which either adults or children could report was within their own family. Therefore, the investigator, decided to focus on parent-child conflict. Further non-scheduled interviews with college students indicated that there was a sudden reduction in parent-child conflict when the children went away to college. This narrowed the focus to high school students living at home. Deeper non-scheduled interviewing showed that it was very difficult to obtain accurate information about conflicts which occurred more than a year in the past. Earlier conflicts were either forgotten or so vaguely remembered that the teenager was unable to give complete information, or he tended to dismiss the whole thing as "just kid stuff" not worthy of discussion. So the quest was further restricted to an analysis of conflicts occurring within the past year. Thus, in this study the non-scheduled interview was used to focus the problem.

Discovering, defining, and testing categories. Often the researcher begins a study with certain general ideas of the questions we want to ask, but with little knowledge of categories appropriate for the answers. For example, in a study of the layman's misconceptions of science we first needed to discover the layman's images of science. This necessitated a set of categories within which the images could be arranged. Since the problem called for classifying the images into two dimensions, we devised a tentative *a priori* set of categories which were to be tested in exploratory interviews. The first *a priori* dimension was called "areas of science" and included the physical, biological and social sciences. The second dimension was called "aspects of science" and included the purposes, methods and results of science. Although this system of cross-categorization was relevant to the problem, it was not clear that all the images or misconceptions people could have would fit into this system.

Therefore, using the categories in the exploratory interviewing was avoided by using a very broad open-ended question followed by a series of neutral probes.[5] The opening question was, "What comes to

5/ A "neutral probe" is a one which indicates that the interviewer would like more information on the topic about which the respondent has been speaking, but it does not restrict the scope of the topic because no specific information is requested (for example: "Tell me more about that." "That's very interesting, could you say more about that?").

your mind when you think of science?" This would be followed by such neutral probes as, "That's interesting!" "Tell me a little more about that." "I see, now why do you feel that way?" etc. The respondent was allowed to follow his own free association as much as possible and very little topic control was used by the interviewer. These interviews were tape recorded and the content of the responses was analyzed to determine whether the *a priori* categories were sufficient or whether they would need some modification. Certain types of statements made by the respondents were considered very relevant to the problem but did not fall into the *a priori* categories. In the dimension of "areas of science" we found that we needed a fourth category, and in the dimension of "aspects of science" we found we needed two additional categories. Thus, in this case, the non-scheduled interview was used to determine the clarity and adequacy of a set of categories.

Once a system of categories is worked out, it sometimes appears to be "obvious" and therefore possible to have been decided in an *a priori* fashion. In some cases, the system appears to be unnecessarily complex or the definitions seem either too loose or too detailed. The only criteria by which to judge any set of categories arrived at by any method are (*a*) how relevant the categories are to the problem at hand, (*b*) whether the categories include the full-range of relevant responses, and (*c*) how reliably the information can be classified by using the system.

Determining range of response. "Range" refers to quantitative variations in response, in contrast to qualitative categories. To illustrate, in a community study of a village in an underdeveloped area, the interviewer wanted an interview schedule in which he could check the appropriate class interval representing a family's cash income per year. As an American, he would have very little idea of the range needed. Should the item on income run from $25 to $200 per year, $100 to $1,000 per year or $500 to $5,000 per year? In some cases, studies of income have already been done so that exploratory interviewing is not necessary. However, sometimes nothing is published on the problem, or only mean or median figures are given with no range. Here the non-scheduled interview can determine the range of responses.

Determining best sequence of questions. In many interviews there is a natural order in which the various subtopics seem to flow. In some studies the natural flow will follow the same sequence for nearly all respondents. In other cases, it will vary depending upon the type of respondent. For example, Schatzman and Strauss[6] found that this pattern varied with social class. In some cases, the order of the topics will be different for each individual. The best way to discover the natural order of topics and the degree to which a given order is either general or individualized is to interview a small sample, exerting *minimal topic control.* Each respondent is thus allowed to follow his own inclinations. If a given sequence of topics is found to be general, it is then feasible to use a more scheduled interview. The more individualized the pattern appears, the freer should be the topic sequence in the interview schedule.

Exploratory interviews sometimes show that information obtained early in the interview is not valid because a "warm up" period is needed. This gives the respondent time for unhurried reflection and free association. In the interview it is often best to begin by discussing related events which occurred prior to whose which are of central interest to the interviewer. For example, in a study of the effectiveness of an employee information program, the main point was to discover (*a*) the amount of factual information absorbed by the employee, (*b*) his general attitude toward the information meetings, (*c*) the degree to which he believed the information he was given, and (*d*) the degree to which the employee passed the information on to other people.

Since the interview took place many days after the meetings, it was necessary to start with a question which was in itself irrelevant; but since it focused on a time immediately before the events in which the interviewer was interested, it stimulated the respondent's memory and initiated a trend of thought leading to the central focus of the interview. The interview was opened with the question, "How did you first hear about the information meeting?" This was followed by, "What happened at the meeting?" These two questions usually laid a good foundation for obtaining information regarding the respondent's attitudes toward the meeting. The information obtained was probably more valid than it would have been if the first question had been, "How did you like the information meeting you attended last week?" This question asked abruptly before the respondent had an opportunity to "re-live" his experience would tend to elicit a response like, "Oh, it was nice," or "I don't really remember much about it."

Similarly, in a study to determine why people bought "Brand X"

6/ Leonard Schatzman and Anselm Strauss, "Social Class and Mode of Communication," *American Journal of Sociology,* Vol. 60, No. 4 (1955), pp. 329-38.

automobiles, it was found that the respondent could talk more spontaneously about his first purchase of a "Brand X" if a thoughtful, permissive atmosphere was established. The interviewer started with "When did you first drive a car?" and later, "When did you first own a car?" This helped establish a reminiscent mood, sometimes quite nostalgic, which always led smoothly into more recent car-buying episodes. By the time the more recent events were reached, the respondent was becoming aware of changes in his own tastes and motivations in car buying as well as certain consistent patterns. All this provided not only a stimulus to the memory, but also a general *context,* enabling the interviewer to make inferences and pose more searching questions.

Discovering special vocabularies. Every social group has its own special vocabulary, or "universe of discourse," which is often not clearly intelligible to outsiders. We are seldom aware of this universe of discourse in our own group unless it is consciously learned as a defense mechanism against the outsider, as is done by professional groups in medicine, education, arts, crafts, and the underworld.

The plumber might complain about the philosophy professor using a lot of "big words," while the plumber himself has a vocabulary equally confusing for the professor. Often these jargons distinguish the initiated from the uninitiated. A person not only has to have the "right ideas," but must also express them in a particular way to be recognized by the group.

These universes of discourse are not always merely a protective jargon, but often provide a type of shorthand or code which may be more efficient and accurate than ordinary language. Special vocabularies are not only associated with professions and occupations, but also with certain social strata and geographical regions.

The non-scheduled interview with minimal topic control is needed to discover these special vocabularies. By carefully listening to the modes of expression the respondent uses to talk about certain topics, the interviewer learns which words can be used in phrasing questions for a more scheduled interview.

Detecting inhibitors and facilitators of communication. Later we will deal in detail with a theoretical framework outlining certain types of inhibitors and facilitators of communication in the interview situation. Now we will merely illustrate the need for using non-scheduled interviewing as an aid in mapping out possible trouble spots in the interview as well as possible "spontaneity producers" which might be brought into play. Experience shows us that attempts to empathize with an imaginary respondent to predict his reactions to certain questions sometimes fail completely. Our empathic hunches should be tested in a few exploratory non-scheduled interviews.

As an example, a social worker was interviewing Puerto Ricans in New York to determine the need for aid to dependent children. Three items of information were necessary to estimate the future budget requirements of certain social welfare agencies: whether the woman of the house was married, how many children she had, and the ages of the children. The social worker assumed that the best order of questioning would be as follows:

a) Are you single, married, widowed, separated?
b) (If ever married) How many children do you have?
c) What are the ages of your children?

She had assumed that the first question should precede the second, because a woman would be embarrassed if she first answered she had three children and then was asked whether she was married. To avoid this embarrassment, it was assumed that the respondent with children would falsely report that she was married even if she were not. In this case, however, the interviewer's own cultural values prevented her from empathizing correctly with the respondent.

During a few exploratory interviews the interviewer discovered that there was a large percentage of couples with children who were not legally married. However, these couples did *not* have guilt feelings. If they lied about their marital state, it was usually to avoid embarrassing the interviewer. The longer the common-law couple had been in the United States, the more they were likely to lie about their marital state to those outside the Puerto Rican community. On the basis of this experience, the interviewer decided to reschedule the sequence and phrasing of questions as follows:

a) How old is your oldest child? The next? The next? etc.
b) Are you married, living common-law, or alone?

This order of questioning indicated to the respondent that the interviewer realized there was no necessary connection between having children and being legally married. If, in addition, the interviewer's attitude was not one of condemnation or shock, the respondent was assured that the interviewer "understood" the situation.

The non-scheduled interview frequently discovers unexpected inhibitors or shows that expected inhibitors are not actually present under the conditions of the interview.

In order to understand why people are willing to talk about some things and very reluctant to talk about others, we must be free to explore many avenues of information in addition to those immediately relevant to the subject of the interview. We need to know:

   ' *a*) how the respondent interprets the interview situation;

   b) how we can influence his definition of the interview situation;

   c) what "meaning" the information signifies for the respondent in terms of his own ego or social status; and

   d) what the respondent can gain by talking to the interviewer.

Sometimes this type of information is obtained through skillful non-scheduled interviewing and sometimes it is stumbled upon by accident. The use of the non-scheduled exploratory interview should considerably increase the probability of obtaining this needed information since, unlike the highly scheduled interview, it does not rule out accidental findings which might be relevant.

Measurement objectives

It is possible to combine the objectives of discovery and measurement in the same interview; but as more emphasis is placed upon one objective, the other must be subordinated. What style is best for the purpose of measurement? Generally, the scheduled interview, with high topic control, is more efficient and effective in obtaining uniform coverage, precision and reliability of measurement. The measurement is likely to be valid if the interview schedule has been constructed on the basis of results from skillful non-scheduled interviews.

Although the scheduled interview where the measurement objective predominates is used more, there are several situations in which the non-scheduled interview would be capable of more valid measurements if done by a skilled interviewer. This would be true in several types of interview situations where communication barriers would arise if the strictly scheduled interview were used.

One of these situations would be where the *universe of discourse* varies so greatly from respondent to respondent that the interviewer must vary the wording of his question and sequence of probes to fit the understanding of the particular respondent. This might be the case in dealing with topics like toilet training of children, sex behavior among teenagers and adults, and other topics dealing with private spheres of experience.

The non-scheduled interview is also needed where communication on the topic is inhibited by the respondent's *fading memory*. The interviewer must be free to exercise low topic control and to vary the sequence of questions, thus allowing the respondent to follow the natural paths of free association. To further stimulate the memory, the interviewer must be free to probe particular vague points in the story. Also, he must be free to create a mood of thoughtful reminiscence and to return to the same topic several times. In this case, a skilled interviewer can be more effective if he is free to devise his own tactics as the interview progresses.

There are other barriers to communication which can be surmounted best by a skilled interviewer unhindered by a schedule. The next chapter deals with eight inhibitors of communication, at least four of which can be handled better by skilled non-scheduled interviewing. They are forgetting, chronological confusion, inferential confusion and unconscious experience.

A basically different situation in which the non-scheduled interview might be more practical for measurement purposes occurs where the measurement is simple and the respondents so few that the construction of a schedule is not necessary or efficient to validly and reliably rank the respondents on the variable being measured.

In deciding whether a scheduled or non-scheduled interview should be used, one argument advanced is that the non-scheduled interview is dangerous because the interviewer is free to bias the responses. This is true if unskilled, careless, or dishonest interviewers are used. However, bias can also be built into the interview schedule itself, offering the doubtful virtue of uniformity to the bias. We must be careful not to simply trade one source of bias for another. Neither should neatness of the interview schedule, efficiency of coding, or reliability of response be confused with the more important criterion—validity of the information.

It is sometimes argued that the scheduled interview is usually more reliable and *therefore* more valid than the non-scheduled interview. This reasoning is not necessarily correct. It can be demonstrated that it is possible to have perfect reliability, in that the same or different interviewers obtain precisely the same answers from the same respondent on two different occasions, yet despite this reliability, the validity of the information may be very low.

In cases where the purpose of the interview is to obtain accounts of deviant behavior, but where the situation or the interviewing methods jeopardize the respondent if he reports the deviant behavior, we can expect the reliability to be high and the validity low. For example, if a manager of a department store used an interview or a questionnaire to ask, "Do you often steal from the company?" the answer would be a simple "no" even if the respondents were reinterviewed. Thus, we could reliably depend upon the falsehood being repeated.

This validity-reliability conflict would also be found when the interview seeks information considered by the respondent as a competitive secret. In this case, the most ironclad guarantee of anonymity for the respondent is of little value, since the object of the secrecy is to prevent the information from getting to a competitor. This situation is found, for example, in governmental secrecy where the object is to keep the information from a competing or hostile nation and in industrial secrecy where the purpose is to avoid leaks to competing corporations. It is interesting that in both of these situations a system develops in which each institution tries to obtain the secrets of its competitors. Thus, it is to be expected that the naive interviewer who asked an employee of the automotive industry questions about the next year's model of his company's automobile, or who asked a member of the State Department what the next move was to be in disarmament negotiations, would not obtain valid information except for the occasional straightforward response, "That is a secret."

A third situation, much more frequently encountered by interviewers, is that in which the information sought has faded from the respondent's memory so that the images he can recall are confused, amorphous or ambiguous. If the situation in which this interview takes place, or the methods used, tend to suggest a plausible or socially acceptable answer, the bias will be in that direction and will persist upon repeated interviewing under the same conditions.

These three examples do not exhaust the types of validity-reliability conflicts which can result from the inhibitors of communication described in detail in the next chapter. Here, we merely wanted to point out that validity and reliability do not necessarily go hand in hand, nor are they necessarily related to whether a scheduled or non-scheduled interview is used.

Both the scheduled and the non-scheduled interview may be reliable or unreliable, valid or invalid, depending on the conditions and purposes. The non-scheduled interview may suffer from bias due to freedom permitted unskilled interviewers. Likewise, the scheduled interview may have a built-in bias which prevents the best interviewer from obtaining valid information. One type of error may be no better than the other.

Use of an interview guide

When using a non-scheduled interview for discovery or measure-ment, the interviewer is not engaging in a completely unplanned trial and error activity. The topics he is exploring or the dimensions he is measuring should be as clearly defined as possible. In addition, an *interview guide* should be prepared to help direct him toward the objectives of the interview.

The *interview guide,* in contrast to an *interview schedule,* provides only an outline or checklist of the topics and sub-topics to be covered but does not specify a sequence. In some cases, it might also include several ways of wording questions or various probes which might be useful in pursuing the subject. The interviewer is not only free to vary the sequence of topics and sub-topics to fit the particular situa-tion, but he may also return to a topic more than once. He is free to omit questions suggested by the guide if he feels that the information was already obtained indirectly. He is also free to add questions and reword others when this will help convey the meaning.

The *interview guide* can have two general functions. It may simply remind the interviewer of the areas to be covered in his investigation. It can also be a form for recording the answers under certain topical areas so that the interviewer can maintain an inventory of what has been covered and what has not. In a sense, the interviewer uses the interview guide as a motorist uses a road map. It reminds him of possible routes to many objectives and is a convenient way of record-ing where he has been and what he has missed. In some cases, the interview guide, once written, is memorized by the interviewer so that his questioning appears spontaneous.

In a series of exploratory interviews aimed at developing a struc-tured interview schedule, the original tentative interview guide may go through several revisions in which the content of the questions, their wording, sequence and context, as well as the response catego-ries, become more detailed, more structured and clearly relevant to the objectives of the interview.

INTERVIEW VERSUS QUESTIONNAIRE

Earlier in this chapter when comparing interviewing with other basic methods of information-gathering, we did not mention the questionnaire. The questionnaire is not a separate basic method; it is an *extension* of the interview.

The most essential difference between an interview and a questionnaire is that the interviewer asks the questions orally, while in a questionnaire the respondent reads the questions. There is nothing about the nature or form of the questions or answers which can reliably distinguish the interview from the questionnaire. Thus, according to this minimal definition, an interview can resemble a questionnaire to the point where the differences are insignificant. For example, the principal of a high school requested each of the teachers to distribute 4 x 6 index cards to students at 10 a.m.; each student was to put his full name in the upper left-hand corner and write the numbers from 1 to 5 in the left-hand margin to designate the answers to five questions which were to be asked by the principal over the intercom system. In this way the answers were obtained from 1,000 students simultaneously without having to duplicate 1,000 copies of a questionnaire or to make up the answer sheets. Whether or not this should be called a "group interview" or an "oral questionnaire" is a fruitless controversy.

There are forms of questionnaires which have many of the attributes ordinarily associated with an interview. Typically, we may think of a questionnaire as being sent to the respondent through the mail, but this is not necessary. Instead, the researcher might give it to the respondent personally with an explanation of the purpose of the study and then leave. The respondent might be instructed to mail it back or to finish it by a certain time when the researcher will return and pick it up. Or, the researcher might distribute the questionnaire to a group of people and wait to collect the questionnaires as soon as they are completed. Or, even more similar to the interview situation, one researcher may personally administer a questionnaire to a single person with instructions that, if the respondent has any difficulty interpreting the questions, he should feel free to ask for help. These different ways of administering a questionnaire represent different degrees of opportunity for the researcher to help the respondent interpret the questions and to motivate him to respond to the questionnaire.

Despite the degree to which a questionnaire and an interview may resemble each other, there are certain general differences which must be taken into consideration in choosing between the two modes of gathering information.

Advantages of the interview

1. The interview provides more opportunity to motivate the respondent to supply *accurate and complete information immediately.*

This motivation factor becomes more decisive as the amount of needed information increases, as the degree of answer-structuring decreases, and as the extrinsic rewards for supplying the information decrease. Thus, motivation supplied by an interviewer would not be needed in a case where the respondent merely has to give his name, address and phone number in exchange for a free chance on a $100 thousand lottery. Similarly, the respondent will promptly and accurately fill out an insurance claim form if it is short and simple and the amount to be collected is high. On the other hand, the probability is small that a member of a random sample receiving a form with 200 complex questions about his premarital sex life would supply the information through the mail.

2. The interview provides more opportunity to guide the respondent in his *interpretation* of the questions. This interpretation factor is more important when the questions are complex or abstract and when the literacy level of the respondents is lower. There are cases where the respondents may be completely illiterate or where the reading skill is so low that the probability of understanding the questionnaire accurately is very low. Also, the more varied the respondents in their understanding, interest, and universes of discourse, the more the interviewer is needed to interpret the general purpose of the interview and the meaning of specific questions.

3. The interview allows a greater *flexibility* in questioning the respondent. The more exploratory the purpose, the greater the need for flexibility in determining the wording of the question, the sequence of the questions, and the direction and amount of probing used. When the emphasis is upon discovery as opposed to measurement, we must give serendipity a chance to operate and allow the interviewer to pursue hunches and clues he may get as the interview progresses.

4. The interview allows greater *control* over the interview situation. For example, it may be extremely important in some cases that the respondent deal with questions in a certain sequence, that he answers one question before seeing a subsequent question, or that he does not change the answer to a question in view of the context or clue furnished by a subsequent question. Or it may be necessary that the respondent not consult others in giving his answers. All of these factors can be more clearly controlled in the interview unless we use a personally administered questionnaire in which the researcher stays with the respondent while he answers the questions to one section of the questionnaire before he is given the questions for the next section.

5. The interview provides a greater opportunity to *evaluate* the validity of the information by observing the respondent's non-verbal manifestations of his attitude toward supplying the information. Although it is possible to supply certain cross-checks in questionnaires to detect the respondent who is not serious or who is deliberately lying, it is much simpler to detect, prevent and rectify such attempts by the respondent in the interview. This type of evaluation is particularly important when the subject matter or the circumstances of the interview tend to be controversial or ego-threatening.

Advantages of the questionnaire

We have mentioned some of the major advantages of interviewing, but there are also several advantages in favor of the questionnaire.

1. The most obvious advantage of the questionnaire is in its *economy.* There are several possible dimensions to this economy. First, if we use mailed questionnaires, we avoid all of the expenses of training and paying interviewers. Also, it eliminates the cost of travel and travel time. This economy becomes more important as the ratio of travel time to interviewing time increases. Thus if we have to ask only two simple questions of a random sample of the United States population, the mailed questionnaire would be infinitely more efficient in getting the questions to the respondents. Another dimension of economy is in the possibility of administering questionnaires to a large group of people simultaneously as, for example, to an audience of a movie.

2. Under certain conditions, the questionnaire can provide a type of *anonymity* not provided by the interview. Occasionally we have circumstances in which the only persons qualified to interview on a topic know all or many of the potential respondents. This was the case when the university foreign student advisors were used to interview Colombian professors regarding their experiences in teaching foreign students in their classes. Some of the questions dealt with the professors' philosophies and practices in teaching, which, if answered frankly, might be negatively evaluated by the Dean of their department or by the Rector of the university. These particular questions were omitted from the interview but included in a questionnaire which could be returned by mail in a self-addressed stamped envelope directly to the research center which had no connection with the university with which the professor was affiliated.

Combined use of the interview and questionnaire

When we design a research strategy, we must not assume that we need to choose between a mailed questionnaire or an interview. It is possible to collect part of the information in one way and part in the other. Even in those cases where a questionnaire is an appropriate data-gathering instrument and most of the respondents will provide required data, it may be necessary to interview those who would not respond to the questionnaire. In other cases, an interview may be needed to complete or clarify the answers, even though the person did respond to the questionnaire.

Another general way of combining the two is to intersperse a questionnaire with an interview at points where the question or the answer structure is so complex that the respondent could grasp it better in writing. This allows him to re-read it as many times as he wishes and to proceed at his own speed. In some cases, the respondent is given only the answer choices in writing after the interviewer has asked the question orally.

Even in those cases where all of the data are gathered by questionnaire, it is usually necessary to do some interviewing to develop a valid questionnaire. Often apparently simple and foolproof questionnaires can be improved by pre-test interviews. It is dangerous to devise "swivel-chair" questionnaires without benefit of pre-test interviewing for several reasons: First, only by trying a question and being able to probe for a full response can we discover whether the question is clear. The vocabulary may not be appropriate, the issue may not be a real one in the minds of the respondents, or there may be a need to provide more context for the question in order to standardize the interpretations. Second, in the cases where structured answers are used, we must actually derive answer choices which are meaningful to the respondent, which do not overlap, which include the full range of possible responses, which do not seem to the respondent to be unduly restricting, which do not suggest answers, and which are clearly relevant to the purposes of the questionnaire. This appropriate structuring of answers often requires exploratory interviewing. And third, while he is face to face with the respondent, the researcher can more easily detect those aspects of the questionnaire which make the respondent *unable* or *unwilling* to give a full, frank response. Exploratory interviewing can demonstrate any need to restructure the questionnaire to be more or less direct, to use more or fewer open-ended questions, to provide more complete or more face-saving prologues to the questions.

In spite of conscientious efforts to pre-test, when the questionnaire results begin to come in, we sometimes discover a need to re-evaluate the effectiveness of a particular question. Additional interviewing may show that a question or its answer structure is invalid and should not be included in the analysis.

Both the interview and the questionnaire have advantages under certain circumstances, but frequently they are used as complementary instruments. Both may be used to collect related data, or the interview may be used as an exploratory tool in building a valid questionnaire or as an evaluative tool after the data have been collected by questionnaire.

This comparison of the interview with the questionnaire is useful to help decide which is more appropriate for a specific purpose. But we will not deal again here with the questionnaire as a separate entity because all of the basic diagnostic concepts regarding the inhibitors and facilitators of communication and most of the tools described under the headings of strategy, tactics and techniques are applicable to the design and administration of a questionnaire as well as to interviewing.

SUMMARY

Interviewing can be seen in five different perspectives. First, it can be seen as one of the most basic modes of collecting data on human behavior along with the other basic modes of empathizing, participating and observing. All of these basic modes are intertwined and are included to some extent in the non-scheduled interview which, therefore, provides an excellent focus for learning basic skills for studying human behavior.

Second, in comparing the interview with ordinary conversation we note that interviewing may include several possible functions of ordinary conversation, but these must be judiciously subordinated to the central purpose of gathering information. Habitual patterns of conversation must be modified in order to maximize the flow of relevant information in the interview.

Third, in viewing the different styles of interviewing we see that one of the most important distinctions is in the amount of freedom allowed in the interview. The interviewer's freedom is controlled by the degree to which the interview schedule is structured in all dimensions. The respondent's freedom is inversely related to the amount of topic control used by the interviewer within the bounds of the interview schedule. In the highly structured interview, topic control decisions by the interviewer are limited to probing for elaboration or clarification of the immediately preceding response, but in the nonscheduled interview the interviewer has considerable latitude in his use of topic control.

Fourth, interviewing has two basically different functions—discovery and measurement. Discovery must always precede measurement. The non-scheduled interview is more effective for discovery, and the scheduled interview for measurement. Both the scheduled and non-scheduled interview may be used reliably or unreliably, validly or invalidly depending on the purposes and conditions.

Fifth, we assume that the questionnaire may fruitfully be viewed as an extension of the interview method. Both have advantages and disadvantages under different circumstances, but the same basic principles, strategies, techniques and tactics can be applied to both.

To develop the skills and insights needed for good non-scheduled interviewing or for building good interview schedules to be used by less skillful interviewers, a person must be free to make his own decisions and then evaluate the result of his performance. Before he can use this freedom fruitfully, he must be guided by some diagnostic concepts regarding the problems of communication in the interview. He must be aware of a variety of interviewing strategies, techniques and tactics available to solve or prevent these communication problems.

3
A frame of reference for communication

This chapter deals only with the _problems_ in interviewing, leaving the tools and skills needed for their solution to the remaining chapters. Basically, the problem is one of maximizing the relevance, validity and reliability of the communication in both directions between interviewer and respondent.

The communication tasks and problems dealt with in this chapter assume an important distinction between simply motivating the respondent to be loquacious and helping him to supply relevant, valid and reliable information. There are several interviewer's tasks clearly related to obtaining relevant information and there are others clearly related to making the information more valid and reliable. We will show how these tasks are accomplished with both verbal and non-verbal communication.

After we have quickly outlined the two basic tasks of the interviewer and the two basic types of communication at his disposal, we will present a conceptual framework of specific social-psychological inhibitors and facilitators of communication which are brought into play in interviewing. Each inhibitor is a force tending to make the respondent either unable or unwilling to give relevant and valid information without special aid from the interviewer. In contrast, each facilitator is a social-psychological need motivating the respondent to report relevant and valid information in the interview. The interviewer has some control over both the inhibitors and the facilitators through the use of appropriate strategies, techniques and tactics to be described in subsequent chapters.

RELEVANCE, VALIDITY AND RELIABILITY

Assuming that we have designed questions relevant to the purpose of the study and that we have found ways of communicating these questions clearly to the respondent, we must then face the problem of obtaining relevant, valid and reliable answers from the respondent. Once he understands the question he has several possible courses of action. In rare cases he might say nothing, as may happen when a psychotherapist interviews a schizophrenic patient. However, a normal person can more gracefully avoid answering the question by saying something irrelevant or ambiguous. If the interviewer does not accept his irrelevancies, but he still does not want to answer the question, he may simply fabricate an answer which is relevant but not valid.

Unfortunately, we cannot use the reliability of the information as a dependable indicator of the validity of an answer. Just because a particular respondent might always give the same answer to the same question does not necessarily mean that the answer is true. He may, under the same circumstances, repeat the same lie in answer to the question, "Did you kill Norman Jacobs?" In this case, the test-retest reliability might be perfect, the answer highly relevant, but the validity is zero because the interviewing method has not been able to discover the reality which is the object of inquiry. It has not been able to penetrate some barrier to communication erected by the nature of the situation.

TASKS AND PROBLEMS OF COMMUNICATION

Tasks of the interviewer

In harmony with the distinction between relevance, validity and reliability, we divide the interviewer's basic tasks into essentially two groups. The first deals with obtaining relevant information and the second with increasing the validity and reliability of the information given by the respondent.

The relevance-related tasks include (*a*) having a clear understanding of the purpose of the interview, (*b*) clearly communicating specific questions in accordance with the purpose, (*c*) detecting and correcting misunderstandings of the question by the respondent, (*d*) distinguishing between the irrelevant, the potentially relevant and the clearly relevant, and (*e*) guiding the respondent to avoid the irrelevant and probing the potentially relevant to convert it into actually relevant information.

The validity-reliability related tasks depend upon maintaining generally good interpersonal relations with the respondent and include (*a*) being aware of the potential inhibitors which make the respondent unwilling or unable to give valid information, (*b*) using both verbal and non-verbal means to help the respondent become more willing and able to give valid information, (*c*) detecting symptoms of resistance in the respondent, and (*d*) refraining from pressuring the respondent for information before he is willing or able to give it.

The interviewer must be constantly alert and ready to modify his own behavior in a way that will maximize the flow of relevant and valid information. To do this he must clearly understand the objectives of the interview, observe the behavior of the respondent and be aware of his own behavior as it influences the respondent.

Problems of communication

Both of these tasks depend upon verbal and non-verbal modes of communication. Non-verbal communication includes the tone of voice, facial expression, gestures, posture, and pacing which accompany the words.

Verbal communication problems. Rarely is there lack of communication because either the interviewer or the respondent does not understand the dictionary definition of a word. More frequently the interviewer's problem is to become acquainted with special jargons currently used by sub-cultures associated with an occupational group, social class, age level, ethnic group, political party, religious group, or geographic region.

The successful interviewer must be willing to learn special universes of discourse. Without the interest and sincerity to master the knowledge needed to make the question meaningful to the respondent and to understand his answer, the interviewer has no right to the respondent's time. Interviewing auto mechanics about the problems of their business without a familiarity with their special, extensive vocabulary is insulting and fruitless. The interviewer cannot show a vital interest in what the respondent is saying if he does not understand what he is being told.

This need of an appropriate vocabulary is more obvious when

interviewing someone with more education or higher social status or when the interview deals with a specialized problem. Nevertheless, the need is often just as urgent in interviewing a respondent of lower social status about a nonspecialized problem. For example, in preparing to interview scientists about recent cancer studies, it is apparent that the interviewer would have to learn a special vocabulary to be effective. It is not so obvious, but just as important to learn a special vocabulary to interview an Arkansas farmer about his experiences in a tornado.

It is sometimes *more* important to know the correct vocabulary when interviewing a person of lower social status. The lower-status respondent feels less free to educate the interviewer, and the interviewer is less likely to perceive his own misunderstandings. Even though the interviewer assumes the role of the "ignorant but willing student," the respondent is still less inclined to assume the role of teacher than if he had higher social status.

As an example of the necessity of special vocabularies, an interviewer planning to interview the personnel of a mental hospital about morale problems should not approach the first respondent without knowing the meaning of common abbreviations such as "EST," "BM," "IV," "GP," "GI," or "GU." Respectively, these usually stand for electroshock treatment, bowel movement, intravenous injection, general paresis, gastrointestinal, and genitourinary. In addition to the medical vocabulary, he would encounter the vocabulary of abnormal psychology and the highly specialized vocabulary dealing with the local physical and social structure of the hospital.

Similarly, if a study of employee morale is to be done in a large telephone company, the interviewer must understand terms such as "CO," "ACO," "PBX," "rate structure," "traffic department," "plant department," "ICC," "A.T.&T.," "employees' concession," and "key-pulse dialing." The same symbol can have entirely different meanings in different universes of discourse; for example, the first abbreviation, "CO," means carbon monoxide to a chemist, chief operator to the telephone employees, commanding officer in the army, and conscientious objector in a Mennonite community.

The examples above have perhaps been misleadingly obvious, since abbreviations are frequently used to express the most unique vocabulary in any occupational group. It is also quite easy to detect special meanings when they are conveyed by words or phrases which are *not common* to the universe of discourse of both the interviewer and the respondent. If a college girl from New York heard a farmer say, "We just built a new water closet"; or a carpenter say, "This ladder needs new dogs"; or a mechanic say, "Your worm-gear is growling"; or a farmer in a semitropical area say, "We use triple-deck farming here"; or one plumber say to another, "Give me the snake, Joe"; or a man on skid row say, "Pete is a snowbird"; she would probably be aware that she didn't understand some of these phrases.

However, the same student might hear an Arkansas farmer explaining his experiences in a tornado with, "I wasn't excited during the big blow, but I studied all night the first four nights afterward." She would probably *not* realize that she did not understand him since only common words are used and the context does not give a clue to the special regional meanings of two of the words.

Another type of universe of discourse is illustrated in the following example. It is more difficult to detect because it is associated with a particular person's life history.

A local women's political organization was studying academic freedom at three colleges in the area by interviewing all members of their social science faculties. One of the interviewers arrived for her appointment with a faculty member and felt that she should first build *rapport* with a friendly conversation before launching into the formal interview.

I: Good morning! I am Mrs. Kirk from the Politics Club.

R: Oh yes, how do you do! I have been expecting you.

I: It's nice of you to give me an appointment. You are helping us with such an important project. We feel that it is important to have academic freedom in our colleges.

R: I can certainly agree with you there. Won't you sit down?

I: Thank you. I am so glad to have a chance to interview someone in the sociology department. When I was young I used to enjoy reading about Eugene Debs and that sort of thing. I think everyone should know how the other half lives. . . . (Pause) Could you tell me how many social workers your department graduates each year?

In this dialog, the interviewer has unintentionally damaged rapport with the professor. Let us consider the last line which, although not part of the formal interview, is the only question. In its denotative aspect, it is simply *asking* for a concrete number of social workers who are graduated in a year. The answer is "zero." However, the context of the question allowed the professor to induce several assumptions on her part that he felt needed correcting.

First, he was amazed by the question but recovered in time to explain the relationship between socialism, social reform, social work, and sociology. Since the interviewer knew she was talking to a member of a sociology department of an undergraduate school, yet expected them to be graduating social workers, the professor knew she did not understand the difference between sociology and social work. Her remark about Eugene Debs implied that she saw a connection between socialism and sociology.

The professor's immediate response was to the *connotative statement,* rather than to the simple *denotative question.* He hastened to explain that sociology had no more in common with socialism than it did with capitalism, vegetarianism, or fascism, except for the first four letters.

The general effect upon the respondent was to make him distrust the interviewer because he doubted that anyone so grossly ignorant of his field could sympathize with the problems of academic freedom or be able to accurately record his opinions on the matter.

These confusions of universes of discourse can be prevented in most cases. Sometimes it is practical to recruit interviewers from the same cultural background as the respondents, interviewers already familiar with the particular universe of discourse. If a large number of interviewers are needed and it is not possible to recruit and train them, exploratory interviewing can be done by a few experienced interviewers. When special words and meanings are detected, they can be taken into account in modifying the wording of the questions and a special glossary can be included in the instructions to warn the interviewers of the special meanings which might appear.

Experimental studies of interviewing[1] show that different respondents sometimes read different meanings into the same questions and, therefore, they are actually answering different questions. These different interpretations are due to differences in the basic assumptions held. C. W. Mills[2] points out that different sets of basic assumptions are expressed in different "vocabularies of motive" used from one historical period to another. Thus, an act that would have been explained in terms of the "battle between God and the devil" in the Middle Ages would be explained in Freudian terms of "the battle between the *id* and the *superego* in the arena of the *ego*" in a later era.

For example, a tornado took a diagonal path (from southwest to

1/ R. S. Crutchfield and D. A. Gordon, "Variations in Respondents' Interpretations of an Opinion-Poll Question," *International Journal of Opinion and Attitude Research,* Vol. 1 (September, 1947), pp. 1-12.

2/ C. Wright Mills, "Situated Action and the Vocabulary of Motives," *American Sociological Review,* Vol. 6 (December, 1940), pp. 904-13.

northeast) across White County, Arkansas, destroying four towns along the highway running in that direction. The disaster team which followed in its wake asked the following question (among many others), "Why do you think the tornado struck the way it did?" This question brought into play the "vocabulary of motives" of this local subculture. Most of the responses were based upon the assumption that God controlled the fate of men and that the tornado was an instrument of God's justice. Based upon this premise, then, the respondents were asked to explain how the inhabitants of one village had been more sinful than those of another and why certain people in their own stricken village were killed and others spared. Some typical responses were, "God does not have to explain his ways to man!" "The youngsters in this town have been going straight to the devil!" "Who am I to judge the ways of God?" In contrast, the members of the disaster study team thought the explanation was to be found in the statistical regularity with which tornados travelled from southwest to northeast through "tornado alley" and could be explained in terms of the rotation of the earth, prevailing winds in the northern hemisphere, local atmospheric conditions and rapid changes in temperature.

The field team members were initially prepared for this question to elicit some pseudoscientific manifestations of anxiety such as: "These tornados are caused by all of that atomic testing!" "They shouldn't seed those hurricanes in Florida because it just broke up one big hurricane which might have stayed out to sea into a lot of tornados which pop up all over the South!" Indeed, such explanations did come from some of the respondents.

With this wide gap between the interviewer's and respondent's silent assumptions, there was a danger of a breakdown in communication if the interviewer was not aware of the respondent's assumptions. The unaware interviewer might think that the respondent did not hear the question correctly, that the respondent was joking with him, or that the remark about the supernatural was merely a manner of speaking rather than a serious intellectual attempt by the respondent. Rapport would have been shattered if the interviewer had laughed, or even smiled, and said, "Really now, why do you think it struck the way it did?"

Garfinkel's study[3] shows how this "cognitive substructure" of silent assumptions is not only associated with the more stable values,

3/ Harold Garfinkel, "Studies of the Routine Grounds of Everyday Activities," *Social Problems,* Vol. 11 (Winter, 1964), pp. 225-50.

beliefs, knowledge and expectations of a subculture; but it is also being constantly reformed and shared in the interaction between members of a group such as the family. Thus, the understanding of the real meaning of today's conversation in a family depends upon having shared yesterday's experiences which provide the unspoken context.

Non-verbal communication problems. We now turn our attention to the interviewer's tasks which relate to non-verbal communication from respondent to interviewer. The interviewer must listen to *how* the respondent says what he does. Auditory clues include changes in pace, pitch, intensity, and volume level. In addition, there are visual clues such as facial expression, gestures, bodily position, and movements of hands, feet and head.

Many respondents have learned to hide certain non-verbal clues to their feelings and attitudes. This control is usually exercised either by maintaining a neutral or noncommittal expression or by pretending an opposite feeling. In exercising such control most respondents manifest this inner conflict by inconsistencies. They are unable to control all of the symptoms of their attitude. For example, the respondent might display a calm facial expression and a casual tone of voice, yet betray anxiety by twisting his hands.

The interviewer can observe these inconsistencies if he develops the habit of watching the *total* bodily response rather than concentrating only on the tone of voice and facial expression. In ordinary conversation, most people look to facial expression more than to other bodily changes for clues to feelings and attitudes. Perhaps it is precisely for this reason that we learn to control the facial expressions more readily.

There is also a problem of accurately judging the meaning of various visual and auditory non-verbal clues. One reason is that respondents vary greatly in their normal range of expressive behavior; unusual tension for one person would be normal for another. The interviewer can deal with this by focusing his attention on *changes* in the level of these expressive symptoms.

Also, if the interviewer has more than one contact with the respondent or can observe him in another setting, it is easier to make more accurate judgments of the respondent's emotional state.

The non-verbal clues noted by the interviewer have little meaning if isolated from the verbal communication and the situational context of the interview. Only when the non-verbal clues and the denotative and connotative verbal messages make a consistent picture to the interviewer, can he feel sure that his interpretation of the respondent's message is correct. If there is some inconsistency, the interviewer should probe further until the matter is clarified for the objectives of the interview.

Thus, for maximal utilization of non-verbal respondent-to-interviewer communication, the interviewer's tasks are:

a) to observe a broad range of non-verbal activity and be alert for inconsistencies;

b) to be alert for *changes* in the respondent's non-verbal activity rather than being aware of only the general level which distinguishes one respondent from another; and

c) to interpret the meaning of any inconsistencies and changes in non-verbal behavior in the broader context of the verbal communication and the situation in which the interview is taking place.

Now let us examine the interviewer's tasks related to non-verbal communication in the other direction, from interviewer to respondent. This aspect of communication will be studied extensively later under "Non-verbal Techniques." Here we will merely point out the nature of the task.

In general, the interviewer must strive to communicate certain positive attitudes toward the value of the interview itself, toward the respondent as a person, and toward his cooperation. This does not imply that an interviewer can turn his attitudes on and off as the chameleon changes his colors. However, several precautions can be taken to minimize negative attitudes which might damage interpersonal relations sufficiently to invalidate the information obtained.

First, the interviewer can be selected to fit the task. From the viewpoint of a field supervisor, this is a matter of selecting the right interviewer for a particular topic and respondent. From the point of view of the single independent investigator, it is a matter of being aware of his own limitations and avoiding interview situations where he cannot control his negative attitudes.

Second, the interviewer may deliberately seek the kinds of topics or respondents toward which he has a negative attitude in order to broaden his views, gain tolerance, and learn to control his expression of these negative attitudes. However, the same interview which is used for this educational purpose will be of little value as a source of valid and complete information.

Third, the interviewer must learn certain techniques to counteract his negative attitudes. Even with ordinary precautions to match the interviewer with the topic and respondent, or to retrain the interviewer's attitudes, there will be some degree of self-control necessary, since it is hardly possible to find any one person who agrees with everything another person believes or has done. Just as it is difficult for the respondent to hide his attitudes with a neutral expression, it is also difficult for the interviewer to hide his attitudes from the respondent.

The interviewer's task is to displace real negative attitudes with equally real positive attitudes. This way, he avoids the problems inherent in attempting to remain neutral or refusing to admit to himself that he has such an attitude. Thus, if the interviewer strongly disagrees with the attitudes and beliefs being expressed by the respondent, he must be so vitally concerned with the information-gathering task that he can show sincere appreciation for the respondent's frankness. Or he can manifest a strong interest in how the respondent arrived at these views, if this is an objective of the interview. In both of these cases, scientific objectivity rather than cold neutrality allows the interviewer to demonstrate positive attitudes of appreciation and interest rather than negative attitudes of disagreement and rejection.

In summary, the interviewer achieves his main goals—that of obtaining maximum relevant information and maintaining optimum interpersonal relations—by being sensitive to both verbal and non-verbal communication. The interviewer's tasks occur in the following cycle:

First phase. The interviewer must accurately receive information through both verbal and non-verbal modes of communication.

Second phase. The interviewer must then make valid inferences regarding the adequacy of the information and the condition of the interpersonal relations.

Third phase. He must then translate what is learned to modify his own behavior at the verbal and non-verbal levels to maximize the flow of relevant information and to maintain optimal interpersonal relations.

It will be noted that although the aim in the third phase is two-fold, we have guarded against interviewer ambivalence or vacillation by not giving the two aims equal weight. The aim is *maximal* information with *optimal,* rather than maximal, interpersonal relations. Optimal interpersonal relations is whatever form and degree of relationship that will maximize the flow of information, or at least not interfere with the flow. Thus, the satisfaction of spontaneous interpersonal relations is viewed as a means to an end.

The precaution of using the word "optimal" is necessary, since there are situations where the best way to *maximize* the feeling of warm interpersonal relations is for the interviewer to "stop asking all those questions!" Often the neophyte thinks he has conducted an excellent interview because "rapport was perfect" and the respondent was "completely at ease, talked spontaneously, and commented that she had enjoyed the interview." Yet when the interview is analyzed for the amount and clarity of relevant data, it is found to be incomplete, superficial, and ambiguous.

Often there may be a conscious or unconscious desire on the part of the interviewer, respondent, or both to avoid any psychological strain in the interview. The interviewer may retreat into rapport-building chit chat or the ritualistic asking of required questions, while uncritically accepting irrelevant, evasive, incomplete, or ambiguous answers instead of probing. The respondent may cooperate with the conspiracy by appearing cooperative while contributing a verbal shower that functions as a smoke screen, obscuring the relevant material.

At times, a respondent may take the initiative in this disguised resistance, inundating the interviewer with meaningless verbiage which he is unable to appraise systematically for its relevance in time to fulfill the objectives of the interview. The loquacious respondent who decides to sidestep the interviewer in this manner often presents a much more difficult problem than the taciturn respondent whose reluctance is more obvious.

Just as it is possible to overemphasize the importance of interpersonal relations, it is also possible for the interviewer to be so concerned with gathering the appropriate information that he neglects to lay even a minimal foundation of interpersonal relations. In this case, the interviewer gives the impression that the respondent is merely a means to an end. The respondent begins to feel like the patient whose medical specialist obviously loses interest upon discovering that the patient does not have a rare disease but merely a common but painful malady.

Thus the interviewer's task is to be approached as the acrobat approaches a balancing stunt. The interviewer must balance his information-gathering task with the rapport-building task. He should develop a sensitive awareness of moments when he should devote more attention to one or the other.

The next chapters will describe, define, and give examples of an array of tools (strategies, techniques, and tactics) available to the interviewer for accomplishing these tasks. But before becoming involved with the "tool kit," it is advisable to view more analytically the main task of maximizing the flow of relevant information so that the tools will be seen for their functional value rather than as ends in themselves.

To maximize the flow of relevant information from respondent to interviewer, the interview situation should be analyzed in terms of general social-psychological factors which inhibit and facilitate the respondent's willingness or his ability to report the relevant information. We can then judge the applicability of specific tools to specific situations.

INHIBITORS AND FACILITATORS OF COMMUNICATION

The writer has frequently heard interviewers on a variety of projects say that a certain respondent did not give much relevant information because he was simply not interested in the topic of the interview. Despite the frequency and apparent clarity of this complaint, the writer has come to feel that the term "lack of interest" is not a specific enough diagnosis to suggest a treatment. There is a type of "lack of interest" based upon the respondent's complete ignorance of the topic. In some cases, this is dealt with at the strategy level by selecting only those respondents who have knowledge on the subject or by designing the interview schedule to include initial filter questions to determine the respondent's qualifications to give relevant information. Also, what appears to be "lack of interest" may actually be due to the presence of one or more of the communication inhibitors. Or "lack of interest" may be a more general lack of motivation which can be dealt with by maximizing the facilitators of communication.

The following conceptual framework presents possible positive and negative forces operating in a variety of interviews. This inductively derived typology is stated at a level of abstraction applicable to all types of information-gathering interviews.

The framework analyzes the general task of maximizing the flow of relevant information by identifying eight social-psychological components which tend to *inhibit* the free flow of information and eight components which tend to *facilitate* the flow. This approach highlights the idea that the interviewer's success will generally depend upon his ability to listen, observe and empathize accurately. Communication from respondent to interviewer is most directly determined by the respondent himself; the interviewer can only indirectly determine the result insofar as he changes the respondent's appraisal of the situation. Therefore, all of the inhibitors and facilitators of communication are described from the subjective viewpoint of the respondent.

Each inhibitor of communication is seen as a barrier or obstacle to be prevented, circumvented, or removed from the respondent's mind. Each facilitator, on the other hand, is *not* merely the absence of an inhibiting barrier but a positive force motivating the respondent to communicate. Within this framework the interviewer's task of maximizing the flow of relevant information is translated into the problem of *minimizing the inhibitors and maximizing the facilitators of communication.*

Inhibitors

The categories listed under this heading operate more frequently to inhibit rather than to facilitate communication. Categories one through four tend to make the respondent *unwilling* to give information, while categories five through eight tend to make the respondent *unable* to give the information even though willing.

Competing demands for time. The respondent hesitates to begin an interview because of other ways he should or would like to be spending his time. He does not necessarily place a negative value on being interviewed, but must weigh the amount of time he is asked to devote to the interview against other activities competing for this segment of time. The interviewer must sell the idea of being interviewed to obtain the respondent's initial cooperation.

This inhibitor functions only in situations where the respondent is free to decide whether to participate in the interview. Sometimes the respondent is obligated to participate, even though he would rather be devoting his time to something else; here, competing time demand is not a factor. This would be the case if the personnel department of a company decided to interview all employees, or if a social worker decided to interview a mother to determine whether she were still eligible to receive certain welfare services, or if a clinical psychologist wished to interview a patient in a mental hospital. In these situations, the problem is not obtaining the respondent's time for the interview, but the sophisticated interviewer knows he must not assume the captive respondent to be *willing* or *able* to give the information needed.

In the free choice situation, the initial problem is to obtain the respondent's cooperation. Once this is accomplished there may be few obstacles to obtaining the information if the amount of time needed is small and if the nature of the interview was clear to the respondent before he gave his consent.

It is possible, however, for an interview to begin without interference from competing demands, but to continue into a block of time where other current or anticipated activities compete for the respondent's attention. In this case, his interest diminishes. For example, the housewife may begin a market research interview gladly, but begin to lose interest and feel apprehensive as it grows closer to the time for her husband to return for dinner.

Ego threat. The respondent tends to withhold information which may threaten his self-esteem. The effect of an ego threat can range from mild hesitancy in giving information to complete repression. Three broad categories may be defined according to the strength of the effect of ego threat.

The strongest effect is repression. The respondent not only refuses to admit the information to the interviewer, but also hides it from himself to preserve his self-esteem and avoid a guilty conscience. He is being honest when he answers that he does not know or that he has forgotten. This level of ego threat primarily occupies the psychiatrist, psychoanalyst, and clinical psychologist, but is sometimes a factor in the information-gathering interview.

A less intense, but more common effect of ego threat is found when the respondent, although he consciously possesses the information, hesitates to admit it because he anticipates that the interviewer may disapprove. Often the respondent is torn between withholding the information and his yearning for catharsis. Since he has not successfully repressed the memory which threatens his self-esteem, he may have guilt feelings. If he is made to feel confident that the interviewer will not condemn him, he may welcome the opportunity to divulge the information.

Sometimes the shrewd respondent indirectly interviews the interviewer to discover the latter's attitudes. For example, the respondent who would like to confess socially disapproved forms of sex behavior may first try to discover the interviewer's probable reaction. He may mention a case similar to his own and may even try to provoke the interviewer into condemning it. If the interviewer condemns the hypothetical case, the respondent will not tell about himself. Confession is usually easier if the interviewer is a stranger whom the respondent never expects to see again. In any case, a generally accepting and sympathetic attitude toward the respondent as a person goes far toward eliciting candid responses.

A lesser threat to the respondent's self-esteem exists if the respondent is willing to give information to the interviewer, but fears losing status if the information becomes public. This respondent must be assured that his anonymity will be respected. This is not always easy to do. The respondent may fear that the interviewer, even with the best of intentions, will be unable to conceal the source of the information. The higher the respondent's status, the more difficult it is to describe his actions in the community without revealing his identity.

This greater fear in higher status people of losing anonymity was demonstrated in the contrast between the attitudes of the officials in disaster stricken towns and those of average citizens toward tape recorded interviews. It was rare to find an ordinary citizen who, as an anonymous number of a random sample, objected to the tape recorder. However, objections from officials were quite common. Even though the official was willing to talk candidly to the interviewer, who was a stranger in the community, he felt that his anonymity would be sacrificed if the tape recording were heard by some member of the local community. He was aware that any of the small town populace could identify the speaker's voice.

Not only must the interviewer assure the respondent of anonymity at the beginning of the interview, but he must also be sensitive to any need for further assurance as the interview progresses. Often the respondent is too shy at the beginning of the interview to show open concern about anonymity; but as he gathers confidence during the interview, he becomes more willing to show hesitancy. This delayed reaction may be more common when the respondent's cooperation is not voluntary. Bain[4] in his analysis of interaction between a research team and workers in a laundry plant, found that the workers' initial cooperation changed to hostility. The researchers did not need the workers' permission to gain access to the plant. Therefore, a thorough, systematic, and convincing explanation of the study had not been given to the workers. Latent doubt flowered into open suspicion when a temporary recession caused the lay-off of a few workers. Rumors spread that the researchers were company spies hired to inform management who should be laid off next. Several

4/ Robert K. Bain, "The Researcher's Role: A Case Study," *Human Organization* (Spring, 1950), pp. 23-28.

weeks were required to rectify this misperception so that the study could continue.

The numerous symptoms of ego threat can be seen as different effects upon the information flow. These effects may range from simply refusing to volunteer any information to fabricating information as a cover-up. A respondent might defend his ego in an interview in various ways. Assume that an interviewer is talking to a person whose home town was destroyed by a tornado. The interviewer asks, "How did you *feel* when your house took off over the pecan orchard?" Here are examples of answers by several respondents.

Evasion. "I looked out the window and could see the tops of the pecan trees below. The roof had blown clean off the house, but it was still holding together. I don't even remember a jolt when we landed in the trees!"

Simple, emphatic denial. "Well, to tell the truth I wasn't scared at all. There's no sense in getting excited 'cause there is nothing you can do. Of course, the women and children screamed, but there is no sense in a man getting scared at a thing like that."

Elaborate, subtle denial. "Ordinarily, anybody with good sense would be scared stiff but I think that it all happened so fast that I had no time to think about it. I couldn't really believe it. Could you believe it if you looked out the window and saw that you were sailing over the trees? I was just trying to hold the door shut and the next thing I knew was when we landed about 300 feet away from where the house left the foundation."

Depersonalization. "I imagine most people would be plain scared at a time like that. People were all scared and excited. Who wouldn't be at a time like that?"

Minimization. "I was nervous, of course, but not really scared like a lot of people were. I'd been through worse than this in the war, so it didn't seem so bad. I'm sort of the calm type, myself, so it didn't have too much effect on me."

Defense. "Of course I was scared! Anyone who had good sense would realize that there was no way to protect yourself. Planks flew right through brick walls and bricks bounced around like pingpong balls. Human flesh is no match for that kind of thing. The worst thing about it is that there is nothing you can do about it. You can't run, you can't hide, and you can't stay and fight it. It is a pure helpless feeling. You feel helpless because for the first time in your life you *are* completely helpless!"

Confession. "When I saw the porch blow off, I was scared to death. I was almost petrified, but I managed to run into the dining room and hold on to the door casing. When the house left the foundation, I was so weak that I could hardly hold on. I prayed out loud and begged God to save me. I'm ashamed, but what else could I do?''

Although in general the respondent's ego-threat leads to omission, distortion, and fabrication of information, there are exceptional circumstances where it is even more ego threatening to withhold the information than to reveal it. For example, when a respondent who has certain information realizes that the interviewer knows he has it and will insist on having the truth, he may give the information even though it damages his self-image. This use of pressure to obtain information becomes more successful as the power and prestige of the interviewer increase and as the respondent has more assurance that giving the information will not result in any reprisals from the interviewer or others. We are all familiar with children confessing to an adult rather than to risk the disfavor of such a powerful figure.

When the interviewer is of a lower social status than the respondent, as would be a newspaper reporter who was interviewing a senator, it is usually impossible to pressure the respondent into giving ego-threatening information. There are even institutionalized responses for handling such a situation. The person of higher status and power merely says, "I don't care to comment on that at this time," or simply, "no comment," or "I'm sorry, but I am not free to give such information."

In general, ego threat is an inhibitor of the free flow of information from respondent-to-interview. Even in cases where pressure seems to succeed, it is unlikely that the response will be as detailed and candid as under conditions where no pressure is applied.

In some cases the purpose of a study is not to penetrate the ego-threat barrier, but to directly study the specific nature of the ego-defense system. We may want to know how people in a particular culture or subculture go about verbally defending their actions which have not measured up to the group or community's expectations. Often, the respondent feels that the interviewer will hold him morally accountable for some untoward behavior which he has admitted or about which the interviewer has previous knowledge. In this case, the respondent tries to bridge the discrepancy between his actual behavior and the ideal by giving an account designed to neutralize any negative feeling toward him. Whether or not this account is honored depends upon the underlying assumptions held by his community regarding the nature of human beings and society. Scott and Lyman[5] give many examples and a refined conceptualization of this process of giving "accounts" in the form of excuses and justifications.

Etiquette. The etiquette barrier operates when the answer to the interviewer's question contains information perceived by the respondent as inappropriate to give to the type of person doing the interview or inappropriate to the situation in which the interviewing is done. Answering candidly would be considered in poor taste or evidence of a lack of a proper consciousness of one's status relationship to the other. The etiquette barrier inhibits the flow of certain types of information both up and down the status hierarchy.

To understand this phenomenon, society must be viewed as not only a web of communication between people in different roles and statuses, but also a pattern of conscious and unconscious barriers to the indiscriminate flow of information. All types of information do not flow equally well among all persons in society. There cannot be a pattern of communication unless there is also a complementary pattern of non-communication.

Etiquette is one of the inhibitors of communication which acts as a qualitatively selective filter, encouraging the passage of certain messages and obstructing the flow of others between two people with a certain relationship to each other. This selectivity may be governed by the nature of the situation as well as the relationship between the sender and receiver.

To a great extent, we learn these subtle patterns of noncommunication unconsciously, but we are painfully aware of them when they are violated. The five-year-old who repeats some bit of intimate family life to his kindergarten teacher learns from her reaction that he has done something wrong. The teenager who uses obscene language in front of the high school teacher knows that the topic is inappropriate for the teacher. However, he often has not yet learned that she does understand his vocabulary, even though she never uses these words in front of students. The teacher may be handicapped in meeting the situation if she is afraid to let the student know that she understands such words.

It is accepted that there are things which men do not discuss in front of women and vice versa, things that married couples do not discuss in front of unmarried people, things students do not tell

5/ Marvin B. Scott and Stanford M. Lyman, "Accounts," *American Sociological Review*, Vol. 33, No. 1 (February, 1968), pp. 46-62.

teachers, things doctors do not tell patients, things parishioners do not tell the clergy, etc. These inhibiting effects of etiquette are often taken for granted as acceptable barriers as long as their inhibiting effect applies to someone else. The problem is that each person's ego, particularly in a democratically oriented society, tends to blind him to his own limitations as a receiver of communication due to the etiquette barrier.

This can be seen in the case of the American returning from a trip around the world who says, "I found nothing but love for Americans everywhere I went." Similarly, a manager of a large corporation may assure the consultant that it is perfectly all right for the middle management people to interview the employees regarding their atti-tudes toward management because, "We have spent years building up good relations between management and workers; we are just one big happy family." And then there is the parent whose child has been charged with a delinquency who tells the social worker, with all sincerity, "But I asked him if he did it and he said he is innocent. I believe him because he always tells me everything he does." Usually, under these circumstances the person involved can admit that the etiquette barrier would *ordinarily* be operant, but he wrongly assumes that in his case, his charm and desire to hear the truth make him an exception.

This desire to avoid embarrassing, shocking, or threatening the other person is quite distinct from the fear of exposing oneself, as in the case of an ego threat. The distinction becomes useful when it is demonstrated that the treatment of one barrier is quite different from the treatment of the other. The ego-threat barrier can be reduced by the interviewer's demonstrating a nonjudgmental attitude toward the respondent's information and by guaranteeing his ano-nymity. This would not facilitate communication if the respondent's information was harmless to his self-image, but was felt inappropriate for the interviewer.

The effect of the etiquette barrier may go beyond simply with-holding information to spare the interviewer's feelings and extend to the point where the respondent tries to please the interviewer by telling him what he wants to hear through selective reporting or fabrication. This desire to please may be particularly detrimental to the validity of the information when the interviewer consciously or unconsciously suggests the "appropriate" answer.

Often the negative effects of the etiquette barrier can be fore-stalled by selecting the appropriate interviewer and situational setting for the interview. Also, if there is a choice of respondents having the desired information, the respondent having the most appropriate relationship to the interviewer should be selected. Sometimes these precautions are not enough in themselves and special techniques and tactics described later can be used.

Trauma. "Trauma" is used to denote an acutely unpleasant feeling associated with crisis experiences. The unpleasant feeling is often brought to the conscious level when the respondent is reporting the experience. This is distinctly different from the fear of losing self-esteem, as in the case of an ego threat, or the fear of shocking the interviewer, as in the case of etiquette. Here, the unpleasantness of the topic results from forcing the respondent to re-live the original emotions associated with the experience. In these circumstances, there is no tendency for the respondent to vacillate between evading a topic and talking about it in order to obtain a cathartic release from guilt feelings. He does not feel remiss for his acts, but has an unpleasant feeling regarding something which happened to him.

The marriage counselor talking to a recently divorced person, the physician obtaining a detailed case history of a person whose close relatives have had untimely deaths, the detective interviewing the widow of a recent murder victim, the social worker interviewing a mother regarding legal charges brought by neighbors against the father for beating his wife and children, the policeman or insurance investigator interviewing the survivor of an auto accident, the personnel counselor interviewing an applicant regarding the circumstances under which he was fired from his last position, the teacher talking to a student suddenly rejected by his peer group because of a rumor regarding the student's family—these and other interview situations are likely to involve some probing of traumatic experiences.

The four inhibitors above (competing time demands, ego threat, etiquette, and trauma) are similar in that they reduce the respondent's *willingness* to talk about a certain topic. The specific recognizable symptoms of unwillingness vary to some extent with the particular inhibitor.

There are four inhibitors which reduce the respondent's *ability*, rather than his willingness, to provide valid information. This inability has two general results. First, and least problematical, the respondent may simply admit that he cannot supply the information at the moment for some reason. Second, the respondent, in trying to cooperate, may supply "information" which is no more than a well-meant mixture of imagination, guesswork, and confusion. The second type of respondent poses a much greater problem for the interviewer. He must learn to anticipate, detect, and counteract this tendency in the respondent. In practice, the solution of the problem is not so difficult as it might seem because much of the respondent's feeling that he has to "say something" is due to a general atmosphere created by the interviewer.

Of the factors which make the respondent *unable* to report relevant information, the first is forgetting.

Forgetting. A frequent inhibitor is the respondent's inability to recall certain types of information. This is not a problem if the objectives of the interview deal only with *current* attitudes, beliefs, or expectations. However, the moment we move into the area of facts we are dealing largely with the past.

This natural fading of the memory (which may be hastened by selective psychological repression) makes it easier for the ego-defense system to reconstruct one's image of his own past by simple omission, addition, or distortion. This idea of the "reconstruction of biography" is a continual theme in the insightful writings of Alfred Schutz.[6]

The memory problem is a much more frequent obstacle than is generally expected by interviewers. Even some of the most seemingly simple and obvious facts cannot be obtained by superficial interviewing methods.

For example, a simple fact such as the date of starting work at a factory cannot be accurately determined in a superficial interview. This was demonstrated in an experiment by Moore[7] in which the respondents' replies to an interviewer were checked against the company records.

Fortunately, the respondent's experience of a particular event is not simply either remembered or forgotten. His ability to remember depends, in general, upon three types of factors. First, the vividness of recall of the experience is related to various dimensions such as its original emotional impact, its meaningfulness to the person at the time, and the degree to which the person's ego was involved. Second is the simple problem of the amount of time elapsing between the event itself and the interview pertaining to it. Third is the nature of the interview situation, including the interviewer's techniques and tactics.

6/ Alfred Schutz, *Collected Papers,* Vol. 1, Maurice Natanson (ed.) (The Hague, Netherlands: Martinus Nijhoff, 1962).

7/ B. V. Moore, "The Interview in Industrial Research," *Social Forces,* Vol. 7 (1929), pp. 445-52.

Knowledge of these factors as they are related to a particular respondent will help the interviewer to *predict* probable trouble in certain areas of subject matter. The second factor, time lapse, is sometimes controllable by the interviewer if he is free to select respondents whose experience is fresh. If he has no control over the amount of time lapse between event and interview, his knowledge of the length of this time span will at least warn him when special techniques and tactics are in order to refresh a respondent's memory. That a once-forgotten event can subsequently be recalled is frequently demonstrated in interviews when the respondent has given a spontaneous and sincere reply early in the interview, only to contradict himself later when his memory has been more adequately stimulated. There are many strategies, techniques, and tactics available to help the alert interviewer overcome the memory barrier.

Chronological confusion. This term refers to the respondent's tendency to confuse the chronological order of his experiences. This may occur in two ways: (*a*) Two or more events may be correctly recalled, but the respondent is unsure of the sequence of their occurrence; or (*b*) only one condition or event is recalled and is incorrectly assumed to have also been true at an earlier point in time.

The second type of confusion is more complicated and merits further explanation. It usually occurs when the interviewer is inquiring into a *developmental* sequence such as relations between people or the respondent's past attitudes, beliefs and expectations, and in his interpretations of past events. Often the original conditions are forgotten and subsequent conditions which are recalled more readily are assumed to have also been true in the prior situation. There is a strong tendency for the respondent to utilize hindsight in interpreting events of the past. Therefore, if we are interested in discovering what the respondent's original interpretation was at the time of the event, special techniques and tactics must be used.

For example, in a suburb of Rochester, New York, leaky gas lines exploded, damaging and reducing the valves which prevent natural gas from entering homes at an extremely high pressure. When the gas pressure suddenly increased 100 times, houses filled with gas and began to explode one at a time over a period of three hours until 45 houses had been completely demolished.

When respondents were asked why they ran from their homes when they first heard an explosion, some said that they wanted to get out of the house before it exploded. Actually, there was no way for people to suspect that the initial explosion was to be the first in a series; the causal connection between the first and succeeding blasts could not have been known immediately. But once the facts were known, running out of the house appeared the rational thing to have done. These respondents, because of chronological confusion, did not realize that they were explaining their behavior at one point in time as being motivated by an idea not gained until *after* they had acted.

This type of problem is commonly encountered in interviews seeking case history information. This would include studies of how people's attitudes and values change, how interpersonal relations in the family or any other group develop, how conflicts arise and are resolved, how people's interpretation of events change, or studies of any problem involving a chronological dimension.

Inferential confusion. This term designates confusion and inaccuracies resulting from errors of inference on the part of the respondent. These errors fall into two general categories: (*a*) due to faulty *induction,* when the respondent is asked to convert concrete experiences into a higher level of generalization; and (*b*) those due to faulty *deduction,* when the respondent is asked to give concrete examples of certain categories of experience supplied by the interviewer.

It is common for the respondent to make a misstep in either ascending or descending the ladder of abstraction. Even though the respondent's memory of his experience might be correct, the moment he begins to interpret, explain, or generalize from these experiences he can make an inferential error. There are two main sources of inferential error, regardless of whether it is the inductive or deductive type. The first is simple; the error may result from the respondent's failure in abstract logic ability. The second is a distortion of thinking which may be produced by strong attitudes and preconceptions.

Errors of the first type are often caused by the interviewer's providing categories of experience which are not clearly defined for the respondent. In this case, the respondent's attempt to provide concrete examples fitting the categories may fail. For example, the interviewer who is studying family conflicts, and who needs to categorize the specific examples of conflict into role conflict, value conflict, and lack of communication, would not be wise to ask, "What are some examples of role conflict in your family?" The probability of the respondent's giving an example which was totally or mainly a case of role conflict is very low, even if an attempt is made to define the term "role conflict" for the respondent. A request for such an example places too much of the burden of analysis upon the respondent.

In order to help the respondent up and down the ladder of abstraction, the interviewer must break the general question into steps which will accumulate relevant details, allowing an accurate analysis to determine which category is appropriate for a specific conflict episode. Often, the respondent is quite adept at giving examples which correctly fit into categories that are his *own*. However, the problem arises when these categories are irrelevant to the purpose of the interview and the respondent is forced to think in unfamiliar terms. The interviewer should use techniques and tactics which either avoid the necessity of the respondent's making inferences or that help him to make them accurately.

Errors of the second type, those involving distortions of inference due to strong attitudes and preconceptions, are common in many types of interviews. These errors usually occur when the objectives of the interview call for some generalized forms of information such as, "How do the black and the white people get along in this school?" "How were the rescue operations handled in the disaster?" "What philosophy of child rearing do you use with your child?" An accurate response to these questions would involve a thoughtful process of inductively reaching a generalization on the basis of a representative sample of observed, concrete events. All of these questions also involve value judgments which are liable to act as premises for a deductive process resulting in the unconscious line of reasoning which says, "This is the way things *should* happen and, in the absence of glaring evidence to the contrary, let's assume that is the way it *did* happen." Thus, the teacher reports that race relations are "tranquil" in her school, the disaster victim reports that the rescue operations were carried out in a "heroic fashion," and the parent reports that she handles the child in a very "permissive and democratic way." In each instance, the respondent may be simply expressing his desire, intent, or assumption. This must be checked by bringing the generalization down the ladder of abstraction to specific concrete events. Often the interviewer will discover that there is no concrete experience to back up the generality.

Unconscious behavior. Often the interview objectives call for information about a person's unconscious behavior. Behavior that is not consciously directed may be classified into three types. The most common is simply custom or habit. The degree to which this is unconscious is indicated by Sapir.[8] Into this category would fall those questions about repetitive behavior such as, "What is the difference between the way you speak to a male and a female on the phone?" "When do you use the prepositions 'of' and 'at' after a verb in the English language?" "Which sock do you usually put on first in the morning?"

Next, there is a type of unconscious behavior which Blumer[9] calls "circular reaction" or the immediate, unwitting response of one person to the subliminal, non-verbal cues furnished by another. This is not usually a repetitious form of behavior, but one which arises only under special circumstances. The following questions would be asking about this type of behavior, "What made you dislike him when you first saw him?" "How did you decide to join the lynch mob?" "How did you know that she loved you?"

The third type of unconscious behavior is found under conditions of acute emotional stress in crises where the behavior does not follow a habitual pattern and where it does not result from circular reaction with others. For example, in a disaster interview a respondent was unable to report how he traveled from his house to a cousin's house in the neighborhood. The evidence indicated that the behavior forgotten by respondent covered a 5-minute interval. The interviewer thought the respondent could have been knocked unconscious and then either blown through the air to that point or carried by a rescue worker. Later, the interviewer discovered that both possibilities were incorrect because other witnesses had seen the respondent climbing frantically over the rubble on the way to his cousin's house and heard him shouting to his wife who had been at the cousin's house before the storm struck.

In general, this type of information is difficult to obtain by interviewing, but is not uncommon for respondents to say that they had never been aware of certain aspects of their behavior until after the interview had been in progress for some time. When interviewing methods fail, the information must be obtained through direct or indirect observation.

These eight inhibitors tend to make the respondent unwilling or unable to give the information requested. They should be viewed as

---

8/ Edward Sapir, "The Unconscious Patterning of Behavior in Society," in E. S. Dummer (ed.), *The Unconscious: A Symposium* (New York: A. A. Knopf, 1927), pp. 114-42.

9/ Herbert Blumer, "Collective Behavior," in Robert S. Park (ed.), *An Outline of the Principles of Sociology* (New York: Barnes and Noble, 1946), p. 224.

forces or tendencies that are not absolute in their effect. Whether or not the respondent gives the information depends not only upon whether the inhibiting force can be circumvented or removed, but it also depends upon the nature and relative strength of certain counter-forces called facilitators.

Facilitators of communication

The facilitators will be approached from the same subjective point of view of the respondent as were the inhibitors. And like the inhibitors, these facilitators are also treated as social-psychological resultants of the relationship between the information and the situation in which it is communicated. Some of the situational stimuli for communication apply to any type of information and others only to more narrow categories of information. Although these facilitators occur in other forms of conversation and can be illustrated with examples from a wide variety of settings, the main concern here is with their value in the interview for both maximizing the flow of relevant information and for maintaining optimal interpersonal relations.

Fulfilling expectations.   One of the important forces in social interaction is the tendency for one person to communicate, verbally and nonverbally, his expectations to another person. The second person then tends to respond, consciously or unconsciously, to those expectations. This may be viewed as one manifestation of the more general human tendency to conform to the group of peers and to the suggestion of higher status persons in the society. It is in this conformity to the group norms that security is sought and usually found. The theoretical and empirical treatments of this basic human tendency are so abundant that we will not attempt to review them here.

More specifically relevant to interviewing is the question of *how* the interviewer communicates *which* expectations to the respondent. In answer to the latter part of this question, we must be aware that the interviewer should communicate both a general expectation of cooperation as well as the more specific expectation of an answer to his specific questions. Although the respondent reacts to his own perception of these expectations, we cannot assume that the response will always mechanically (in a stimulus-response fashion) fulfill the expectation. Instead, by the steady and consistent communication of his general and specific expectations to the respondent, the interviewer will exert a steady, and often cumulative, force affecting the respondent's cooperation. This expectation may be communicated between persons of equal or unequal status, but cooperation requires a type of creative reciprocity that has been described as *dyadic creativity* by Murray.[10]

When we turn to *how* the interviewer communicates his expectations, we must clearly distinguish between *asking* for cooperation and *expecting* it. The former is mainly a verbal communication while the latter is mainly non-verbal. As pointed out by Rogers[11] there must be harmony between what one says and what one feels if the interviewer is to be "dependably real" to the respondent. The inexperienced interviewer who lacks confidence, or who fails to see the importance of his task, will often ask only verbally for the information. He dutifully poses the question, while his whole non-verbal manner communicates his doubt that he has any right to expect an answer. It is this neutralizing effect of the verbal and the non-verbal communication which often causes the novice to lose faith in the "power of positive expectations." He may say, "I told him it was all right to tell me anything that was on his mind, but I'm sure he was withholding important information." This problem persists where the interviewer is not aware that he is also communicating non-verbally with the respondent.

In some cases, the interviewer's negative expectations also interfere with his ability to observe the respondent accurately. His attitude so colors his interpretation of the respondent's behavior that he imagines resistance. This makes him more doubtful and the reinforced attitude is then communicated unwittingly to the respondent. Thus, a form of circular reaction is set up with one aspect reinforcing the other until the interviewer feels it almost unbearable to contact another respondent.

The following example shows how one interviewer projected his expectation of failure into his interpretation of the respondent's behavior:

"I knocked on the door and explained what I wanted. She had a skeptical look on her face. Then a male voice mumbled something from behind her. Then she said that she couldn't do the interview at that time, but that I should come back

10/ Henry A. Murray, "Dyadic Creations" in Warren G. Bennis, *et al., Interpersonal Dynamics* (Homewood, Ill.: The Dorsey Press, 1964), pp. 638-46.

11/ Carl R. Rogers, "The Characteristics of a Helping Relationship," *On Becoming a Person* (Boston: Houghton Mifflin, 1961), pp. 39-58.

the next day. I just knew that she was lying because you could see that she was afraid and she had a sort of weak, high-pitched voice. The man was probably trying to protect her so that gave her an excuse to offer.

I didn't expect to find her there the next day and was I ever surprised when she came to the door and invited me in! I could see that I had been wrong in my original judgment of her, because she was very willing to talk. That tone of voice I had heard the day before was natural for her, even when she was talking about something humorous.

Usually interviewers gain confidence with experience. However, the experience must be mostly successful. The wise novice accepts his limitations and begins with easier assignments and with increasing confidence and skill, he progresses to more difficult ones. Confidence is not all that is needed, but it is one of the positive forces in the interview situation. When the interviewer gains a better understanding of the numerous factors which make an interview successful or unsuccessful, he is less likely to lose confidence through failures caused by forces beyond his control. Just as the physician, lawyer, and minister, in their roles, can expect and receive privileged communications, the interviewer learns his role and is able to communicate it in a subtle way to the respondent.

Recognition.   All human beings need the recognition and the esteem (as distinct from affection) of others. Much of literature of social anthropology, social psychology and sociology is concerned with concepts which involve this element of recognition. Studies of such factors as competition, social status, prestige or approval all involve this element. W. I. Thomas[12] was one of the early sociologists who consciously conceptualized the idea as one of the "four wishes" basic to human motivation. The desire for recognition is fitted into a carefully developed theoretical framework of *social exchange* by Homans,[13] who shows that social interaction often depends upon an exchange of social goods such as esteem and admiration for certain activities. In short, people will "perform" in exchange for recognition and other social rewards. Parsons and Bales[14] use the words *approval* and *esteem* to cover what we refer to as recognition. In their scheme, approval refers to that positive attitude

12/ Edmund H. Volkart (ed.), *Social Behavior and Personality* (New York: Social Science Research Council, 1951), pp. 125-29. Thomas's "four wishes" are the desire for new experience, security, response, and recognition.

13/ George C. Homans, *Social Behavior: Its Elementary Forms* (New York: Harcourt, Brace and World, Inc. 1961), pp. 51-82.

14/ Talcott Parsons and Robert F. Bales, *Family, Socialization and Interaction Process* (New York: The Free Press, 1955), pp. 86-87.

in response to *specific* performances by the other person, while esteem is reserved for the positive *overall* evaluation of that person. Sutherland[15] has demonstrated that even criminals find ways to gain esteem, approval or recognition (and hence self-respect) by conforming to the norms of the underworld.

The need for recognition is fulfilled by attention from people outside the individual's intimate circle. Being appreciated and loved by one's wife is gratifying, but does not fulfill the need for recognition as we use the term. People may enjoy recognition even though it is based upon notoriety or upon a good reputation which is not deserved.

The skillful and insightful interviewer takes advantage of every opportunity to give the respondent *sincere* recognition. Experimental studies of interviewing have shown that praising the respondent's cooperation has a definite positive effect on the interview.[16]

In addition to direct, sincere praise, there are many sources of ego gratification for the respondent. For example, the respondent may be flattered that he was *selected* because he has some information that is *needed*. The same feeling may result because the respondent's town, his place of employment, his school, or any other group with which he identifies is being studied. It is no accident that there have been several magazine articles on the theme, "I was interviewed by Mr. Kinsey." People who have had such an experience are unique in the eyes of those around them.

Altruistic appeals. There seems to be a human need to identify with some high value or cause that is beyond immediate self-interest. This may be a form of identification with the objectives of some larger group. The group may be real or imaginary, contemporary or not. Altruistic deeds usually increase self-esteem whether or not the person's deeds have been public. This distinguishes altruism from recognition.

In every case, the individual is responding to some group value which he has internalized. In some cases, value may be *latent* in that the holder seldom acts upon it because more immediate practical values take precedence. Often the interviewer, if he understands the respondent's value system, can use strategy, techniques, and tactics to reactivate the latent value.

Altruism is of major importance in motivating many respondents

15/ E. H. Sutherland, *The Professional Thief* (Chicago: University of Chicago Press, 1937).
16/ Joan B. Field, "The Effect of Praise in a Public Opinion Poll," *Public Opinion Quarterly,* 1955, pp. 85-90.

in sociological, psychological, and anthropological studies. For example, the Martin brothers gave detailed case history material on their crimes, feeling that this might help other youths stay out of the underworld.[17] In some cases, respondents have volunteered information that was obviously painful to give because they felt it would be of value to others. In a study of marital adjustment, it was obvious that some of the husbands and wives volunteered information beyond what was asked and accepted the blame for an unsuccessful marriage because "it might help someone avoid the mistake I made." Also members of a disaster-stricken community willingly gave information with the hope that it might help future disaster victims.

Sympathetic understanding. Human beings need the sympathetic response of others. They like to share their joys, fears, successes, and failures. This need of understanding differs from the need for recognition which requires success and increased status in the eyes of people with whom one does not share an intimate relationship; in fact, a person can feel "famous" without knowing any of his "fans" personally. In contrast, sympathetic understanding may be obtained in connection with failures and shortcomings as well as successes, and it is usually extended by a member of the primary group, but it may also be extended by the therapist or interviewer.

This need for sympathetic understanding has been incorporated into many schemes of human needs and it has been given several names. Some of the concepts most closely synonymous with sympathetic understanding are: the "desire for *response,*" as used by W. I. Thomas,[18] and a combination of the desire for *acceptance* and for *approval,* as used by Parsons and Bales.[19]

This desire to be understood and to have someone offer a "sympathetic ear" is seen not only in the therapeutic interview but also in many information-gathering interviews. Teenagers often need someone who "really understands" them and who knows what they mean by "problem parents." Old people are often easy to interview, not only because they are retired and have more time, but also because they have problems which no one takes time to hear. Also, until recently their problems have received much less attention than the problems of youth in the American culture. Shut-ins, socially deviant persons, and other types of isolates often cause the public opinion

---

17/ Clifford R. Shaw, *Brothers in Crime* (Chicago: University of Chicago Press, 1938).
18/ Volkart, *op. cit.,* p. 129.
19/ *Op. cit.,* p. 86.

pollster great difficulty because they want to chat about everything but the subject of the interview. In this case, the need for sympathetic understanding interferes with the efficiency of the interview, and the interviewer must decide to what extent he should allow the respondent to talk about his own problems in view of the effect upon interpersonal relations and the adequacy of the information.

People do not have to be obviously isolated to have a pent up need for a sympathetic ear. In their routine pattern of living, many people have few opportunities to meet a good listener. Ordinarily, when they begin to talk about their problems, the listener retaliates with a long list of his own grievances which tend to pale the first person's difficulties. Often, people refrain from expressing their feelings because "my husband hears that from me all the time," or "he hears people's gripes all day long at the office and doesn't want to hear more of the same thing when he comes home."

Interviewers who reflect a sympathetic attitude and who know how to direct it toward the objectives of the interview will find their percentage of successes much higher than those who cannot.

New experience. All human beings welcome some form of new experience.[20] Even though variety may not be the only spice of life, escape from the dreary routine is sought by everyone. In interviewing personnel in hospitals, industry, and schools, there have been many cases where the interview appeals to the respondent's need for new experience. For example, educators who were cosmopolitan by training and who found themselves temporary captives of a small, local community, found it stimulating to be interviewed on such subjects as academic freedom, foreign trade, or trends in the development and application of social science.

When interviewing industrial employees, it was often obvious that they welcomed a coffee break during which they could discuss anything. After the formal interviews were completed respondents commented, "Do I have to go back to work now?" "That was very interesting. I had never thought about a lot of these things before." "I hope I didn't bore you with all this talk, but I found it very exciting." "I'm not much of a talker, but if we can talk on company time that's fine with me." "This is a lot more fun than what I do all day at the plant."

Similarly, as market research people know, the housewife has a certain pattern of activities, and although these may vary in detail

20/ Volkart, *op. cit.,* p. 121.

from tenement house areas to suburbia, a break in this routine is often a welcome relief. In suburbia, many of the women rarely see a man in the neighborhood during the day, much less have the opportunity to be interviewed by one.

Sometimes the respondent is motivated by his curiosity regarding the interviewer, and the interviewer should consider this in deciding what to say about himself.

We must not assume, simply because an interview is a new experience for a particular respondent, that is will satisfy his need for new experience. There are some negative effects when certain aspects of the respondent's perception of the new situation are ego threatening. The respondent may be anxious about whether he will make a good impression on the interviewer or whether there may be some hidden purpose in the interview. This apprehensiveness can often be detected by the interviewer at the beginning of the contact. Once these fears are dispelled, the respondent frequently finds the interview a new and interesting experience.

Catharsis. By "catharsis" we mean the process by which one person obtains a release from unpleasant emotional tensions by talking about the source of these tensions and expressing his feelings. The psychotherapist is most often concerned with catharsis as a release from guilt feelings which may be repressed in the subconscious. Similarly, the religious confession usually involves an expression of guilt in an attempt to relieve the pangs of conscience. Although catharsis is often associated with deep personality disturbances, in its broadest concept it is found in the everyday experience of most people. We have mild guilt feelings over the way we have treated someone during the day, or we have pent up feelings of frustration and inhibited aggression against our associates. This tension may be released by kicking the cat or by pouring out our difficulties to another person.

Although we are all familiar with the frequent need for catharsis in ourselves, we do not always perceive the same need in others. Most people dealing in human relations know that this need to "air our gripes," to verbalize our feelings of hostility, guilt and frustration, is omnipresent. The sensitive field worker frequently recognizes his role as the itinerant "father confessor." For example, a college professor, whose colleague was fired during loyalty hearings, feels guilty for not having come to the defense of his friend. Although he knew his colleague had no communist connections, he was afraid he, too, might lose his job. A mother of a delinquent son might blame herself for his behavior. More commonly, a mother might feel frustrated because her three children keep her so exhausted that she cannot be a good companion for her husband or use her college training creatively. In any of these cases, the need for catharsis increases the spontaneity of the interview once an atmosphere of sympathetic understanding has been established.

The need for sympathetic understanding and the need for catharsis are related, but they are not the same thing. A person may satisfy his need for sympathetic understanding by sharing with the interviewer his joys, plans, and achievements that do not involve any past frustration, aggression, guilt or repression. Since no moral connotations are involved, it is not so necessary for this respondent to feel assured that the interviewer will respect his confidence. He is mainly concerned with finding someone to talk to and does not consider whether the interviewer will divulge the information or not.

Frequently, motivation behind the conversation may move by imperceptible degrees from the simple need for a sympathetic listener to the need for catharsis. Although at some points in this process it is difficult to distinguish which motive is dominant, this does not make the distinction between the two motivations meaningless.

There can be a situation in which the need of sympathetic understanding is being fulfilled without catharsis. However, it is impossible to fulfill the need for catharsis without first establishing an atmosphere of sympathetic understanding. For this reason sympathetic understanding usually *precedes* catharsis. The interviewer who does not have time to listen to what he considers inconsequential egocentric talk will not find the respondent ready to share important confidences.

The need for catharsis is usually a positive factor, but once the proper atmosphere has been established, there is sometimes a detrimental delayed reaction, and the respondent begins to feel embarrassed or resentful toward the interviewer for "making" him talk about ego threatening topics. Once his need for catharsis has been fulfilled, the respondent may become concerned about the possible results of having given the information. The respondent's doubts grow when the interviewer is no longer present to provide the constant reassurance of anonymity, and to display his own non-judgmental attitude toward the respondent. As a result, any second contact with the respondent may begin with coolness or hostility. In cases where no second contact is needed, the respondent may still damage the study by negatively influencing other potential respondents. Ways of minimizing this possibility will be shown later.

The need for meaning. Another general human trait is the need for meaning. The desire for an answer to such questions as "Who am I?" "Where did I come from?" "Where am I going?" or "Why do events happen as they do?" often tempts a person in higher status to give a person in lower status an answer that he does not believe himself but which he thinks will satisfy his questioner. For example, a child may ask his mother, "What holds up the moon?" and in desperation she may reply, "It hangs on a string," or "It is full of gas like a balloon." Most primitive tribes have a myth which explains the origin of their tribe, if not of the whole universe, which fills the void between desired knowledge and available knowledge.

Every society has a set of assumptions, values, explanations, and myths lending order to the confusion of reality in which the members of that society live. Cantril[21] has spelled out in some detail the interrelationships between different parts of the system as they are internalized in one personality. Particularly relevant to the problem of interviewing is his general observation that under changing social conditions, the individual's system of meaning becomes inadequate to explain real events from which he cannot escape. When the social matrix is disturbed, the individual embarks upon a search for meaning which often makes him highly susceptible to suggestion and a likely candidate for some social movement.

This concept of the *need for meaning* has been dealt with experimentally by Festinger[22] and others as the need to resolve *cognitive dissonance.* They point out that there is a psychological tension set up in the individual when he becomes aware of any incongruence of facts, assumptions or interpretations. This tension is painful and its reduction is rewarding to the individual.

As the interviewer with wide experience knows, these disturbances of an individual's belief system result from wars, depressions, catastrophes, and other large scale crises. Disaster interviews often show that the crisis left the members of the disaster-stricken town groping for the meaning of what has happened. They would wonder, "Why did some people get killed while others were spared? Why was I spared? How could a just God allow this to happen to innocent

21/ Hadley Cantril, *The Psychology of Social Movements* (New York: John Wiley & Sons, Inc., 1941), pp. 53-77.

22/ Leon Festinger, *A Theory of Cognitive Dissonance* (Stanford: Stanford U. Press, 1957), p. 13.

children who are too young to be sinners? What would have happened if Robert had been late to the high school dance as he usually was . . . would he have been killed on his way?"

This need for meaning and the tendency to search for answers was noted in these people's increased attendance at several different local churches for some weeks after the disaster. Usually, each minister responded to his congregation's expectation of an explanation by showing how these events could be reconciled to the concept of a "just and loving God." The need for meaning was also shown in the respondents' reflections during the interview.

More common sources of insecurity accompanying loss of meaning are seen in the life cycle of individuals. In a dynamically changing society, the adolescent is beset by confusion as he tries to adjust to the process of becoming an adult. The examples set by his own parents no longer apply to conditions of life in the atomic age. Similarly, the graduate from a teachers college is shocked in his first teaching job when he finds a great discrepancy between his idealistic expectations and the actual operation of the school in which he teaches. He might wonder, "Is this what I went to school for? Do parents really want their children to be educated, or do they merely want them to be taught the same things they learned? Are teachers hired mainly to keep the kids off the streets, out of the labor market and away from their mother's bridge game? Is it really possible to teach, thinking of the individual needs of each child, while trying to prevent bedlam in a class of forty children? Why didn't anyone mention these things in our courses on teaching methods?" During this initial disillusionment he may seek someone to talk to as an aid to thinking through the problem and deciding on a future course of action. Likewise, it is found that people who never felt pressed by questions about things such as sickness, loneliness, and death, begin to face some new questions as they approach later maturity. Their philosophy of life sometimes needs to be reevaluated when it becomes apparent that they will not live forever.

In those cases where the interview topic deals directly with the sources disturbing a person's system of meaning, there is a strong motivation for the respondent to talk it through, once he is convinced of the interviewer's interest in his search for meaning. It is sometimes possible for the interviewer to elicit the respondent's interest by pointing out contradictions, inconsistencies, dilemmas, or facts that might stimulate the respondent's need for meaning. In other words, the interviewer may try to disturb the respondent's equilibrium by involving him in a problem. This is usually more difficult than dealing with a problem in which the respondent is already involved. Valid public opinion polls on "controversial issues" are often difficult to do, because problems defined as public issues by the information collectors may not concern those who are answering the questions.

Once the interviewer has been sensitized to this omnipresent need for meaning, he can use skills, techniques, and tactics to maximize the stimulation and fulfillment of the need, thus utilizing another basic motivation to communicate.

Extrinsic rewards. This term refers to those rewards motivating the respondent other than those he gains directly from interaction within the interview itself. These extrinsic rewards are helpful insofar as the respondent sees the interview as a means to an end. Even though the objectives of the interview may not coincide with the respondent's objectives beyond the interview, the interviewer may skillfully utilize various extrinsic rewards in order to obtain the respondent's cooperation.

Many forms of extrinsic rewards have been used. Money may be given in exchange for the respondent's time, or the interviewer's study may help solve some problem in which the respondent is interested. A respondent may submit to an interview, or even seek it, as a means of obtaining a job. A recently divorced mother may agree to an interview with a social worker, hoping that she will be able to obtain financial aid and psychotherapy for her daughter. A businessman may cooperate in an interview because he is interested in reducing juvenile delinquency, particularly shop-lifting from his own store. A college professor may have an interest in being interviewed on the topic of academic freedom, hoping that the study might stir up public sentiment for the protection of this freedom.

Extrinsic rewards are usually not needed to obtain cooperation in studies involving human interest, but they become more necessary as intrinsic rewards decrease and as the amount of time and thought demanded from the respondent increase. For example, it is more necessary to pay people to submit to a psychological study of sensory perception or reaction time than to pay respondents to cooperate with an opinion poll on a current issue. Sometimes an extrinsic reward is desirable even though the respondents are members of a captive group who do not give their permission as individuals. This is true particularly if the reward is given by the agency sponsoring the interviewer rather than by the agency that allowed the interviewer access to the respondents. The extrinsic reward sometimes helps overcome initial resentment or allows a series of contacts without causing the respondent's increasing resentment of time spent.

There are circumstances in which any extrinsic reward, particularly money, is detrimental. If the offer of a reward has the effect of attracting one type of respondent and repelling others, this selectivity may bias the study. Offering money may damage the prestige of participating in the study or may encourage bargaining by people who are interested only in the money. The effective use of extrinsic rewards will be explored in the next chapter on field strategy.

Extrinsic rewards are rarely needed and then mainly for obtaining the initial contact. Once the interview begins, the interviewer must bring as many of the intrinsic rewards into play as possible.

SUMMARY

From the interviewer's point of view, there are two basic tasks to be accomplished. The main one is to *maximize* the flow of relevant and valid information. As a means to this end, he must maintain *optimal* interpersonal relations between himself and the respondent. Unlike a social conversation, the task of maintaining optimal interpersonal relations is subordinated as a means to the end of maximizing the flow of useful information.

It is helpful to view the interaction in the interviewer-respondent dyad in the broader theoretical framework of *social exchange* to which we have referred from time to time.[23] This framework helps us focus upon the essential fact that the interviewer must take stock of the social-psychological rewards he can offer in exchange for the information he seeks from the respondent. From the point of view of the respondent, we can see that the exchange in the interview involves both *costs* and *rewards*.

The *cost* to the respondent is represented by his effort to overcome the inhibitors classified as (1) competing time demands, (2) ego threat, (3) etiquette, (4) trauma, (5) forgetting, (6) chronological confusion, (7) inferential confusion, and (8) unconscious experience. The *rewards* to be offered by the interviewer to offset the costs consist of the facilitators classified as (1) fulfilling expectations, (2) giving recognition, (3) providing altruistic appeal, (4) supplying

---

23/ Peter M. Blau, *Exchange and Power in Social Life* (New York: John Wiley and Sons, Inc., 1964), contains one of the best formulations of social exchange theory.

sympathetic understanding, (5) providing new experience, (6) facilitating catharsis, (7) fulfilling the need for meaning, and (8) supplying extrinsic rewards when the preceding seven intrinsic rewards are not sufficient.

In a nutshell, the interviewer's task consists of *reducing the costs* to the respondent by minimizing the inhibitors of communication and *enhancing the rewards* by maximizing the facilitators of communication. The rest of this book provides a wide variety of strategies, techniques, and tactics which can be used by the interviewer to perform these two basic functions in the dyadic social exchange we call the interview.

4
Interviewing
strategy

The central task of the interviewer is to minimize the eight inhibitors and to maximize the eight facilitators of communication to increase the flow of valid, relevant information. The tools for this task are of three general types: strategies, techniques, and tactics. These three can be distinguished by thinking of *strategy* as the making of those decisions which determine the general social-psychological setting of the interview.

In dramatistic terms, we would say that strategy determines the *plot* (purpose or objectives), the *scene* (time, place and definition of the situation), and the *cast* (who is to interview who). However, it does *not* include writing the *script* (the interview guide or schedule). The script, or who says what to whom, includes both techniques and tactics as will be defined here. Unlike the cast of a stage drama, the interview is usually limited to two persons and only one has a script.

DEFINITION OF STRATEGY

In making strategy decisions we must specify the purpose of the interview as clearly as possible since the selection of the cast and scenes depends upon the plot. Even though the research director may seem free to determine the purpose of a study, he is never completely so because he may be limited by the availability of funds, by theoretical problems, and by methodological shortcomings in view of the particular field conditions in which the research must take place. A particular type of research may be fairly simple in one culture and impossible in another.

Once we have a tentative formulation of the plot we can then choose the actors. In selecting potential respondents we must think about who has the needed information, who is most likely to give the information, and who is most accessible in terms of the efficiency of the project. In selecting the interviewer we must think of the types of persons who will have the best understanding of the purposes of the study and the best relationship to the people who have the needed information.

We cannot mechanically proceed from the consideration of the plot, to the selection of the cast and then to the specification of the scene. Instead, realistic choices of scene, in view of the actual field conditions, must be taken into consideration in selecting interviewers or respondents and in revising or specifying the purpose of the research. The researcher, unlike the playwright is not completely free to create the scene from his imagination, but must consider the actual field conditions in which he must operate. Nor can he proceed effectively without creative imagination to conceive of ways to exercise some control of the scene by the selection from among real possibilities of time and place and by devising effective ways of influencing the interviewer's and respondent's definition of the situation in a way that will minimize the inhibitors and maximize the facilitators of communication.

The researcher does not have a choice of either making or not making strategy decisions. He uses a strategy whether he is aware of it or not, whether he consciously selected from among alternatives or not, whether it was guided by any theoretical rationale or not. The fact that a particular interviewer is not aware of these problems does not mean that the decisions have not been made by someone. In large scale research projects these strategy decisions are rarely made by the corps of hired specialized interviewers. Instead, they may be made by a research director, a supervisor for the specific study, or a special consultant-interviewer. Regardless, the person making the strategy decisions should be someone intimately familiar with the purposes of study, with the types of potential respondents, and with various possible settings in which the interviewing might be done. Frequently it is necessary for the strategist to do some pilot interviewing and usually some of the early pretesting of the first drafts of the interview schedule, if it is to be used by a team of specialized interviewers. The larger the research organization and the greater the amount of data to be collected on a particular study, the smaller the proportion of the total personnel involved in the strategy decisions.

Whether it is a small team effort or a large scale survey, it is advisable to clearly specify all of the strategy decisions as part of the instructions to the interviewers. It is not uncommon for the instructions for a 10-page interview schedule to be as long as 40 to 50 pages. The neophyte is often unaware of the importance of this manual of instructions for a particular interview study. It is important to their performance and morale for the interviewers to understand what decisions have been made regarding strategy, techniques and tactics and why these are necessary.

ASSUMPTIONS UNDERLYING THE TREATMENT OF STRATEGY

It may be assumed that other sources of information such as personal documents, official records, census data, questionnaires, participation, and observation have been considered and that there has been a decision that some or all of the information must be collected by interviewing.

A myriad of practical specific questions must be resolved to meet minimum requirements of any field operation. Specific problems such as how to select a random sample of respondents, if such a sample is needed; how to obtain a list of special respondents; how to locate respondents once they have been selected, will not be taken up here, not because they are considered unimportant, but because the concrete answers to these questions vary infinitely, owing to the variety of specific settings, and the questions themselves do not deal with the central problem of minimizing inhibitors and maximizing facilitators of relevant information.

It is useful to discuss *general* types of problems and an array of problem-solving tools without giving rules to cover the multitudinous specific situations which might arise. These general problems must be considered by the designer, field supervisor or sophisticated interviewer so he can effectively select from among several possible strategies. The principles which we might illustrate in only one or two cases are often applicable to many different specific settings.

CONTRASTING TYPES OF FIELD SITUATIONS

It has already been pointed out that the researcher, unlike the playwright cannot create the scene completely from his imagination, but must operate within the limitations of the realities of the field situation in which the study must be done.

The following classification of field situations sensitizes us to three vital dimensions of the broader context in which studies operate. Each dimension has important consequences in that it places different types of limitations and poses different types of problems calling for different types of strategies. These three dimensions are: friendly versus hostile, open versus closed, and single versus multiple contacts.

Friendly versus hostile territory

Logically, there might be three points on a continuum which indicate community attitude toward the interviewing. At one extreme would be the completely hostile situation with a minimum of cooperation expected. This would be approximated in the military interrogation of a prisoner of war or in the policeman's questioning of a suspect. Less extreme would be the case of the sociologist interviewing the president of a college to discover flagrant violations of academic freedom. Similarly, a social scientist studying the effects of the "sit in" against restaurant segregation would encounter hostility in interviews with leaders of a restaurant association formed to combat the "sit ins."

At the other extreme of the continuum would be a group inviting a social scientist to help them achieve some goal they have spontaneously agreed upon. This type of field situation, as long as it remained one of pure cooperation, would not pose any particular problems for the strategist. However, even though the interviewer had been invited to do the study, initial cooperation might change as the interviewing progressed and disturbed the social equilibrium. The good strategist is prepared for this possibility.

Between the two extremes of hostility and complete cooperation is a middle ground encountered more frequently. Three classes of intermediate types can be delineated. The first is simply a form of *limited cooperation* where the cooperation has certain implicit or explicit limits. These limits may consist of certain quantitative or qualitative conditions which are imposed. For example, the middle-management people in a large corporation might be happy to be

interviewed by a consultant regarding problems of management training programs if a "reasonable limit" was placed upon the amount of
time or the number of interviews involved. If this limit was exceeded,
the initial cooperation might turn to mild hostility.

The implied limitation may be qualitative. A civic organization
that invited a consultant to interview a sample of suburban residents
later withdrew its support because he asked "personal questions"
such as the source of the respondent's income and his religion.

Another type of intermediate point might be called *ambivalence*.
This is a more volatile circumstance in which individual respondents
have the potential for both excellent cooperation and explosive hostility. The respondent's ambivalence may be due to either conflicting
values and desires within himself or potentially opposite perceptions
of the interview situation. This type of ambivalence was sometimes
found in respondents recounting their marital difficulties; they
would feel torn between confessing certain actions to obtain catharsis and cutting the interview short to avoid confessing such ego-
threatening information.

A third type of middle ground might be called the *polarized* situation. Here, as in ambivalence, both ends of the hostility-cooperation
continuum are actually or potentially present in the group. However,
each individual is consistently cooperative or hostile depending upon
his attitude toward some issue related to the interview topic. The
split in the community or organization might occur between strata of
power or prestige, between subcultural groups, or between occupational categories. The polarized situation would be probable in a
study of labor-management conflicts. In this case, if the interviewer
were perceived as partial to the union, he would also be perceived as
unsympathetic or hostile to management, and vice versa.

Open versus closed communities

Here, "closed" refers to the degree to which persons of power or
prestige can prevent the interviewer from contacting or gaining the
cooperation of subordinates in the group. If a group is open, each
individual respondent is free from any legal or other direct social
pressure determining his decision to cooperate with the interviewer.
The degree of closedness of a group, organization, or community
depends upon the degree to which the power figure has absolute
control over members, the degree to which the membership of the
group overlaps with other groups, and the degree to which the mem-

bers feel committed to the wishes of the power figure, even though they can be contacted through other groups or in the open residential community.

To illustrate these dimensions, assume that we wish to interview prison inmates. The prison warden has absolute control over the inmates in his institution; during their stay in prison they are not members of any other group through which the interviewer might gain access to them as respondents. However, if the criminal were interviewed after his release from prison, he would not feel any obligation to the warden.

On the other hand, in doing a social-psychological study of certain monastic orders, we would find a different pattern of closedness. In some orders, the person in charge of the monastery may grant or deny permission to anyone who wishes to enter or leave and each monk's total life pattern may take place within the monastery walls. In these characteristics, the organization is as closed as the prison, but if a brother were to leave the order and return to the outside world, he may have internalized the point of view of the church hierarchy and still be strongly under its influence. A different pattern of closedness prevails in a delinquent gang not in custody. No one's permission is needed to make contact with any members of the gang, since they all have homes and may even go to school regularly. Nevertheless, obtaining information about their illegal operations is very difficult unless the informal leader gives an affirmative nod.

The closed community is not always easy to recognize or to anticipate because of various possible complications. The community may be polarized between two nearly equal power groups, one favoring and the other opposing the interviewing. The opposition may be hidden from view, while the favoring group may be reluctant to acknowledge the opposing group's existence. The control over the respondents may be either legal or extralegal, while the sanctions for violation may be either positive punishment or withdrawal of certain privileges or status. The followers may perceive their leader's desires as external pressure or as "the right thing to do."

Strategy problems are not necessarily greater in the closed community than in the open, but the problems are different. Regardless of the quality or amount of closedness in a group, certain common strategy must be planned to obtain the goodwill of the power group which can allow contact with respondents and give some assurance of their cooperation. If this sanction is given by the leaders, plans must be made for maintaining their support throughout the study. If the community is not only closed but also polarized between power strata, an interesting dilemma arises. The support of the super-ordinate group, which must be obtained to gain access to the sub-ordinate group, is double-edged; the interviewer may be suspected by the respondents *because* he has the approval of their superiors. Fi-nally, if the power group does not give its support, plans must be made, if no other community can be substituted, to gain access to respondents without the leader's sanction. The extent to which this can be accomplished depends upon to what degree the respondents are completely controlled by the one closed group or community.

Single versus multiple contacts

Whether or not each respondent must be contacted more than once depends upon several conditions. For example, if the interview calls for a wide variety of special respondents, the first contact may be devoted to checking the respondent's qualifications in terms of the experiences he has had and his ability and willingness to report them. Or, if the type of information needed requires a more intimate relationship than can be established quickly, the first contact may be devoted mainly to building a suitable relationship. In other cases, multiple contacts are required simply because the amount of infor-mation to be obtained is too great to obtain in a single interview without encountering fatigue or competing time demands. Another common type of information requiring multiple contacts is the panel study or any study where the objective is to trace changes in individ-uals over a period of time. Also, the study may be in the initial stages of exploration so that the interviewer does not know during the first interview all the questions which must be asked. Finally, there are times when the interviewer needs to return to the respondent to clarify or to verify some of the information obtained in the first contact.

There are certain strategy problems associated with both the sin-gle- and the multiple-contact field situation. If only one contact is to be made, there may be a problem of building good rapport in the short time available. However, there are advantages to the single contact in that the interviewer is usually perceived as a stranger who will leave the local scene soon and therefore not become involved in local matters.

In some circumstances the single contact seems to be advisable regardless of the large amount of information to be collected from each respondent. A very long interview makes it more difficult to find a sufficient block of time uninterrupted by competing time demands. However, the efficiency of the interview might be improved by using auxiliary questionnaires or check lists, by pruning out all unnecessary questions, and by carefully selecting a time and place for the interview which will minimize competing time demands. Of course, the latter solution will often spread the same number of interviews over a longer period of elapsed time.

A danger to guard against in the long interview is simple fatigue or loss of interest by both the interviewer and respondent. Fatigue is not necessarily a result of the length of the interview; there is considerable evidence that fatigue is often more the result of the presence of the communication inhibitors and the absence of the facilitators. It has been demonstrated that it is possible to interview one person for eight hours at a time without fatigue seriously interfering with the flow of information.[1]

In making strategy plans involving the possible use of extremely long interviews, pilot interviews should be done to explore any negative effects of fatigue. It might be found necessary to abandon plans for a single contact and split the interview into two sessions.

When single contacts are to be made with a large number and variety of special respondents, a much larger proportion of the interviewer's time will be spent locating and contacting than would be the case where a series of contacts is made with the same person. This is an unavoidable consequence which must be recognized in planning the rate of progress of the field study.

Let us now examine some of the potential problems present when the interviewer makes multiple contacts and stays longer in the community. First, we must guard against the contamination effects of one respondent directly or indirectly influencing another. This influence may be negative. For example, a respondent might feel uneasy about confidences given even though the interview had a pleasant cathartic effect at the time. His delayed reaction may cause him to warn others in the community about "that interviewer who makes you say things you don't mean." Often, this possibility can be reduced by ending each interview with a short informal conversational period aimed at building the respondent's ego. In some cases, the respondent will use this ego-building period to rationalize or "explain" things he said but "didn't really mean." If the interviewer simply accepts these rationalizations without question and praises the respondent where he can do so conscientiously, there is less

1/ N. Gross and W. Mason, "Some Methodological Problems of Eight-Hour Interviews," *American Journal of Sociology,* Vol. 59, No. 3 (November, 1953), pp. 197-204.

tendency for the respondent to try to retaliate after the interviewer leaves.

Another contamination effect is found where one respondent tries to explain to a potential respondent the purpose of the interview, the sponsorship, and so on. Although his intentions are good, his account may distort the facts so that the interview is seen as simply worthless or even ego threatening. This difficulty can sometimes be forestalled by preparing a written explanation, combined with a note of appreciation, to be left with each respondent after completing the interview. This pamphlet or letter should contain clear information on the purpose, sponsorship and anonymity of the interview. Perhaps more important, it should include the name, address, and phone number of some locally-trusted person who endorses the project and who can quell any doubts. Another safeguard is to give news releases to local papers explaining the study, reporting its progress, and praising the community for its cooperation. Also, the possibility of contamination can be reduced by maintaining contact with key informants regarding any developments of rumors or opposition.

Another problem arising when the interviewer stays longer to make multiple contacts might be called "role confusion." On the first contact, the interviewer may be given confidential information because he is perceived as a stranger who will not remain long enough to carry confidential information to others in the community. When the same interviewer is in the community weeks later talking to neighbors, a respondent might temper his remarks in the next interview or show suspicion of the interviewer's purpose.

Much of this role confusion can be prevented by stating clearly at the start how long the interviewer intends to stay in the community, by reassuring respondents regarding the interviewer's integrity, and by showing the necessity of interviewing all types of people. Also, the topics to be covered in a series of interviews may be planned to leave the most ego threatening information to the last in the series.

Another strategy is to use different interviewers to contact respondents who fear the possibility of information being passed among them by the interviewer. This problem is greatest when the community is polarized or fractionalized over issues conceivably related to the topic of the interview. The interviewer's association with members of one group is perceived by members of another as "fraternizing with the enemy." When this polarization is extreme, multiple contacts with each respondent become almost impossible. In this case, one interviewer could specialize in respondents on one side of an issue and another interviewer could deal with the opposite camp.

In addition to the contrasting types of field situations, another important dimension of strategy is the type of respondent needed for the purposes of the study.

GENERAL TYPES OF RESPONDENTS

Broadly, the types of respondents can be said to correspond, in general, to the kinds of information sought in a study. Here, we are not concerned with personal characteristics of the respondent, but with the general type of information he can offer.

Key informants

The key informant is any person who gives information relevant to any of the strategy problems of a study. In this role, the person does not give information directly related to the objectives of the interview. Instead, he helps by supplying information on the local field situation, by assisting in obtaining cooperation, by locating or contacting respondents, and by relaying information during the progress of the study to help meet its objectives. Key informants are particularly necessary in hostile and closed communities.

Special respondents

The special respondent is any person who gives information directly relevant to the objectives of the study and who is selected because he occupies a unique position in the community, group, or institution being studied.

The special respondent is needed because his unique position qualifies him to give special information, either on his own thoughts and actions as he functions in that particular position, or on his observation of others' feelings, thoughts, and actions from his special vantage point.

The special respondent also provides information on the *structural* aspects of the group, institution, or community. Such special respondents would be useful in discovering the difference between the formal and informal organization of an industrial plant, mapping out the channels of political influence in a community, or analyzing the structure of a boys' gang.

A different type of information may be obtained from each special respondent since his unique perspective is his chief contribution to the study.

Representative respondents

The representative respondent, like the special respondent, gives information directly relevant to the objectives of the interview. The representative respondent is chosen because he is *like* other respondents, in that he belongs to a certain category, universe, or population. The representative respondent, as one of a sample of representatives from the same class, contrasts with the special respondent who might be the only member of his special class to be interviewed.

Several important characteristics distinguish the use of special respondents from the use of representative respondents.

a) Representative respondents are worthwhile only when there are enough of them to represent certain variations in the universe or population from which they have been selected.

b) The same questions must be asked all members of the sample.

c) The sample is considered as an *aggregate* of individuals having a range of characteristics similar in variation to the universe. Likewise, the universe is also conceived as an aggregate rather than a *structure* of relationships between individuals.

d) Since the sample is an aggregate, the measurements obtained from individuals are subject to mathematical and statistical operations such as addition and multiplication or to finding a mean, standard deviation, and measures of association.

None of the above characteristics applies to the use of special respondents.

Uses of kinds of respondents

It is important to realize that a single study might require the use of key informants, special and representative respondents. Furthermore, the same person may be a key informant at one time in the study; later he may be a representative respondent, and even later a special respondent.

To illustrate the use of key informants, special respondents, and representative respondents, let us examine a field study in which all three types are needed. In studying teenagers' conflicts with parents and the relationship of these conflicts to juvenile delinquency, we might begin by contacting key informants, such as the staff of the state juvenile authority, to help select a location for studying the problem. These informants might help find locations with extremely high and low delinquency rates; they might also estimate the extent to which the differences in the official rates reflect actual differences in delinquency rather than in booking systems.

In addition, these key informants could furnish the names of special respondents in the local areas, such as the superintendents of schools, juvenile parole officers, truant officers, and family case workers, who deal directly with known delinquent children. Additional special respondents such as high school counselors, teachers, playground directors, and local police would be able to provide information on many unrecorded delinquencies. Another class of special respondents would be each delinquent's closest friend or the whole gang to which he belongs.

The representative respondents could include a sample of teenagers and their parents from each of the two communities. These teenagers and their parents could supply information on the number and types of conflicts they have experienced. If the two communities were large, with a population of more than 100 thousand, a 1 percent sample of teenagers and their parents might easily include some of the special respondents.

It is possible to have a study requiring only special respondents, such as a study of a small community's division of labor pattern. At the other extreme, a public opinion poll for predicting election results usually involves only representative respondents. Thus we see that the types of respondent depend upon the purposes of the study and the types of information to be collected.

STEPS IN FIELD STRATEGY

After the problem of the study is clearly formulated and the types of information needed are specified as precisely as possible, the next step is to determine the types of respondents required. With the ideal types of respondents decided upon, it is then necessary to determine the means of locating and contacting them.

Locating and contacting representative and special respondents

If the study calls for a sample of anonymous representative respondents, locating and contacting them may involve merely knocking on the doors of a random sample of an area's dwelling units. If special respondents are needed, there are usually several channels through which they may be identified, located, and contacted. In this case, the advantages and disadvantages of one channel must be weighed against those of other channels.

For example, in studying the process of professionalization of occupational therapists, there are several possible channels of contact. The interviewer might obtain the names and addresses of OT's from the national or local association and interview them at their homes. This would avoid seeking the permission of the administration of the hospital where they work. If the study also requires interviewing physical therapists, physicians, nurses, and orderlies working in the same hospital, it would be desirable to obtain the hospital administration's approval so that the names of all of these employees in the local hospital could be acquired. It might also increase the efficiency of the project if some or all of the special respondents could be interviewed at the hospital. This would require additional cooperation from the administration.

After discovering which channels of contact exist and how cooperative each will be, further consideration must be given to the possible effects of each channel of contact upon the respondent's motivation to cooperate.

Securing the cooperation of key informants

If a key informant's permission must be obtained to gain access to several respondents in a closed community or organization, we should try to learn as much as possible about him. The following questions should be answered: Would the study threaten him in any way? What competing time demands might make him reluctant to give access to the respondents? Would this person take an ambivalent position because of conflicting desires or because of an ambivalent picture of the study's purpose or effect? If this person gives his wholehearted permission for the study, what might be the effect of this knowledge upon the respondents?

Some information relevant to these questions might be obtained from written sources if the key informant is a leader or professional person in the community or organization. Company newspapers, college catalogs, local newspaper files, local newspaper reporters, and directories of professional, administrative, business, and occupational groups are all useful sources of information about a person's status and function in a given social setting. Available public documents may yield such facts as the person's full name, his address, correct title and position, phone number, age, race, organizational affiliations, educational background, job history, public activities, and possibly a photograph. Further information might be obtained from other key informants who have contact with the person and can give impressions of his probable attitudes toward the proposed study.

Prepared with this background information, and guarding against prejudices, preconceptions, and stereotypes, the interviewer can approach the person whose approval he desires. The interview with this key informant may accomplish several objectives. It may explain the purpose of the study, the sponsorship, and show how the information is to be used. It may demonstrate how the study can help the key informant, or the interviewer may appeal to an altruistic motive and show precisely how the key informant can help the project. It might also be desirable to show the extent of anonymity involved in the collection and the publication of the information.

The interviewer may also want to ask for advice on such things as the best time and place for interviews. He should also take advantage of every opportunity to show sympathy for any of the problems confronting the key respondent in his decision to cooperate and should probe to clarify the precise nature of the problems instead of trying to discount them as imaginary or inconsequential. This information allows the interviewer to deal more intelligently with the obstacles, and his interest in the key informant gives a sympathetic and responsible impression.

This interview should create an atmosphere encouraging the informant to ask questions and clarify any doubts. It is always good strategy to leave written materials covering the same points as the oral explanation along with details of where the interviewer and the sponsor might be contacted. In this way, channels of communication remain open.

If there is reason to believe that serious resistance will be offered by the target community, it is often practical to do a small pilot study in a similar community or organization at a distance to obtain perspective and forewarning of some of the potential strategy problems. For example, if a university sociology department wishes to study the problems of public school superintendents in five counties surrounding the university, it would be useful to do a small pilot study in a remote county of the same state where a serious strategy error would not damage the final study.

If there is reason to suspect opposition from leaders of a closed community, plans should be made to meet it with constructive counterstrategies. One of the most problematic situations occurs in the study of a closed community in which the power figures are not in sympathy with the study, but do not feel free to publicly refuse cooperation. In this case, covert measures such as keeping the interviewer busy with irrelevant activities, stalling, red tape, and subtle threats to respondents may be used to sabotage the interviewer without directly refusing cooperation. It is well to anticipate, if possible, some of these potential evasions and have countermeasures ready. For example, it is useful to prepare face-saving explanations for the person of influence in case his initial resistance weakens and he wants to avoid the appearance of having acquiesced to pressure. In some cases, it is even necessary to prepare for a hasty retreat if a final rejection seems imminent. If possible, a final "no" should be avoided even at the cost of a temporary retreat.

If permission is refused. If the leaders' formal permission or informal approval is not obtained, there are still several paths toward the next step. At this point it is necessary to deal with several inter-related questions: Is it crucial to study this particular community or organization or can the study be carried on equally well in more friendly territory? Is the leader's power so complete that all channels of contact to the respondent are closed, or is it still possible to contact the respondents as individuals rather than through the group? If the respondents can be contacted as individuals, will the influence of the power figure still prevent their cooperation? These judgments must be made on the basis of information obtained in the local setting.

We must never forget that refusals to cooperate with the formal interviewing of a study may, nevertheless, provide much relevant information. In the discussion of the person's public reasons for non-cooperation, real fears and suspicions or some of the powerfully competing time demands will frequently be manifested. In spite of the respondent's adroit mixing of public information and official explanations, the interviewer can find clues to some of the underlying causes of resistance.

In addition, it is possible to obtain relevant factual information while the person is refusing to cooperate. For instance, if an interviewer wished to study conflicts in a small town during desegregation of the public schools, the local mayor would be a good key inform-ant regardless of his attitude toward the study. Even though he would not give confidential information about the performance of the local police force, for example, he would probably be willing to review specific incidents, name parties to the dispute, and give his official interpretation of the events. Regardless of the accuracy of his interpretations, the verifiable facts of time, place, and names would provide leads to other special informants on both sides of the issue.

On rare occasions, it is necessary and effective to challenge the power figure by pointing out that his resistance appears defensive in view of the guaranteed anonymity. In equally rare cases, it can be pointed out (where it is true) as a last resort that the study will have to be carried out with or without his sanction. Of course, in a completely closed community such a statement could not be made.

If permission is given. Plans should be made to maintain cooperation, once it has been obtained, because initial approval, either in an open or closed community, may turn to resistance. For example, people who originally assumed the study to be a survey of public opinion may subsequently feel that "confidential" information is being collected. They may simply be unable to see the relationship between the stated purpose of the study and the specific information gathered, and feeling threatened, they may accuse the interviewer of misrepresenting the nature of the study. This problem must be guarded against early by providing a written explanation which can be referred to later. This explanation may cover the range of information to be collected, or it may allow for more detail to be added from time to time with each interview with the same respondent.

Often, while not objecting to a particular question, the respondent objects to what he believes are certain implications in the relationships between the questions. An example is provided in a study of the social-psychological factors determining the success of rescue operations after a community-wide disaster. The officials of the city were not reluctant to give figures on the number of men and the amount of police, fire, and medical equipment sent to the scene. However, these facts were often viewed differently by the respondents after they had been asked the extent of the disaster, the time when the rescue workers and equipment were needed, and the precise time of their arrival on the scene. Initially, the rescue work was often carried out informally before any of the official organizations (such as the National Guard, Red Cross, Civil Defense, or local police) could mobilize; thus, manpower and equipment in excess of the need were sent, draining the surrounding area of its normal fire, police, and medical personnel. Even though the information was not to be used in judging, praising, or penalizing officials for their performance or for assuming responsibilities outside their jurisdiction, the interview questions were ego threatening to people who liked to think of themselves as always having things under control.

In this type of situation the ego threat can be reduced by separating the facts so that the ego-threatening relationships are not perceived by the respondent. This may be done by having a series of interviews with the same person. In this way the relevant facts are collected in widely dispersed time, or parts of the picture are collected from different respondents and later assembled into a meaningful whole.

In some cases, the initial cooperation of the power figures of a closed community precludes the enthusiastic cooperation of the respondents. This happens if the community is polarized between the superordinates and subordinates. Since the interviewer must have the permission of the leaders to gain access to the community members, the respondents may view the interviewer as a representative of the superordinate group. This difficulty can be ameliorated by the interviewer's frankness in explaining to the respondent that he is not sponsored by the power group but had to gain their permission to do the interviewing. This explanation in itself, truthful and logical as it is, will not necessarily gain the immediate trust of the respondent. The interviewer will have to show by his interest in the respondent's point of view that he is not a spy for the dominant group.

This discussion of possible steps in field strategy has presented a necessarily pessimistic picture, since its aim was to warn of certain problems which might arise and to suggest possible solutions. At each step the worst was assumed by supposing (*a*) that the respondents could not be contacted directly, but were in a closed and potentially hostile community; (*b*) that the situation within a community was complicated and sometimes polarized; (*c*) that it was necessary to persist in the study even though cooperation was refused; and finally (*d*) that even if permission were given, it might turn into resistance unless certain precautions were taken. Fortunately, it is rare to find all of these complications arising in any one field study.

All the possible strategy problems are never encountered in any one study. However, it can never be assumed that any information-gathering project will lack resistance merely for being a good cause in pure or applied human relations. Nor can we assume that all potential respondents will be disarmed and freed from ego-threat by the fact that the social scientist is not going to use information for his personal gain or for penalizing any individual or institution.

Instead of the naively optimistic or the hopelessly pessimistic approach to the strategy problems, a constructively cautious approach will be more useful—preparing for the worst and expecting the best.

Successful strategy involves doing the right things in the correct order and avoiding assumptions about the nature of the field situation without first checking available facts. The researcher must obtain reliable information about the field situation in order to prevent the rise of misperceptions, rumors, and suspicions before he has had an opportunity to explain the study to persons whose cooperation is needed. Unless there is a degree of success at the strategy stage, the interviewer will not have an opportunity to use his skills in interviewing.

So far, the discussion has dealt broadly with strategy by defining strategy in contrast to techniques and tactics, discussing some of the general types of field situations, delineating three type of respondents, and discussing some of the possible steps in field strategy as a decision-making process. This serves as a background for a more detailed treatment of four basic tools of strategy: selecting appropriate respondents, selecting appropriate interviewers, selecting the optimum time and place for the interview, and structuring the interview situation.

SELECTING APPROPRIATE RESPONDENTS

The type of respondent needed depends mainly upon the type of information sought. The interviewers available and the setting for the interview will also have a bearing; but in discussing the selection of respondents, we will assume that the optimum interviewer and interview situation obtains.

If a special respondent occupies a unique position, then he is irreplaceable. If representative respondents comprise a sample which cannot be altered without damaging its representativeness, then each individual in the sample is irreplaceable. If both types of respondents are irreplaceable, there is no choice in selecting respondents. Then the query becomes, why deal with the *selection* of respondents?

Special respondents are *chosen* in two senses. First, it is necessary to determine which of the many unique positions (role, status, or function) are relevant to the purposes of the study. Second, similar positions are frequently occupied by more than one person. Thus, the special respondent is not a unique individual, but any person occupying a special position in society giving him access to certain observations, actions and knowledge.

Representative respondents, on the other hand, offer fewer opportunities for purposive selection other than determining whether each is a member of the universe as defined for the study. However, there is an opportunity to maximize the flow of relevant information by "selecting" cases even after the complete sample has been chosen. This is done by deciding which respondents are to be interviewed by which of the interviewers (who are also already selected).

Logically, there are at least four basic criterion questions which must be answered in selecting respondents: Who *has* the relevant information? Of those having the information which are physically and socially *accessible?* Which persons having the information are most *willing* to give it? Which persons having the information are most *able* to give an accurate accounting?

The first two of these questions depend so heavily upon the specific information needed and the specific nature of the field situation that we will deal with them only superficially and then devote the remainder of this section to the last two criterion questions.

Who has the relevant information?

This question is simple to answer in some cases because everyone has it. For example, in a psychological study of normal vision, anyone can be a respondent by participating in a simple laboratory experiment.

The rarity of people having the information is determined by two dimensions: first is the number of people having the experience about which we are gathering information, and second is the degree of directness of the experience required for the purpose of the study. If direct experience by the respondent is necessary for the kind of information sought, there will be fewer respondents than when observations of another's experience will also suffice. Still more respondents are available if information *about* an experience of either the direct participator or the observer will provide relevant information.

There are two important reasons for eliminating non-relevant respondents at the strategy phase of the study. It is a waste of time to locate and interview a respondent, only to discover then that he does not have the relevant information. It is also possible in some cases for the respondent who could not possibly have the information to fabricate it in an attempt to hide his own ignorance or to aid the interviewer.

There is an important distinction to be made between *fact* and *opinion*. The latter is probably more available on many topics. When we are seeking detailed facts regarding any event which was exciting, interesting, or controversial, the respondent often fails to distinguish between fact, rumor, and opinion in his account of the event. The more successful we are in eliminating ineligible respondents before the interview begins, the less effort must be spent in each interview verifying the respondent's credentials and checking the verity of the information.

Who is accessible?

The problem of *accessibility* of respondents is often great. Although a respondent must be accessible if he is to be interviewed, there is a danger that the most easily accessible respondent might not have the other qualifications. In public opinion polls and market research, for example, there is frequent danger of a systematic bias in the selection of respondents when quota sampling is used. For example, the interviewer who must obtain a quota of 10 males between 30 and 50 years of age from a certain neighborhood might choose those who are conveniently near the subway station or other artery of transportation. Or he might select those who are most psychologically accessible in that they seem to be middle-class educated people who can "express themselves more clearly." Numerous studies indicate that the opinions of these people differ markedly on many subjects from other socioeconomic classes.

Respondents in the upper socioeconomic class are often difficult to reach. They are highly organized and feel no obligation to respond to the desires of a lower status person. Furthermore, they are suspicious of "con" men or burglars who might be disguised as interviewers, or may fear that information given might be used to their economic disadvantage. In this stratum of society, sponsorship, recommendations, and introductions are extremely important.

It is also difficult to obtain access to lower socioeconomic class respondents under certain conditions. For example, in ethnic-group neighborhoods of urban areas, the interviewer might be suspected of being a bill collector, a salesman, a detective, or truant officer. To complicate matters, some families live in tenement houses or apartments, and the interviewer has no opportunity to speak to the respondent face-to-face before being refused. When someone shouts down the stair well or speaking tube, "Who is it?" the interviewer can only hope that the door does not slam as he shouts back the shortest and most enticing version of his purpose.

Who is willing to give relevant information?

In dealing with this question we will assume that it is known who has the relevant information, and that those who have it are physically and socially accessible. It will also be assumed that the study requires special respondents, but that more than one of each type of special respondent are available.

The question then becomes that of how to select from among the *available* special respondents those that are most *willing* to give relevant information? A more refined version of this question is how to best circumvent the four inhibitors (competing obligations, ego-threat, etiquette and trauma) which tend to make respondents less willing to give information?

Competing time demands. Often it is possible to reduce the pressure of competing obligations in the interview situation by choosing a lower-status person if he can provide the same information as a higher-status person. The lower-status person will feel more obligated to spend time in the interview.[2] In addition, certain facilitators of communication are more likely to be brought into play in an interview with a lower-status respondent. For example, it is more likely to be a release from boring routine, thus appealing to the need for new experience. Also, the lower-status person is more likely to feel he is gaining recognition in the experience.

It is possible in some circumstances to reduce the competing time demands by selecting a respondent who has large blocks of unoccupied time. If the same information regarding a teenage gang fight could be obtained either from firemen or drugstore employees who witnessed the event, it would be better to go to the firehouse than

2/ Lewis A. Dexter, "Goodwill of Important People: More on the Jeopardy of the Interview," *Public Opinion Quarterly,* Vol. 28, No. 4 (Winter, 1964), pp. 556-63. Some of the dangers of intruding upon the time and privacy of high status persons are cited here.

the drugstore for an interview. Again, if equal information is possessed by a mother of five children or a retired senior citizen, the latter would feel fewer time pressures.

Ego threat. The ego threat barrier can sometimes be reduced by the proper selection of respondents. The general principle is to find some person whose ego is not involved in the information sought. There are many kinds of information given much more freely by one person than by another who feels threatened by admitting the truth. The most obvious example is the choice between a respondent who actually perpetrated an act of which he is ashamed and a respondent who saw another commit the act, but is neither identified with the perpetrator nor afraid of any reprisals if he gives the information. This is a situation familiar to the legal profession where the witness for the prosecution has less ego threat than the defendant.

Perhaps more familiar to the social scientist is the situation where one person reports information withheld by another because he does not realize the stigma attached. He is not consciously "tattling" nor acting as a witness against the other, but merely giving a straightforward answer to a question. This is seen in cases where a child or youth tells the straight truth, while the adult, who realizes the implications, tries to alter or completely deny the facts. For example, in a study of teenagers' adjustment problems in school, the child is likely to admit having been suspended from school for three days. In contrast, the middle class *mother,* who feels that the child's bad behavior is actually due to her own failure, is less likely to be truthful. Also, children are often more free in admitting sibling rivalry than are the parents.

This difference between the frankness of children and adults seems to be just one example of a general principle. The greater the responsibility a person assumes for some deviation from the public norms, the greater the pressure to pretend that actual behavior conforms with the norms.

Concrete examples will illustrate this principle. The public relations office of a college is more reluctant to admit any conflict between the administration and the faculty over academic freedom than is the student body president. Also, public school superintendents are less likely to admit their school's basic problems in achieving high-quality education than are the young teachers. Similarly, the superintendent of a state mental hospital testified before a state legislature that there was adequate staff to give good care to the patients, an opinion which shocked the nonadministrative staff.

Unfortunately, there is sometimes a dilemma when the person who has the most accurate information will be the least likely to give it because he is most directly connected with the events being studied. This leads to the danger of depending upon more indirect sources of information. In these cases, strategies, tactics, and techniques other than selecting the nonthreatened respondent must be used.

Etiquette. In some cases, it is possible to avoid the etiquette barrier by selecting the appropriate respondent. The problem arises in situations where the interviewer is perceived by the respondent as a person who would be surprised, shocked, or chagrined by candid answers.

The etiquette barrier commonly appears when a person in a responsible position sincerely attempts to evaluate the human relations aspects of his organization by interviewing his own subordinates. If a junior executive in a large firm wants to evaluate a new employee information program, he would wisely select respondents who do not know him as the designer of the program, since there would be a tendency for the respondents to avoid hurting his feelings by giving any negative impressions. If the information needed calls for representative respondents, this method of eliminating the etiquette barrier is not available. Instead, the *interviewer* must be carefully chosen to avoid selecting anyone who might be perceived by any of the respondents in the sample as having a vested interest in the program to be evaluated. In rare cases, the employees in the sample might fall into two or more distinct types requiring different types of interviewers to minimize the problem.

Often, the etiquette barrier is more effectively minimized if we are free to select the appropriate interviewer, rather than the respondent; but an administrator, or any authority, often finds himself in a position where some knowledge is better than none and must proceed to gather it himself. In such situations, we cannot warn too strongly against the effects of the etiquette barrier. If it is necessary to minimize the etiquette barrier by selecting the best respondent, the interviewer must be intimately acquainted with the norms governing what can be politely communicated from whom to whom. Lack of this knowledge results in serious miscalculations.

Often such knowledge is not possessed at the outset, in which case it becomes part of the strategy phase to discover the relative validity of information coming through certain channels. This can frequently be done in a small pilot study where two or more categories of respondents are asked for the same factual information. The frequency with which the two groups mention events tending to discredit or embarrass the interviewer can be compared. It is also possible to compare written comments from a group of anonymous individuals with oral statements made by the same group to the interviewer. This difference for one category of respondents could be compared with that of another category of respondents.

In general, if a respondent is not inhibited by the etiquette barrier which would usually apply, it is because of one of the following reasons:

a) He does not realize that the information he gives has a negative value in the eyes of the interviewer. Children are often immune to this type of inhibitor for this reason.

b) He might be so in accord with the interviewer's effort to obtain accurate information that he will be candid although being truthful may be painful.

c) He may have a desire to embarrass, belittle, or hurt the interviewer's ego and therefore welcomes the opportunity to elaborate upon all of the details which tend to threaten the interviewer. Although this might be a strain on the interviewer, it often has a cathartic effect, reducing the respondent's hostility toward the interviewer.

d) He may have a relationship with the interviewer which permits such information to flow freely on the particular topic as long as the interviewer's questions are considered genuine rather than rhetorical, and sincere rather than designed to obtain a compliment.

Trauma. The trauma barrier is not so rare in interviewing as we might think. Of course it is rarely found in the opinion poll on current public issues or in the practical surveys made in most communities. However, certain interviewers, because of the problems with which they deal, frequently encounter the trauma barrier: these would include the police investigator of homicides and suicides, the coroner who holds inquests, the insurance investigator, the case worker attached to the family relations court, the industrial safety investigator, the minister, the Red Cross disaster worker, and the social scientist investigating such problems as causes of auto accidents, causes of suicide, or adjustments to mental illness in the family.

Often, the problem cannot be circumvented by selecting respondents because the person with the most direct knowledge of the crisis also had the most traumatic experience. But there are occasions when the interviewer can select a respondent with no traumatic experience to supply the relevant information. A police investigator of auto accidents might needs facts such as the time of the accident or the number of passengers in the car which hit a child crossing the street while her mother watched from the curb. In this case, the investigator can choose between interviewing the mother or the two shop keepers who were eye witnesses.

It should not be assumed that merely because a respondent has had a traumatic experience he will refuse to report it or will stint on detail. This has been shown untrue in interviews with families who have just lost children in a disaster. In these cases it seemed that the respondent's altruism and his needs for meaning, sympathetic understanding, and catharsis were stronger than the urge to repress the memory.

Who is most able to give the information?

Even though two people have the same experiences and are equally willing to report them, there may be a wide variation in the precision or efficiency of their reports. Having had the appropriate experiences does not guarantee the person's ability to report these experiences.

Forgetting. If the interview seeks information on events repeatedly experienced by many people, respondents who have experienced the event most recently can be selected in order to minimize the problem of stimulating the memory. Of course, if the event experienced is a rare one, we may need to wait for it to happen and be ready to interview people immediately while their feelings and images are fresh.

Assume we are studying the changes in family relationships resulting from the arrival of the first child. In an interview one year after the child's birth, it would be difficult to obtain an accurate and detailed picture of these subtle changes. It would be better to obtain from local hospitals a list of patients who have been discharged from the maternity ward long enough to have recovered physically, but who were still establishing their new family routine.

In addition to selecting respondents who have been most recently exposed to the experience, we can select those for whom the event was the most meaningful, problematical, ego-involved, or direct. For example, in studying childhood diseases of primary school children in the Puerto Rican district of New York, the information would be more accurately obtained from the mother than from the father who feels strongly that raising babies is the mother's complete responsibility.

Chronological confusion. Since chronological confusion is partially a function of a fading memory, any method of selecting respondents which reduces the memory-fading process will also reduce the amount of chronological confusion. There are other safeguards in selecting respondents which can minimize chronological confusion.

First, we might cross check chronological accuracy by selecting more than one person to give the same information. The two or more respondents selected should have participated in, or observed, the same situation. For some purposes, it may be more revealing to interview those whose observation or participation was completely independent of each other, and for other purposes, it is necessary to select people who interacted in the situation. In either case, the cross checking of one respondent's story with the other will alert the interviewer to problems of chronological confusion. It is sometimes effective to have the two or more respondents discuss the event in a group interview. Whether the group interview should precede, follow, or replace individual interviews is decided in the specific setting.

Second, it may be possible to select a person whose role in the situation provides a special perspective for remembering details in chronological order. In an investigation of crowd reactions at an air show where a stunting airplane had crashed into the full grandstand, it was desirable to discover the precise chronology of events immediately preceding the crash. The one person capable of doing this was the master of ceremonies for the show. He was aware of the order in which events had originally been scheduled and the deviations from this order. Also, he could relate the informal, non-scheduled events to the scheduled events, thus establishing a complete chronology.

Inferential confusion. Any selection of respondents which reduces the fading of memory or chronological confusion is helpful in reducing distortion of the facts upon which inferences are to be based. This does not necessarily mean that the inferences made by the respondent will be logically correct.

Most of the solutions to inferential confusion lie in the areas of tactics and techniques; however, we may still reduce the interviewing problems by selecting the respondent who has the best understanding of the types of generalizations to be made, and has no strong prejudices on the topic to bias his logical processes.

Unconscious behavior. The reader will recall that we use "unconscious behavior" to refer only to actions that were automatic at the time they were performed rather than to memories of actions which, although accompanied by a high level of awareness when they were being performed, have been *repressed* into the unconscious because they would constitute a severe ego threat. This aspect of the unconscious has been subsumed under the inhibitor category of ego threat.

If the objective of the interview is to study some segment of human behavior which is experienced at a low level of consciousness, it is often impossible to obtain a valid account in retrospect, even though the behavior was very recent. For example, if we need to know which shoe a person put on first this morning, it is rare to find a person who is sure that his guess is correct later in the day.

It may be impossible to stimulate recall of certain behavior. A different approach is often more valid and practical. Instead of dealing with respondents' past behavior, we can select respondents who are about to undergo certain relevant experiences and will report them, or who can observe others carrying out the behavior in question.

The participant-respondent is asked to participate in the event or situation, observe his own behavior of which he is ordinarily unconscious, and then report it to the interviewer. This approach would be useful for describing such unconscious patterns of behavior as tying one's tie, doing a complicated dance routine, playing a musical instrument, or shaving with a safety razor.

When an observer-respondent is used, he is first given the problem and then sent to observe others' unconscious behavior. The best observer-respondent is one who is interested, unbiased, acute in his observations, and who has access to the situation in which people indulge in the type of unconscious behavior being studied. The observer-respondent is needed only if the interviewer himself does not have access to the situation.

This approach is particularly useful in cases where the act of self-observation might change the pattern of behavior being observed or where self-consciousness might completely invalidate the information.

It would be invalid to ask a mother to observe her own behavior toward her two-year-old son to note how frequently she attempts to avert undesirable behavior of the child by physically removing some object of his attention rather than by first using a verbal command, request, or distraction. The mother, consciously posing this question to herself and observing her own behavior toward the child, might recognize her reliance on the physical method which became a habit before the child learned to speak. In this situation using an older sister as observer-respondent would probably yield more accurate information.

In some instances, a combination participant-respondent and observer-respondent is needed. For example, to study the subjective experiences of Mr. X during a bit of social interaction, we might have Mr. Y observe him and report Mr. X's overt behavior, some of which Mr. X himself was not fully aware. This information can then be used as cues for interviewing Mr. X to stimulate sensitivity to his own overt behavior and to report the accompanying covert behavior.[3]

Thus far the problem has been in choosing the respondent to minimize the inhibitors which make him less willing or able to supply relevant information. The respondent was selected with regard to his relationship to both the relevant experiences and to the interviewer. Here, it was assumed that the interviewer-respondent relationship could be manipulated only by the selection of the respondent. In the next section, the assumption will be that the respondent is predetermined. In this situation, the relationship can be manipulated only by selecting from among possible interviewers or by the interviewer selecting the most appropriate role from his repertory.

SELECTING APPROPRIATE INTERVIEWERS

The field supervisor, the self-directed research team, and the individual researcher must all be concerned with selecting appropriate interviewers. The field supervisor may find some of the suggestions useful for hiring interviewers for a special project, for selecting

3/ A similar result can be obtained in some cases by using one respondent and a tape recording of the situation. For example, a meeting might be tape recorded and one of the participants interviewed later without prior warning. If he is allowed to listen to the tape recording, the overt behavior will act as stimulus to reproduce the same subjective reactions he had during the meeting. The playing of the tape recording can be interrupted at crucial points to probe the respondent about his subjective reaction. In this way, it is possible to obtain information about the effect of different remarks on the respondent. Ordinarily, he would be unable to report directly because of his vague consciousness of the exact source of the stimulus or his reaction at the moment. We have used this strategy to discover what an interviewer does to obtain certain reactions from the respondent.

from among the continuing staff of interviewers the one best suited for a particular project, or for deciding which ones might be most easily trained for certain types of studies.

When a new interviewing team is being organized, it is important that they be selected for their information-gathering potential. When a study calls for contacting a wide variety of special respondents, it is often more effective to allow each member of the team to specialize in one or two types of special respondents with whom he has the most effective relationship.

The criteria suggested below are useful to sensitize the interviewer to some of his immutable characteristics such as sex, race, and physique, which limit the possible role relationships in his repertory. This in turn restricts types of studies he personally should undertake and suggests the need for collaborators on certain aspects of information gathering.

Some of the suggested criteria will point to areas in which the interviewer must prepare himself before contacting the respondent. Specific knowledge of the interview topic or of the type of respondent and situation in which the respondent is to be contacted fall into this category. In addition, criteria such as the role repertory, attitudes, and situational skills will suggest a long range program of personal development for the serious student of human behavior.

For this discussion, it will be assumed that skill in interviewing is possessed by all interviewers. Not all possible personal characteristics are considered relevant to selecting interviewers. The criteria will be limited to those having a *direct* bearing upon the problem of maximizing the flow of relevant information between respondent and interviewer. These criteria will be grouped under four headings: overt characteristics, basic personality traits, attitudes, and knowledge. These areas are all interrelated and are significant in that they affect the role repertory as it relates to the interviewing task.

It should be noted that the selection of an appropriate interviewer does not affect as many of the inhibitors as does the selection of an appropriate respondent. This is true because selection of the appropriate interviewer does not affect the respondent's *ability* to give the information, but only his *willingness.* Although there are four inhibitors (competing obligations, ego threat, etiquette, and trauma) which generally reduce the willingness to give information, only two of these, ego threat and etiquette, are clearly influenced by the choice of an interviewer. In addition, it is possible to maximize three of the facilitators of communication (recognition, sympathetic understanding and new experience) by choice of interviewer, quite independent of skill in interviewing techniques and tactics.

It is not enough to accurately assess the qualities of an interviewer; it is also necessary to know how these characteristics will be perceived and evaluated by the potential respondent. During the strategy phase, and within each subsequent interview, we should be alert for clues to the respondent's perceptions of the interviewer. It is often possible for the interviewer to make tactical corrections within an interview which will clarify his role or to correct misperceptions. If not, it is frequently possible to change the strategy of the approach toward future respondents or more effectively match interviewers with respondents.

It should be noted that the relative importance of the interviewer's overt physical characteristics is greater in single-contact than in multiple-contact field situations. These overt characteristics are also more significant in the scheduled than in the non-scheduled interview. The less structured the schedule, the more freedom the interviewer has in expressing basic personality traits.

In discussing the effects of certain characteristics of the interviewer on the flow of relevant information, we are using a shorthand expression for "probable effects in general" or "effects possible under certain conditions," or "tendencies which may or may not be counteracted by certain tactical and technical skills." We must assume intelligent and empathic use of these suggestions which, in specific situations, are to be treated as hypotheses checked by feedback from key informants, by observation of the respondent, and by analysis of the interview results.

Overt characteristics of the interviewer

Such characteristics as sex, age,[4] race,[5] ethnicity, social class,[6] manner of dress and speech are important. Not only do they create an immediate impression and help determine whether or not the

4/ Mark Benney, David Riesman and Shirley Star, "Age and Sex in the Interview," *American Journal of Sociology,* Vol. 62 (September, 1956), pp. 143-52.

5/ Aaron Bindman, "Interviewing in the Search of Truth," *Social Quarterly,* Vol. 6, No. 3 (Summer, 1965), pp. 281-88. This deals with the effects of using Negro versus white interviewers.

6/ Daniel Katz, "Do Interviewers Bias Poll Results?" *Public Opinion Quarterly,* Vol. 6 (Summer, 1942), pp. 248-68. This classic study compares the results of using "white collar" and working-class interviewers to obtain opinions on war and labor issues.

respondent will consent to be interviewed, but they also place certain limits upon the roles which the interviewer may successfully occupy. Many studies on interviewer bias have shown differences in the results when the interviewers vary in these overt characteristics. One of the most systematic studies has been done by Hyman[7] and his associates at the National Opinion Research Center.

In reading and evaluating the many studies done on interviewer bias, we often find apparently contradictory results. Often this is because there is no guiding theory to relate type of interviewer and type of respondent with the type of information to be obtained. Often, studies try to determine the effect, for example, of a "white collar" interviewer versus a "blue collar" interviewer in a random sample survey. The results are likely to be ambiguous since the random sample is composed of both "white" and "blue collar" respondents. Even if the effects were separated according to type of respondent, the effect would be different depending upon whether the topic of the interview were attitudes toward labor unions or preferences for types of shaving cream.

Here, we will try to show how the overt characteristics are meaningful only insofar as they affect the relationship between the interviewer and respondent, which in turn affects the potential barriers to communication.

Sex. Selecting an interviewer of the proper sex can sometimes reduce the etiquette barrier. For example, male market research interviewers can obtain more spontaneous information about men's shaving habits than female interviewers. Likewise, female interviewers are more successful in obtaining information on feminine hygiene from women. The use of a female interviewer for a market research survey on shaving methods and materials would not be as serious a strategy error as using male interviewers on the feminine hygiene study.

The sex of the interviewer may also operate to increase the facilitators of communication. It would appeal much more to the need for *new experience* to use a male interviewer with respondents in a women's prison or to have an attractive Wac interview soldiers in an isolated garrison post, or to send a male interviewer to an electronics plant where 90 percent of the workers and supervisors are women.

Also, the sex of the interviewer may determine the extent to

7/ Herbert Hyman, et al., *Interviewing in Social Research* (Chicago: University of Chicago Press, 1954).

which the respondent will perceive him as a person capable of giving *sympathetic understanding* to certain problems covered by the interview. A female interviewer would probably be more welcome in interviewing mothers regarding the problems of the housewife. A male interviewer would probably be perceived as more sympathetic in an interview with crane operators about their grievances.

In some cases, the use of a male interviewer appeals to the respondent's need for *recognition*. This was found in several interviews when male respondents expressed surprise that the interviewer was a man instead of a woman as they had expected. They made such comments as, "This must be an important study if they are sending out men to do the job." In this case, a woman, regardless of her qualifications, would have had a disadvantage. Further conversation indicated that the respondent had stereotyped women interviewers as "housewives with a gift of gab, a big curiosity, and time for a part-time job."

In some cases, the sex of the interviewer is important not so much because of the effect it will have upon communication in the interview as upon the probability of even starting the interview. In single-contact interview studies in metropolitan areas, one of the large problems is gaining entrance to the home. For example, it is not rare for the male interviewer in an urban poverty area to notice someone peeking out the window as he comes up the sidewalk; then the radio is silenced and no one answers his knock. This may be because the occupants of the house think he is a bill collector, a truant officer, parole officer, or a salesman. Sometimes in areas which have had recent violent disturbances, whether man-made riots or natural disasters of some type, a male interviewer is mistaken for a newspaper reporter. All of these mistaken identities of the male interviewer usually present problems.

Female interviewers should not be used in areas with a high crime rate, particularly at night when male interviewers are most likely to be available. Even though statistics show that most of the major crimes of violence are committed against family members, there is still a greater chance that a woman who is obviously an outsider in the neighborhood will be robbed or harmed in some way. Perhaps most important is the effect of this possibility upon the morale and performance of the female interviewer.

There are rare studies which might require a female interviewer to gain rapport with respondents in this type of area. There are several possible ways to avoid problems under these circumstances. For example, interviewing might be done only during certain hours of the day, interviewers might be sent out in pairs, respondents might be interviewed in another place (perhaps where they work), or having indigenous sponsors vouch for the interviewer might improve safety.

Age. The main social significance of a person's age is that it limits the roles which he can assume and the status he has *vis-à-vis* with another person. In general, an older person has higher status than a younger person when other visible signs are equal and when neither knows the other's function in society. The effects of status difference on communication will be discussed when we focus on the status dimension of the relationship.

Since age offers both possibilities and limits to the role repertory, the individual investigator may examine a typical life cycle of a person of the same sex in his culture and realize that at one time in his life he will be a better interviewer on one set of topics, at another time he will excel at another. A high school student doing a study of family relations might find the etiquette barrier arising in the interview with parents regarding child-rearing problems. Yet the same high school student, with minimal skills in interviewing, could do an excellent job of interviewing students about "problem parents."

Often, it may be necessary to interview people in a very different age bracket because there are few interviewers among the age group being studied and the interest in the specific problem is not widely shared. The interviewer, by skillful tactics and techniques, can often overcome this initial disadvantage. For example, Krause[8] found that as a graduate student, when she interviewed people over 60 years of age on problems of personal adjustment in old age, she had to exercise care to avoid conveying the feeling of superiority because of her higher education. She learned to show by every word and gesture that she appreciated the wisdom they had gained with experience. They were quick to appreciate her sincere respect which they felt was rare in the younger generation. In effect, she had to escape the stereotype of university student and become a personal disciple of the respondent.

Race or ethnicity. Whether or not an interviewer who appears to be of a certain race or ethnic group is an appropriate interviewer de-

8/ Luise Krause, "Problems of Interviewing Older People," in her unpublished M.A. thesis *Personal Adjustment in Old Age,* prepared under the auspices of the Department of Sociology, University of Chicago, 1950.

pends upon the respondent's perception and evaluation of that group and the role he feels appropriate for the interviewer to assume. Since this affects the status relationship between the interviewer and respondent, there is the possibility of the barriers of ego threat and etiquette inhibiting the flow of certain types of information.

For example, it might be a distinct advantage to be a Negro in studying nationalistic attitudes of Africans or attitudes of Indian students toward racial discrimination in the United States. Conversely, in an industrial relations study, a white field worker might find it very difficult to obtain spontaneous information from Negro workers even after spending months in the plant.[9]

Racial differences between interviewer and respondent not only affect the respondent's attitude toward the interview, but also the interviewer's attitudes and stereotypes of the respondent. If the respondent is a member of the minority race, he is quick to sense the stereotyping by the interviewer. He may resent it, conform to it, or both; but in any case, it will affect the flow of information.

There is the additional communication problem caused by differences in the universe of discourse. Racial or ethnic group cultures are quite distinct in some ways from the middle class white cultures, and this difference impedes communication.

The effect of race of the interviewer and respondent depends, of course, upon the meaning of those particular racial differences within the culture in which the interview is taking place. The problem would be quite different in Hawaii, Brazil, and Arkansas. Only insofar as race is a symbol of role and status will it affect the flow of information in the interview. Whether this effect is positive or negative depends upon the meaning of race, in general, and its significance to the topic of the interview.

An example of clear experimental effects of the race of the interviewer is shown in two studies by Athey[10] in which the white respondents scaled down their expressions regarding non-whites for both the Negro and Oriental interviewers in comparison with white interviewers.

Speech. It is common knowledge that the vocabulary, accent, and diction of a speaker are glaring signs of ethnicity, status, and role. As such, they affect the flow of information in the interview. In some

9/ Robert K. Bain, "The Researcher's Role: A Case Study," *Human Organization,* Vol. 9 (Spring, 1950), pp. 23-28.

10/ K. R. Athey, J. E. Coleman, A. P. Reitman, and J. Tang, "Two Experiments Showing the Effect of the Interviewer's Racial Background on Responses to Questionnaires Concerning Racial Issues," *Journal of Applied Psychology* (Spring, 1960), pp. 244-46.

cases, an accent is sufficient to nullify the effect of obvious racial characteristics. Identical Negro twins born in England and speaking with a crisp British accent would encounter different reactions in a southern railroad station if one freely demonstrated his accent and wore a turban while the other said nothing to betray his accent.

The converse of this was demonstrated when a white graduate student studying at the University of Chicago was doing his master's thesis on a Negro Muslim cult hostile to white Americans. Upon first contact with the group, the researcher was trying to locate their meeting place in the basement of a vacant building. There he was caught by surprise, frisked and taken to their leader who explained that the "snooper" was fortunate to have a foreign accent or they would have dealt with him more harshly. Upon discovering that the student was from Baghdad and was a wrestler, they invited him to teach in their "college," which he did for a few months while writing his thesis on the development of the movement.[11]

Dress and grooming. These factors of appearance are symbolic of social status and role as well as the subculture to which a person belongs. The more superficial the contact with the respondent and the stronger the solidarity of the respondent's "in-group," the more important the effect of dress and grooming. Part of the strategy phase of a field study must sometimes include getting information on the most appropriate way to dress. However, it is usually not possible, practical, or ethical to try to pass oneself off as a full-fledged member of the group being studied. Nor is this usually necessary, although it is often advisable to prevent the interviewer's being falsely perceived as an outsider in a threatening role.

For example, a person studying the activities of teenage gangs in a city's high delinquency area might give the impression that he is a detective by wearing black shoes. Or, if he carries a brief case, he might be suspected of being a bill collector. Without trying to impersonate the members of the respondent's group, the interviewer must discover how to dress to prevent mistaken identity. In addition, it is possible to reduce the social distance between the interviewer and respondent by dressing more nearly like the respondent without trying to imitate him. A person studying the problems of controlling migrant children from farm areas in an urban neighborhood might do well to dress like the local graduates of the junior college rather than like an Ivy Leaguer.

11/ This account was given by Hatim Sahib, now returned to Baghdad, in a personal conversation with the author.

Basic personality traits of the interviewer

An excellent interviewer need not conform to the popular image of a pleasing personality. The sparkling personality is sometimes a valuable asset in making the initial contact or getting in the door, but the same qualities might interfere with communication by stealing attention from the respondent.

Basic personality traits are relevant only insofar as they help or hinder the performance of the interview. Three important assets would include flexibility, intelligence, and emotional security. Flexibility allows the interviewer to assume a very active role when it is called for and to assume a more overtly passive role when this will facilitate communication. Intelligence permits the interviewer to clearly appreciate the objectives of the interview, to learn to evaluate critically the information he is receiving, to remember what information has been given, and to probe for greater clarity and completeness. Emotional security frees the interviewer from anxiety about himself and allows him to direct his full attention toward the tasks of maximizing the flow of information and maintaining optimal interpersonal relations.

The absence of flexibility severely limits the interviewer. Some personalities find it impossible to slow down the pace of an interview, allow relatively long silences, and permit the respondent to say what he wishes when he wishes. For this type of person, silence is intolerable; it is a vacuum which must be filled at any cost. He panics when the respondent does not immediately respond in an appropriate manner. This type of interviewer tends to dominate the situation in a way which threatens the respondent's ego. He does not build a permissive and thoughtful mood, and frequently, he unknowingly distorts the information by suggesting answers.

Some interviewers tend to be rigidly passive. This type of person does well as long as the task calls for letting the respondent take the lead, but he can be easily lured into irrelevant bypaths or sociable conversation when this is neither necessary nor desirable. He is reluctant to assume an active role by holding the respondent to the topic, to evaluate critically the information he receives, and to probe for completeness and clarification.

The importance of sufficient intelligence to the tasks of eliciting the information, evaluating it in terms of interview objectives, and probing for clarity and completeness is obvious. This does not imply that any intelligent person will carry out these tasks efficiently at the first attempt. Rather, he must have the basic ability to learn once the task is clear and he has the opportunity to practice.

The interviewer's emotional insecurity could have several detrimental manifestations in the interview. He may display a compulsive urge to dominate and challenge remarks unnecessarily. In some cases, the challenging response is compulsive and unconscious. The insecure person is often so anxious about himself that (*a*) he fails to observe the respondent's emotional needs, (*b*) he communicates his own insecurity to the respondent rather than a positive expectation of cooperation, (*c*) he may be unable to empathize with the respondent at crucial points in the interview, (*d*) he cannot communicate warmth which leads the respondent to reach for sympathetic understanding and perhaps cathartic communication which might bring relevant information; and (*e*) he is incapable of giving sincere praise to the respondent for his efforts or his performance.

This is not to suggest that anyone having personal insecurities will always manifest them in these detrimental ways, nor does it necessarily indicate that any person who commits any of these errors is a hopeless victim of personal insecurity. As a neophyte interviewer, any conscientious person is likely to be doubtful, self-conscious, and anxious. An experienced interviewer may feel the same way about the first few interviews of a new study. Before one can devote full attention to the respondent's needs, he must take care of his own anxieties which arise in a new situation or with a new study.

Some people show these symptoms of insecurity only in certain types of interviews. Often, the distinguishing factor is the status relationship between the interviewer and the respondent. Some find it very easy to interview people of lower status, but if a respondent tends to assume an equalitarian relationship, the interviewer finds it intolerable. Some find that they cannot interview anyone who is not a peer, while others function most adequately in a subordinate role such as student or seeker of advice.

Ideally, the interviewer should have a flexible personality, free of defense mechanisms which limit his sensitivity to the respondent or his ability to shift roles as the situation requires. If the well rounded interviewer cannot be found, we should at least recognize the limitations and avoid assignments which demand behavior of which a particular person is not capable.

Much personal insecurity can be controlled to suppress detrimental manifestations. The best prescription is to master some of the basic interviewing techniques, tactics, and skills and to prepare thoroughly for a particular interview by being completely familiar with its purpose, by planning some tentative alternative tactics, and practicing whatever recording techniques are to be used.

Attitudes of the interviewer

Since the positive attitudes intentionally displayed by the interviewer will be discussed later, this section will focus on only those uncontrollable negative attitudes which can be eliminated only by selecting the appropriate interviewer. These attitudes may be negative toward the type of respondent from whom the information must be obtained, toward the topic of the interview, or toward some particular information given by the respondent.

To speak of selecting an interviewer devoid of such negative attitudes does not imply that one must be completely free of such attitudes to be effective. Nor should it be said that training of the interviewer does not help overcome these attitudes or at least teach how to avoid displaying them so they affect the interview. Whether we depend upon selection or training depends upon the availability of interviewers, the time available for training, the strength of the negative attitudes, the delicacy of the interview topic, and the degree to which the interview is scheduled.

Here the intent is not to quantify these factors but to give some examples of their symptoms and the direction of their effects. Often a strong attitude toward a certain type of respondent is accompanied by strong stereotypes. The attitude may be toward certain religious, racial, occupational, ethnic, educational, or political groups. Leighton[12] found that some research workers in the Japanese relocation centers were unable to lose their stereotypes of Japanese even after living in the center for months. This stereotype acts as a barrier to communication, since it represents a form of insensitivity to individual differences which prevents the interviewer from adjusting his behavior to that of the respondent.

In training social scientists for field work in mental hospitals, high delinquency areas, and foreign cultures, the author has often found fear, suspicion, or a feeling of superiority toward the respondent. Even though these feelings may be controlled to the point of not being manifested to the respondent, nevertheless they may have an effect upon the interview.

The interviewer's attitude may be so strong that is perceived by the respondent and brings ego threat or etiquette into play, inhibiting the response. The attitude toward the respondent may cause the interviewer to use loaded questions in a way which biases responses.

Even if the interviewer suppresses all visible manifestations of his

12/ Alexander Leighton, *The Governing of Men* (Princeton, N.J.: Princeton University Press, 1945).

attitude so that it is not perceived by the respondent, there are three important ways in which his attitude still may minimize the flow of relevant information. (1) The interviewer's effort to control his negative attitude may succeed at the price of failing to manifest the positive attitudes of recognition, appreciation, sympathetic understanding, and the expectation of cooperation. Thus, some of the most important facilitators of communication are neglected. (2) The interviewer may attempt to exude a warmth which deceives the respondent, but still fail to empathize with him enough to probe points important to both the respondent and the objectives of the interview. (3) When the completely structured interview prevents the interviewer from using loaded questions, when he is experienced enough to avoid letting his personal attitudes show in the interview, and when the respondent actually gives ample relevant information, there is still the possibility that the interviewer will bias the result in taking notes on the respondent's replies.

An excellent experimentally controlled study done by Fisher[13] shows that the interviewers with strong political attitudes did not accurately record the responses and that the direction of the error was consistent with the direction of the interviewer's political attitudes. This bias in the recording phase of the interview is most likely to occur when the interviewer is attempting to take verbatim notes on responses to broad questions and the respondent is speaking too rapidly to allow the interviewer to actually write everything.

The negative attitude toward the topic of the interview need not be in the form of taking sides in a controversial issue. Just as common is the apologetic attitude which seems to say, "I'm sorry to ask such questions. I'm not sure I have the right to expect you to answer them." This communicates the expectation of failure and may stimulate precisely the anticipated reaction. Such an apologetic attitude would have scuttled studies such as the Kinsey[14] report or Becker's study of marijuana users.[15]

Special knowledge possessed by the interviewer

Special knowledge refers to specialized information or skills needed by the interviewer in order to gain access to the situation

13/ Herbert Fisher, "Interviewer Bias in the Recording Operation," *International Journal of Opinion and Attitude Research,* Vol. 4 (Spring, 1950), p. 393.

14/ Alfred C. Kinsey, et al., *Sexual Behavior in the Human Male,* chap. 2 (Philadelphia: W. B. Saunders Co., 1948).

15/ Howard S. Becker, "Becoming a Marijuana User," *American Journal of Sociology,* Vol. 59 (July, 1953, and May, 1954).

where the respondent can be interviewed, to gain the respect of the respondent, or to understand the topic of the interview. This special knowledge often goes beyond any superficial knowledge or skills which can be gained by the interviewer for the occasion. For example, Howard Becker's study of the jazz musician would not be as thorough and insightful if Becker had not played in dance bands at the time.[16] Again, Hatim Sahib's study of the Negro-Muslim sect was greatly facilitated by his knowledge of the Koran and of Arabic as well as his skill in wrestling and his ability to teach Iraqi cooking.

Not only does special knowledge act as key to gathering information through sustained contact with the respondents, but it also is needed for certain types of single-contact interviews. For example, in a study of the performance of state police in a local crisis, the interviewer should have considerable knowledge of the usual function, organization, and jurisdiction of the police. To understand their accounts of their activities during the crisis, the interviewer should also be familiar with the local geography and relevant locations such as police headquarters, the radio transmitter, and the highway system.

Regardless of whether he has one or many contacts with the interviewer, the respondent often judges him not on the basis of his skill in interviewing, but on the basis of his knowledge and interest in those subjects in which the respondent is an expert. Where continued contact is needed in a participant-observer field study, the interviewer has an advantage if he can show competence in an area which is understood and respected by the community.

Sometimes it is practical for the interviewer to acquire the special knowledge needed for a specific assignment. At other times, the topic is so technical and complex that it would be more practical to select a person who is already a specialist in the area. For example, to discover some of the problems of coordinating a team of researchers, it would seem advisable to use a social scientist who had previous experience in team research. To discover some of the problems of the adjustment of American students in Latin America, the interviewer would need to be familiar with the Latin American culture and the Spanish language.

Special knowledge, then, helps the interviewer gain access to the respondent *in situ,* helps him understand the respondent who refers to local detailed information, provides him with the universe of dis-

16/ Howard P. Becker, in *The Professional Dance Musician in Chicago,* his unpublished M.A. thesis, Department of Sociology, University of Chicago, 1949.

course needed, and gives the respondent respect for and confidence in the interviewer. If the interviewer shows that he has not bothered to familiarize himself with needed special knowledge, it may be difficult to persuade the respondent to devote serious time and effort to the project.

When interviewing special respondents, especially those in high status, the interviewer will do well to obtain some advance information on the respondent's personality, life history, and position, particularly as they relate to the topic of the interview.

SELECTING THE APPROPRIATE INTERVIEWER ROLE

Role is probably the most important characteristic of the interviewer. All other characteristics (such as sex, age, race, speech pattern, basic personality traits, knowledge, and attitudes) gain some portion of their significance from the fact that they all create opportunities or limitations for the role behavior of the interviewer.

The nature of role-taking

Selecting the proper role for the interviewer to assume might involve selecting the appropriate interviewer, or the interviewer might need to select from among his role repertory the one or ones most appropriate for the task at hand. Role-taking is distinct from role-playing. The former refers to selecting from among a person's actual roles those which are most appropriate to display under the circumstances; the latter refers to taking a role which the person has never assumed in real life or which he is assuming in an artificial situation. Role-playing is done in psychodramas, sociodramas, and ordinary dramatic productions and games. Role-taking is done in everyday life, usually quite unconsciously. The minister in the pulpit does not usually choose to behave in the role of a father or a husband. Within his minister role he may choose to display certain aspects or to withhold them; he may act as a Christian, as a Protestant, as a mentor, or as a chastiser.

Role-taking should not be confused with an unethical form of deceptive play acting, a childish game of cops and robbers, or a romantic cloak-and-dagger operation. In interviewing, role-taking[17] is a conscious selection, from among one's actual role repertory, of

---

17/ It should be noted that in discussing the role repertory of the interviewer we are concerned with auxiliary roles peripheral to the *central* interviewer role.

the role thought most appropriate to display to a particular respondent at the moment. Most of us have no occasion to take an inventory
of the roles we play, but if we do so, the number is usually much
larger than expected. A man scanning his own experience could find
that he has had the following roles from time to time: child, sibling,
husband, parent, neighbor, social scientist, consultant, tax payer,
consumer, voter, teacher, student, client, patient, card player, employee, employer, tourist, foreigner, native American, advisor, committee member, writer, musician, photographer, swimmer, subscriber, contributor, translator, insuree, driver, bicyclist, pedestrian,
or cook.

Functions of the auxiliary role

All of these roles constitute the role repertory from which one or
more may be selected as auxiliaries to the principal role of interviewer. For example, the Fund for the Republic sponsored a study of
the state of academic freedom on the campuses of American colleges.
Twenty of the sample of 180 colleges had refused to allow interviewers on campus to interview the social science faculty. One interviewer was assigned to visit some of the 20 reluctant colleges to try
to convince the president to change his mind and to interview faculty
members and students to discover what, if anything, the college was
hiding. Which of his many roles should the interviewer display to
which respondents on the college campus? He could, in honesty,
present himself as "a representative of the Fund for the Republic,"
"a consultant hired by Elmo Roper Associates," "a college professor
interested in theoretical problems of social conflict," "a sociologist,"
"a grandson of a Presbyterian minister," "a specialist in interviewing
methods"—these roles and many others would be equally true.

Actually, many of these selections from the role repertory proved
valuable at certain times with certain respondents. In contacting a
sociology professor, it was helpful for the interviewer to mention
that he, too, was a sociology professor working as a consultant for
the Fund for the Republic. In dealing with the President at one
college, it proved an asset for the interviewer to be the grandson of a
Presbyterian minister, since the President was a Presbyterian minister
himself. In no case did it seem advisable to be presented as "a specialist in interviewing methods," since this would probably cause some
ego threat. Even the role of bicyclist was useful in breaking the ice

with one professor when the interviewer commented that he, too, rode a bicycle to work if the weather permitted.

The respondent often wants to know "What kind of person is this who is asking the questions?" In a study of family relations, the respondent is relieved to know that the interviewer is not a bachelor but married and the father of two children. Even though this does not necessarily qualify the interviewer to understand the particular respondent's problems, that respondent is less inhibited by the etiquette barrier than if he perceived the interviewer as a bachelor.

A field situation may require the interviewer to actually *function* in an auxiliary role for the duration of the study, rather than merely presenting himself as a person who has a role other than interviewer. The interviewer may choose to function in an auxiliary role in order to gain access to respondents in a certain situation. For example, a researcher studying the professionalization process in a group of occupational therapists might work with several occupational therapists in the hospital in order to discuss their work *in situ.* Or instead of interviewing the "OT" as she works in the hospital, he might have formal interview sessions after working hours in the respondent's home. In the latter case, the interviewer's work in the hospital one or two days per week would have several useful functions. It would acquaint him with the universe of discourse of the hospital setting, clarifying communication in the interview. Furthermore, the interviewer would be more capable of sympathetic understanding. The etiquette barrier would be reduced, since the interviewer now would be considered more of an equal, and this greater equality would usually reduce the ego threat. Also, if the interviewer carefully arranged his working hours so that he actually reduced someone's work load, this might be an effective extrinsic reward to the respondents or their supervisors and make the interviewer's continued presence more welcome.

In general, when taking an auxiliary role, it is advisable to make it clear from the beginning that the main purpose is to study the situation and that the auxiliary role is a way of gaining a more intimate and sympathetic view. Often the key informants in a closed community and prospective respondents are favorably impressed by the interviewer who will take the assignment seriously enough to get his hands dirty in the situation. This is something perceived as a form of recognition and often reduces the respondent's defenses against an "ivory-tower" approach to his problems.

Interviewers have taken jobs as factory workers, custodians, life-guards, hospital orderlies, psychiatric aides, dance band musicians, taxicab drivers, and have even posed as mental patients or criminals to gain an inside view.

Dimensions of role relationships

Rather than attempting to show the relative values of an almost endless list of specific roles to be taken by interviewers, it is more useful to deal with two salient dimensions of role relationships. The significance of the interviewer's central role as interviewer and his auxiliary roles lies in the *relationship* generated with the respondent. Two of the most important dimensions of the relationship may be conceived of as the horizontal or "in group-out group" relationship and the vertical or subordinate-superordinate dimension.

The effect of the interviewer's presenting himself as a physician cannot be predicted unless we know whether the respondent is, for example, another physician or a nurse. The difference is these two pairs can be expressed in terms of relative status. The physician-physician relationship is one of equality. The physician-nurse relationship is one in which the physician is superordinate. To view these same relationships in the "in group-out group" dimension would require additional information. For example, the physician-physician pair would be furthest toward the in-group end of the continuum if both were members of the American Medical Association, lived in the same town, and constituted a clinical team. They would tend to view each other as outsiders, however, if one were a physician from the Soviet Union wanting to practice in the United States, or if one had lost his license through malpractice.

In many instances, it may appear that two people have an in-group relationship *because* they are of equal status. Upper-class people may welcome other upper-class people into their homes, but will erect barriers to keep lower-status people at a distance. On the other hand, there are instances where two people have an out-group relationship because they are of equal status. This is often true in competitive situations where there is conflict between equals. If the chief body designer for X Motor Company were sent to interview the chief body designer of Y Motor Company, the interviewer would be treated politely perhaps, but would be suspected of spying.

These two basic dimensions of role relationships can either inhibit or facilitate the flow of various types of information.

Ingroup-outgroup relationships. There are advantages and disadvantages to either type of relationship. Which is more desirable depends upon the type of information needed. In some cases, we need information from both vantage points and must use two interviewers to obtain complete results. Since the outsider role is often the easiest for the interviewer to attain, it is valuable to begin by indicating some of its advantages.

Advantages of the outsider role. The outsider has the advantage when he is seeking information on violations of the in-group code. Here, the outsider, not bound by these codes and with no power or desire to enforce them upon the respondent, has an advantage over the insider. The interviewer is not an ego threat to the respondent. Thus, a criminal would more willingly admit to a sociologist than to a member of the underworld that he once squealed on a partner to reduce his own sentence. In another situation, members of a teenage gang admitted to an interviewer that they had never been to a prostitute, but this fact was never admitted to the other members of the gang who would have considered it a sign of inferiority.

This tendency to make one's verbal behavior conform to the perception of the group norms has been experimentally demonstrated in several settings. For example, the writer[18] demonstrated that when the interviewer asked members of a group for their opinions on Russia, they tended to compromise their private attitudes to conform with what they perceived to be the group norms with respect to Russia.

Another general circumstance in which the outsider has the advantage is in obtaining information on methods of manipulative control used by those in power to keep subordinates in line. Anthropologists have found that adults of one tribe will give totemic secrets to neighboring tribes, but not to their own children.[19] Similarly, it was found that ministers gave information on how they manipulated their congregations by interpreting and re-interpreting scripture, yet they vehemently denied any such purposive manipulation in a men's club discussion of the minister's role in the church. To give such information to the in-group in which he has status would constitute an ego threat to the minister.

The outsider again has the advantage over an insider when the

18/ Raymond L. Gorden, "Interaction Between Attitude and the Definition of the Situation in the Expression of Opinion," *American Sociological Review,* Vol. 17, No. 1 (Spring, 1952), pp. 50-58.

19/ Marcel Griaule, "L'enquette Orale en Ethologie," *Revue Philosophique de la France,* Vol. 142 (October, 1952), pp. 537-53.

group is looking outward for some type of assistance. This is often experienced by social workers. The outsider in this case has some potential extrinsic reward to offer.

Often, the outsider does not have the disadvantage of facing the etiquette barrier which exists between certain in-group members. For example, a sociologist whom the respondents have never seen before can obtain detailed information of the premarital sex lives of a husband and wife which they have never discussed with one another because it was considered bad taste.

The outsider may also have a certain advantage in that the respondent's need for new experience can be fulfilled by talking to an outsider. Anthropologists, sociologists, public opinion pollers, and social workers all have moments when they feel that the respondent is more curious about them than they are about the respondent. The respondent may waver between excited curiosity and apprehension. When a later maturity study was done in a deteriorating apartment house area of Chicago, a charming old lady of 80 years shyly admitted to the interviewer, "I saw you talking to Mrs. Podolsky and I was curious about what you were talking about, but I don't think I would have let you in if you weren't talking to a friend of mine."

Often a respondent will perceive the interview as means of getting recognition. He may not be appreciated in his home, at the office, or in his community. Or it may be that he has already told all his friends, neighbors, and coworkers about certain highlights of his life. In this case, if the interviewer is interested in obtaining a life history the respondent will welcome the chance to have the complete attention of another human being. Such an opportunity to talk about oneself is rare indeed. An insider who already knows certain public facts and perhaps more intimate aspects of the respondent's life has little reason to ask him to "begin at the beginning and tell me everything you feel is significant in your life."

In some circumstances, a strong in-group feeling is developed in a group of people who have suffered together some catastrophe, hardship, or persecution. This common experience is the badge of membership for the in-group. In this case, there is no possibility of an outsider's becoming a full-fledged member of the group unless he too has shared the same experience. If the interviewer has not had the experience, it is sometimes harmful to rapport if he pretends to appreciate the respondent's experience. In this case, the interviewer's approach should be as a sympathetic outsider.

For example, in interviews with respondents who had experienced a community-wide disaster, resentment could be detected in the respondent's manner if the interviewer pretended to fully appreciate the horrors of the experience. It proved a better tactic if the interviewer admitted that he was an outsider striving to catch a glimpse of what it was like to live through a devastating tornado. When a respondent told her listener, "You have no idea how horrible it was. The only way to know is to go through it yourself," the interviewer's best response was that of a sincere and concerned outsider, shown in his reply, "Yes, I've never been through anything like that in my life. I'm sure I can't begin to really grasp what it was like. I can only hope to learn through someone who has lived through such an experience. What would you say kept you going through all this?"

In this kind of situation the interviewer who takes the humble approach has a distinct advantage over the insider, because those who have shared the experience feel little reason to talk about their misfortunes to someone who has been equally unfortunate. The respondent seems to feel that he has more of a right to demand sympathy from the outsider.

In some instances, respondents of an in-group welcome the outsider hoping that he can fulfill their need for meaning by raising meaningful questions, by clarifying confusion, by settling a controversy, or by sharpening the issue. The outsider is more trusted than the insider, who is suspected of taking sides if the group has been polarized, or who is considered too close to the problem to have the required perspective.

Even in situations where the respondents belong to a closely knit in-group suspicious toward all outsiders, there are still certain kinds of information which can be obtained by the outsider. He may discover the official line given to the outsider, the extent to which the group is interested in recruiting or proselytizing others, and the in-group's fears and stereotypes of the outside world.

Advantages of the insider role. With all the advantages of the outsider role, there are still many situations when the insider has a distinct advantage. Most of these advantages revolve around situations where the outsider is perceived as an ego threat, where communication with an outsider is restricted by etiquette, or where he is perceived as a person incapable of sympathetic understanding. In some instances, even though the respondent is able and willing to give the relevant information, an outsider is unable to use the jargon fluently enough or is ignorant of the local facts needed to understand what he is told. This last possibility has already been discussed, so let us examine more closely those situations in which communication with the insider involves less ego threat, fewer etiquette restrictions, and a greater satisfaction of the need for sympathetic understanding.

An outsider may constitute an ego threat to the respondent guilty of violations of public norms (laws and mores) who is afraid that such information might be used to damage his reputation. Thus, a person studying social organization in a slum would not have access to much information on underworld activities until he had achieved the status of insider. This might be called a form of in-group defensive secrecy. Thus, Whyte[20] spent months becoming accepted as a friend by the "corner boys" in an Italian-American slum section of a large city before he began to obtain information on certain organized crime activities in the area.

Similarly, studies[21] of Japanese-Americans interned in relocation centers during World War II recorded the difficulties interviewers had becoming accepted as "friends." Some Caucasian researchers never achieved this status. Others succeeded within four or five months. Even the Nisei members of the research team had difficulty avoiding being perceived as "informers" by the camp members although none of the information they received was ever given to the government. Much of the relevant information could not be elicited until the insider role was established.

Another type of information withheld from outsiders might be called trade secrets. These are not withheld for being distasteful, immoral, or illegal, but because they give the possessor advantages in the competitive struggle. This information must not fall into the hands of a competitor. If the interviewer were perceived as a person who could not conceivably pass on the information to a competitor, the respondent would be less reluctant.

Another disadvantage to the outsider role lies in the etiquette barrier. Even though no ego threat is involved in the outsider's presence, there may be a tendency to treat him as a guest or a "visiting fireman," and the respondent tends to put on his company manners.

Finally, the interviewer from the outside is perceived as a person unlikely to sympathize with the in-group's problems and who has no real interest in the respondents except for what they offer the study. There is a feeling that there is nothing in common upon which to

20/ William F. Whyte, *Street Corner Society: The Social Structure of an Italian Slum* (Chicago: University of Chicago Press, 1943).

21/ Dorothy S. Thomas and R. S. Nishimoto, *The Spoilage* (Berkeley: University of California Press, 1946).

build rapport. Students studying some of the social-psychological aspects of the church meetings in store-front churches report this "feeling of emptiness" between themselves and their respondents. In this case, the respondent correctly senses the lack of any sympathetic understanding on the part of the middle class college student. Although an interview can be conducted under such conditions, little information on the more subtle feelings, aspirations and beliefs of the respondent can be obtained, because the answers are not motivated by a desire to share experiences with a sympathetic person. Therefore, responses tend to be short, unspontaneous, and not always relevant.

Establishing the insider role. In spite of the advantages of the outsider role, there are purposes for which the interviewer must have an insider role. How is this role established? There is no simple formula for attaining it with respect to an individual or group, but there are general ways to approach the problem.

The first general way to be accepted as an insider is to participate in the group, institution, or community being studied. The intimacy of the interaction demanded depends upon the nature of the information sought. If the group is very closely knit, the intimacy of participation needed before one is considered "in" is very great. For example, to become an insider in a religious sect actively opposed to existing religious institutions requires more intimate association and active participation than being an insider in a conventional denomination. Joseph Zygmunt[22] found in studying the Jehovah's Witnesses that faithful attendance and participation in the weekly meetings was not enough. He had to spend additional time "witnessing" on street corners and distributing the literature where there was opposition before he was considered really sympathetic.

Religious groups differ not only in their degree of hostility toward the "outside" world but also in the degree to which they are interested in recruiting new members. For example, the Jehovah's Witnesses are both hostile toward conventional religion and actively proselyting for new members. The Negro-Muslim sect mentioned previously is hostile to the white Christian world, but is not interested in trying to convert the enemy. Not hostile to the outside world, the Bruderhoff communities in the United States and England want to explore a new communal way of life and welcome the outsider as

22/ Joseph F. Zygmunt, *The Role and Interrelationship of Symbolic and Structural Processes in the Development of a Sectarian Movement,* unpublished Ph.D. dissertation, University of Chicago, 1960.

long as he participates in their work. The Hutterite communities in the United States and Canada are not at war with the larger world, do not seek recruits, but are withdrawn and generally want to be left alone.

When groups practicing protective secrecy are suspicious of outsiders trying to gain entrance, it is often necessary for the field worker to enter in a subordinate role or not at all. One convenient subordinate role is that of student. By showing a sincere desire to learn from the members of the group something in which they excel and something which distinguishes them, the interviewer can reduce hostility and suspicion by reducing ego threat.

The language of the group can often be learned to gain rapport. This was found true by Whyte in his study of "Cornerville," where he found that learning Italian helped to gain the group's trust. Thomas and Nishimoto also reported that in their study in Japanese relocation centers, the Caucasian interviewers found it useful to learn Japanese, even though they did not become fluent enough to use it in interviews.

This role of student can be adapted to a variety of situations. Bain found that in interviewing workers in industry, the role of student could take the form of asking the respondent to explain his job and the equipment. In interviewing senior citizens, Krause, as a person sensitive to problems of interpersonal relations, found it quite natural to assume the role of a youth seeking insights and perspectives possessed only by her elders.

In addition to the approach of becoming an insider through direct participation, it is often possible to be perceived as an insider through an indirect method of being sponsored or recommended by some trusted person. The degree to which this entrance by sponsorship is successful depends upon how hostile, how closed and how locally autonomous the group is, and the nature of the information sought. These problems of sponsorship will be dealt with later in this chapter.

Subordinate-superordinate relations. Any two persons having functionally related roles, directly interacting with each other can be located on a continuum showing that one is superordinate, equal, or subordinate to the other.

In the following pairs having a reciprocal relationship, it can be seen that in each pair there are superordinate-subordinate roles: captor-captive, master-slave, captain-lieutenant, manager-worker, physician-patient, teacher-student. Note that the first three might be called power relations, since they are based upon the use or the threat of force. Even though the subordinate in each case might like to escape his role, he would be forcefully restrained from doing so. The second three might be called dependency relationships. Although the subordinate in each case may break off the relationship he usually endures the subordinate role because it is more beneficial than breaking it off. This attribute alone is not enough to determine the existence of the superordinate-subordinate relationship; it would be possible to have a mutually beneficial relationship where both would suffer equal injury if it were broken. Therefore, to be an unequal relationship, termination must clearly be more injurious to the subordinate.

For the purposes of interviewing, we are interested in this dimension of the interviewer-respondent relationship only insofar as it inhibits or facilitates the flow of relevant information. It is not always clear when the interviewer is in a superordinate, equal, or subordinate role. The reality of the relationship depends not only upon the respondent's perception of the interviewer and upon the interviewer's perception of the respondent, but also upon the degree to which these two perceptions agree.

Upon initial contact between interviewer and respondent, there may be mutually agreeable or clashing perceptions of each other. This relationship develops and fluctuates as they size each other up. For this reason status relations may develop clarity or even reverse directions in the progress of a single interview. This is particularly true when the situation is not clearly defined at the outset and when the interviewer has wide latitude in techniques and tactics.

It is possible to initiate an interview in a superordinate position to gain initial cooperation and then shift to a more equalitarian role to obtain information which would be withheld from superordinates. The initial social distance can be reduced by a skilled interviewer who finds among his role repertory status attributes comparable to those of the respondent or which at least help in conveying to the respondent a non-threatening image. It is probably easier for the interviewer to move from a superordinate position to an equal or subordinate one than vice versa.

Advantages of the superordinate position. In general, it is easier to make contact, to obtain an appointment, or to begin the interview, if the interviewer is perceived as occupying high status. The obligation to the higher status person tends to reduce the effect of competing time demands. This does not necessarily mean that the interview, once begun, will be successful.

In some cases, the higher status of the interviewer will not only make the initial contact easier but will also facilitate the flow of information, because the interviewer's position symbolizes a moral obligation so strong that refusing to give accurate information would threaten the respondent's self-esteem. The reality of this ego threat depends upon the extent to which the respondent has actually internalized the moral obligation. For example, a child will sometimes lie to a peer, but when confronted with his mother's sternness, will admit the truth.

Sometimes the high status of the interviewer does not have this happy effect because the respondent has not internalized the norm. Or, the ego threat involved in giving a truthful answer would be more painful than the conscience pangs generated by lying. In this type of conflict, the respondent can show great creativity in developing rationalizations for not giving the information. If the ego threat involved is due to the authority position of the interviewer, then the superordinate role is double-edged. This is often the situation where the witness in a trial has taken an oath to tell the truth, but feels threatened if he does.

In some circumstances, the superordinate interviewer has the advantage of appealing to the respondent's need for recognition. The respondent may even hope for some publicity as a result. Of course, this, too, can be double-edged in rare cases where he believes a more sensational tale has a better chance of being published. This was occasionally encountered in interviewing "heroes" in disaster situations. More often, however, the respondent who had been featured as a hero in the local newspaper showed embarrassment over the exaggerations or fiction furnished by an enthusiastic and creative reporter who had found his human interest story for the day.

If the interviewer's higher status is based upon his higher education, his specialized knowledge, or his experiences in a certain area related to the interview topic, the respondent may be motivated by his need for meaning. The father of a delinquent child being interviewed by the social worker, the teenager feeling the first emotional attraction to a member of the opposite sex being interviewed by the high school counselor, or the supervisor who did not receive an expected promotion being interviewed by the personnel department

—all might be motivated to talk by a need to orient themselves to the realities and to make sense of the events.

If the interviewer's higher status is of the non-threatening type, the respondent will be more inclined to show his puzzlement than he would be to equals or lower status people.

Finally, the interviewer in the superordinate position has the advantage of being able to offer extrinsic rewards while the lower status interviewer cannot. The interviewer or sponsor may pay respondents a flat rate per interview "as a symbol of our appreciation of the time and effort you have given us." Other inducements— paying transportation and lodging for respondents to come to a central point to be interviewed, offering to obtain appointments with influential people, or taking the respondent to lunch—have been beneficial in some instances. Gross and Mason's[23] study of the role of the public school superintendent illustrates this.

Service in some form may also be rendered by the field worker in exchange for information. For example, Oscar Lewis[24] found that to establish good rapport with the people he was studying in the Mexican village, Tepoztlan, it was necessary to help them. Similarly, Albert De Graer[25] found that his role as medical doctor gave him an acceptable reason for intimate contact with both the patients and "doctors" of the Azande tribe in the Belgian Congo. This technique is not only useful when working in exotic cultures but also in our own culture, whether in a factory, hospital, school, or community.

In general, the fact that the researcher is rendering a service to the group or individual he is studying gives a reason for his presence that is much more understandable to many people than the abstract idea of research on human behavior. The service function gives him an opportunity to do more than formal interviewing. It also allows him to be a participant observer with access to certain situations which might be considered taboo even if he were accepted as a researcher.

In some cases, it is possible for the service to take the form of giving useful information; however, there are some important safeguards which must be observed. First, the information must not have been confidentially obtained from a previous respondent, even if that respondent is anonymous. There is always the danger that the cur-

23/ N. Gross and W. Mason, "Some Methodological Problems of Eight-Hour Interviews," *American Journal of Sociology*, Vol. 59, No. 3 (November, 1953), pp. 197-204.

24/ Oscar Lewis, *Life in a Mexican Village: Tepoztlan Restudied* (Urbana: University of Illinois Press, 1951), p. v.

25/ Albert De Graer, "L'art de Guerir Chez les Asande," *Congo*, Vol. X, pp. 220-21.

rent respondent will be afraid that his information will be passed along. Second, there are many situations in which it is harmful to even give the respondent a statistical summary of the type of data which has been found up to that point in the study. For example, some disaster interviewers tried to reassure a respondent, who felt guilty because he had become so frightened that he could not eat or sleep for two days, by pointing out that "more than 60 percent of the people in other communities studied have shown these same symptoms." This is dangerous for several reasons. In some cases, the respondent may not have been aware that he had been communicating his guilt feelings. Also, he may resent being "just another statistic" and want the interviewer to view his case as unique. And from a psychotherapeutic standpoint, the respondent finds it difficult to obtain catharsis if the very basis for his guilt is denied by the interviewer. Finally, there is the danger that giving certain kinds of information will confuse the respondent about the interviewer's role.

Many harmless forms of information can be supplied. For example, an interviewer in a factory may become quite popular during the World Series games by giving the latest report on the scores. Or, an interviewer in an academic institution may pass along some interesting information on new publications and current research projects in the respondent's field.

The effect of extrinsic rewards may often depend upon whether they are of the discriminating or non-discriminating type. Those discussed previously are non-discriminating, in that all respondents receive the benefits regardless of their performance in the interview. This type of extrinsic reward is more common in the social science interview in which the interviewer is not in a power position even though he may have high status. The discriminating extrinsic reward is one which is given only to those respondents who have completed the interview successfully according to certain criteria set up by the interviewer. This is often the situation when the social worker is interviewing a respondent; the information obtained may be used to determine eligibility for welfare measures. The personnel interviewer speaking to the job applicant holds out the hope of a job if the respondent is successful according to some criteria which may or may not be known to the respondent. The prison parole officer; the administrator of loans, grants, or fellowships; the manager in charge of promotions; or the physician examining a person to determine eligibility for medical insurance—all these and others interview people to determine whether they are deserving of some reward.

It can readily be seen that the non-discriminatory extrinsic reward is more clearly an asset to the interviewer than the discriminatory reward. In the latter case, the respondent is highly motivated to pay attention, to comply with requests and to devote extended periods of time, but there is always the ego threat of possible failure in reaching an admitted objective. To avoid failure, the respondent is tempted to withhold information he feels might be damaging to his case or to exaggerate certain points while distorting others. Whenever it is feasible, information should be collected in situations where no discriminatory rewards are used.

Advantages of equality. The advantages inherent in an equality relationship assume the absence of a competitive or conflicting relationship between equals. Thus, the advantages of equality are gained when there is an in-group relationship between the two. The principal advantage under these conditions is the absence of ego threat.

There is an advantage also in the absence of certain etiquette restrictions. There may never be any relationship completely devoid of etiquette restrictions, but for the purposes of interviewing we are interested in eliminating only those which inhibit the flow of relevant information. Abstractly, we can say that in the equal relationship the quality of the etiquette restrictions is different from that of unequal relationships.

The absence of any power or prestige leverage by the interviewer may make it difficult to obtain the cooperation of an equal unless some bond of friendship, sentiment, or symbiosis is present. The interviewer must depend upon some intrinsic reward to obtain the cooperation. In the equality relationship at its best, it is possible for the respondent to be a true collaborator in a common problem, and once his interest is captured, it can be sustained.

Advantages of subordinate role. The principal advantage in the subordinate role for the interviewer is the absence of any threat to the respondent's ego. If the interviewer demonstrates a high level of competence, he can be respected although in a subordinate role. The respondent who is not pleased by the purpose of the interview, the sponsorship, or some aspect of the strategy is often more apt to express his displeasure to an interviewer "who is just doing a job assigned to him" than to someone in higher status where etiquette might interfere.

Sometimes the respondent gives the information because he feels sorry for the interviewer who has such a "distasteful" job. Or, the respondent may feel no obligation to furnish more than a modicum of information and dismiss the interviewer. Since there is no possibility of applying direct pressure to the respondent, indirect pressure in the form of an appeal to his altruism may be used. To do this successfully, the interviewer must know which values, reference groups, or membership groups might be legitimately identified with the purpose of the interview in the respondent's mind.

The low-status interviewer is not in a position to offer any of the discriminatory extrinsic rewards as is the high-status interviewer, but he is not completely without resources in offering non-discriminatory extrinsic rewards. If he is familiar with the type of respondent and the general setting, and if he is sensitive to opportunities to offer small favors in a non-discriminating way, he may smooth the path of the interview for the single contact or be more sure of appointments for a series of contacts with the same person or organization.

As mentioned previously, the interviewer's auxiliary role might involve a form of participation which is beneficial to the organization or the individual respondent. There are also many types of small services which can be rendered upon a single contact. Helping the respondent bring in the groceries, watching the baby while the respondent puts the groceries away, bringing an armload of wood from the barn into the house, explaining the latest treatment recommended by the Department of Agriculture for a parasitic corn fungus, bringing the newspaper from the foyer to the respondent's third-floor apartment—these types of services, depending upon the setting for the interview, can have a positive effect where the interviewer does not have to worry about losing a superordinate position.

Just as it is possible for the interviewer initiating the interview in the superordinate role to move toward a position of equality as the interview progresses, the subordinate interviewer can also move upward to a position of equality during the interview. The downward shift of the superordinate interviewer is most likely to be accomplished by emphasizing auxiliary roles the interviewer has in common with the respondent. The upward shift of the subordinate interviewer is more often accomplished not by emphasizing auxiliary roles but by performing well in the central role of interviewer.

The central role of the interviewer

Thus far, we have focused the discussion upon the *selection* of the appropriate role for the interviewer, which involves both the selection of the right person to do the interview and the selection of the most appropriate roles from the interviewer's natural role repertory. Since the *selection* process required us to focus upon the background characteristics of the interviewer, the emphasis was upon his auxiliary roles. With the attempt to sensitize the reader to these factors we have perhaps overemphasized the importance of the auxiliary roles and neglected the central foreground factor of the person *qua* interviewer.

In the final analysis, the auxiliary roles are important only as they impinge upon the central role of interviewer. More directly relevant to the problem of maximizing the flow of relevant information is the way in which the interviewer plays his role of interviewer vis-à-vis a particular respondent. It is often apparent that the respondent has only a very hazy notion of the interviewer's role. This is unavoidable since respondents rarely have extensive practice in their role as a respondent. One exception is the respondent who has undergone treatment by a psychiatrist or clinical psychologist; these respondents are often more secure in a non-scheduled, low topic-control interview, aimed at collecting information on subjective experiences.

The general vagueness of the average respondent's concept of the interviewer's role has advantages and disadvantages. If the concept is vague, the interviewer at least has a clean slate upon which to communicate his expectations of the respondent. If the respondent does have a strong conception of the interviewer's role, often it is a stereotype not appropriate to the particular situation in which he is being interviewed. These incorrect expectations must be detected and corrected by the interviewer.

The optimum performance of the interviewer's role depends not only upon specific techniques and tactics, but also upon the interview setting. Insofar as the interviewer controls this setting by selecting the time and place and by planning his explanation of the situation to the respondent, he is making strategy decisions that will inhibit or facilitate his central task of obtaining relevant information.

We now will assume that the respondents are chosen, that the interviewers are chosen, and that thought must be given to the most appropriate time, place, and explanation of the interview situation.

SELECTING THE APPROPRIATE TIME AND PLACE

In discussing the selection of an appropriate time and place for the interview, we will concentrate upon the circumstances that often link the spacial and temporal dimensions with the specific social-psychological dimensions of communication. No attempt will be made to deal with aspects of time and place which affect the *costs* of the information-gathering enterprise.

Although the spacial and temporal dimensions contain physiological and psychological aspects that influence the communication flow, a list of such factors to be considered by the interviewer will suffice. The time and place should maximize the respondent's physical comfort as well as the interviewer's, with the temperature, humidity, light, and odors conducive to comfort. Also there should be no visual or auditory distractions that make concentration difficult for the interviewer and respondent. In addition to these physiological aspects, occasionally we must consider physical characteristics such as the spacial relationship between the interviewer and respondent; and if a recording machine is to be used, we should check the location of a functioning electrical outlet, whether there is alternating or direct current, and where the machine and microphone can best be placed. Once these details are known, the more important problem is the social-psychological *meaning* for the respondent of the prospective situation.

There are several interesting and relevant connections between the time-space aspects of a situation and the communication problems which result. These general relationships are pertinent to many interviewing problems.

Some effects of place

Minimizing inhibitors. The selection of an appropriate place for the interview can minimize the competing time demands. This statement may appear to be a contradiction of terms in that it proposes to deal with the *time* dimension by manipulation of the *space* dimension. This is possible only because places contain people, things, and interests that might compete with interview time. Although the aphorism "out of sight, out of mind" is not completely true, there is a tendency in this direction.

To illustrate this, an interviewer studying morale problems of the public school teacher could arrange to interview her in her classroom during a free period, talk with her in the faculty lounge, or interview her at home in the evening. In the first setting, the desk may be stacked with unread English themes or the bulletin board may contain a display a week behind schedule; the blackboard may contain an assignment for which she too must prepare. Although the faculty lounge may be free from these distractions, it may have less privacy than either the classroom or home. In any case, the types of competing time demands activated by each situation are qualitatively and quantitatively different.

The appropriate selection of place can also minimize ego threat. Place is connected with ego threat insofar as it influences the respondent's conception of the role and status of the interviewer and the purposes of the interview, or reminds him of certain values he must uphold or roles which he must perform. In addition, the place may suggest various probabilities of information leaking out to some ego-threatening audience. This suggests that the *place*, like a stage set in a play, provides the context in which the interaction takes place and therefore gives support to each actor's role. The interview setting should be chosen to reinforce the respondent's perception of the interviewer's most appropriate auxiliary role. If inappropriately chosen, the impression of the setting can overpower any attempt of the interviewer to communicate a non-threatening image of himself.

For example, in studying the reasons why high school students choose nursing as a career, the interviewer should not arrange appointments with new recruits in the office of the director of the school of nursing if he wants to avoid identification with the authority of the nursing school. In one study, the interviewer did accept the invitation to use the director's office for the interviewing. He tried to overcome the handicap by explaining that he was not working for the hospital, but was doing research on his own initiative. Later, it was discovered that several of the girls still did not understand that the interviewer was not on the hospital staff. Some remembered and believed his explanation, but assumed that the interviewer was interested in administration of hospitals or schools of nursing. While some very real reasons for going into nursing were given to the school counselor over a cup of coffee in the cafeteria, they were not mentioned in the more formal interview. For example:

R: Letha and I were talking the other night about her home background and were surprised to find the same things. We are both from strict farm families. In our home town, the Lutheran church does not allow boys and girls to mix in the teenage Sunday School classes. Things are pretty dead in the country and the boys get to run around while the girls just sit at home. The only way you can get away from home is to get married, go away to college, or go into nursing.

I: Why not get a job as a stenographer, waitress, or store clerk?

R: You don't know my dad. He doesn't think waitresses are respectable. And you can't get a job in an office unless you can type well. I went to a school where they don't teach typing, bookkeeping and that sort of thing. All the girls working in the offices in this town are graduates of the city high schools.

In contrast, in the formal interview situation there was a strong emphasis on such factors as the social usefulness of the nursing profession, the desire to "work with people," and the practical combination of the nursing profession with marriage. Here, the place of the interview considerably affected the information obtained.

Similarly, an interviewer should consider carefully invitations to use the principal's office to interview teenagers on their adjustment problems, the dean's office for interviewing college students, or a management conference room for interviewing employees on their morale problems and perceptions of management. More neutral ground should be used for the interview, if possible.

Of course, if ego threat is to be minimized, it is usually necessary to find a place where privacy is assured. Sometimes the person's home, if there is privacy, provides the greatest security. In other cases, lower status respondents may feel defensive about their economic condition as reflected by the home. This is particularly true of minority groups who are forced to live in slum housing, even though they dress well and drive a late model car. Also, crowded living conditions may make privacy rare in this kind of home except at certain times.

Sometimes there is the problem of achieving the proper balance between privacy and complete isolation. For example, when males are interviewing female respondents, either the respondent or others in the community or organization may become fearful or suspicious of the intimacy that might result.

Considerable ingenuity is often required to find privacy needed for the purposes of the interview. It is very difficult and sometimes impossible to obtain valid information from a subordinate when his superordinates can listen. This obstacle is familiar to the public opinion poller who finds that wives more frequently have "no opinion" on controversial issues when their husbands are present. If it is essential to the results, the need for privacy should be tactfully and firmly explained to the respondent.

Just as the situational setting tends to influence the respondent's perception of the interviewer's role, it also makes the respondent more conscious of one of his own roles than of another. Therefore the ideals, obligations, expectations, and other subjective orientations connected with that role are brought into the foreground of the respondent's consciousness. A respondent who is a father, a business-man, and a deacon of the local church might give different answers to questions from the same interviewer on controversial issues such as local option liquor sales, taxes for schools, or federal aid to religious education, depending on whether he was interviewed at home, in his business office, or in the office of the church. In each setting it is possible that different moral frames of reference gain ascendency in weighing issues. What is considered threatening to the ego depends upon the person's self-concept, which he strives to maintain. It is highly probable that individuals vary considerably in the degree to which their self-concept remains stable and consistent as they move from one role to another. Therefore, whatever flexibility exists will be associated with those changes in setting that highlight different roles.

Many of the same points regarding the connection between the place, role emphasis of interviewer and respondent, and ego threat can be said of the relationship between place, role, and the etiquette barrier which acts as a filter of communication allowing some items to pass and prohibiting others, depending upon the role relationship between the two communicators. Any change in the role of either the interviewer or the respondent will have some effect upon limiting communications. To apply this principle, the interviewer must know how the selection of the place for the interview will affect the respondent's perception of his own and the interviewer's role. In addition, the interviewer needs to be familiar enough with the situation to know which etiquette restrictions are attached to which role combinations.

Although seemingly complex, which it is in theory, in actual practice every mature adult is able to govern his behavior according to many of the subtle requirements of etiquette. The problem becomes acute, however, when an individual in the role of interviewer is required to operate in situations where he is not familiar with the nature of the etiquette restrictions. A vital part of the strategy phase of any study is to become familiar with the restrictions in the new settings.

Simple forgetting and chronological confusion may both be reduced, in some cases, by the selection of an appropriate place. It is important that the place be quiet and private so that the interviewer can establish the appropriate pace and mood for careful recall of events. Without this quiet privacy it is impossible to use some of the techniques and tactics useful for stimulating recall.

Another way of utilizing place to stimulate recall is to effect a return to the scene with certain physical objects prodding the memory. It is sometimes possible to interview the respondent while walking through the actions in their original setting. Where this is impractical, it may be possible to use photographs, maps, tape recordings, and other physical traces of settings and events that relate to the interview.

Often an accurate presentation of the spacial arrangements of the original scene (regardless of whether these are seen in the real setting or in a photograph) will facilitate the untangling of the chronological order and perception of events. This was observed in interviews with building contractors to discover the types of conflicts they had with clients. By either visiting the house he built or by looking at photographs and floor plans, the respondent was stimulated to remember in considerable detail misunderstandings and issues of conflict with the client.

Maximizing facilitators. If the type of information to be obtained requires the establishment of a sympathetic and understanding mood, the place must be quiet and private. In some cases, the location may represent a new and interesting experience for the respondent. Or, the trip to the place of the interview might be an extrinsic reward that attracts respondents. The main value in the location of the interview, however, is the absence of distractions.

Some effects of time

Many of the effects of *place* also apply to the selection of a *time* for the interview, in that the relevant characteristics of a particular place change from time to time. Therefore, this aspect of time in relationship to place was assumed as a consideration in selecting the place for the interview.

There is another important aspect of selecting a time for the interview. This is the relationship between the point in time when the interview takes place and the events or experiences about which the interviewer is seeking information. In assessing current opinions and attitudes, this time dimension is not involved. However, in many interviews the time of the interview in relationship to events and experiences determines both the respondent's *ability* and his *willingness* to give relevant information.

The most significant effect of timing is upon the respondent's ability to remember, accurately and completely, avoiding chronological and inferential confusion. To avoid simple forgetting, the interview should take place as soon after the relevant events and experiences as possible. Much psychological research indicates the distorting effects of fading memories. Specific facts, if remembered, may be quantitatively or qualitatively distorted. Complex events may be retained in an essentially correct pattern with non-essential detail omitted; or the whole gestalt of the event may be distorted, thus reversing its significance.

What is forgotten depends not only upon the recency of the experience but also upon how ego-involved it was, whether it was a completed task, whether it was considered a success or a failure, and whether it was routine, dramatic, or traumatic. Regardless of the cause of the forgetting, in general, time is an important factor, in that the longer the period since the event, the greater the probability of quantitative or qualitative distortion in the person's memory. Therefore, to obtain a detailed and accurate report, the interview should take place as soon as possible after the event.

Events are not simply forgotten or clearly remembered. Often the faded memory can be revived by special interviewing techniques and tactics. At the strategy level, information on events more than a month in the past is more efficiently obtained by giving the respondent some advance notice of the interview topic. If the topic of the interview is explained when making an appointment (with or without the suggestion that the respondent might like to think it over), and if this is one or two days in advance, it is often easier to obtain more complete detail in the interview. The advance notice may be given to all respondents at once in the form of individual letters, a public announcement in a newspaper or on a bulletin board, or by radio or any other available public channel. Whether or not the advance notice should be individualized or simply made public depends on the topic of the interview and the nature of the group, community, or institutional setting.

Generally, immediate interviewing will not only reduce the loss of accurate detail, but will also help to avoid chronological confusion, which becomes a major problem in studies of changes in attitudes and beliefs over a relatively long period of time. There is a tendency to forget or repress previous attitudes, beliefs, and expectations. The writer has had occasion to interview the same persons on international relations at six-month intervals. People who at one time vehemently expressed a conviction that war with Russia was inevitable would deny with equal vigor six months later that they had ever taken such a "defeatist position."

In this case, two interviews six months apart discovered shifts in the respondent's attitude that would not have been revealed by simply asking the respondent, "What is your opinion on the probability of war with Russia?" and "What was your opinion on this issue six months ago?" The respondent tends to feel that his present position is rational and right and, therefore, the same as it has always been.

Similarly, attempts to discover why a person "chose" to work for his current employer, why he "selected" the college he now attends, or why he "elected" to enter his particular vocation, are all fraught with the danger of chronological confusion. Each in-group, whether it is an industry, college, profession, or community, supplies its members with certain ready made rationalizations for how and why they came into the group. The virtues of the in-group may be systematically extolled in rhapsodic indoctrination by its myths and ideals, or the individual may develop his own self-congratulatory version of why he made such a wise decision. In either case, it is extremely difficult in retrospect to uncover the original forces accounting for the final decision.

Even though the respondent has selectively forgotten certain things because he desires to forget, we nevertheless classify this in a later interview as an *inability* to give the information. Although originally the memory was repressed, the respondent is being perfectly honest when he says he has simply forgotten since he is not consciously withholding or distorting information. If at the strategy level, we can eliminate the need for extensive retrospection, the technical and tactical problems in the interview will be greatly simplified.

The strategy planner must always keep in mind that sometimes it is either impossible or impractical to depend upon interviewing to obtain information that has been forgotten and that other sources such as diaries, public records, personal letters or other documents should be used, either as a principal source or to supply cues to stimulate the respondent's memory and to guide the interviewer's probing.

There are many other situations in which not only the respondent's ability to remember, but also his willingness, depend upon *when* he is interviewed. Information which could be given freely at one time becomes an ego threat to the respondent at another. When the writer was interviewing college presidents and faculty to discover why the college had refused permission for interviews about academic freedom, he was given an important observation by one of the professors:

It's a peculiar thing—perhaps if I weren't a social scientist I wouldn't have noticed it—when there was the big dispute on campus about firing Professor X, several faculty members besides myself defended his right to academic freedom. Some of them continued to criticize the administration after the professor's services had been terminated. All of these people except myself have since left, more or less voluntarily. The others who defended Professor X up to the time of his dismissal, but then dropped their objections, are still here. My point is, that of those who are still here, most of them will not admit *now* that the action of the administration was a violation of academic freedom. Yet no new evidence has been admitted to change their original point of view. To me it is quite simple. These people do not want to admit that they would continue to teach in a place which does not have academic freedom because this would be an admission that they are willing to knuckle under; so to save face, they deny that there has been any restriction of academic freedom. Perhaps I am just projecting, but that is the only way I can make sense out of their change in behavior.

If this respondent's assessment of the situation is correct, interviews with the faculty would have been much more fruitful *before* the administration had made the decision to dismiss Professor X. It is now an ego threat to the respondent to admit that X's dismissal was a breach of academic freedom.

Selecting an optimum time for the interview can also increase the respondent's conscious willingness to give the relevant information. One of the simplest ways is to select a time when the respondent has the fewest competing time demands. To do this, the interviewer must be familiar with the daily, weekly, monthly, and seasonal patterns of the respondent.

These patterns vary with the culture, the person's roles in that culture, and personal preferences. The interviewer who sets out to interview students the last week before the semester ends, farmers during harvest season, fishermen leaving in two days for a six-week's voyage, lifeguards on duty, factory "graveyard shift" workers at 11 a.m., housewives at 5:30 p.m., or a fireman immediately after a fire, shows either ignorance or a lack of sympathy with the respondent he is approaching.

The interviewer should not assume that he can guess what the competing time demands will be in a strange situation. Often, the most obvious common sense assumptions are completely wrong. For example, it was assumed that respondents who had experienced a disaster of major proportion (such as the burning of their house, the injury or death of members of the family, the crashing of an airplane into their home) would be reluctant to spend one or two hours in an interview the next day. The assumption seemed sensible, in view of the fact that under these circumstances such respondents would have many new tasks to complete as a result of the disaster.

This assumption is essentially correct *if* the disaster involves only one person, one family, or only a few families in a community. The assumption is completely fallacious, however, in large-scale disasters where the total community is devastated; the community is not yet functioning as an organization, each individual is unable to play his normal roles, and therefore, has few competing time demands. The man whose house has blown away, whose horse and cow have been killed, whose barn and tractor are damaged beyond repair, and whose strawberry patch is covered with heavy debris cannot begin to do anything about his condition. His every move depends upon someone else's making a move. He would like to go to the next town to make arrangements with the insurance adjustor for a new tractor. Ordinarily he would phone, but the telephone lines were destroyed by the tornado; he would drive his car, but it is damaged; although a bus line ordinarily passes the house, the highway is obstructed by fallen utility poles, trees, and high power lines; he would use his power chain saw to remove some of the trees from the road, but he has no gasoline for the motor and since the electricity is off, there are no pumps working at the local gas station, so he cannot refuel. Thus, he is caught in the paralyzing web of a non-functioning community. In his frustration, he is perfectly willing to talk about his troubles and has ample time to do so. Under these conditions, there is no difficulty in obtaining a two- or three-hour interview from the average respondent.

Sometimes an etiquette barrier arises in cases where the interviewer is asking for information before it has become public. Etiquette often requires that a hierarchy of people be notified of an event or decision before it becomes public. If the interviewer attempts to obtain the information too soon, his request may be denied. This problem often arises when the interviewer is studying some on-going community action program *in situ*. If he must continue work in the same community or organization over a long period, repeated requests for advance information could become a serious source of irritation.

In rare cases, the time for the interview may be selected to minimize the inhibiting effects of trauma by providing sympathetic understanding which will lead to catharsis. Immediately after a traumatic experience, the respondent is often more willing to talk about it than he will be later. Perhaps this is because the event is vivid in the respondent's mind and he cannot repress it. Since his mind is full of images and internalized conversation about the event, it is no more painful to externalize these thoughts in conversation with the interviewer. Later, when the experience is less fresh and the respondent can cast the thoughts from his mind, he is reluctant to renew the pain by discussing the topic. For example, after a community-wide disaster, interviewers noted a sudden decrease in respondents' willingness to discuss their experiences once the funerals were over. The funeral ceremonies seemed to symbolize the community's return to normal routine.

An interview may be timed to maximize the appeal to the respondent's need for meaning by catching him while he is still undecided, confused, and trying to pin down a future that is in a state of flux. If the purpose of the interview is to study value systems, decision-making processes, role conflicts, or processes of defining situations, then although it might be possible to wait until after the decision has been made before interviewing the respondent, this delay would allow greater memory distortions and deprive the respondent of the opportunity to use the interviewer as a sounding board for his ideas, dilemmas, and ambivalences during his struggle for meaning.

This immediate timing would be fruitful in studying such problems as decisions to marry or divorce, occupational choices, selection of a college, labor turnover, migration, and other major decisions that change a person's life pattern.

Thus far, we have discussed some of the implications of the time of the interview in relation to the individual's pattern of time demands and his experiences to be reported in the interview. Another aspect of the time dimension is selecting the most appropriate *sequence* of interviews with the different respondents.

If a random sample selects representative respondents who are so widely dispersed socially and geographically that they do not communicate with one another, the chronological order for contacting them is usually a matter of convenience and efficient use of the interviewer. But, if there is a possibility of contact between the respondents, so that they might discuss the interview either in prospect or retrospect, the effect of this communication upon the flow of relevant information should be carefully considered in the strategy planning.

Several types of questions should be answered in terms of the specific field situation in which the interviewing is to be done. Should the respondent of higher or lower status be interviewed first? Should the most willing or the most reluctant be interviewed first? Should certain respondents be interviewed first because they will not be available later? Should those special respondents who can give the broadest picture of the situation be interviewed first?

Ordinarily, it is best to interview the people of higher status first. Those of lower status may wish to wait to see if those higher up are going to cooperate by being interviewed. Also, those of higher status may be insulted if they are the last to be asked for their opinions on some community issue. This resentment, in extreme cases, might make it impossible for the interviewer to continue if the offended person has the power or prestige to blacklist the study.

Where the status of the prospective respondents is equal or irrelevant, it might be desirable to select the most willing respondents first in order to build a background of experience with the interview topic and the type of respondent. This experience might be useful in dealing with reluctant or resistant respondents. Also, the fact that all the others have cooperated and found it painless and even interesting might exert some pressure or arouse the curiosity of the reluctant.

In some situations, the interviewer knows in advance that some segments of the community or the institution will be moving or going on vacation and should be approached first. Also, certain special respondents might have the type of information which gives a broad view of the situation helpful in understanding the more specialized experiences of the respondents to follow. Such respondents may also give information on the relationships between the other respondents or information about them as individuals.

If there is a possibility of collusion between two or more respondents, this can sometimes be prevented by interviewing them separately and simultaneously. This method was used by Burgess and Wallin[26] in gaining information on sexual adjustment in marriage. A husband and wife were given questionnaires and were interviewed at the same time in different rooms. Each knew that the other was asked the same questions. This technique was able to elicit private information with great accuracy, and it provided validity checks.

In this section, some possible effects of the place and time of the interview were pointed out along with some of the problems in this phase of the strategy and their possible solutions. The next section

26/ E. W. Burgess and Paul Wallin, *Engagement and Marriage* (Philadelphia: Lippincott, 1953).

will assume that the respondent, the interviewer, and time and place have been selected. We will focus on structuring the interview situation so that it will have the most advantageous beginning.

STRUCTURING THE INTERVIEW SITUATION

Here, "structuring the interview situation" refers to only the final phase of strategy, from the moment the interviewer first contacts the respondent through the opening question of the interview. What the interviewer says and does during this time provides the immediate context of the interview and can greatly affect communication. Decisions must be made in advance relating to eight questions: (*a*) How should I introduce myself? (*b*) How should I explain the purpose of the interview? (*c*) How should I explain the sponsorship of the study? (*d*) Should I explain how and why the respondent was selected? (*e*) Should the respondent be anonymous? If so, how should this be explained? (*f*) Should any extrinsic reward be mentioned? (*g*) How should the interview be recorded, and how should the recording technique be explained? (*h*) What are some appropriate alternative wordings for the opening question?

Interviewer's introduction

In presenting oneself to the respondent, what is said is significant mainly in helping the respondent crystallize his perception of the interviewer's role. Therefore, all that has been said regarding selection of the most appropriate role from one's repertory applies to the introduction. In addition, the manner of the introduction will preview the interviewer's degree of aggressiveness, responsiveness, competence, self-assurance, warmth, or objectivity.

Giving one's name to the respondent helps reduce suspicion that might arise if the interviewer remained anonymous. This is true even though the respondent may remain anonymous. This common courtesy personalizes the relationship to some extent. If the respondent is not to remain anonymous to the interviewer, and if his name is known, then the interviewer should use the respondent's name as he presents himself. Generally, the following two phrases would leave considerably different impressions:

"I'm interviewing residents of this community on. . . ."
"Hello, Mrs. Bishop, I'm Mr. Rolph. I'm helping X Organization with a survey of this community on. . . ."

It is often necessary to remind the neophyte interviewer, with his enthusiasm or anxiety to obtain the information, of the desirability of observing such common amenities.

If it is essential that the respondent remain anonymous to the interviewer, the interviewer may nevertheless give his own name and proceed in a way that makes clear that the respondent's name is not needed.

Sponsorship

Often the next phrase of the introduction includes the sponsorship of the study, if it has one. The value of having an organization as a sponsor generally increases in more urban settings and when the interviewer is a stranger to the respondent. In a small village, folk society, or primitive groups, organizational sponsorship is often meaningless. The only meaningful sponsor in this case would be a *person* known to the respondent.

The central strategy problem here is to obtain information on the field situation. Which type of sponsorship and which organization or person will be helpful? Which might be fatal? Again, the significance of sponsorship is its effect upon the respondent's conception of the interviewer's central and auxiliary roles and the effect of this upon the inhibitors and facilitators of communication.

It may be helpful to have both a formal organization and a local person as sponsors. For example:

Mrs. Jones, how do you do! I'm Mrs. Beals from the Association for the Aid of Crippled Children. Reverend Rolf said that you would be a good person to talk to about some of the problems in Yellow Springs.

If the respondent is to remain strictly anonymous, it is still possible to use a personal sponsor in the following manner.

How do you do! I'm Mrs. Beals from the Association for the Aid of Crippled Children. Perhaps you have read in the paper that Reverend Rolf is the Yellow Springs representative for the study now under way here. I would like to talk to you about some of the problems of crippled children in your neighborhood.

In some cases, it is advisable for the interviewer to carry some written credentials including his name and the sponsor's. Respondents will rarely ask, but will be reassured, when identification is routinely shown. Even in cases where the sponsoring organization is unknown to the respondent, he may be favorably impressed by the interviewer's willingness to give information. The credentials may be a lapel button with either an official or an informal look depending on the nature of the study; or they may be a letter of introduction.

If the interviewer expects to spend several days in the community or organization under conditions where the respondents and potential respondents do not see him every day, it may be advisable to have the credentials reproduced in a form to be left with each respondent, along with a thank you note, so that questions from potential respondents can be answered accurately. This prevents the rise of rumors regarding the identity, sponsorship, or purpose of the interviewer.

Although the optimum sponsorship may be very helpful for getting in the door, it will have to be followed by good interviewing performance to maintain the initial advantages. Since the same sponsorship may not impress all respondents equally, some additional explanations will have to be given.

One of the most difficult situations in which to select sponsorship occurs when studying a group which has polarized for and against an issue related to the topic of the interview. Special care must be taken to find a sponsor perceived as neutral or disinterested. If a disinterested organizational sponsor can be found, it sometimes also helps to find a personal sponsor in each of the opposing camps of the controversy.

Explaining the purpose of the interview

The purpose of the interview should be explained in terms the respondent can understand and in a manner which will account for *all* the types of questions which are going to be asked. If the initial explanation is too narrow or vague, the respondent may not be able to connect certain questions with the stated purpose. His suspicions may be aroused because he feels the interviewer is hiding his "real" purposes. This is particularly likely to happen in a hostile or polarized community.

In order to keep the initial explanation as simple and clear as possible, it may be necessary to plan additional explanations as the interview proceeds, pointing out the relevance of each new line of questioning to the originally stated purpose. In the interests of clarity, the language used should be appropriate to the background of the respondents and free of any technical jargon.

The next problem is to include as many points as possible which will maximize the facilitators and minimize the inhibitors of communication. In the explanation, it is often possible to avoid ego threat while appealing to the need for recognition, sympathetic understanding, new experience, the need for meaning, or some combination of these. For example, if the problem is to discover why one area of a city has much higher delinquency rates than another, and the hypothesis is that social control functions of the family break down when these are not supported by an organized community, we could use the following type of explanation to open an interview with a parent in a high-delinquency area:

You have probably read in the newspaper that Metropolitan Community Studies is interested in the problems of youth in our city. We are talking to parents all over the city to discover if it is more difficult nowadays for parents to bring up children than it used to be when your parents were raising you. What do you think are some of the problems in bringing up children nowadays?

This explanation of purpose is designed to help the interviewer get inside the door. It is short and directly connected to the opening question. It indicates that the study is publicly supported, is a good cause, and is interested in the respondent's practical problems. It appeals, therefore, to the respondent's altruistic impulse, promises sympathetic understanding and possible recognition. Further explanation may be needed and given at transitional points in the interview where the questions in a new topical area are not obviously related to the initial explanation. For example:

Some people feel that there are different problems for parents living in different parts of the city. Do you feel that there are any problems which you have with children in this neighborhood that parents in other neighborhoods might not have?

The type of explanation needed, the sequence, and the timing of the various vital points depends upon the situation.

Explaining the selection of the respondent

It is not always necessary to explain why and how a particular respondent is selected. Often, the respondent does not question the point, particularly in the more traditional census or opinion poll. But it is especially important to give a clear explanation when interviewing in potentially hostile or polarized territory. In this case, if the *representative* respondent can be persuaded that he has been chosen in an objective and impartial manner and that he will remain anonymous, ego threat and hostility will be minimized. If he is a *special* respondent, and therefore not anonymous to the interviewer, it would be helpful to mention that he had been recommended by some person he knows and trusts.

Even in the most friendly territory, the respondent may suggest that the interviewer contact "somebody else who knows more about the problem," or "who has more time." In this case, it is particularly important to explain to the *representative* respondent that he was selected by an impartial sampling procedure and that it is necessary to obtain the point of view of everyone in the original sample, including people who are very busy and do not have time to be experts on the topic at hand. If the person is a *special* respondent, it is usually easier to appeal to his ego by recognizing his unique value to the study. Often, an appeal can be made by pointing out that he was selected because he has, by implication, certain altruistic tendencies. For example, "You have been recommended as a person who has done a lot of volunteer work with youth of the community," or "You have shown an interest in the problems of the senior citizens of Akron," or "You have taken an active interest in the PTA."

There are also ways of explaining the selection of the *representative* respondent that will give him recognition as a member of a particularly interesting or meritorious local group, community, or institution. In a study of the causes of delinquency, the interviewer was collecting information to compare a high-delinquency area of a large city with an equal population in a village. Although a random sample of villagers was interviewed, each one was made to feel somewhat unique by the following explanation:

We are analyzing some of the causes of juvenile delinquency by comparing places with very high delinquency rates with those having very low delinquency. You can be very helpful to us, since you live in a town with the least delinquency in this part of the state.

The explanation can communicate positive expectations of cooperation by assuming that everyone will cooperate since, thus far, everyone else has. For example:

We have been able to interview the families in every ninth house in this area and it looks like we will be able to finish today.

This strategy must be used with caution. To avoid being interpreted by the respondent as pressure tactics, careful wording and the appropriate context must be employed. The expectation should be mentioned casually as an interesting sidelight.

Thus we see that even though the respondent is willing to cooperate without an explanation of how and why he was selected, it is often desirable to provide an explanation appealing to altruistic tendencies, giving him recognition, and communicating positive expectations of cooperation. All of these precautions, although not always 100 percent successful, should help to assure optimum interpersonal relations at the outset.

Providing anonymity

It should not be assumed that the respondent, whether special or representative, desires or should be given anonymity. Often, the respondent does not care to be anonymous because this might detract from his recognition. At times, it might be necessary to make clear that the results will be anonymous even though the respondent prefers to tell the world what he has on his mind. This is the case where the respondent sees the interview as a means to some personal gain and colors his report hoping for approval of superordinates or for the discreditation of peers. Under these conditions, his motivation is not to give an objective report but to select, censor, exaggerate, and rationalize, as it best fits his purpose.

There are circumstances where the respondent would prefer to remain anonymous, but should not be granted his wish by the interviewer. This would be the case in studying a controversial issue in a community and attempting to predict who will take what public stand. If the respondent does not feel strongly enough or is not courageous enough to give his point of view to the interviewer, he is less likely to take a public stand later than the person who gives his views in a forthright manner. This principle may be carried further by having the interviewer bring up arguments of the opposition and ask for permission to quote the respondent in his report to some public body or the press.

Thus, we see that the granting or withholding of anonymity is not decided upon the basis of tradition or the respondent's desires, but upon the purpose of the interview. One ethical point must be observed in any case. If the respondent is promised anonymity, that promise should be scrupulously kept; if he is not to be given anonymity, this should be clear to him before the interview begins.

Anonymity is not an all-or-none factor. There are several degrees or types of anonymity which have practical and theoretical implications. The most extreme degree of anonymity consists of the interviewer's being ignorant not only of the identity of the respondent, but also of where he might be contacted again. This would be the case if a sociologist who was studying the underworld had a contact person, who trusted him, bring unapprehended criminals to be interviewed about the practices of the professional criminal.

Another example of this degree of anonymity would be interviewing a random area-sample of the sun bathers on the beach regarding their preferences in bathing suits. Or, people waiting at a railroad station might be interviewed on their opinions of the services to passengers.

This degree of anonymity has a disadvantage in that the same respondent cannot possibly be recontacted if additional information is later needed to complete the picture. There are ways of arranging to recontact the same person while he remains anonymous to the interviewer. The respondent may be identified by an address only, or by a phone number. Also, some "go between" selected and trusted by the respondents might arrange the recontact. In any case, where anonymity is vital to the flow of communication, the respondent must have no doubts of the anonymity. This assurance is always more difficult to provide if the respondent is to be recontacted.

There are lesser degrees of anonymity in which the respondent is known to the interviewer, but not to the sponsor or client; and there is still less anonymity where both interviewer and sponsor can identify the respondent, but where any report either to a select body or the general public keeps the individual anonymous. Still less anonymity is involved when knowledge of the identity of the respondent is restricted to an official or professional group who is to use the information. This is often the situation where case study materials collected by a social worker are available to clinical psychologists or juvenile authorities.

Another important dimension of anonymity is the degree of identification of groups versus individuals. In some cases, the respondent is almost as reluctant to have information published about his particular group, organization, or community as he is about himself. This may be because his role in the group is so conspicuous that he too would be identifiable, even though he was not named, or he may simply be so ego-involved in the organization that he feels any threat to its reputation as a personal threat. Here, it is difficult to assure anonymity for the organization if only one such organization is studied. Organizations are easily kept anonymous when many of the same type are studied, and the results reported as either a statistical summary or as case studies which are frankly camouflaged by changing non-essential details and omitting unnecessary identifying materials.

Even though one of the above methods of preserving the respondent's anonymity may be used, there are occasions when a particular respondent is not convinced of the interviewer's sincerity. Sometimes the interviewer's promise is put to a severe test. One respondent may quiz the interviewer for information obtained from another respondent. A management person may ask for some "off the record" information about one of the workers who has been interviewed. In rare cases, the interviewer will be threatened with jail or persecution for not giving the information. This situation arose in a study of a disaster-stricken community where the chief of police ordered an interviewer to surrender her tape recordings for him to hear. After refusing and explaining that the information was confidential and that the respondents had been promised anonymity, she was threatened with persecution for "withholding evidence." Of course, such a charge was groundless, since no crime had been committed for which evidence was needed. Probably, the chief was anxious about the possibility of people reporting the shortcomings of the police department during the crisis. Knowing that he was not on firm legal ground, the chief did not attempt to use physical force to obtain the tapes. When the field supervisor explained the situation to the chief, he reluctantly relinquished his claim.

The foregoing discussion on maintaining various degrees of anonymity indicates the need for some serious strategy planning to avoid problems in this area. Closely related to the problems of anonymity in general are the problems that arise regarding tape recording of interviews, which bring up the question of how the interview should be recorded and what explanation of the recording technique should be made to the respondent.

TAKING NOTES ON THE INTERVIEW

The best method for recording the interview must be decided on the basis of various criteria. For example, the method that obtains the most complete and accurate detail may be chosen or which affords optimal interpersonal relations, or which makes the analysis of the data most efficient. We assume the most valid criterion is that of obtaining complete and accurate information, regardless of the effects upon the problems of analysis. Information collected efficiently is of questionable value if it is not also valid. Of course, there are degrees of reliability and validity which must be considered in relation to the purpose of the project and weighed against the merits of efficiency.

"Taking notes" may consist of either recording the respondent's statements in his own words, noting important relevant central ideas, classifying the responses by checking some predefined answer categories, or taking "probe notes." Probe notes are specific points jotted down to be elaborated or clarified later, rather than notes taken to record detailed relevant information.

Note-taking on informal interviews

Recording the interview covers many kinds of activities. In the case of informal interviewing (as in anthropological studies), where the respondent does not see the researcher in the formal role of interviewer, the researcher should not take notes of any kind during the interview. It is typical in participant-observation to make notes on one's observations of others and of his own reactions after leaving the scene.

Note-taking on structured interviews

In a more formal interview, the problem of noting the relevant information varies according to the scope of the questions to be asked and the degree to which the answers are structured. Where the scope is broad and the answers left open-ended, there is greater difficulty in recording the answers, unless the breadth and openness are used mainly to facilitate the spontaneous flow of communication and the proportion of relevant information is low and falls into anticipated, clearly recognizable categories. In this case, recording the relevant data can be efficient and does not tend to interfere with the interviewer's tasks of critically listening and evaluating the information. The interviewer may be simply required to check a box or to circle a number.

Sometimes the response is not clearly codable into the response categories given. In this case, the interviewer should give the response as completely as possible, and in some cases, check the category which seems nearest to fitting the response. This then becomes a coding problem.

In cases where it is advisable to let the respondent know the answer choices, they may be included as part of the question or the choices can be printed on a card to be handed to the respondent, as illustrated in the chapter on interviewing techniques.

Verbatim notes. For some purposes, it is necessary for the interviewer to record the responses "verbatim." In many situations, it is not humanly possible for the interviewer to record the total interview verbatim. When the respondent is highly emotional, ungrammatical, or erratic in his verbal pacing, and yet a complete report is needed, the only solution is to use a tape recorder. The verbatim recording of responses in longhand that is a common practice of many survey-type studies is valid only if

a) we need the exact words and phrases used by the respondent;

b) the responses cannot practically be categorized in advance;

c) the scope of the question is narrow enough that the relevant response is short and uncomplicated;

d) the essence of the relevant response can be written without damaging rapport in the interview;

e) the interviewer can complete any missing words immediately after the interview before going on to the next;

f) the interviewer's handwriting is corrected or clarified before going on to the next interview so that the people who code the responses may reliably read them.

Under these conditions, when verbatim notes are needed, the interviewer must carefully discipline himself to avoid paraphrasing or summarizing the respondent's ideas.

One method of obtaining verbatim or other fairly detailed notes without either being distracted from listening to the respondent or using a tape recorder is to use a two-person interviewing team, with one person asking the questions while the other takes notes. In some cases, it is useful for the two to exchange roles from time to time. A few of the pros and cons of these "tandem interviews" are discussed by Kincaid and Bright.[27] Although this system has advantages, in that it leaves the interviewer free of note-taking to give full attention to what the respondent is saying while avoiding possible objections to a tape recorder, we must carefully evaluate the probable inhibiting effects of the third person in the context of a particular interview situation.

Probe notes. Another type of note-taking is the use of probe notes. In contrast to verbatim notes (which are aimed at storing the

27/ H. V. Kincaid and M. Bright, "The Tandem Interview: A Trial of the Two-Interviewer Team," *Public Opinion Quarterly,* Vol. 21 (Summer, 1957), pp. 304-12.

information received), the probe notes are taken to remind the interviewer of specific points which should be elaborated or clarified later in the interview. They are similar to verbatim notes in that they include the exact word or phrase used by the respondent rather than a paraphrase or summary. The less the interview is structured by a detailed interview schedule and the more important it is to not interrupt the respondent's association pattern by immediately probing any unclear or incomplete response, the more necessary it is to take probe notes so that the relevant points may be elaborated and clarified later.

Effects of note-taking on rapport. Taking notes in an interview may have several effects. Intense note-taking may distract the interviewer from his task of observing and listening to the respondent. Also, the respondent may feel the interviewer should not neglect him and should show more spontaneous appreciation. When few notes are taken, the respondent may feel that, when the interviewer is writing, something important has been said. In hostile territory, it is usually better to leave note-taking until after the interview if the session is short and the details are few. The interviewer can often detect the respondent's positive or negative reaction to the note-taking by the latter's tendency to elaborate at those points where the interviewer is taking notes, to go back and qualify or "correct" those points, or to quickly pass on to a new topic.

In some situations, the poised pencil seems to act as a non-verbal probe to "tell me more about that." Where note-taking seems to have a negative effect, the interviewer can ameliorate some of the effect by devoting his full attention to the respondent and taking as little notice of his own note-taking as possible. The interviewer should never attempt to take notes secretly. If the effect of taking notes is detrimental, then the danger of being caught or even suspected would be much more detrimental. The best approach is to assure the respondent of anonymity and to explain that notes must be taken to insure completeness and accuracy. When he does not accept this idea, it is better to refrain from taking notes.

Tape recording the interview

The tape recorder is not used in most interviewing, not only because of the cost of tape and recording machines, but also because of the high cost per interview for transcribing and coding the relevant information. If every word of the interview is to be transcribed, it may require from three to 12 hours of typing for each hour of recording. This ratio varies with the speed of the speech, clarity, pacing, complexity of vocabulary, accents of the interviewer or respondent as well as with the background knowledge and technical skill of the typist.

Despite these disadvantages of economy, particularly for large-scale projects, the tape recorder is an invaluable tool for certain phases of interviewing. Even on those projects which depend mainly on highly structured interview schedules, the tape recorder is an excellent tool in the initial exploratory interviewing and subsequent pretesting of the interview schedule.

The tape recorder is almost indispensable for the teaching and supervising of interviewing. It would seem ludicrous to try to teach painting without seeing the student paint a picture, or to teach swimming without seeing the person in the water, but people are often taught to interview without the advantage of having any experienced person actually hear them interview. Instead, an attempt is often made to learn by reading detailed instructions or basic theoretical ideas, perhaps doing some role playing, and then going out to learn by doing. Also, the supervisor of the interviewers on a large project may determine the interviewer's skill by noting such objective indices as whether all the questions have been answered, whether verbatim notes are clearly legible, and whether the quota of interviews is completed on schedule. All of these indices do not tell us whether the interviewer unwittingly loads the questions with his tone of voice, whether he interrupts the respondent, whether he probes for more information at appropriate points and whether he correctly codes or records what the respondent has said.

Also, for the person who wants to improve his interviewing independently, the tape recorder is a boon. Without it, he cannot be fully aware of where he accepted inadequate information without probing, where he missed specific opportunities to probe, and where he failed to note important non-verbal cues from the respondent. All of these can be recorded on tape and heard more accurately by the interviewer later when he is free from the strain of listening, recording and deciding what to say next. Another unique advantage is that precisely the same behavior can be analyzed several times by the same or different people.

In addition to being used as a tool for teaching, supervision and self-instruction, the tape recorder is sometimes needed for all of the interviews in some types of data-gathering projects. In deciding whether the tape recorder should be used in this way, there are many variables to consider. Objective evidence has been accumulated showing that much of the apprehension about the inhibiting effects of using the tape recorder are valid only under certain limited circumstances. One of the most comprehensive and thoughtful treatments of the pros and cons of using the tape recorder is given by Bucher, Fritz, and Quarantelli.[28] Another article by Engle[29] deals with the advantages of using the tape recorder in consumer research, and Womer and Boyd[30] show the value of the tape recorder in the simultaneous training and selection of interviewer for a particular field study. These and other more atomistic experimental studies can be subsumed under some general principles to guide our decision as to whether or not we should plan on using a tape recorder on a specific project.

The more complex the information, the less the method should depend upon the interviewer's memory. The more rapid the flow of relevant information, the less we should depend upon taking longhand notes. The more we wish to explore for unanticipated types of responses and the less sure we are of what categories of information are relevant to the problem, the more we should use a tape recorder which omits nothing and allows the relevance of the responses to be decided later. The greater the significance of the precise words used and the order in which ideas are expressed, the more necessary it is to use a tape recorder. The less topic control is used, and the less the sequence of topics is controlled, the more important it is for the interviewer to be relieved of verbatim reporting in longhand and allowed to devote more attention to probe notes. The more important it is for the interviewer to devote full attention to the respondent to obtain optimal interpersonal relations, the more important it is to use the tape recorder.[31] However, because of the time consumed in transcribing or coding, the tape recorder should never be used if all relevant data can be validly recorded on the spot by the interviewer. One exception would be the situation where the inter-

28/ Rue Bucher, Charles E. Fritz and Enrico L. Quarantelli, "Tape Recorded Interviews in Social Research," *American Sociological Review*, Vol. 21, No. 3 (June, 1956), pp. 359-64.

29/ J. F. Engle, "Tape Recorders in Consumer Research," *Journal of Marketing*, Vol. 26 (April, 1962), pp. 73-74.

30/ S. Womer and H. W. Boyd, Jr., "The Use of a Voice Recorder in the Selection and Training of Field Workers," *Public Opinion Quarterly*, Vol. 15 (Summer, 1951), pp. 358-63.

31/ Charlotte H. Wilkie, "A Study of Distortions in Recording Interviews," *Social Work*, Vol. 8, No. 3 (July, 1963), pp. 31-36. This study shows how distortions in recording seriously limited the worker's understanding of the client's problems.

viewer tape records in order to improve his technical and tactical skills.

Thus, even though the vast majority of interviews done by both specialized and auxiliary interviewers are not done with a tape recorder, the writer feels that it has a unique function in the exploratory interviewing phase of many large-scale projects, for teaching, supervision and self-instruction in interviewing, as well as for collecting all of the data on certain types of projects. Thus, it is worthwhile to deal with some of the basic ideas involved in using the tape recorder for any one of these purposes.

Tape recording and interpersonal relations. When a tape recorder is to be used, here are several precautions that should be taken to facilitate optimal interpersonal relations:

a) The interviewer should become thoroughly familiar with the machine so that he does not feel insecure in its use or devote too much attention to it.

b) The physical setting should be arranged, if possible, so that the tape recorder is out of the respondent's sight.

c) The microphone should be inconspicuous and out of the direct line of sight as the interviewer and respondent face each other.

d) The use of the recording machine should be explained in forthright and matter of fact way.

e) Once the interview begins, the interviewer should show no awareness of the tape recorder's presence.

In explaining the use of the tape recorder to the respondent, the interviewer realizes with experience that it is rare to find a respondent who will object to its use. It is possible for the interviewer to raise doubts in the respondent's mind by *asking* for the respondent's permission to use the machine rather than *explaining* why it is used. The interviewer should show by his manner that it is merely routine procedure. Some explanation such as one of the following is usually sufficient:

I am interested in getting all the details of your story in precisely your own words. Since I can't take shorthand and don't want a third person present, the best way is to let this machine do all the work.

or:

We always record the interview so that the information will be accurate. I listen to it and type the relevant material so that the tape can be used over again.

It sometimes breaks the ice to let the respondent hear himself and to assure him that he is right when he says the recording seems to distort his voice.

Transcribing tape-recorded information

The most satisfactory system for transcribing the material from the tape includes the following features.

The transcribing should be done by the same person who did the interview. First, if because of field conditions there is some lack of perfect audibility in the tape, the person who did the interview is much less likely to make errors in transcribing. Second, if the interviewer has been careless in those details essential to obtaining a clearly audible recording, he then directly reaps the results of his carelessness. This supplies a strong motivation to get good audibility in subsequent interviews. Third, if there are peculiarities of speech, such as regional, or foreign accents, the interviewer is more likely to be able to understand it. Fourth, it is an excellent training device, since it makes the interviewer acutely aware of his errors in tactics and techniques. Fifth, the interviewer becomes aware of the amount of missing information and is strongly motivated to probe more persistently in subsequent interviews.

The relevant material should first be transcribed in the order it occurred on the tape with no attempt to organize it systematically. Keeping the information in sequence is not only more practical than attempting to code it as we go, but this also preserves the unique context. This practice assumes that the interviewer who is doing the transcribing has a clear grasp of the problem and therefore is capable of selecting the *relevant* information. This assumption is warranted since, as we pointed out previously, unscheduled interviewing cannot be done successfully by anyone who does not thoroughly understand the problem. This selection process sharpens the interviewer's awareness of the problem and makes him acutely aware of any shortcomings in the information he has obtained. As a general rule, unless material is clearly irrelevant, it should be transcribed. It can later be rejected in the coding process.

The transcribed material should then be coded by the interviewer and another person familiar with the problem. As a reliability check, the material should be coded by independent coders who are familiar with the problem. There is a real danger in using the test-retest measure of reliability if this is done only by the original interviewer, because in many cases he tends to read into the material more than is there. If the second coder does not code some material in the same way, it is often because he sees less information in the material than the interviewer does. In this case, the interviewer might become aware that he is judging on the basis of additional information and insights which have not been transcribed from the tape. Often, there is a certain *gestalt* in the total interview which is lost in the transcription, thus possibly making the original interviewer's judgment more accurate. At any rate, the cross-check between the interviewer and the non-interviewer provides a more balanced view and forces the interviewer to support his interpretations with clearer evidence. Often, the interviewer becomes aware that he should include in the transcription significant non-symbolic cues which influenced his interpretation of the material. This usually increases the agreement between the interviewer and the non-interviewer coding the material.

The interviewers on the project should transcribe and code their first interview as soon as possible so that subsequent interviews will benefit from the experience. This practice is beneficial whether the main purpose of the project is to learn interviewing techniques or whether the main aim is to obtain complete, reliable and valid information. Having the interviewing, transcribing and coding all done by the same people improves the quality of the data in situations where non-scheduled interviewing is needed; therefore, the sooner these experiences are combined in one interview, the sooner the next interview will be improved.

Another distinct advantage of alternating interviewing and transcribing is that it provides a more balanced variety of activities throughout the life of the project and saves the interviewer from continuous long hours of tedious transcription and coding of data.

Sometimes the objection is made that having the interviewing, transcribing, and coding done by highly skilled people will make the cost of the operation prohibitive. This argument can be reduced to, "It costs too much to get accurate information so let's spend less and get inaccurate information." We have no choice if we decide that tape-recorded non-schedule interviews should be used only to get information that could not be obtained just as effectively by a questionnaire or a highly structured interview. Open-ended data cannot be reliably coded by people who do not thoroughly understand the problem. Nor can non-scheduled interviewing be done by people who are merely following mechanical rules. Since it takes a considerable investment of time to familiarize someone with the problem, it is more efficient to use the same people for both the coding and the interviewing. But why shouldn't we use professional typists to transcribe the data? Here the answer is not so clear cut.

There are certain conditions under which it is more efficient to have typists do the transcribing. If the audibility of the tape is extremely clear, if the typists are sufficiently impressed with the importance of accuracy, and if the proportion of relevant data is so high that it is quicker to transcribe the whole interview than to select out the relevant material, then the use of typists may be satisfactory.

We have found the proportion of directly relevant interview material to vary from five to 90 percent. For a number of reasons, the use of typists is probably not economical when, for example, only 40 percent of the information is relevant. They often make errors at crucial points in the interview which can be checked only by having someone familiar with the interview situation listen to the tape and check it against the type script. Also, the length of time required to type the total interview is sometimes greater than that required for the interviewer, who may not be as good a typist, to select and type 40 percent of the interview. The coding process is cumbersome when there is a large proportion of extraneous material. Also, the amount of inaudible material will be much greater if the interviewers are not responsible for doing their own transcribing.

Poor audibility is one of the main causes of transcribing difficulty! Sometimes one hour of tape recorded material can be transcribed in as little three hours if the rate of speech is average and the audibility perfect. However, 10 hours might be needed to transcribe one hour of tape with poor audibility.

Planning the opening question

Even though the interview is not scheduled to the extent of providing exact questions or an order for covering subtopics, it is advisable for the interviewer to prepare several opening questions. The importance of the opening question is too great to leave to caprice, yet neither should it be rigidly predetermined.

There are several important and unique functions of the opening question. It may either be broad enough to delineate the entire topic of the interview, or it may select a single point of departure. In either case, it should be clearly connected with the explanation of the interview so that the respondent is immediately aware that the interviewer is pursuing the stated purposes. If possible it should ask for information which is relatively easy for the respondent to give so that there is no chance of ego threat at the outset. The opener may also begin with a point on which the respondent feels particularly qualified to speak, thus appealing to his need for recognition. A well-phrased question might also demonstrate sympathetic understanding of the respondent's problems. Finally, if the interview requires free-flowing and detailed answers rather than simple yes-no responses, it is important that the respondent realize this at the beginning.

In studying the attitudes and problems of the community's senior citizens, an excellent opening question was found to be, "Do you think there is some age at which people should stop working?" A question equally appealing to teenagers in a study of parent-child conflict was, "What are some of the things you feel parents and other adults should know to get along with teenagers?"

It is often desirable to plan opening questions for different categories of representative or special respondents, so that each can begin the interview at a point that concerns him.

In interviews where the main problem is to stimulate the respondent's memory of experiences during a certain period of time, it is useful to begin the interview with a question regarding a point in time prior to the events the interviewer wants reported. This "lead-in" helps establish associations and builds an appropriate mood and pace before dealing with the critical time period. The lead-in portion of the interview may last from 30 seconds to 10 minutes, depending on how far in the past and how detailed the experiences to be reported. The time needed for the lead-in discussion increases when it functions to supply certain background information about the respondent or the event providing a context for the interview.

When approaching each respondent, the interviewer should make it a point to get to the opening question as quickly as possible. The introduction, the explanation of the purpose and sponsorship of the study, the explanation of how the respondent was selected and the extent to which he is anonymous, and any explanation of the recording should be as economical and clear as possible in order to get into the opening question. In some cases, not all of these preliminaries are needed because the respondent understands the situation. At other times, the explanation needed is so long and involved that further explanations of the objectives of the interview, the use of the data, the respondent's anonymity or the recording method might be made as the interview progresses at points where the context makes it more meaningful.

SUMMARY

Strategy includes the overall planning done before the actual interview is underway. This planning is done carefully on the basis of information gained regarding the field situation, but the strategy plans must be considered tentative and subject to revision on the basis of additional information gained after the interviewing begins.

Three dimensions of the general field situation (friendly-hostile, open-closed, and single-multiple contacts) affect the general strategy to be used. These general types of field situations provide a backdrop for making basic decisions.

These basic decisions include the selection of appropriate respondents, of appropriate interviewers and interviewer roles, choosing an appropriate time and place, and structuring the interview situation. All of these decisions are made on the basis of their probable effect upon the respondent's willingness or ability to give the relevant information. All of them are strategy tools which can be used to minimize the inhibitors and to maximize the facilitators of relevant information. All these decisions, and their effect depends upon their meaning to the respondent.

In selecting appropriate respondents, a distinction must be made between *key informants,* who provide strategy information on how to obtain information and respondents who provide information directly relevant to the objectives of the interview. Respondents are either *special* respondents who have specialized types of information which can be obtained only from people in a certain role or status, or *representative* respondents who are chosen because they share certain characteristics defining a group or category of people.

In selecting respondents, the problem is to determine who has the needed information, who is most able to give it, and who is the most willing to give it. Whether or not the person has the relevant information depends upon his experiences in relation to the purposes of the interview. His ability or willingness to report his experiences depend upon the degree to which the facilitators and inhibitors of communication are present.

Once we know what information is needed, the field situations where it must be sought, the kinds of respondents who possess such information and are most able and willing to report it, the next problem is to decide what type of interviewer is most likely to be able to obtain the information completely, validly, and efficiently. Certain overt characteristics such as sex, age, race, ethnicity, speech patterns, dress and grooming place limits upon the role repertory of the interviewer by determining the respondent's perception of him. Of these overt characteristics, only dress and grooming are easily changed. The others can be controlled only by selecting the appropriate person as interviewer. The interviewer's basic personality traits are also important insofar as they determine his ability to perform his interviewing task. Since, by definition, these traits cannot be changed to fit the interview situation or the type of respondent, the problem must be solved by selecting the right interviewer for a particular task. Interviewers may also be selected on the basis of certain special knowledge needed and for the presence or absence of certain attitudes. To a certain extent, the relevant knowledge can be acquired for the particular interviewing task and attitudes can be controlled by training, but there are practical limits upon both.

From the point of view of a particular interviewer, his task is to determine which auxiliary role or roles in his own natural role repertory he should present to the respondent, or which new auxiliary role he can or should take to facilitate interviewing. The particular role taken by the interviewer is important only insofar as it puts him in a different relationship with the respondent. Role relationships exist along at least two dimensions: the in-group—out-group dimension and the superordinate-subordinate dimension. In appraising the in-group—out-group dimension certain conditions can be specified giving advantages to both ends of the continuum. Similarly, there are advantages and disadvantages in both the superordinate and the subordinate role. The desirability of a particular role relationship depends upon how it affects the respondent's willingness to give relevant information.

The place of the interview provides the opportunity to communicate and, like a stage set, acts as a context for action which brings certain auxiliary roles to the foreground for both the interviewer and the respondent. The respondent's self-perception and his perception of the interviewer has an effect upon the degree to which certain information is inhibited because of ego threat or etiquette. In addition, the setting may minimize competing time demands, stimulate recall, and provide the conditions needed for the interviewer to use his techniques and tactics to full advantage.

The temporal setting of the interview is significant in its relationship to the time of the experiences which the respondent is reporting. When the interviewer asks the question determines to a great extent both the respondent's ability and his willingness to give the information. The selection of an appropriate time can minimize the inhibiting effect of forgetting, ego threat, and competing time demands, as well as maximize the facilitating effect of sympathetic understanding, catharsis, and the respondent's need for meaning.

The final phase of strategy consists of structuring the interview situation before the actual questioning and probing begin. To assure best results, the interviewer must have planned how to introduce himself, how to explain the sponsorship and purpose of the interview, how to explain the selection of the particular respondent, how much anonymity should be promised, how to record the interview, and several possible opening questions. These aspects influence the respondent's views of the interviewer's role and of what information is relevant, as well as his willingness to give relevant information.

Strategy problems have many dimensions. It is impossible to provide a specific solution for each possible problem. Instead, we have pointed to some of the available strategy tools and must leave their application to multitudinous specific situations to the interviewer. The writer's experience in consulting and in training interviewers shows that many of the strategy errors were avoidable in that the interviewer had at his command resources to solve the problems. Failures most frequently resulted from not raising the right questions before leaping into the situation.

5
Techniques in interviewing

Earlier we defined *techniques* as specific forms of verbal and non-verbal behavior used during the interview and *tactics* as the way in which specific techniques are varied to meet problems as they arise in the context of a particular interview. Techniques can be classified in isolation from the larger context of the interview, while tactics are the patterns or sequences of questions as they relate to the progress of the interview as a whole. Thus, each question or statement by the interviewer has a technical form in itself and is part of a larger tactical pattern.

Techniques and tactics are functionally intertwined in the dynamics of interviewing, but to simplify the exposition, the two will be separated. In an actual non-scheduled interview, the interviewer must direct his attention toward tactical problems as they arise unpredictably; therefore, the successful interviewer must have mastered a wide range of specific techniques so that their use is automatic before he attempts the more complex task of adjusting the pattern of questioning to the on-going context of the interview. These techniques include the use of silence, the verbal forms used by the interviewer, and the attitudes manifested by him.

SILENCE AS A TECHNIQUE

It might be argued that silence cannot be a technique of interviewing because it consists of doing nothing. Experience and research in

187

social interaction indicate that silence is as meaningful in verbal communication as rests are in a musical score. Research by Gorden[1] and by Matarazzo and Wiens[2] indicates that there is positive correlation between the amount of silence used by an interviewer and the respondent's general level of spontaneity. Hall[3] presents an interesting discussion of the cultural differences in the rhythm and pacing of communication and interaction which causes misunderstandings between people from different cultures.

In interviewing, silence not only acts as punctuation but also communicates a mood. The lack of any pauses in the interview often indicates that the interviewer is anxious and insecure. This tends to make the respondent feel the same.

One of the first skills the interviewer must learn is *not to interrupt* the respondent. To interrupt, the interviewer need not begin speaking while the respondent is still talking. Psychologically, an interruption is any audible or visible activity initiated by the interviewer before it is clear that the respondent has finished the thought he is expressing and does not intend to continue without direction from the interviewer.

The interviewer can pause for two to 20 seconds before asking the next question and yet be interrupting. Ordinarily, if the respondent has completed a sentence with a tone of finality and then looks at the interviewer expectantly, a two-second pause assures that he has finished the comment; but if the respondent stops obviously in the middle of a sentence or is gazing thoughtfully into space, a silence of 10 seconds before asking the next question is no guarantee against interruption. For example:

I: How did you know you shouldn't light a cigarette in the area of the plane crash?

R: Well, I just know there was gasoline all over the ground where the crowd had collected and. . . . (15-second silence). . . . Hmm, I guess it was the master of ceremonies of the air show who announced on the public address system that we shouldn't light cigarettes or try to start any of the cars in the parking lot beside the airstrip.

This is typical, in that a respondent often interrupts his own re-

1/ Raymond L. Gorden, *An Interaction Analysis of the Depth-Interview,* unpublished Ph.D. dissertation, University of Chicago, 1954, p. 170.

2/ Joseph D. Matarazzo and Arthur N. Wiens, "Interviewer Effects on Interviewees' Speech and Silence Durations," *Proceedings of the 74th Annual Convention of the American Psychological Association,* 1966.

3/ Edward T. Hall, *The Silent Language* (New York: Doubleday & Co., 1959).

sponse with a pause while he recalls a more accurate version of the event. In this example, the respondent first assumed that he knew there was gasoline on the ground from his own astute observation, but actually he was reminded by the master of ceremonies who was a veteran United States Air Force ground crewman.

Just as an interruption may occur in spite of a prolonged pause, it is also possible for the interviewer to speak at the same time as the respondent *without* the psychological effect of interrupting. This is the case when the interviewer reacts with "noises" and verbal expressions indicating interest in what the respondent is saying, as in the following expressions: "Uh huh," "hmm," "I see!" Of course, these verbal expressions must be accompanied by the appropriate nonverbal attitudes if they are not to interrupt the flow of information from the respondent.

Besides serving as insurance against interrupting the respondent, silence as an interviewing technique has several other vital functions. It creates a slower pace; this is conducive to a more *thoughtful mood* than could be achieved at a more rapid pace. This mood shows the respondent that the interviewer *expects* him to take time to give thoughtful answers, and it allows time for the respondent to retrace his own paths of association to revive faded images and feelings.

Silence also allows the respondent to *control* the direction of the next step in the conversation. This allows the interviewer to note the order of the respondent's association and the degree to which the respondent is willing to talk without probing. It maximizes the possibility of obtaining relevant information which the interviewer does not anticipate. Often, a silent probe used in an exploratory interview obtains answers to significant questions which the interviewer would never have thought of asking.

If the silence is accompanied by a facial or postural expression of interest and thoughtfulness, it gives the respondent the impression that the interviewer is vitally interested in the story. The opposite practice of interrupting usually gives the respondent the impression that the interviewer is not interested in him or his story.

Too much silence is also possible. The interviewer must develop a sensitivity to the respondent's pace and expectations so that excessive silence will be avoided. The respondent may feel the pressure of expectancy in the silence and yield to it reluctantly by merely repeating what he has already said or by giving a very short statement, as if to say "I've done my part, it's your move." In this case, the interviewer's use of silence has ceased to be a way of creating an informal, permissive, and thoughtful atmosphere and has become a source of embarrassment for the respondent. He may feel that the interviewer is not holding up his end of the conversation. In extreme cases, he may view prolonged silences as a weapon which the interviewer is using to force him into submission, and he may retaliate by trying to outwait the interviewer and beat him at his own game.

The interviewer must develop a sensitivity to the use of silence so that he can adjust appropriately to the pace of a particular respondent and so that he may take the initiative in establishing a more thoughtful mood or in jolting the respondent out of reminiscences not relevant to the objectives of the interview.

VERBAL FORMS USED BY THE INTERVIEWER

In spelling out specific verbal forms and attitudes comprising the interviewer's kit of techniques, we will also indicate their purposes and probable effects upon the respondent's ability and willingness to give relevant information. The verbal forms and their effects to be discussed here will include (*a*) providing specific *context* for the question, (*b*) selecting the appropriate *vocabulary* in wording the question, (*c*) delimiting the *scope* of the question, (*d*) supplying *answer categories,* and (*e*) *suggesting answers.* All of these verbal forms when appropriately used help the interviewer with his two major tasks of maximizing the flow of relevant information and maintaining optimum interpersonal relations.

Contexts aimed at communicating the question

Every specific question occurs in a context which helps convey its meaning to the respondent. Context is furnished at the strategy level by the respondent's perception of the purpose of the study, the sponsorship, the interviewer's auxiliary roles, and the time and place of the interview. As the next chapter explains, context is also furnished at the tactical level by the sequence of questions and answers in a particular interview. At this point, we are concerned only with the context provided at the technique level by wording a particular question to include the context or by supplying a contextual statement which immediately precedes the question.

Several useful functions can be performed by the provision of an appropriate context with the question. The context may simply clarify the meaning of the question; it may increase the respondent's ability to give the relevant information by stimulating his memory, by decreasing the chronological confusion, or by bringing unconscious norms and assumptions to the surface; it may also increase the respondent's willingness to give the information by decreasing ego threat, removing the etiquette barrier, appealing to the need for meaning, or stimulating altruistic motives.

Defining terms. It is often necessary to preface a question with a contextual statement defining crucial terms which might be unclear to the respondent. Ego threat is prevented by giving the definition before the respondent shows that he needs it and without asking whether he understands the term. For example:

There are cases where a man and woman live together as man and wife, set up housekeeping, have children and take care of them, but do not get a marriage license or have a wedding ceremony of any kind. *Do you think children of these common law marriages should be entitled to the legal rights of inheritance?*

This is better than either asking if the respondent knows what a common law marriage is or assuming that he understands the term.

The same question might have different meanings to different respondents who use different sets of assumptions to interpret the meaning of the question. Garfinkel[4] shows how, in different situations in everyday social interaction, people interpret the actions of others in terms of common sense theories. These theories are composed of assumptions about human behavior, as they know it, which help them to make sense out of what people say and do. He goes further to show that this *context* of unstated assumptions, particularly the cognitive assumptions, changes within a group as a result of the members' past interactions. Each person, therefore, brings to any communication situation a set of assumptions (normative and cognitive) which are derived both from his general cultural background and from the more unique experiential background of the groups of which he is a member. Usually, in the interview situation the respondent and interviewer are establishing a new relationship in which neither knows the unstated assumptions of the other that would bear upon the interpretation of the particular questions to be asked. Under these conditions, if the interviewer does not explicitly furnish a context for interpretation of a question because he unwittingly assumes that there is only one possible context, he is leaving the respondent free to use his own set of assumptions which are unstated

4/ Harold Garfinkel, *Studies in Ethnomethodology* (Englewood Cliffs, N.J.: Prentice-Hall, Inc., 1967).

and unknown to the interviewer. Thus, not only is the question different in the minds of these two people, but also the response has a different meaning to each.

Of course, the context for the interview as a whole is partially established by those dimensions of the situation previously treated under the heading of strategy, but at this point we are concerned only with contexts as a verbal technique for more clearly communicating the question.

Studies involving controversial issues on a national and international scale often involve terms not clearly understood by many people. In a random sample of the population such words as "monopoly," "savings," "profit," "free-trade," "mandate," and "right of way" carry only a vague meaning for the majority. In many cases, the respondent will not ask the meaning because he thinks he knows or he is embarrassed to ask.

Providing a time perspective. Often the answer to a question can be completely reversed by a shift in the time perspective. This is particularly true when obtaining facts or opinions on *trends* of any type. For example, in response to the question, "Do you think that the amount of academic freedom on American college campuses has increased, decreased, or stayed about the same?" A respondent's answer might be "increased" or "decreased" depending on the period of time the interviewer has in mind. To bring about a clearer time perspective, the context could be, "Try to remember some of the things happening on this campus five years ago, in 1956, and compare that with the present time. Think of the general psychological atmosphere and its effect upon academic freedom."

If the interviewer has information on some specific events in the local, national, and international scene occurring in 1956 this would be helpful in providing a more vivid time perspective.

Providing a spacial perspective. Just as an answer could be reversed by the time perspective, it could also be reversed by the spacial perspective of the respondent. A citizen's civic improvement organization interested in knowing the public's reaction to its efforts in one section of a large city questioned a random sample of respondents in and near the area where its work was going on, asking, "Do you feel that your neighborhood has got better, worse, or stayed about the same in the last years?" The problem here was that the psychological boundaries of each respondent's neighborhood varied. If the respondent's own psychological boundaries did not coincide with the area the organization had in mind, the answer could be negative since the surrounding area was rapidly deteriorating in its physical and social condition. This was easily remedied by preceding the question with this clarifying context: "Perhaps you are familiar with the area between Wentworth and State streets from 43rd to 57th. Just think of this area and forget for the moment all the areas right around it."

The responses to this question after the context was furnished would be significantly different, particularly for respondents residing near the outside edges of the designated area.

Supplying a social-psychological perspective. A myriad of examples could show that a question in its logical purity, even with clearly defined terms could be answered differently depending on the circumstances which the respondent has in mind. For example, we could define "bureaucracy" as a pure form of social structure and then attempt to discover people's attitudes and opinions on the desirability of such a form of human organization by asking the question, "Now that we have defined the bureaucracy as we will use it in this discussion, what do you think of it as a general form of organization?"

The answer to this question would vary depending upon whether the respondent was thinking of the probable effects of such an organization when manned by "those government bureaucrats in Washington" or by "the managers of America's great business enterprises such as X Motors." The respondent might very well have no opinion on "bureaucracy" in the abstract, and in order to give the question some meaning he would supply his own context if none was supplied by the interviewer.

Supplying criteria for judgment. Closely related to the previous type of context is one which clearly specifies the criteria the respondent is to apply in making a judgment. Of course, in the previous example the respondent might use different criteria in judging a business bureaucracy versus a government bureaucracy, but the interviewer has no way of knowing in advance what the criteria are. The following example is an attempt to focus the respondent's attention on one of many possible criteria for making a judgment.

As you know, there are some counties in this state which have not yet integrated their public schools. Many reasons are given for favoring and opposing the integration, but I am interested in your opinion on the economic efficiency of integration. I am not asking whether you favor or oppose integration. Just assume for the moment that the only problem is one of getting the best education for the most people for the least money from the taxpayer. Do you think integrated schools would be a more efficient or a less efficient use of public funds? (Probes: Why do you say that? Could you explain that a little more?)

It will be difficult to persuade the respondent to use the criterion of efficiency if he is strongly opposed to integration on other grounds. For this reason, it would be necessary to probe carefully as to *why* he feels the integrated system would be more or less efficient.

Supplying needed facts. Many times, the point of an interview is to discover how a person will decide an issue if he has certain relevant facts. Instead of either assuming that he has them or asking him if he is "well informed," the interviewer supplies the salient facts. Thus, he is sure they were taken into consideration insofar as the respondent gives them weight.

For example, in a study of public opinion formation in a small community, the following question was one of those asked of a carefully selected group of opinion leaders:

As you probably read in the *News-Sun* the Village Council must make a decision at next month's meeting on whether to put in a new gravity-flow sewer system at the cost of $400 thousand which will still serve the population 25 years from now, or to put in a new sewer pumping station at the cost of $100 thousand but which will have to be enlarged at the cost of $50 thousand in five years. With each five-year period, the cost of enlargement would be greater so that the total cost at the end of 25 years would be about $600 thousand. Do you personally favor the gravity-flow or the pumping station? (Probes: Why do you favor that? Is there any special reason you favor that? Could you explain that a little further?)

The use which the respondent makes of the supplied facts varies depending on the additional facts he has, the knowledge he has of the general problem, and the questions he is able to generate in his analysis of the information he has. For example, in the discussion brought out by the probing, one of the better informed respondents said:

If you look at it from the standpoint of long-run efficiency of service, it is difficult to decide which would cost the taxpayers the most because the total cost of either system depends upon how much money must be borrowed, at what interest rate, for what period of time and, finally, how much inflation or deflation there will be in the local economy during the period for which the money was borrowed. Since I don't know these things, there is no way to make an intelligent choice.

More typical responses were in the direction of the two below representing both those who favored and those who opposed the gravity-flow sewer.

I think it is best to do what is cheapest in the long run. If it is going to cost the taxpayers $200 thousand more within a 25-year period to use pumping stations, I think we should put out a little more money right now by getting the gravity-flow sewer and saving in the long run.

I have heard the argument that it would save us money in the long run to get the gravity-flow sewer, but who is "us"? I may not be here in 25 years or even 10 years. Also, this might be a ghost town by that time and not even need as big a sewer system as we have now. I don't believe in these predictions of the future.

It is clear that both respondents considered the facts but reached opposite conclusions by putting these facts in different perspectives.

Discovering the respondent's own contexts. So far, we have shown how the interviewer may need to provide some context with a particular question in order to define terms, provide a time perspective, give a spacial perspective, locate a particular social-psychological circumstance, supply criteria for judgments, or furnish specific facts to be used in making a judgment. All of these uses of context are aimed at communicating the meaning of the question more precisely to the respondent. Thus, we assume that the interviewer has a particular context in mind which he desired to make clear to the respondent.

There is a contrasting purpose of the interview where the main objective is to discover the respondent's own context which gives meaning to certain words, facts, slogans, or any form of abstraction. In this case, it would *not* be appropriate to furnish the context; special tactics may be needed to discover the respondent's context without appearing to be cryptic or non-supportive. This problem will be dealt with in the next chapter.

Contexts aimed at motivating the respondent

The preceding types of contexts are aimed primarily at communicating to the respondent the precise meaning of the question. Once the respondent clearly grasps the question, it is sometimes also necessary to make him either more *able* or more *willing* to answer fully. The respondent's willingness may be increased by a context which arouses his interest in the topic, acknowledges the respondent's special qualifications, or reduces any ego threat or etiquette barrier.

Contexts may also increase the respondent's ability to give relevant information by stimulating his memory, by obviating chronological confusion, and by stimulating unconscious behavior patterns and attitudes.

Arousing the respondent's interest. Often a respondent has a low level of motivation because he fails to see significance in the information he is giving. If it can be done without "loading" the question, supplying contexts from time to time in the interview can help motivate the respondent. For example:

There has been a lot of discussion in Congress recently about free trade. Slogans such as "Trade not aid to the underdeveloped areas" have been invented. There are two bills before Congress at the moment dealing with the problem. *What does the term free trade mean to you?*

This context does more than arouse interest; it provides a perspective suggesting international free trade rather than interstate free trade in the United States. If the international perspective is correct for the purpose of the interview, then this context would not distort the information.

Recognizing the respondent's special qualifications. It is not only useful to remind the respondent of his qualifications at the beginning of the interview when explaining how and why he was selected, but it is also helpful to remind him of his special qualifications at other points in the interview. One way of doing this is to preface a question with a reminder of the respondent's qualifications as is done in the following examples:

You have had much more experience with life than I and can see things in a broader perspective. What advice would you give to young people today to make the "senior citizen" period of their lives more full and happy?

Since you were at one time a member of the gang with the biggest "rep" in East Harlem, could you give me some idea why teenagers join these kinds of gangs?

Within one interview, different aspects of the respondent's qualifications can be mentioned in order to support the respondent's need for recognition.

Reducing ego threat. Questions can be worded to include a face-saving preface to reduce the ego threat. For example: "I know people nowadays do not have time to keep up on everything that is going on in the world, but would you tell me if you have read anything about the Near East crisis?" Several studies of the validity of people's statements regarding current events have demonstrated that they exaggerate the amount of reading they have done and tend to feel guilty about how little they know about current world issues. A preface of this type will reduce the urge to overestimate one's reading and reduce the ego threat involved in an admission of ignorance.

Another approach is to show that "even the Gods have clay feet," and celebrities, too, have failures. This helps place a respondent's possible weaknesses in a non-threatening perspective. For example: As you probably know Winston Churchill, Albert Einstein and others of that calibre failed in some of their college courses. How many courses have you failed so far?

Depending on the purposes of the interview, the interviewer's knowledge of the respondent, and the general setting of the interview, this principle can be adapted to soften many potentially ego-threatening questions.

Preventing falsification. It often saves a tremendous amount of time and energy to prevent the respondent's committing himself falsely. Once he has taken the false position, he will feel honor bound to defend it even though he may regret his falsification. Often, an elaborate web of lies has to be built up to preserve consistency with the original lie. It is mainly in detective stories that the culprit breaks down when inconsistencies are discovered in his story. In the interview situation the respondent is not obligated to submit to continual pressure. Neither is a suspicious attitude on the part of the interviewer considered within the bounds of etiquette. Under these conditions prevention is more efficient and less embarrassing.

For example, an employer is interviewing a prospective employee who has been fired from his former job. If the interviewer wants to know something about the respondent's relationship with his former employers, he should let the respondent know that the former employer has informed him the respondent was fired. A straightforward question, after rapport has been built up, would not only save time but would also indicate to the intelligent respondent that the interviewer has no desire to trap him. The interviewer could simply say, "I was told by your former employer that you were fired. They gave me their side of the story, but I would like to hear it from your point of view."

Reducing the etiquette barrier. In the strategy phase, the interviewer-respondent combinations should be selected to avoid role relationships which erect an etiquette barrier. However, there are still situations in which the respondent may identify the interviewer with a role which would damage the flow of information. If the interviewer takes advantage of opportunities to clarify his role as the interview progresses, the probability of the etiquette barrier arising can be reduced. For example, a college professor who was interviewing students regarding their experiences in a new foreign extension of the college conducted a group interview with five students recently returned from abroad. The professor was the designer of the program and this fact was known to most of the students. He assumed that students would be reluctant to criticize the weaknesses of the new program and therefore introduced the discussion as follows:

As you probably know, I was instrumental in designing the original program set up in Guanajuato in 1958. I have had no official connection with it over the past three years and I am somewhat out of touch with what is going on there. I am interested in doing what I can to improve the program at this time. I suspect that in its actual operations the program has certain weaknesses which should be brought out in the open and discussed. That is why I have invited you here today, not to obtain a pollyannaish report of the program, but to get some insight into your personal experiences so that I can see it from the point of view of the students it is supposed to benefit. What are some of the things that should be done to improve the program there in Guanajuato?

Of course, beginning the discussion with a one-paragraph statement aimed at reducing the etiquette barrier is not to be depended upon completely. The group began with some minor criticisms as well as some praise of certain aspects of the program. The interviewer's success in obtaining criticism of the program rested heavily upon his reactions to the group's initial criticisms. When they observed that he did not swell with pride when the program was praised, nor attempt to defend it against their criticisms, they were encouraged to express themselves more candidly. All etiquette barriers were not eliminated by this technique. For example, students interviewing the same group discovered objections not raised in the discussion with the professor, but these were matters withheld because he was a member of the older generation and not because he was the originator of the program.

We have dealt with several ways in which an appropriate context might reduce the respondent's resistance to giving relevant information. Now we will examine some of the ways to increase his ability to report his experiences.

Stimulating the memory. By reviewing some of the objective facts about a certain situation, the interviewer often can stimulate the respondent's memory of his experiences in that situation. In the following example the interviewer is attempting to reconstruct the pattern of interaction between members of a family when a tornado struck their rural village. He needs to obtain an accurate report of the actions of each person and the extent to which other family members were taken into consideration.

Now after the wind stopped blowing and the house had crashed into the pecan orchard, it was still dark, raining very hard and someone outside the wreckage was shouting, "Anybody in there?" At that moment did you know where your husband was?

It is not always necessary for the interviewer to know that the respondent was conscious of all the circumstantial facts mentioned as long as all the facts are accurate and were occurring at the time of the respondent's relevant experiences. In contrast to the example above that describes *events* occurring at the relevant time, the context might focus upon a description of the physical *scene* of the event. In any case, the interviewer should attempt to include those circumstantial facts most salient to the respondent.

Reducing chronological confusion. Often the respondent is less aware of the chronological order of his actions and observations than he is of their relationship to certain salient observations of events not directly related to the objectives of the interview. Even if the respondent does not know the correct order of the irrelevant events, the interviewer who knows their order can use this information to unscramble the respondent's sequence of experiences.

We have been able to clearly establish the order of some events that you might remember from the day of the explosions here in Brighton. First, there was the explosion in the reducing-valve vault under the sidewalk at Twelve Corners, then the gas jets in people's stoves, furnaces and gas dryers began to make a hissing noise, then the Mellinger house exploded, the next house exploded about 12 minutes later. The first explosion was south of your house, the second was directly west. What were you doing when you heard the first explosion? Where were you when you heard the second explosion?

This technique of preventing chronological confusion is simply an extension of the general principle of using known facts to stimulate recall of additional actions and observations.

Discovering unconscious factors. Of the types of unconscious experience a respondent might have, the one most amenable to verbal techniques is that of the values or norms which govern a person's behavior. Frequently, they cannot be clearly reported because the respondent is not aware of the norm in the abstract, but expresses it in his behavior toward concrete situations. In this case, it is often helpful to use a hypothetical case as the focus for discussion. Several hypothetical cases may be required to delineate the particular norm or pattern of norms in question.

Suppose our problem is to discover the norms governing the relationship between nurses and doctors in a large metropolitan hospital. The interviewer might ask a nurse how the higher status of the doctors is shown in their behavior toward nurses and in their treatment by the hospital administration. The following is one hypothetical case:

Suppose a maternity patient in the hospital is about to give birth to her baby, but the physician in charge of her case has not yet arrived. Her labor is in the final phase and the child will be born in a few minutes. This is the patient's fourth child, she is in good health, and her medical history is known to the nurse in charge of her case. Three hours previously, the physician called to say he would arrive at the hospital in four hours which would be in another hour. (1) What would the nurse in charge of her case do? (2) What would the supervising nurse on the maternity ward do? (3) What would the physician probably say if he could be reached by 'phone and it was explained that the birth was going to take place before he could arrive?

If the interviewer has some hunches of what would constitute a violation of the norms in this situation, he might suggest these to obtain the respondent's reaction. Very frequently, we are more aware of specific actions which would constitute a *violation* of a norm than we are of the norm itself. In some problems of this type, the interviewer can simply ask, "What would be the wrong thing for the nurse to do in this situation?" or "What could you say for sure the physician would *not* suggest for the nurse to do in this case?"

To stimulate discussion of this hypothetical case, it might be useful to suggest possible actions to obtain a response. For example, "Would the nurse go ahead and deliver the baby herself, if she knows there are no complications in the case?" "Would the supervising nurse ask one of the physicians on the ward who was not busy at the moment to perform the delivery?" "Would the nurse in charge, by previous arrangement with the physician, retard the delivery until the patient's regular physician arrived?"

This extension of the hypothetical case by suggesting possible action solutions must, of course, be constructed so that a full range of action is included, or so that each action or action alternative involves the norms in which the interviewer is interested. Otherwise, we may bias the responses by suggestion or by exclusion of certain relevant alternatives. If the interviewer is not sure of the adequacy of the alternative actions, they could be used only as possible answer choices for the interviewer to check without mentioning any of them to the respondent.

The hypothetical case is often an excellent focus for discussion and will, if well chosen, stimulate salient responses. Good hypotheses often cannot be constructed from a swivel chair but must be built upon previous knowledge. Often it is not until the later stages of a study, or at least until after several interviews have been done or some participant observation used, that relevant hypothetical examples can be produced, since they should contain problematical situations which could really occur.

Selecting appropriate vocabulary

Without becoming enmeshed in a multitude of possible examples, let us look at some of the main problems in selecting an appropriate vocabulary for the interview.

a) The words should be clearly understood by the respondent.

b) The words should aid in establishing an optimum role relationship between the interviewer and respondent.

c) In some cases, the question should be worded to include the vocabulary needed by the respondent to give his answer without violating the etiquette of the situation.

d) Emotional words which might unintentionally "load" the question should be avoided.

These apparently simple principles may be very easy or very difficult to put into practice.

The first principle can be thwarted by very subtle differences in the universe of discourse of the interviewer and the respondent. For example, the two questions below obtained quite different responses from rural victims of a tornado:

What were some of the problems which arose during the rescue operations right after the tornado struck?

What sorts of trouble did people have trying to help folks who were hurt or trapped in the wreckage?

The second question obtained a straightforward and spontaneous response relevant to the purposes of the study. The first wording of the question seemed to puzzle some respondents because the word "problems" had a connotation narrower than intended by the interviewer.

The second principle, using a vocabulary that will establish an optimum role relationship between interviewer and respondent, has many manifestations, but it can be viewed in the same two-dimensional system suggested in the previous chapter. The interviewer must recognize that the respondent can quickly classify him as an "insider-outsider" or "subordinate-equal-superordinate" on the basis of his choice of words. For example, in an interview to obtain voters' attitudes toward certain policies of the Department of Agriculture, the interviewer might ask, "What do you think of our policy of allowing farmers to vote on alternative types of farm programs we administer through the Department of Agriculture?" In exploratory, non-scheduled interviews, the interviewer noted that most of the respondents referred to any department of the federal government as "they" rather than "we" as did the interviewer. This prevented the interviewer from being perceived as an "insider" by the farmer. On certain controversial issues, this brought the etiquette barrier into play.

It is often helpful to word the question so that it is clear to the respondent that the interviewer understands the local universe of discourse. This allows the respondent to speak more spontaneously without having to "translate" for the interviewer. Usually, only the more educated or experienced respondent will bother to do this, while the respondent with a narrow range of experience does not realize he has a special jargon. The interviewer can indicate that there is no need to "translate" by using the local jargon in the wording of the question. For example, in an interview with a supervisor in a telephone company, the interviewer said, "I understand, according to one of the CO's, that they expect to install key-pulse dialing when the new rate structure filed with the ICC is approved. When do they expect the ICC to give its decision?" Immediately the respondent was aware that the interviewer understood "CO," "key-pulse dialing," "rate-structure," and "ICC."

There is danger in using the local jargon if the interviewer does not actually understand it or if it puts him in the insider role when it would be more desirable to be an outsider. Often, the outsider role can be retained without forcing the respondent to translate if the interviewer explains that he has learned as much of the jargon as he can for the occasion and will ask for further explanations from time to time. Only a few questions early in the interview will clearly indicate that the interviewer is an outsider.

In some cases, the vocabulary used is crucial in helping the respondent classify the interviewer as an equal or a superordinate. In cases where the interviewer is perceived as a superordinate, the respondent is sometimes reluctant to answer a question because he senses that his vocabulary would be considered vulgar outside his own group, yet he does not know what vocabulary would be considered appropriate by the interviewer. In this case, the interviewer can be careful to supply the vocabulary by his wording of the question so that the meaning is obvious. Then the respondent can use the same vocabulary in answering. For example, in a study of child-rearing practices of mothers in the lower socioeconomic level, the question, "How did you go about toilet training your child?" was ineffective. Instead, it was necessary to use a series of questions to provide the polite vocabulary needed by the respondent. Mothers were asked, "When were you first able to depend on Johnny asking to go to the toilet to have a bowel movement?" and then, "When did he quit wetting himself and going to the toilet instead?" Once these questions were answered, a more detailed discussion of the mother's attempts to toilet-train the child followed rather smoothly, since "bowel movement" had become a common phrase.

It is common sense to avoid using emotionally loaded vocabulary in wording the question. The actual implementation of the principle is not so simple, but depends upon the interviewer's knowing which words have a biasing effect upon the respondent. For example, in a study of communication between North Americans and Latin Americans, the use of the word *gringo* in Mexico to refer to North Americans would have a strongly negative emotional loading. *Gringo* would not have this effect in Colombia where the word *yanqui* is reserved for negative connotations.

There are times when it is appropriate to use emotionally loaded words as long as it is intentional and the direction of the effect is known. This intentional use of the "loaded" question will be discussed later.

Delimiting the scope of the question

Questions and probes by the interviewer may vary tremendously in their scope. A question may be so broad that it includes within its confines more than the total objectives of the whole interview, or it may be so narrow in scope that hundreds of minutely specific questions are necessary to cover the same topic. The scope of each question used in an interview is not automatically determined by the objectives or the topic of the interview. People experienced in non-scheduled interviewing realize that it may require twice as many questions to obtain the relevant information from one respondent as from another. In one case, broad questions provide sufficient stimulus for the respondent to cover many specific points within the scope of the general question, while in another the interviewer must specify each bit of information needed.

It is important for an interviewer to become aware of this dimension, called "scope," since most people have an unconscious habit, developed in social conversation, of being unnecessarily restrictive in the scope of their questions. Perhaps it is a way of saving time or of restricting the other person's remarks so that we may express our point of view sooner. Or perhaps the efficient businessman, the incisive lawyer, or the police detective who "get to the point" in mass media portrayals influence our conversational patterns. Regardless of the source, in training interviewers the writer has found that it is usually more difficult for them to ask broad questions than to ask each specific point separately. Frequently, the neophyte interviewer behaves as if his motto were "never use a general question if several specific questions can be used instead." By developing a sensitivity to how apparently small differences in the wording of a question make vast differences in its scope, the interviewer may guide his own behavior in accordance with the objectives of the interview, rather than be guided by unconscious habit.

To illustrate this difference in scope, let us compare three opening questions used by different interviewers in an interview with teen-agers to discover some of the educational values of the county fair for city children.

a) Tell me what happened at the Greene County Fair when you were there last Saturday.

b) Tell me what you did at the Greene County Fair when you were there last Saturday.

c) Did you like the horse show at the county fair?

Regardless of which question is the best opener for this type of interview, the vast difference in scope is clear. The first question, by using the term "what happened," leaves the topic open for the respondent to report what he did, what others did, what he saw, what others saw, what he felt or thought about what he did or saw, and what he felt and thought about what others did and saw.

The second question logically restricts the area of discussion as much as 90 percent by asking only what the *respondent did*. This unnecessary restriction of the topic might constitute an ego threat in this case, because the respondent probably was mainly a spectator and could more spontaneously report what he saw than what he did. Also, the impersonality of "what happened" versus "what did you see, do or think" often makes the respondent less self-conscious.

The third question restricts the conversation to some fraction of 1 percent of the respondent's impressions of the fair. It also inhibits the spontaneous flow of information, because it prevents the respondent from talking about what, for him, were the most memorable aspects of the fair. It also implies that a simple "yes" or "no" answer is required.

Dimensions of scope. Rather than examining scores of illustrations of differences in scope and discussing their possible effects on the flow of relevant information, we have devised a scheme to show some of the important abstract dimensions of scope. This allows the reader to generate his own examples. The chart delineates four dimensions of scope, represented by the column headings, which apply to all questions. The columns are arranged in the order each dimension usually appears in the sentence structure of a question.

	Question	*Actor*	*Action*	*Scene*
A	What?	Unspecified actor	Happened	General topic of interview
B	Why or how?	You	Do (overt)	Restricted area of time
C	Where or when?	Others (in general)	See, feel, or think (covert)	Restricted location
D	How much? How many?	You (or specific others)	Specific verb	Specific event or situation
E	Did. . . . ?	You (or specific others)	Specific verb	Specific object or characteristics of an object in a specified situation

Whenever possible, within each column the categories are arranged with the broader ones at the top and the narrower ones at the bottom. With some imagination, the reader can construct questions for a hypothetical interview using all possible combinations of the four dimensions.

To illustrate some possible combinations of these four dimensions, we will resume the interview on the educational effects of the county fair. The type of question being illustrated will be designated by giving four letters, for example AABB, representing the rows selected from each successive column.

Type AAAA: Tell me what happened at the county fair?

Type ABBD: What did you do at the fair last Saturday?

Type ADBD: What did your father say to you when you were at the fair with him last Saturday?

Type BDBD: Why did your father go to the fair last Saturday?

Type EBCE: Did you see the draft horses at the fair last Saturday?

Not all logical combinations of the four columns would make sense. Also, the number of categories is different in each of the four dimensions and in some cases may be arbitrary depending on how finely the distinctions are made. In spite of the lack of refinement, this scheme can help sensitize the reader to the fact that the scope of a question can be expanded or contracted by gradual degrees and that the answer to several of the narrower questions could be logically included in the answer to one of the broader questions.

Consciously or unconsciously the interviewer makes a choice in the non-scheduled interview between (*a*) using broad questions and encouraging the respondent to elaborate to obtain specific details, or (*b*) using many narrow questions to cover the same topic The tactical problem of shifting from broader to narrower questions or vice versa will be discussed in the next chapter. At this point we will examine some of the most probable values of broader and narrower questions and indicate some of the limiting circumstances for the use of each.

Values of broad questions. Broad questions have two general values: first, they must be used to obtain certain types of information which would be distorted by the effect of many specific questions; second, they have certain motivational effects upon the respondent under certain conditions.

Interviews with any or all of the following objectives often require the use of broad questions: (*a*) discovering the respondent's paths of association regarding a certain topic, situation, or event; (*b*) discovering the relative importance of various aspects of a topic, situation, or event experienced by the respondent; (*c*) discovering the frame of reference used by the respondent in observing, analyzing, or acting in a situation; (*d*) discovering the chronological order of the respondent's experiences in a given situation; (*e*) discovering the vocabulary used by the respondent in discussing certain aspects of a topic, situation or event.

In each of these objectives the interviewer must be careful not to impose his own organization upon the topic but must encourage the respondent to discuss the topic in his own terms. It is practically impossible for the interviewer to divide the topic into many specific questions without imposing his own frame of references, without using a vocabulary he is not yet sure is appropriate, without interrupting the respondent's natural paths of association, and without imposing different perspectives or hierarchies of importance upon the specifics reported.

Broad questions not only help the interviewer to avoid giving rather than receiving information, but also help to increase the respondent's ability and willingness to give relevant information in several ways.

Reducing ego threat. Often certain facts regarding a topic, situation or event might constitute an ego threat to the respondent if the interviewer calls his attention to the significance of the relationship between these facts. If the interviewer asks for each fact, the respondent may become concerned with how the interviewer is going to evaluate the information. However, if the interviewer does not ask for but is given the facts, the respondent does not know the interviewer attaches any particular significance to them. In rare cases it might be necessary to pose a broad question that focuses on an area only indirectly related to the specific facts needed so that the respondent will not feel threatened by direct questioning on sensitive areas.

Stimulating memory. The objective of the interview may not be to discover the respondent's individual paths of association. Still it is often advisable to allow him to follow his own inclinations in order to assure that he is not forced to give information before he has had an opportunity to recall it. When specifics are asked for before the respondent volunteers them, there is a danger that he will fill the gaps in his memory with his imagination. The respondent may be reporting what he assumes he must have done in view of the logical or moral requirements of the situation, he need not be consciously fabricating.

Giving the respondent recognition. By merely introducing a broad topic of discussion and allowing the respondent to tell his own story, the interviewer implies a respect for the respondent's ability to report relevant material. This lack of restriction also allows the respondent to mention information to his credit even though it may not be directly relevant to the objectives of the study.

Giving sympathetic understanding. Giving the respondent more freedom to tell his own story in his own way usually implies to him that the interviewer is more interested in him as a unique person than as a source of information. He perceives that the interviewer is "interested in what is important to me" and is encouraged to take advantage of the opportunity. The more that specific, narrow questions are asked, the more likely that the emphasis of the interview will shift away from each respondent's unique concerns.

Encouraging catharsis. Once an atmosphere of sympathetic understanding is established, the respondent will be encouraged to "get certain problems off his chest" if they are important to him at the moment and are related to the topic of the interview. Of course, whether or not the interviewer should encourage this catharsis depends upon whether the information is relevant, whether the catharsis is helpful or harmful to the optimum relationship between interviewer and respondent, and how efficient the interviewer must be.

Need for meaning. In some cases, the freedom from the restrictions of specific questions and a generally permissive atmosphere will encourage the respondent to soliloquize. He begins to think out loud and expresses his doubts, fears, and even his decision-making process in forming answers to questions he has. This usually occurs when the interview topic itself or the life situation of the respondent touches upon confusion or crisis. If the interviewer needs to stimulate the respondent's need for meaning by pointing out problems and dilemmas, the broad question does not always allow him to do this.

Values of narrow questions. As in the case of the broad question, the value of the narrow question depends to a great extent upon the type of information sought and the type of motivation which must be stimulated. In general, if specific facts and opinions are needed rather than more complex structural relationships, a more specific question will be more efficient. For example, if we wish to know a person's age, religion, and marital status and if such information is not ego threatening under the circumstances, then it would be ridiculous to attempt to obtain the information by asking, "Would you please tell me about yourself?" On the other hand, if we wanted to know which were the most salient aspects of a person's self-concept, we would need to know not only his age, religion, and marital status but also many other characteristics, as well as their relative importance and interrelationships in the mind of the respondent. In this case, the broader question would be more appropriate. However, under certain circumstances the narrower question has advantages in motivating the respondent.

Reducing ego threat. There are circumstances where the topic and the respondent are such that broad questions have little meaning to the respondent. He may feel at a loss to begin his report or to organize it into some meaningful whole. This is particularly true when the topic itself is not vital to the respondent or is put in terms that are too abstract. Under these conditions the ego threat is not in the information itself but in the fact that the respondent is embarrassed because he feels he has nothing to say. He is given encouragement and support by the interviewer who dissects the topic into more manageable specifics.

Reducing the etiquette barrier. In some interviews, the respondent is willing to give any information as long as he is sure that it is considered useful or necessary by the interviewer. If the interviewer has a relationship with the respondent that makes him reluctant to report certain information, he will tend to omit it unless the interviewer specifically asks for it.

Stimulating the need for meaning. Often a person's interest in the topic of the interview can be increased by stimulating his need for meaning. This can be done by asking specific questions posing dilemmas, inconsistencies, or problematical relationships. The respondent can often be enticed by the realization that things are not as simple as they might appear at first glance.

Structuring the answer

Questions may include varying degrees of answer structure. The categories of acceptable answers may be explicit or implicit. The respondent may be instructed to choose one or more than one. The answer categories may be mutually exclusive or overlapping. The respondent may be given the choice of either using the answer categories supplied or giving a more detailed answer in his own words. The categories may be qualitative or quantitative.

In general, questions which do not supply the answer categories are called "open-ended" and those that limit the answer choices are called "closed." An example of an open-ended question would be, "What did you see at the County Fair?" An example of a closed question would be, "Which of the following did you see at the county fair: sulky racing, the hog show, the milking machine display, the fruit exhibit?"

The answers to a question need not be either completely open or closed, but may fall in between. Rather than supplying categories, the wording of the question may imply choices as in these two examples: "How many times a month, on the average, do you go to church?" and "Do you go to church every week?" The first example implies that the answer should be in terms of times per month. The second implies that either a "yes" or "no" answer is needed. A more completely structured form would be as follows: "How many times, on the average, do you go to church: more than once a week, once a week, two or three times per month, once a month, or less than once a month?"

Of course, none of the above three forms should be used unless preceded by a filter question to determine whether or not the particular respondent did in fact attend some religious body that would be appropriately called a church.

In deciding upon the amount of structuring to use, it is necessary to consider the type of information sought and the effects of the structuring on the respondent's ability and willingness to give the relevant information.

Some of the same information objectives requiring questions with a broader scope also require open-ended questions discovering the respondent's paths of association, frames of reference, and universe of discourse.

If the information can be obtained equally well by either open-ended or closed questions and if there are no inhibitors of communication to overcome, then the closed question should be used because it increases the efficiency and reliability of the coding and analysis of the data.

In a semischeduled interview in which specific items of information are to be obtained but no wording of the questions or sequence is specified, it is still possible for the interviewer to structure the answers and to record the responses on a multiple choice code sheet. This eliminates having to convert verbatim notes into code categories. Also if the correct category for the answer is unclear to the interviewer, he can probe for further clarification.

Structuring answers can have several possible effects upon the facilitators and inhibitors of communication.

Competing time demands. The use of structured answers not only saves time for the interviewers, coders, and analyzers but also for the respondent. If the information is of the type where it is appropriate to structure the answers, the respondent is often happy to see that the interviewer knows exactly what he wants and is businesslike and efficient.

Ego threat. Under some conditions respondents feel threatened by open-ended questions which sound "as if they would require a dissertation to answer." The respondent's insecurity can often be reduced by placing the choices before him.

Etiquette. Often the etiquette barrier can be reduced by supplying specific answer categories which show that the interviewer expects such information. Answer categories can supply the respondent with a vocabulary compatible with the etiquette requirements of the situation. For example: "With which of the following did you have your first complete heterosexual intercourse? (1) With a prostitute? (2) With an intimate acquaintance before marriage? (3) With a girl 'picked up' for the occasion? (4) With your wife before you were engaged? (5) With your wife after engagement and before marriage? (6) With your wife after marriage?" Such a question put in a matter of fact tone by a mature interviewer would be more likely to elicit a valid response with less strain on the respondent than would the open-ended form of the same question. If there is no reason why the information must be collected by interviewing, a questionnaire would probably be still more effective in reducing both the ego threat and the etiquette barrier. A compromise between an interview and a questionnaire can be arranged by stating the question orally and then handing the respondent a card with the answers on it and asking him to give the *number* of the correct answer.

Forgetting. Under certain circumstances it is more efficient, valid, and reliable to obtain facts which have faded in the respondent's memory by asking him to choose from among several specific alternatives. It is usually easier to *recognize* the correct answer when it is presented by the interviewer than it is to *recall* it without a suggestion of the possibilities. This is a valid procedure only if the interviewer knows in advance that the suggested choices include the correct answer and that only one answer could be correct. It is also helpful to eliminate as many incorrect answers from the list as possible and to offer possible answers clearly different in their meaning or their sound. For example, students returning for a summer session in Guanajuato, Mexico, were interviewed to determine some of the effects of the cross-cultural experiences. The interviewer wanted to establish where the person stayed during his six weeks there. After learning that it was "some hotel with a Spanish name, but I can't think of it at the moment," he asked:

I: Was it at El Orozco, La Posada de Santa Fe, or El Castillo?
R: Oh, yes, La Posada de Santa Fe, we called it the Posie, or the hotel, because it had such a long name.

Once a memory has faded, it is not always possible for the respondent to recognize the correct answer even though it is included in the choices. A good interviewer can often detect when the respondent is unsure or simply guessing.

Chronological confusion. The interviewer can often help the respondent avoid chronological confusion by supplying a set of events known to be arranged in chronological order and then asking the respondent whether the event in question occurred before or after each event in the list. For example: "Let's see if we can get a little more exact age at which Johnny had the skin allergy. Was it before he could walk, after he could walk but before going to nursery school, or after he was in first grade at Mills School?"

If the events arranged chronologically are also meaningful to the respondent and have some connection with the event to be recalled, this technique may be very helpful to the respondent and save considerable interviewing time.

Thus far, we have indicated some of the conditions under which closed questions are particularly useful. The conditions for using open-ended questions are the same as those calling for the use of broad questions and these have already been discussed.

Using leading questions

The term "leading questions" refers to any question, including its context and answer structure, which is phrased so that it appears to the respondent that the interviewer desires or expects a certain answer; yet the interviewer's expectation could not have been derived solely from what the respondent has already said in the interview.

Forms of leading. A question may be leading because of the *context* in which it appears; this leading context may be of a personal or impersonal type. The following is an example of the personal context.

The President has made several public statements advocating freer trade between nations. Do you think we should eliminate some of the tariff barriers that have been erected against free trade?

The direction of the effect of this loaded context cannot be predicted unless the respondent's attitude toward the President is known. Nevertheless, it is highly probable that changing the context as in the example below would obtain a different response from many respondents.

Socialists have historically advocated free trade among nations. Do you think we should eliminate some of the tariff barriers that have been erected against free trade?

In contrast, the impersonal context does not mention the point of view of any individual or group, but brings into play certain facts and logical relationships which tend to influence the answer in one direction. The next question is put into two different contexts tending to bias the response in opposite directions.

In view of the fact that the United States is the richest country in the world do you think that the defense budget should be cut as much as 25 percent?
In view of the fact that about 80 percent of the total federal taxes are spent on past, present, and future war expenditures, do you think that the defense budget should be cut as much as 25 percent?

There is little doubt that a random sample poll of the United States, using the two forms of the question, would show significantly different results.

Even when no leading context is provided, the question may be loaded by simply using *emotionally charged* words. For example, compare these two questions:

How do you feel about Negroes moving into this area?
How do you feel about Negroes invading your neighborhood?

Even though in sociology *invading* is not an emotionally charged term, to the respondent *moving into* would appear more neutral.

A third way of loading a question is to structure the answer in a way that restricts the respondent by *omitting a category* most appropriate for him. Compare these two questions:

What is your religion? Protestant, Catholic, or Jewish?
What is your religion? Protestant, Catholic, Jewish, agnostic, atheist, or free-thinker?

It is highly probable that the second form would elicit a smaller number of Protestant, Catholic, and Jewish responses.

A fourth way of leading is to make *challenging statements.* The respondent will often change his general point of view expressed in the interview if the interviewer consistently challenges one type of statement and allows the opposite type to go unchallenged. Any of the following would be considered a challenge to some degree: "How do you know that?" "Do you think you could back up that statement with evidence?" "Give me a specific example of that." "That sounds very unusual, I have never heard of such a thing happening. How do you account for that?" "Are you sure that your observations are correct?" "That seems to contradict what you said before."

The effects of such challenges depend upon how sure the respondent is of his rapport, the extent to which he is inclined to show deference to the interviewer, and the tone of voice in which the challenge is made.

Effects of leading questions. In the literature on interviewing there seems to be a preponderance of opinion, usually based upon direct experience in interviewing, that the leading question should be avoided. For example, Cannell and Kahn suggest that "Questions should be phrased so that they contain no suggestion as to the most appropriate response."[5]

Kinsey takes an opposite position at one point in his discussion of interviewing methods used to obtain information on the respondent's sex behavior. He advocates putting the burden of denial on the respondent:

The interviewer should not make it easy for a subject to deny his participation in any form of sexual activity. It is too easy to say "no" if he is simply asked whether he has engaged in a particular activity. Consequently we always begin by asking when they first engaged in such activity ... and since it becomes apparent from the form of the question that we would not be surprised if he had had such experience, there seems to be less reason for denying it. It might be thought this approach would bias the answer, but there is no indication that we get false admissions in forms of sexual behavior in which the subject was not actually involved.[6]

Becker, who takes the position that challenging the respondent in an aggressive manner does not necessarily bias the response, points out some of the conditions under which he could obtain more valid information from public shcool teachers regarding race relations problems in the school. He says that a basic condition for success was

... the professional bond of courtesy which the teacher feels obligated to extend to the interviewer. She felt she must avoid being unpleasant. Such tactics

5/ Charles F. Cannel and Robert L. Kahn, "The Collection of Data by Interviewing," in Leon Festinger and Daniel Katz, *Research Methods in the Social Sciences* (New York: The Dryden Press, 1953), p. 346.

6/ Alfred C. Kinsey *et al.*, "Interviewing," *Sexual Behavior in the Human Male* (Philadelphia: W. B. Saunders Company, 1948).

will not prove effective in all situations nor would one want to use them . . . where, for example, your research places you in continuous contact with those being studied, as in a long-term community study, it might be wisest to avoid the possibility of antagonizing informants which lies in this stratagem. . . . Finally . . . the informant must not be of a higher social status than the interviewer because the unspoken etiquette of such a relationship leaves the informant free to be rude through evasiveness and implausibility, free to ignore the demands of the questioner who is stepping out of the confines of his deference role.[7]

None of the authors cited base their conclusions on experimental studies aimed at testing the relative effectiveness of using leading versus non-leading questions. Richardson[8] and Dohrenwend[9] have done experiments which show that the question, "Should leading questions be used?" is not well put, since the answer can be neither "yes" nor "no." Instead, we should try to account for the conditions under which they are successful or unsuccessful. After reviewing much of the literature and his own experiences, the writer suggests that the following factors account for the different effects of leading questions.

It is helpful to distinguish between three types of situations, one in which the leading question helps to obtain more valid information, another in which valid information is obtained in spite of the leading question, and a third situation where the leading question actually distorts the answer. Here are some of the most important characteristics of the type of situation in which the leading question helps to obtain more valid information:

a) Respondent has accurate information clearly in mind,

b) but there is a tendency to withhold it, either because reporting the correct answer would violate the etiquette requirements of the situation, or because the correct answer is potentially ego threatening, since it admits a violation of public ideals of some type.

c) The respondent either accepts these ideals as valid or assumes that the interviewer does so.

d) Under the above three conditions the leading question is useful *if* it leads in a direction contrary to the public ideals.[10]

7/ Howard S. Becker, "A Note on Interviewing Tactics," *Human Organization* (Winter, 1954), pp. 31-32.

8/ Stephan A. Richardson, "The Use of Leading Questions in Non-schedule Interviews," *Human Organization,* Vol. 19, No. 2 (1960), pp. 86-89.

9/ Barbara Snell Dohrenwend and Stephan A. Richardson, "A Use for Leading Questions in Research Interviewing," *Human Organization,* Vol. 23 (1964), pp. 76-77.

10/ Lois R. Dean, "Interaction, Reported and Observed," *Human Organization* (Fall, 1958), No. 3, p. 36, demonstrates the tendency of the respondent to falsify his report in the direction of the acceptable norms.

Regardless of whether the bias of the question is toward or away from the correct answer in the case of a particular respondent, such a leading question will be helpful. If the respondent's correct answer happens to be in violation of the public ideals, then the question is biased *toward* the correct answer and the respondent is more likely to admit his deviant experience. This is particularly true when the interviewer's manner shows that he expects the respondent to have had such an experience and that he does not condemn him for it. If the respondent has not had the deviant experience, he is less likely to pretend that he has committed a violation of public ideals. Thus the use of the leading question under these circumstances is based upon the assumption that in general people are less likely to falsely plead guilty than they are to falsely plead not guilty; therefore the bias should be toward guilty.

There are circumstances in which valid information is obtained in spite of the use of leading questions. Here the following conditions are important:

a) The information is clear in the respondent's mind, free from fading memory, chronological or inferential confusion.

b) Neither the information to be reported nor the relationship between the interviewer and respondent constitute an ego threat.

c) There is no etiquette barrier between respondent and interviewer.

To illustrate these circumstances let us assume that an interviewer is attempting to discover what happened at a meeting attended by the respondent and how he felt about what transpired. Further assume that the meeting lasted one hour, that 15 people attended and that it consisted of a short speech and a discussion of the pros and cons of an increase in the public school tax levy. The meeting occurred the night before the interview. Note that all the questions are leading in that they either suggest possible answers or exclude other possible answers, yet none of them cause distortion in the respondent's information.

I: How many people were at the meeting, about 100?

R: Oh no, there were 15 including the speaker; I know them all. There are very few people interested in the public schools, particularly in the summertime.

I: What time did the meeting start, 8 or 8:30?

R: We always start at 7 as we did last night.

I: Did you just have an informal discussion?

R: No, we also had a speaker from Columbus.

I: Was his talk about the usual sort of things which education people have to say about child psychology?

R: The topic was "What can the taxpayer buy for his school tax dollar."

I: Oh, I see. Did you feel that the speaker had little of value to say as is so often true of people speaking on this topic?

R: No, he had quite a bit to say; we selected him because of his analytical objectivity.

I: Do you feel that an excellent speaker of this type will exert a strong influence on improving the public schools?

R: He won't have any strong *direct* influence on the community since he was speaking to only 15 people, but there is a possibility that this will spark some activity among the vitally interested people.

To avoid being led astray by the "harmless" leading question, the interviewer should be reminded that often he will not know in advance that all the necessary conditions are present for rendering the leading question harmless. In some situations the interviewer may know in advance that a certain condition is present, but he often cannot know in advance that other conditions are also present. In any case, it is a good plan to avoid the use of leading questions rather than hope they are of the harmless variety unless the situation calls for their intentional use.

There are types of situations in which leading questions are definitely harmful because they bias the response away from the truth. The following conditions are significant:

a) The respondent does not have the information clearly in mind because of fading memory, chronological or inferential confusion; he is, therefore, susceptible to suggestions from the interviewer.

b) The information requested is not important to the respondent, and there is little motivation to strive to remember the accurate information.

c) The respondent does not feel free to say "I don't know" because he has an ego-threatening relationship with the interviewer or because the etiquette of the situation requires that he show deference to the interviewer.

d) The question leads in the direction of a false answer.

These conditions typically prevail in settings where the respondents are subordinates in the same community or organization as the interviewer.

For example, Company X, a large corporation, has been carrying on an intensive "educational" program pointing out the virtues of working for Company X—such as its pension plan, job rotation plan, retraining for automation, and family health insurance. In the excerpt below the interviewer is working for the personnel department and is studying the problem of recruiting workers to reduce labor turnover. Four years ago when the respondent came to work for the company, the same interviewer had talked with him. The objective of the present interview is to obtain a complete picture of the factors accounting for why the respondent came to work for Company X. In the course of the interview the following loaded questions obtained these responses:

I-1: We are doing a study of why people come to work for Johnson Electric and why they stay so long. How long have you been working for us?

R-1: About four years, I guess.

I-2: Why did you pick this company to work for?

R-2: Gosh, that was a long time ago. Let me see . . .

I-3: Yes, it was quite a while ago. Who were you working for before you came here?

R-3: For Central Electric.

I-4: Why did you leave there? Didn't you like it?

R-4: No, it wasn't a very pleasant place to work.

I-5: Did they have a pension plan like ours or a job rotation plan, training for automation, family health plan, or that sort of thing?

R-5: No, they didn't have any of those benefits like we do here.

I-6: What did your wife think about your choosing Johnson Electric?

R-6: She was glad I could get the job . . . she likes the family health plan very much, and I like the system of rotating jobs every three months after you have been here a couple of years. It makes things interesting. I learn a lot that way about the company as a whole. I can't understand people who like to hold down one job all the time.

I-7: Did you hear about this company through ads in the paper?

R-7: I spent a lot of time looking at the ads to find a good job.

I-8: Why did you choose to work for Johnson Electric?

R-8: It is a very progressive company. It has a lot of good personnel policies like I mentioned before. For example, I hope I can benefit from the in-service training program so I can be upgraded when we get more automated.

With question 1 the interviewer begins to furnish a biasing context in the phrase "why they stay so long" rather than "why people come and go." Question 2 is loaded with the assumption that the respondent "picked" the present company to work for when actually he might have preferred another but was not accepted. Question 4 suggests an easy way for the respondent to avoid the ego threat of saying that he was fired. Question 5 supplies the answer for questions

6 and 8. In questions 5 and 6 the interviewer does not probe to distinguish between what the respondent and his wife like about Johnson Electric now that he is here and what they knew about it before he applied for the job. Only the latter could have been a reason for coming to Johnson Electric.

Question 7 supplies an answer to what would have been a less biased question: "How did you first hear about Johnson Electric?" After four years the respondent's memory might be vague on how he heard about Johnson Electric and any suggested answer would be tempting. In question 8 the interviewer again assumes that the respondent chose to work at Johnson Electric. Response 8 gives the "company line" answer suggested by the interviewer in question 5 even though response 2 indicates a possible fading of memory.

The overall effect of the leading questions in this situation is to suggest invalid answers which are readily given by the respondent due to the type of communication barriers operating.

The following conditions describe another type of situation in which the leading question has a distorting effect upon the response.

a) The information is clear in the respondent's mind and he is, therefore, *able* to give it accurately.

b) The correct report would constitute an ego threat since it is in violation of public ideals or the apparent wishes of the interviewer.

c) Or, the correct report would violate certain etiquette requirements of the situation.

d) The question is slanted toward the public ideals and, for the respondent, toward a false answer.

These conditions frequently prevail in situations where the interviewer is perceived by the respondent as a superior. The main difference between this situation and the preceding one is that here the ego threat, the etiquette barrier, or the leading must be stronger to distort the response since the respondent has the correct information clearly in mind. He must consciously distort his report to compromise in the situation. In this case, he often produces rationalizations for his falsification such as, "He doesn't really want to know the truth anyway, so why should I give him the benefit of it." "He wouldn't do anything constructive with the information so why give it to him." "He just wants to find out how to get me to work harder; why should I whip myself?" "I don't want to be a stool pigeon!"

By specifying and illustrating some of the relevant conditions determining the positive, neutral, and negative effects of the leading question, we have hoped to demonstrate the uselessness of the over-simplified query, "Should leading questions be used?"

Thus far, we have focused the discussion upon the *verbal forms* of behavior involved in the interviewer's technique such as furnishing specific contexts with the question, selecting an appropriate vocabulary for wording the question, delimiting the scope of the question, structuring the answer, and using leading questions. All of these verbal techniques were evaluated with respect to their effectiveness in communicating to the respondent what information was considered relevant and with respect to their probable effects upon the respondent's ability or willingness to give the relevant information. Now we will discuss expressed attitudes as part of the interviewer's technique.

ATTITUDES EXPRESSED BY THE INTERVIEWER

The interviewer's attitudes, as well as the verbal forms of the question, constitute an essential portion of his technical tools. No amount of clever verbal technique or strategic preparation can compensate for an interviewer's negative attitudes expressed consciously or unconsciously in the interview. Conversely, strong positive attitudes persistently manifested by the interviewer can both overcome and prevent many a verbal *faux pas*. To a great extent the respondent listens to what the interviewer *means* rather than to what he *says* and the attitudinal accompaniment to the strictly semantic aspects of the interviewer's questions helps to complete the meaning.

As techniques, attitudes differ from the verbal forms of the question in that they may persist beyond one particular question. Also they may be manifested both verbally in statements to the respondent and non-verbally in the tone of voice, gestures, and facial expressions which accompany statements and questions by the interviewer. For this reason we will not be able to illustrate many of the manifestations of attitudes on the printed page.

Attitudes are similar to the verbal forms of the question in that they have an effect both upon the meaning of the question and upon the respondent's motivation (ability and willingness) to answer the question.

Let us proceed by discussing some of the manifestations and possible effects of the interviewer's positive or negative attitudes toward (*a*) the general task of interviewing on a particular topic, (*b*) specific items of the information received from the respondent, and (*c*) the respondent as a person.

Attitudes toward the interviewing task

Attitudes toward the interviewing task tend to prevail throughout a series of interviews on the same topic; in some cases, an interviewer has certain attitudes toward the interviewing task in general regardless of the particular topic at hand. In extreme cases, the attitudes may be a function of the interviewer's basic personality pattern.

Regardless of the pervasiveness of the source of the attitudes, we will first look at some of the negative attitudes commonly manifested toward the interviewing task. Negative attitudes often held by interviewers toward the task can be grouped into two types: those that indicate a general lack of *desire* to obtain the relevant information, and those that indicate a basic anxiety over one's *ability* to obtain it.

The interviewer's lack of desire may be based upon his initial lack or subsequent loss of interest in the topic of the interview. For example, an interviewer discovering housewife's motivations in buying soap might feel that the problem is inconsequential to the future of mankind and be bored with the procedure. Even in studies of people's behavior in disaster situations, the writer noted a tendency for the interviewers' interest in the problem to decrease once they had done enough interviews to obtain a fairly clear picture of the chronology of events and the variety of reactions to the crisis.

Sometimes the lack of interest in the topic springs from the interviewer's naive assumption that he knows what the respondent's answer is in advance. This dangerous attitude has been noted in cases where the interviewer is interviewing a friend or acquaintance. The interviewer's lack of interest may lie in the intrinsic nature of the topic or in the formulation of the problem. If the problem was formulated by someone else, the interviewer may have no vital interest in the topic, or he may not agree with or understand the formulation of the problem.

Regardless of the cause of the lack of interest in the interview, there are two results: The interviewer often fails to probe beneath the surface, and accepts incomplete information; also, the respondent often receives the impression that the interviewer is not serious or is incompetent or that the topic is not important. As a result he is not motivated to give complete, thoughtful, and accurate information and may even resent having to devote his time to such unimportant pursuits. The interviewer's boredom can be conveyed to the respondent by his tone of voice, posture, facial expression, and other gestures.

Attitudes reflecting the interviewer's basic anxiety over his ability to obtain the information are found in several common forms. He may feel apologetic for asking the types of questions required by the objectives of the interview. This apologetic attitude is seen in statements selected from two interviews: "You might not want to answer this question but. . . ." "You probably don't see much sense to this question. . . ." "I am supposed to ask you if. . . ." "Would you mind if I asked you. . . ." "This next question is a dilly. . . ." "You probably don't remember this but. . . ."

This attitude of apology and embarrassment often negatively affects the flow of information. The respondent may feel a lack of the support and recognition he desires. Or sensing the interviewer's embarrassment in asking the question, the respondent may think the answer will shock him. The etiquette barrier then arises. Another possible effect is for the respondent to perceive the interviewer's reluctance as an indication of guilt over some possible hidden purposes of the interview. Thus the respondent may feel some potential ego threat in the situation which puts him on guard and inhibits the flow of information. Another frequent effect is that the respondent simply tends to fulfill the interviewer's expectations by finding the information very difficult to give. The interviewer's anxiety also manifests itself in a rapid-fire pace which invites superficiality and destroys any chance of building the thoughtful mood needed to recall memories.

The remedy for boredom is often gained with experience. For example, it is the neophyte interviewer who assumes that he knows in advance what the respondent is going to say. With experience he becomes sensitized to clues which should be probed further to bring out the individual respondent's unique point of view. Once this is accomplished, the interviewer can see for himself the difference between the initial, superficial responses and the more complex and fundamental underpinnings which emerge with further exploration.

It is also helpful if the interviewer has a vital stake in the study he is doing. He should understand any practical or theoretical significance of the study and have an appreciation of some of the more subtle methodological problems involved in obtaining complete and valid information. He should have the purpose and specifications of the study so clearly in mind that he is highly sensitive to what is relevant, potentially relevant, and irrelevant to the objectives.

To avoid an attitude of embarrassment or apology the interviewer should ask himself the following question: "Would I be willing to answer all of these questions if I were approached by an interviewer under the same conditions?"

By "under the same conditions" we do not mean that the interviewer should necessarily be willing to answer the questions if the respondent were to reverse their roles during the interview. Instead, this means that the interviewer should be willing to answer the questions in a study planned to render useful knowledge, in which the sponsorship and purpose of the study were clearly given, and in which the anonymity of the respondent were guaranteed.

If he would not be willing, the interviewer will not be successful in hiding his attitude from respondents. Many field workers, including the writer, feel that such an interviewer has no moral right to ask questions he is not willing to answer himself. Regardless of the moral issue, it has been demonstrated that interviewers' attitudes have an effect upon the degree of candidness of the respondent.

The interviewer must realize in advance that there is likely to be some inconvenience and psychic strain at times for both the interviewer and respondent but that this is necessary to advance applied or theoretical social science. The writer has noted on several occasions that the neophyte interviewer's questions regarding his ethical rights to "ask those questions" typically arise when he is beginning to feel some of the tension involved in overcoming the inhibitors of communication. This tendency to feel that if it is difficult it might be unethical is understandable in terms of psychological mechanisms of guilt, punishment and rationalization. Nevertheless, it should be avoided by the social scientist.

Now let us examine some of the manifestations and possible effects of the interviewer's *positive* attitudes toward his task. Instead of being bored, apologetic, or embarrassed, the successful interviewer shows that he expects to be successful. He is strongly interested in the topic and assumes responsibility personally for the questions he asks rather than attempting to hide behind the sponsor. He is so "sold" on what he is doing that there is a higher probability of appealing to the respondent's altruism. His competence is a compliment to the respondent who realizes that he is not in the presence of a casual inquirer but an incisive prober with a purpose and a method.

Most of these positive attitudes, just as the elimination of the negative ones, grow from the interviewer's instruction and experience.

Attitudes toward the information received

Here, the problem is the interviewer's attitudes toward specific statements made by the respondent rather than toward the interview topic as a whole or toward the questions which must be asked. In general, the interviewer should have a non-judgmental attitude rather than being shocked by the information received; he should show a lively interest in what the respondent is saying rather than being bored; he should usually maintain an analytical attitude toward the information and the degree to which it fulfills the specifications of the study. He should give praise and recognition to responses which are of a high quality in terms of their detail, completeness, depth, and candidness regardless of the moral implications of the report.

It is sometimes difficult for the interviewer to avoid showing his personal values when the respondent makes some completely unpredicted statements which catch the interviewer off guard as illustrated below. In this example a group worker from a settlement house in the slums of a large city is talking to the person indicated in the records as the mother of a boy who has recently committed another delinquency.

I: Hello Mrs. Johnson. I am Mr. Brown from Roger Booth House. I would like to talk with you about John.

R: Come in, Mr. Brown.

I: John spends quite a bit of time at Roger Booth House. We are sorry to hear that he is in trouble and I was wondering if there is anything we can do.

R: That's right nice of you, but I don't think anything can be done now. I have had trouble with him for years. He seems to be just a born renegade. I have done my best but he just can't stay on the beam.

I: How's that?

R: Ever since he was two days old he has been trying to kick over the traces.

I: What does his father think of this?

R: I really can't say. You see, I never met his father.

I: (Making a quick recovery) I see, how old was he when you adopted him?

R: I didn't have to adopt him because I took care of his mother—she was my aunt's sister-in-law. I took care of her since she was nine years old and I made her promise that when she got married she would give me her first son. Well, she wasn't married, but John was her first son. In fact, she had him right in this house. This was a much nicer neighborhood then.

The social worker with extensive experience with lower socio-economic status people of various ethnic backgrounds would not be shocked by the respondent's last statement. However, in this case the interviewer had little experience with people in metropolitan slums and was unable to conceal the fact that he was taken aback by the casual attitude displayed toward middle class ideals of parenthood and the red tape of adoption procedures. From this point on, the respondent ceased to express herself so candidly and any constructive working relationship was made more difficult.

We could supply many examples in which the interviewer is caught off guard and shows surprise, shock, morbid curiosity, inappropriate amusement, or disapproval of something the respondent has said. The probability of such material entering the conversation depends upon the topic of discussion and the difference in experience, cultural background, and auxiliary roles of the interviewer and respondent. The interviewer must be sensitive to the problem and have wide experience before he can take all the respondent's statements in stride.

It is easier for the interviewer to learn to inhibit the expression of embarrassment, boredom, shock, disapproval and gullibility in reaction to a respondent's statement than it is to pretend the opposite attitudes when they are not actually felt. However, pretense is not necessary. The most constructive approach is for the interviewer to *learn to express* the following generally productive attitudes.

The non-judgmental attitude. Generally, the interviewer should not express agreement or disagreement, approval or disapproval of anything the respondent says. He should remember that his goal is to obtain accurate and complete information and that any show of disagreement with the respondent constitutes an ego threat.

The interviewer must learn the fine but important distinction between disapproving of a certain value held by the respondent and rejecting him as a person. At the same time, the interviewer should not assume that the respondent makes this distinction; therefore, it should be expected that any disagreement with the respondent's point of view will be interpreted as a disapproval of him as a person.

It is not suggested that a good interviewer is a chameleon-like character lacking his own values and merely reflecting those of the person he is interviewing. On the contrary, the interviewer, in order to discipline himself so that he will not indulge in unplanned demonstrations of approval or disapproval, must feel secure in his own value position, at least to the point where he does not need to defend it or seek support for his position.

The very values which the interviewer holds and may be working for in the interview can be foiled by his expression of these values during the interview. For example, a person interested in reducing the juvenile delinquency rate thwarts his chance of gaining insight into the social-psychological process by which a child becomes a delinquent by expressing a disapproving attitude toward the delinquent he is interviewing.

The main value of the non-judgmental attitude is that it frees the respondent from ego threat, taking him off the defensive and allowing him to candidly review his own behavior. There are *rare* occasions when it is appropriate to the objectives of the interview for the interviewer to express approval and disapproval. In learning to interview, however, the non-judgmental approach is the basic discipline which must be mastered first so that any deviations from it are consciously calculated to meet interview objectives rather than emotional reflexive actions.

Showing an interest in the information. The interviewer's demonstrating or withholding his display of interest in certain aspects of the information is a technique of guiding the focus of the discussion. Also, the general level of interest shown in the information influences the amount of spontaneity shown by the respondent. Here "interest" covers a syndrome of more specific attitudes: a desire to understand how the world looks to the respondent; an appreciation of the things experienced by the respondent; sharing in the respondent's struggle to recall, organize, and express his experiences; appreciating the difficulties involved; and a desire to accurately reflect the respondent's opinions, feelings, and beliefs.

Various aspects of the interviewer's interest in the information can be demonstrated verbally as well as non-verbally. A few examples will illustrate this.

R: At that time I had three babies still in diapers and that made it a bit difficult to adjust to the divorce.
I: Three babies all in diapers! How did you manage?

The interviewer who is less sensitive or less appreciative could have merely said, "I see," or "What were some of the problems?" or "How is that?"

The following exchange is taken from an interview with a disaster victim where the objective was to obtain a complete account of the respondent's experiences during the period of crisis.

R: Jim and I were going down highway 67; we didn't see the tornado, but just as we came to one of those banked turns we couldn't make it because the car was off the ground. We were jerked up in the air and I remember seeing a flash as our car hit the high-tension lines. Then we landed bottom side up in a swamp about four feet deep. One more gust of wind came and just flipped the car right side up again.

I: Were you going north or south on highway 67?

After a large number of interviews this interviewer had become insensitive to the experiences of disaster victims. He shows no appreciation for what the respondent is saying. True, this respondent's experiences, although dramatic, are not unusual for people in an area hit by a tornado. But from the point of view of the individual respondent there is little encouragement to elaborate and clarify the details of his experiences. An appropriate responsiveness on the part of the interviewer would have shown that he *expected* more detail at this point, that he *sympathized* with the respondent's traumatic experience, and that he *recognized* the respondent's unique qualifications to report how it feels to fly through the air in a car. All of these facilitators of communication could have been triggered by a natural expression of candid amazement on the part of the interviewer.

Fortunately, the interviewer's temporary lapses into insensitivity were not fatal to the flow of information on this particular topic because of the tremendous need for catharsis which leads most respondents to concentrate their attention on the most devastating portion of their experience. However, the better interviewers seemed to build up "credit" by showing interest in the respondent's account of the impact period of disaster. This credit carried over to the later portion of the interview dealing with information not nearly as important to the respondent himself.

The verbal techniques of showing interest, responsiveness, empathy, sensitivity, appreciation and recognition are often very simple as long as the non-verbal accompaniment rings true. For example: "That's very interesting to me." "That's exactly what I want to know; could you spell out more of the details?" "That's amazing—how did you do it?" "That's a very unusual experience, to say the least. Now let's see if I have the correct idea." "You must have been really angry by that time!"

All of these expressions of interest in the appropriate context are perfectly natural. For this reason interviewers are sometimes either suspicious of their use or do not think of them as "techniques." We must be careful to avoid the conception of techniques as tricks or insincere play acting. Instead, *techniques consist of increasing one's empathic sensitivity to the respondent's story and a disciplined with-holding or expressing of real attitudes.*

There are occasions in some interviews when an undisciplined ex-pression of interest, sympathy, or curiosity by the interviewer, even though sincere, will derail the interview so that the interview is very interesting but the information received is not relevant to the objec-tives of the interview. Here the over-concern with building rapport reduces the interview to a sociable conversation.

Critical analysis of the information. The non-judgmental ethical neutrality and the disciplined interest in the respondent's story must be balanced by a third attitudinal stance we will call critical analysis of the information. By "critical" we denote the process of evaluating the adequacy of the information for fulfilling the objectives of the interview.

It is not enough for the interviewer to be vitally concerned with evaluating the adequacy of the information; he must communicate this attitude to the respondent. When this attitude is perceived by the respondent, it helps prevent his temptation to give vague, super-ficial, incomplete replies which would require an inordinate amount of time to unscramble. The interviewer must prevent the respond-ent's perceiving him as a simple-minded, superficial, disorganized, or easily misled person.

The interviewer's attitude of critical evaluation is shown in his interest in precise facts, his concern for correct inferences, and his painstaking care in establishing accurate sequences of events when they are relevant. He also demonstrates it in his desire to get beneath clichés or instantaneous conclusions, in his willingness to help the respondent's memory, and in his conscientious attempt to correctly reflect the respondent's attitudes. These persistent efforts of the interviewer establish an appropriate mood. In order to help the re-spondent give the quality of response expected, the interviewer may have to slow down the pace of the interview and establish a thought-ful mood to facilitate memory. He may have to tactfully call the respondent's attention to apparent inconsistencies, contradictions, or omissions in the report.

This critical attitude has two general functions. First, it can be thought of as a balance wheel governing the two previous attitudes of non-judgment and interest. The interviewer must discipline himself by restricting his interest to those experiences which are relevant to the problem. Similarly, he must restrict his non-judgmental approach to expressions of approval and disapproval of the respondent or the information given rather than to the completeness, accuracy, or general relevance of the information as measured by the objectives of the interview. The critical attitude reserves expressions of sympathetic understanding for only candid information; it prevents the misplaced expression of appreciation for efforts not up to the capabilities of the respondent.

The second function of the attitude is in its motivation of the respondent. He sees that a high level performance is expected of him by the interviewer. He sees more potential ego threat in being caught in an attempt to falsify than in a candid report, and this forestalls fabrication. The memory barrier is minimized by impressing the respondent with the importance of an accurate report. Indirectly, the respondent is given recognition since, if he perceives the interviewer as being competent, he is apt to feel that he was respected enough to merit a good interviewer. The appeal to an intelligent respondent's altruism is enhanced because he is more likely to be willing to give his time for a good cause if he feels the cause is in the hands of competent people who will see it through to a successful conclusion. For some respondents a careful interview which insists upon achieving somewhat difficult objectives constitutes a challenging new experience. The interviewer's attempts to get beneath a superficial level often stimulate the respondent's need for meaning by pointing out certain inconsistencies of thinking of which the respondent had not previously been aware.

Now that we have examined some of the manifestations and functions of three general attitudes toward the information received by the interviewer, let us turn to some important aspects of the interviewer's attitude toward the respondent as a person.

Attitudes toward the respondent as a person

It is not possible to make a perfectly clear distinction between the interviewer's attitudes toward the information received and toward the person giving the information because, as has already been pointed out, the interviewer may tend to dislike the respondent if he dislikes many things he says and the respondent may tend to feel ego threat if the interviewer disagrees with some of his ideas.

For the purposes of this discussion we will use the phrase "attitudes toward the respondent" to refer only to those attitudes toward the respondent that are independent of anything the respondent has said in the interview and are based upon the interviewer's image of an attitude toward a particular type of respondent. The type of respondent may be distinguished by such characteristics as sex, race, age, personality type, role, social class, and educational background.

There are several specific manifestations of the interviewer's attitudes which hinder communication with one class of respondent. An attitude may range in feeling from a strong dislike, through indifference, to a strong affinity. A negative feeling makes it difficult for the interviewer to empathize with the respondent. The writer has found in the analysis of tape-recorded interviews that interviewers with some experience rarely express a negative attitude toward the respondent in a *direct* manner. Even though they learn to control such direct expressions, there are several indirect ways which betray a lack of interest. An awareness of these indirect manifestations will help an interviewer control his negative attitudes toward a particular category of respondent.

Forgetting previous responses. This is a typical indirect manifestation of a lack of interest in the respondent. In the non-scheduled interview there is always the danger of asking the same or similar question twice. However, the writer has found that some interviewers, when interviewing certain types of respondents, were more prone to forget what the respondent had already told them even though it was something extremely important to the respondent. For example:

R: I called out "Victor, Victor, Victor" . . . as loud as I could yell. The next door neighbor was trying to calm me down, but I just couldn't control myself.

I: What was your husband doing meanwhile? . . . Oh yes, that's right you said he was unconscious all this time.

In this case the interviewer caught his own mistake and softened the blow. Such lapses of memory on the part of the interviewer are readily detected by the respondent when the information he has given is vitally important to him. This is ego threatening to some respondents, and if it happens more than once, it is often interpreted as an indication of the interviewer's lack of sympathetic understanding.

The interviewer can give this unsympathetic impression even when he has not forgotten that he has asked the question and is asking a slightly different question for clarification. There is a danger that the respondent will feel or say, "I told you that once." To prevent this, the interviewer may positively give the respondent recognition by acknowledging the information previously given before probing further. He might say, for example, "You told me that your husband was unconscious after being hit by a board off the barn. What was he doing before that time?"

Neglecting to probe in crucial spots. This neglect communicates a lack of empathy for the respondent. If often pays to probe for elaboration and clarification of ego-involved or emotionalized responses even though the information does not seem to be directly related to the objectives of the interview. Showing an interest in what is important to the respondent is a good rapport-building technique. For example, in an interview to discover some of the factors contributing to the low morale of workers in a steel plant, the conversation was as follows:

I: Are there some supervisors the men find hard to get along with?

R: You have to take a lot of guff off the foreman here. I don't know who he thinks he is—and he has been here only two months.

I: What do you mean by that?

R: Well (with great hostility), the bastard actually violated some of the agreements the union has with the company!

I: Are there any other things that you dislike in the management or supervising system?

The interviewer's last question veers away from one of the respondent's favorite gripes. When the respondent is just beginning to gather momentum and before the interviewer has discovered the actual nature of his complaint, the interviewer rushes on as if he had only a limited amount of time. From the respondent's point of view, this behavior might indicate that the interviewer is not actually interested in his morale problems, and this could discourage the respondent from elaborating on other incidents.

Using a condescending tone. There is a certain saccharine tone heard in tape recordings of interviews where the interviewer is trying to patronize the respondent who is considered in lower status. This tone is often used in an attempt to conceal outright disapproval or complete lack of interest in the respondent as a person. It is rarely successful in convincing the respondent that the interviewer is interested or impressed.

Being rigidly cautious. Although male interviewers rarely use what we called the "saccharine tone," they often become rigidly cautious in the same type of situation. In this case, the interviewer shows little spontaneity, perhaps because he fears betraying his own feelings in an off-guard moment. In some instances we traced this rigidity to the interviewer's feeling that he might lose status in the respondent's eyes by being too informal and spontaneous. This behavior was found in corporation managers while interviewing employees, in sociology students interviewing members of low status ethnic groups, and in social work students interviewing mental patients.

Having shown some common manifestations of the negative attitudes toward the respondent, we now examine some of the ways of manifesting positive attitudes toward the respondent.

Interest in the respondent as a person. Often it is impossible to motivate the respondent by treating him strictly as a means to an end. This is particularly true where the objectives of the interview make heavy demands upon the respondent. Here, the task of the interviewer is to reconcile the apparently conflicting goals of the interviewer who wants to obtain information and the respondent who wants to be understood and considered as a unique individual rather than as a statistic or case. The solution is to show a vital interest in the respondent and his story at those points most relevant to the objectives of the interview. This interest, to be appropriate, must not be an idle curiosity nor a chummy intimacy but should be mainly confined to a keen interest in the relevant, unique experiences of the respondent. Such interest is characterized by the desire of the interviewer to see the relevant experiences through the respondent's eyes.

The respondent can be reminded of this attitude not only by its non-verbal manifestations such as the interviewer's paying close attention, responding with facial expressions and tone of voice, but also by such verbal expressions as, "I want *your* side of this story!" "How do you, *personally*, feel about this?" "Tell me what happened to *you* in the tornado." "What is *your* reaction to the rising cost of living?" "Which of these things seem most important to *you?*" "I want to be sure I understand *your* point of view on this issue!"

All of these questions and statements could be worded in an impersonal manner, but with less appeal to the respondent's ego. Personalizing the request for relevant information is one way of showing interest in the respondent as a person without encouraging irrelevant responses.

Interest in the respondent as a person can also be indicated by making statements at appropriate points showing appreciation of the respondent's role, status, or values. This does not mean that the interviewer must agree with the respondent's values. In the following excerpt an interviewer with a Protestant background is interviewing a

Catholic woman who has felt the pressures of prejudice from fellow college students.

R: I recall one incident where two girls were talking about how only unintelligent people could be Catholics because they had to accept dogmatic pronouncements no matter how illogical they may be. Then one of them turned to me to see if I didn't agree. I just said, "You can't expect me to agree because I'm a Catholic myself." Were they ever embarrassed! They sputtered out something about they didn't realize I was a Catholic.

I: That reminds me of the time I heard a conversation on the bus where one woman said, "How was I to know! She didn't look like a Catholic at all!"

R: That's it exactly! They think that Catholics have two heads or something. That's why, in this community, I make a point of being known as an individual *before* I mention what church I belong to. People are less likely to be prejudiced then.

Note that the interviewer did not mention any of his experiences where the same thing had happened in relation to Jews, pacifists, socialists, or any other minority group. It is often a mistake to assume that one minority member sees any similarity between his situation and that of other minorities. And there is always the danger that the comparison will be resented.

Showing appreciation of the respondent's effort. The interviewer should be sensitive to the respondent's need for appreciation and recognition at two points in the interviewing process. First, the interviewer should show that he realizes a particular question places great demands upon the respondent. In doing this, he should not imply that he expects the respondent to fail to meet the demands. If the objectives of the question demand careful searching of one's memory, untangling chronological and inferential confusion, or reporting semiconscious experiences, the interviewer should give some indication that he appreciates the difficulty of the problem. For example, he might say, "This is a difficult question, but I'm quite sure you can give me some good ideas if I just let you think it over for awhile. Let's go back to the time you mentioned when you joined the Black Hawk gang . . . that was about six years ago. Why would you say you joined the gang?"

The second phase of showing appreciation is in praising the respondent for the *effort* he has made and is making. Interviews with respondents regarding their experiences in a non-scheduled interview showed that frequently the respondent himself did not understand why he was having difficulty in reporting some of the relevant information. Furthermore, he was often insecure not knowing whether he was considered successful by the interviewer. In these cases, it is important that the interviewer show his appreciation of the respondent's efforts to give the information.

The interviewer must be sensitive to opportunities to praise the respondent sincerely throughout the interview. The praise need not be lavish nor even direct, but should be given at those points where the respondent has exerted special effort. For example: "That was difficult and you did it very well!" "You seem to understand exactly what I want!" "You have given me an unusual amount of detail on your experiences. This is very valuable information!" "I know it was hard for you to talk about these painful experiences and I appreciate it." "I am grateful for your candid accounts of the conflicts and disagreements you have had with your parents!" "You have done an excellent job in giving me some insight into this problem. Is there anything else you would like to add before we go on to the last topic?" "You have given me a wealth of relevant information!" "You make interviewing very easy!"

It is easy for the interviewer to be so concerned with what information is lacking that he forgets to appreciate what has already been given and the amount of the respondent's effort expended. It encourages the respondent to go beyond the superficial level if he feels that it is expected and appreciated.

A DEMONSTRATION OF TECHNIQUE PLANNING

To connect the theoretical principles just discussed with the actual operations in the interview, we will demonstrate the kind of technique planning necessary for one specific interview. An interviewer may unconsciously arrive at some of the specific techniques needed. But those interviewers who become self-conscious in their application of theory will create the most appropriate solutions to interview problems a higher percentage of the time.

A general approach to planning techniques

The objectives of any study are first expressed in terms of "what we want to know" and must always be translated into more concrete terms of "how to word the question." The techniques of wording the question include deciding upon the type of verbal *context* needed, the *vocabulary* to be used, the *scope* of the question, the degree to which the answer should have *structure,* and whether to use a *leading* or *non-leading* form of question.

When deciding which techniques are most appropriate, we should keep in mind two basic objectives: (*a*) *communicating the question* to make clear what information is relevant, and (*b*) *motivating the respondent* to give the relevant information as accurately and completely as possible.

Specifying the objectives. The logical first step is to convert the apparently simple problem into a range of possible specific objectives and select from these the one felt to be most relevant. There are always several different interpretations of a problem when it is stated in common sense terms. Each problem has several facets, perspectives, dimensions, aspects, frames of references or contexts which have not been clearly specified. This leaves much of the creative process of problem-raising to the interviewer himself. Accepting a particular interpretation of the problem determines the remaining steps in the solution.

The particular perspective can be arrived at by a "brain storming" process of running up and down the ladder of abstraction. For example, instead of trying to arrive at an abstract delineation of the problem before converting it to specific questions, it is better to make a *tentative* abstract definition of the problem and then quickly write as many questions as possible without any immediate concern for "techniques" as such. Next, consider the following questions to see what different aspects of the problem they suggest and ask what specific details might be relevant to each aspect: (*a*) What are some of the different interpretations of the meaning of this problem? (Any others?) (*b*) What difference does it make whether you interpret the problem one way or the other? (effect on communicating the question? effect on the respondent's willingness or ability to answer? effects on the techniques to be used?) (*c*) Give a specific question to get at this interpretation. After this, it would be wise to look again at the abstract delineation of the problem to see whether it suggests additional questions not yet included. Once this is done, try to obtain a correspondence between a revised statement of the problem and some of the questions which seem relevant to this new statement.

Anticipating the inhibitors and facilitators. Only after specific bits of needed information have been decided upon can the interviewer attempt to empathize with a specific respondent to anticipate some of the potential inhibitors which must be guarded against, or some of the potential facilitators which might be activated by the appropriate technique. He should ask himself, "If we assume interpretation A in this problem, what are some specific questions bringing the objectives down to an operational level?" "Now if you were to have interviewer X ask that question of respondent Y, what are some of the potential inhibitors of communication? Facilitators?" "Would this be different if you were to assume interpretation B in this problem?"

Reviewing the basic tools of technique. Once the interviewer is aware of the specific information needed and the potential inhibitors and facilitators, he should consider how each category of techniques may be applied to facilitate communication. We have discussed seven uses of contexts: (1) contexts aimed at *communicating the question,* (2) contexts aimed at *motivating the respondent,* (3) the effects of specific *vocabulary,* (4) the effects of narrow and broad *scope* questions, (5) implicit and explicit ways of *structuring* the answer by wording the question, (6) the conditions under which questions should be *leading* or *non-leading,* and (7) the importance of certain *attitudes* being expressed by the interviewer. On paper we cannot demonstrate the non-verbal communication of attitudes, but only the ways in which attitudes might be inferred by the respondent from the wording of the question. The interviewer might ask himself such questions as these:

Now let us assume that we have decided upon objective B and we want to know _____. How then could we provide a contextual statement followed by an appropriate question in order to minimize ego threat and maximize sympathetic understanding?

Is there any way that we could change the vocabulary to make the question more effective?

Is the scope of the question appropriate or should it be broadened or narrowed?

Should we use a leading form of the question? If so, how should we word it?

He should try to devise several wordings of the same question in which techniques are applied in different ways and then select among the techniques building a composite of two or more of them. One must constantly guard against covering too much in one question, particularly when trying to devise an "opening" question to a topic.

A specific interview situation

This situation involves a wide range of interviewing techniques. A discussion of possible solutions to the problems presented follows the description of the situation.

Objectives of the study. Assume that you are to plan an interview to *discover* the sources of intergenerational conflict in the American culture by interviewing high school students regarding the kinds of conflicts they have with their parents. You are interested in all types of conflicts from the most mild to the most violent and want to discover the range of issues involved. You are to carefully explore all the conflicts between the teenager and his parents in the year preceding the interview. A comparison of the nature and the frequency of the conflicts in different types of communities may render important clues to some of the causes of mental illness and delinquency in teenagers. The respondent is a 16-year-old high school girl being interviewed by a 22-year-old college student.

The interviewer says, "My name is Linda White. I am helping with a study of family relations sponsored by the U.S. Public Health Department. We want to get the teenager's point of view on family relations and that is why we are talking to hundreds of high school students. Your name was one of those picked out of the hat for an interview."

Problem 1. What question will open up a free discussion of the types of conflicts the respondent has had with her parents in the past year? This is to be the opening question following the introductory explanation above.

Problem 2. Design a question to discover which kinds of behavior the teenager hides from her parents to avoid open conflict.

Problem 3. Design a question which will also be asked of the parents and will allow you to compare the teenager's point of view with theirs in the area of economic responsibilities and privileges. How you would word the main question? What subsidiary questions are needed? To limit this problem deal with only one type of economic responsibility or privilege, some economic issue over which parents and teenagers are likely to have conflict.

Problem 4. Design a question to discover the respondent's criteria for judging the relative seriousness of conflicts she has had with her parents in the past year. Use one or more questions, whichever is most appropriate. Omit any neutral probes.

Some tentative solutions to the problems follow. These are not intended as the only or the best solutions, but are offered to share the writer's views. Perhaps more important than the examples of the specific solutions is the account of the assumptions upon which they are built. Several patterns of solutions might be generated by the application of the same basic principles.

This discussion follows the same format as does the general approach to planning techniques.

Discussion of specific techniques for this interview

Problem 1—the opening question. We assume that the main purpose of the "opening question" is to motivate the respondent to talk in the *general area* of the subject matter.

Interpretation and specification of objectives. The first question need not clearly delineate the problem, but it must be related to the *area of conflicts* between teenagers and parents. This contrasts with trying to start the topic in some area other than conflicts hoping to later move into the topic in some indirect way. The latter is not only unnecessary but runs a risk of making it increasingly difficult to shift from one tactic to another. Instead we will begin directly in the area of *conflicts.*

We might use a degree of indirectness by starting in the direction of "conflicts between teenagers and their parents" without asking "what conflicts have *you* had with your parents?" If we have some familiarity with conflicts, we know that they cover a wide range, from slight disagreements on how to mow the lawn, to basic disagreements over the dating practices or sex life of the teenager.

Anticipating inhibitors and facilitators. There is the possibility of ego threat since the girl may hide certain types of behavior to avoid conflict, or she might feel that parents and children should not have disagreements, or that this is a symptom of personal weakness. There is also the possibility of the *etiquette* barrier if she perceives the interviewer as a person who might be shocked, embarrassed, or insulted by the report of certain types of conflict. A third possible inhibitor of relevant information is *inferential confusion.* Here, the danger is that the interviewer will not clearly communicate what is meant by "conflict." Therefore, the respondent will fail to see that certain concrete events are in fact examples of "conflict" in terms of the interviewer's definition. If the respondent feels that conflict is evil, this attitude will tend to bias her reporting of conflicts in which she felt she was justified or where the conflict was so mild or "natural" that it had no pathological implications.

On the positive side, there is a potential opportunity to appeal to several facilitators of communication. First, through *sympathetic understanding,* an atmosphere may be established in which the respondent's *need for catharsis* may motivate her to go into great detail regarding the conflicts. Also, a correct approach can appeal to the girl's need for *recognition* and her need for *meaning.* Here are several examples of opening questions:

As far as we know, all parents and teenagers have some sort of disagreements with each other at some time or other. As you think of your own observations of people you know and your own experiences, what are some of the disagreements, arguments, or conflicts between teenagers and their parents?

In every family there seem to be times when there is not complete agreement between the parents and teenagers and there is either some small disagreement, an argument, a big fight, or just hurt feelings without any open argument. What are some of the disagreements you have had from time to time with your parents?

I am interested in some of the causes of disagreements between parents and teenagers. Do you think that most parents actually understand teenagers?

What are some of the ways you feel teenagers are not understood by parents?

What are some of the disagreements between parents and teenagers caused by a lack of understanding by the parents?

Techniques. Note that either the contextual statement, the question, or both often tend to be *leading* to show that the interviewer assumes that teenagers have conflicts with parents and expects the respondent to report them. The vocabulary used aims at giving the impression that conflict of some sort, mild or severe, is assumed to be normal and is not judged moralistically by the interviewer. There is an attempt in most of the examples to keep the *scope* broad, at least in a way which will avoid giving the impression that the interviewer is interested only in the dramatic or physical conflicts.

Problem 2—hidden behavior. Since the first topic already establishes the types of conflicts which might occur between parents and teenagers, there is already a clear context for the meaning of *conflict* as used in the second topic.

Interpretation and specification of objectives. Where the focus is upon the teenager's attempt to *avoid* conflict by hiding certain behavior from his parents.

We could interpret the phrase "hides from his parents" to mean everything the parent does not know which might be a source of conflict. This broad interpretation could include both those things which the parent has never asked about and those cases where the parent asked and the teenager lied. We must decide whether the distinction between the two kinds of "hiding" is necessary. If we decide on the distinction, we then have a more difficult problem of obtaining an admission from the respondent that he has lied. We are assuming that no such distinction is needed, thus simplifying the task somewhat.

Inhibitors and facilitators. Even though we do not need the admission from the respondent that she lied to her parents, we can still assume that there is potential ego threat. The teenager has some degree of fear, anxiety or apprehension over his behavior or he would not hide it from his parents. If he claims that the parents are wrong, he still must find some rationalization to protect his ego against the idea that hiding his behavior is cowardly. Thus the interviewer's task is to use techniques which will minimize ego threat and maximize sympathetic understanding. Insofar as possible, the questions should be worded to express a non-judgmental attitude toward the act of hiding one's actions, show sympathetic interest in the respondent as a person, and show that cooperation is expected as the natural course of events. In some cases the respondent may be motivated by his need for catharsis to "tell all."

Techniques. We can use a contextual statement with the question which gives the respondent a readymade ego defending rationalization. The *vocabulary* should be simple and non-ego threatening and, insofar as possible display the interviewer's role of "member of the younger generation." The *scope* of the question must be broad in order to prevent the exclusion of relevant information. The question should *structure* the answer as little as possible to prevent excluding unanticipated categories of hidden behavior. Finally, the question should be *leading* in the direction of violations of parental norms. Example of a possible series are given here:

1) Sometimes in order to keep peace in the family we feel it is better to do certain things without telling our parents because we know they would be against it. What are some of the things the teenagers you know do without even mentioning them to their parents?

   a) I see. That's very good. What other things do they do?

   b) Are there any things you suspect they might be hiding from their parents but you don't know for sure because they just don't talk to you about it?

   c) What are some other things they might hide?

   d) Is that the worst kind of thing they hide?

   e) Isn't there anything more disapproved by the parents that at least some of them might do?

2) Now here is a checklist including the kinds of things you have just mentioned. Check all of those things which you have done without telling your parents.

The intentional loading of question *e* to encourage the respondent to mention the most deviant behavior may in some cases result in distortion or exaggeration in an attempt to please the interviewer. However, this is not damaging to the interview since the purpose of question 1 is to prepare the way for the second question. Question 1 gives the respondent a chance to talk about himself directly or in disguise, while giving the interviewer an opportunity to manifest a non-judgmental attitude toward a range of deviant behavior. It also provides a specific list of deviations to be discussed more directly in question 2. The checklist for question 2 can be devised on the basis of exploratory pre-test interviewing and still allow for write-in items to be included in the discussion with a particular respondent.

The series of questions given in the example was based upon the assumption that a partially indirect approach of asking about the behavior of *others* before asking directly about the behavior of the respondent would be best. This is not necessarily so. Under certain conditions that the experienced interviewer can detect, the more direct and time-saving approach would be equally successful. The interviewer might begin with, "Sometimes in order to keep peace in the family we feel it is better to do certain things without telling our parents because we know they would disapprove. What are some of these things you have done without telling your parents?" Note that the context gives the respondent a rationalization for not telling the parents, and the interviewer used "we" to include herself and the respondent in an in-group versus the out-group of "parents." This basic question could then be followed with an adaptation of questions *a* and *c.*

Another opener for this topic might be as follows: "Do you think parents really know *almost everything* their teenage daughters do? (IF NOT EVERYTHING.) What are some of the things the parents don't know about?" This also used the indirect approach with a challenge to parental infallibility which might appeal to many teen-agers. This could be followed by more direct questions about the respondent's own behavior.

Much of the success of any of these verbal techniques would depend upon the general emotional atmosphere developed in the first topic and the non-verbal expression of attitudes at the moment.

Problem 3—issue of economic responsibility and privilege. The problem to "compare the teenager's point of view with his parents' point of view in the area of economic responsibilities and privileges" is intentionally imprecise. This gives the interviewer the full responsibility of clarifying and limiting the objectives of the interview.

Interpretation and specification of objectives. One crucial phrase which needs interpretation is "point of view." It contains several possible dimensions. For example it could refer to the respondent's view of the moral restrictions within which he must operate. Or it could refer to positive responsibilities or rights and privileges—all viewed from the perspective of what the respondent himself thinks is right. On the other hand, these same factors may be viewed from the perspective of what the respondent feels others expect of him regardless of whether he, personally, agrees with these expectations. These "others" might include members of his own family, other families in the community of the same social class, teenagers in general, or some other relevant reference or membership group. Another quite different interpretation would be to obtain the respondent's views of some ideal pattern of economic responsibility and privilege under better material circumstances.

Once we are aware of the various interpretations of "point of view," another basic problem arises in analyzing the notion of "comparing" the teenager's point of view with his parents'. Here we must decide whether we are trying to discover (*a*) differences between the parents' and the teenagers' frames of reference for judging economic responsibilities and privileges, or (*b*) differences between their judgments when they are held to the same frame of reference.

This problem specifies that we "deal with only one type of economic responsibility." This still allows a tremendous range of interpretation in what is meant by "one type." This could be as broad as any disagreement over how the teenager obtains and spends money or as narrow as who selects and who pays for the formal dress the respondent is going to wear to the senior prom.

The next decision to make is which of several economic issues to discuss. In an actual study this might be decided by a preliminary empirical investigation or by previous studies in the same culture. Here we must make an *a priori* judgment in choosing among such issues as use of the family automobile, saving money for college, working for pay outside the home, or getting an allowance.

We have chosen to illustrate with the topic of receiving and spending an allowance, hoping to touch upon all of the most important aspects of the problem where conflict might be involved.

After we have decided as clearly as possible the exact purpose of the interview, we can begin to think of the types of specific questions we might need to ask. At this point it is possible to empathically anticipate some of the inhibitors and facilitators.

Anticipating inhibitors and facilitators. Although there may be several potential inhibitors in this type of topic, some of them such as competing time demands and etiquette should have been dealt with mainly in the strategy phase. Here, in planning techniques, it is advisable to guard against both ego threat and inferential confusion. There is a possibility of ego threat to the parent who may feel that he is either being too lenient or too restrictive in money matters, or that he is too strongly influenced by the teenager or other parents in the community. The teenager may also feel threatened if he thinks he is permitted too much freedom or has been manipulating his parents by selectively reporting what other families do.

Inferential confusion is a potential danger if the interviewer does not make clear which of the several frames of reference is relevant to the problem. He should provide specific concrete dimensions of the issue falling within the appropriate frame of reference.

Techniques. It is probable that the potential ego threat of the economic topic is not nearly as great as in discovering what the teenager has hidden from his parents. Nevertheless, we should minimize ego threat by providing an appropriate *context,* using a nonthreatening *vocabulary* and by *leading* in the direction of assuming that the teenager has had certain conflicts.

Most of the labor of planning the techniques in this problem is in minimizing the inferential confusion. So that a comparison will be valid, the parent and the teenager must both be responding to precisely the same questions. Probably answers which are clearly and completely structured would best do this. Also, structured answers would allow a quantitative comparison between parents and teenagers.

An example: The interviewer begins with a verbal introduction then hands the respondent a list of statements about the allowance issue to which she is to respond on a structured five-point scale.

In modern society we expect to find a wide range of ideas and opinions on many matters including how parents and teenagers view money matters. One of the points of frequent disagreement is over the teenager's spending money. Here is a list of opinions on teenagers' receiving allowances of spending money. Think in terms of what you think should be done in your own family under the usual financial situation, not in terms of some ideal time when things are more prosperous. Do not be concerned about what other parents or teenagers or your own family might think about this. We want to know how *you* personally feel about it! (*Hand list to respondent.*) Just put the number, according to the directions, in front of each statement to show how much you agree or disagree with the person making the statement.

LIST

Directions: Show how much you agree or disagree with each statement by using the following key.

1. Agree strongly.
2. Agree to some extent.
3. Not sure whether I agree or disagree.
4. Disagree to some extent.
5. Disagree strongly.

1. ___ I think teenage girls should not have any allowance from parents. If they want cash for spending money they should work for it outside the home!

2. ___ Teenage girls should have some regular allowance of spending money as long as they do certain chores around the house; but they should not be paid by the hour or by the job for working at home!

3. ___ I think that parents should give teenagers some regular allowance only if they are willing to work outside the home for part of their spending money!

4. ___ If any teenager gets a regular allowance, it should be cut off or reduced temporarily any time the teenager doesn't do as her parents tell her!

5. ___ I feel that it is all right for a teenager to borrow on future allowances to meet emergencies, as long as she pays it back every time!

6. ___ If any teenage girl gets a regular allowance she should either save some of it for the future or not get it!

7. ___ Parents should give "emergency" increases in a teenager's allowance to cover such occasions as school dances.

Directions: Show where you think the money should come from to pay for the following items used by the teenage girl.

1. The boyfriend should pay for it.
2. Girls should earn own money for this.
3. Should come from girl's regular allowance.
4. Should be given by parents in addition to regular allowance.
5. Not needed.

8. ___ buying new clothing.
9. ___ repair and cleaning of old clothing.
10. ___ snacks and meals outside of home.
11. ___ school lunches.
12. ___ money for dates.
13. ___ gasoline for car.
14. ___ damage to household items caused by teenager's carelessness.
15. How much should teenage girls get for a weekly allowance? ___
16. How much do you (or your teenage child) get? ___

Even though the techniques suggested above are highly structured, they are also highly tentative and would need extensive revision after being tried in the field.

If an interviewer is not familiar with the types of issues of economic responsibility and privilege prevalent in a population, he would need to precede the suggested structured approach with a more open-ended exploratory approach to discover the exact nature of the issue.

Problem 4—criteria for judging seriousness of conflicts. Here we must keep firmly in mind that we are not to discover whether the respondent has certain criteria that we have in mind but to discover what her own criteria happen to be. Neither are we to discover what criteria she applies to some abstract idea of parent-teenager conflict, but rather those criteria which she applies to concrete conflicts she has had with her parents in the past year.

Interpretation and specification of objectives. We will proceed on the assumption that the interviewer has been able to accumulate a sizable list of conflicts between the girl and her parents in discussing problems 1, 2, and 3. Nevertheless, some last attempt might be made to increase the list, particularly at the extremes of the most and the least serious.

Anticipating inhibitors and facilitators. The two most likely inhibitors in obtaining the criteria are *inferential confusion* and *unconscious behavior.* First, we cannot expect the respondent to correctly infer what is meant by "criteria for judging the seriousness of conflicts." Instead the interviewer must assume the responsibility for inductively deriving the criteria. Even though some respondents might be capable of giving a valid answer to the direct question, this would be rare. Often the person's report will be clouded by wishful thinking that he should have some clear rational criteria, or that the criteria should meet some ideological standards.

Second, even if the respondent clearly understood the meaning of "criteria for judging the relative seriousness of conflicts" and could recognize them if given a multiple-choice test, his own use of these criteria is mainly a form of unconscious behavior. This means that the respondent cannot be expected to report them directly but must, with the interviewer's help, inductively arrive at the criteria after noting certain specific conflicts, making judgments regarding their relative seriousness, and then discussing why one conflict was classified as "more serious" than another.

Techniques. A *context* can be provided to connect the problem of criteria to concrete conflicts already mentioned by the respondent earlier in the interview. This will make the respondent's judgments more realistic in that they will more accurately reflect the criteria used in real situations.

When referring to previously mentioned conflicts, the *vocabulary* used in the contextual statement and the question should include the exact words used by the respondent. This will help the respondent more quickly associate with the real experience.

In deciding on the *scope* of the question for trying to discover the criteria for judgment, we should be careful not to make it any narrower than necessary. We must allow for obtaining unanticipated types of criteria which might be ruled out intentionally by excluding certain dimensions or categories.

We should still avoid *structuring* the answer even though the scope is broad and the answer categories logically cover the total scope, because the respondent's categories covering the same scope might be sliced in a different way.

There is no need to use a *leading* question unless we wish to first try to discover the most serious conflict the respondent has ever had with her parents.

EXAMPLE OF APPROACH

1. You have mentioned several disagreements you have had in the past year with your parents. I have a list of them here. Let me read them to you. (Have a list of those conflicts mentioned in the interview up to this point, using the respondent's own words.) As you think back over it, were there no conflicts more serious than these?

2. Were there any less serious than these?

(*After making any additions to the list, hand the list to the respondent and ask the following questions.*)

3. Look at this list and decide which is the most serious conflict as you see it, and put an "M" in column A. Which is the least serious? Put an "L" for that one. Which is the next most serious? Put a number 2 for that one. Number the rest from 3 on down to the least serious.

(*After respondent finishes ask him for the list.*)

4. Now I would like you to explain to me why you personally feel that _____ is the most serious type of conflict.

Why is _____ the *least* serious?

Why is number 2 less serious than number 1?

(*Continue this process until all adjacent pairs are compared.*)

5. Now that you have had a chance to discuss what makes a conflict serious, could you sum it all up in a general statement on what makes one conflict more serious than another?

(*If his general statement does not seem to correspond to some of the specifics, these confusions should be cleared up if possible.*)

It should be reiterated that these sample solutions are offered to illustrate the applications of techniques to the solution of basic problems of communication in the interview. The examples should suggest other approaches. In any case it should be clear that (*a*) there are varying interpretations of each problem, (*b*) that different interpretations and even the same interpretation lead to different solutions which may be equally good, (*c*) that any solution to the problems made before the first interview should be regarded as highly tentative. However, a serious attempt to anticipate and solve potential problems will increase the interviewer's success in the long run.

SUMMARY

Silence, question forms, and attitudes are used as techniques by the interviewer to communicate the question more clearly and to increase the respondent's ability or willingness to answer it.

Silence as a technique is important because it is insurance against the negative effects of interrupting the respondent, its use helps to create the appropriate mood and pacing for stimulating the memory, it allows the respondent to take the lead and follow his own inclinations, and it can give the impression that the interviewer is interested enough in what the respondent has to say to allow him great freedom.

Among the verbal forms used as techniques are providing context with the question, selecting an appropriate wording, defining the scope of the question, structuring the answer, and using leading or non-leading questions. Providing the verbal context with a question is one technique for communicating the question more accurately to the respondent by providing definitions of terms, time perspectives, spacial perspectives, social psychological contexts, criteria and facts to be used by the respondent in making judgments. In questions where the objective is to discover the respondent's own frames of reference, definitions, criteria and perception of the facts, the interviewer must scrupulously refrain from providing the context.

Verbal context provided with the question may also motivate the respondent by arousing interest in the topic, by giving recognition to the respondent's special qualifications, reducing ego threat, preventing falsification, stimulating memory, reducing chronological confusion, and discovering unconscious subjective orientations of the respondent.

In wording the question itself the interviewer should try to use a vocabulary which is clearly understood by the respondent, which aids in establishing an optimum relationship and which does not unintentionally load the question in favor of a particular response.

The scope of a question may vary from the broad type which includes the whole topic of the interview to one which delimits some particular aspect of a particular person's behavior in relation to a particular object at a specific time and place. Broad questions are useful in discovering the respondent's paths of association, hierarchy of values, perspectives, universe of discourse, definitions of terms, perceptions of facts, and chronology of personal experiences. Under some conditions, the broad question can reduce the respondent's ego threat, stimulate his memory, give him recognition, provide sympathetic understanding, encourage catharsis, and stimulate the need for meaning. Under other conditions, the narrow question can help reduce ego threat, circumvent the etiquette barrier, and stimulate the respondent's need for meaning.

In structuring the responses, the interviewer should consider the type of information sought as well as the effects upon the respondent's motivation to give such information. The open-ended question is sometimes more useful in discovering unanticipated responses, the respondent's paths of association, his universes of discourse, perspectives, definitions of terms, hierarchy of values, and perceptions of facts. Closed questions are preferred over open ones when equally valid information can be obtained because of the greater efficiency in coding and analyzing the results.

Under certain conditions, the closed question has great motivational value. By speeding up the interviewing process and shortening the interview, the probability of encountering competing time demands is reduced. Providing answer choices reduces the size of the task for the respondent and the ego threat which might be involved when the boundaries of the response are unknown. The structured answer is useful in stimulating the respondent's memory if the correct answer is among the choices. Similarly, choices provided in chronological order may be helpful in reducing the respondent's chronological confusion.

Leading questions are those which tend to indicate that one answer is expected or preferred over another when such expectations or preferences are not based on previous information given by the respondent. The question may be loaded by associating it with a personal or impersonal context having emotional meaning to the respondent. Questions can also be loaded by providing answer categories which stack the cards in favor of a particular response. In extreme cases, the question may be loaded by an accompanying direct challenge.

In some circumstances the leading question seems to obtain more valid answers than a non-leading one. This is true when the respondent has the information clearly in mind, but tends to withhold it because it violates certain public ideals which the respondent either accepts himself or assumes that the interviewer accepts. Under these conditions, if the question leads in the direction contrary to the public ideals, it can often obtain more valid results than the non-leading question. Under other conditions, the leading question seems to have no effect; valid information is obtained in spite of its use. More common, however, are situations in which leading questions distort the response.

In addition to silence and verbal forms, the third general technique is in the interviewer's attitudes expressed toward the general task of interviewing, toward specific information given by the respondent, and toward the respondent as a person. These may all help or hinder the flow of information.

The interviewer must learn to avoid expressing surprise, shock, embarrassment, or disgust in response to any information received. He must strive to maintain a generally non-judgmental attitude toward information given by the respondent, to maintain a strong interest in the information, and to critically analyze the information in relation to the objectives of the interview. This attitude of critical analysis should be communicated to the respondent in order to prevent carelessness or fabrication in giving responses.

Negative attitudes toward the respondent as a person are frequently shown in the interviewer's errors of omission (such as forgetting a previous response and neglecting to probe in areas important to the respondent), or in his condescending tone of voice or cautious rigidity. These negative manifestations should be displaced by a strong verbal and non-verbal expression of interest in the respondent as a person rather than exclusively as a "case," a "statistic," or "source of information," and by showing appreciation of the respondent's effort to give relevant information.

Even though the interviewer may unconsciously use some of these essential techniques, their conscious mastery and application will significantly increase his interviewing success.

6
Tactics in the interview

Those *chronological patterns* of techniques in the give-and-take of the interview that are aimed at facilitating the flow of relevant information while maintaining optimum interpersonal relations with the respondent are here defined as interviewing *tactics*. Many auxiliary interviewers are responsible for all the tactical decisions in their interviewing. In large-scale survey projects all or most of the tactical decisions are planned in advance by the research director, consultants, or supervisors, leaving only a few of the tactical decisions to the judgment of the specialized interviewer. The proportion of the tactical decisions which can be legitimately frozen into the interview schedule and instructions to the interviewer depends upon the type of information sought, the types of respondents and interviewers available, and the amount of data which need to be collected. In any case it is helpful for all members of a research team to share an awareness of tactical problems and possible solutions.

ADVANCE TACTICAL PLANNING

Assuming that the interviewer knows precisely what bits of information are needed, there are several areas in which he may do advance planning. However, all of these plans must be considered as tentative in the non-scheduled interview. The interviewer must decide how many subtopics there actually are in his broad topic. He should decide which one to begin with and perhaps work out pivot questions to determine whether subsequent subtopics are relevant to the particular respondent. He might devise lead-in questions which are designed to psychologically prepare the respondent for questions which will follow but which do not intend to directly obtain information relevant to the purposes of the interview. When getting chronological material from the respondent, the interviewer must decide whether to begin the discussion precisely at that point in time relevant to the objectives of the interview or to go back further and do a lead-in designed to help the respondent reconstruct the scene and the situation immediately preceding the relevant period of time. Once the order of topics and the means of getting from one subtopic to another are decided, tentative plans must be made for developing the discussion within each subtopic area. Here the interviewer must decide on all possible alternative wordings of questions, on how contexts can be provided when needed, on alternative sequences of questions; and above all he must select some clear way of recording what has and has not been covered in the progress of the interview. The latter will be a problem particularly when the interviewer does not follow a fixed sequence of specific questions.

In addition to deciding what subtopics are needed, possible orders of these subtopics, and methods of expanding each of these subtopics to cover all of the specific information needed, the interviewer must also prepare to meet certain infrequent crises which require special treatment. For example, we might find a question which unexpectedly constitutes an ego threat to the respondent. What do we do? Or what do we do if the respondent simply says, "I'm sorry, I'm too busy now to be interviewed"? What do we do if he says, "Ask someone else who knows something about this topic; I don't know anything about it"? Or if he says he does not want to have his voice tape recorded or he stops in the middle of the interview to ask, "Why are you taking notes?" If he responds to a question by saying he does not remember or does not know, are we to take this literally? If, in response to a question, he uses the Yankee system of asking you the question, what tactics should be used? Or what if we merely suspect that the respondent is resisting, that he is not giving all the information he has and is withholding something? What can we do to test a hypothesis of this kind?

This chapter deals with these problems of arranging topics and subtopics, pivot questions, lead-in questions, and transitions; developing each topic to cover the specifications of the interview; meeting resistance by the respondent, and testing whether or not he is actually resisting. To a certain extent, successful use of tactics depends upon basic skills which have been developed, but perhaps to a larger extent it depends upon an awareness of what kinds of tactical problems might arise and planning some possible ways of meeting these problems. Once we know how to make these plans, all that remains is to practice planning for a wide variety of interviews so that required basic skills can be developed.

ARRANGING TOPICS AND SUBTOPICS WITHIN AN INTERVIEW

It is possible to have an interview so simple in its objectives that there are no topics or subtopics. The simplest possible interview might contain only one question:

"As you know, —————— and —————— are running for President of the United States. For whom do you intend to vote?" At the other extreme, an interview's objectives might include the opinions of the respondent on several public issues, certain personality traits that he might have, some of his social background characteristics such as religion, social class, political views, the amount of influence he has on others, and his position in the community. The number of topics or subtopics perceived within such a complex interview depends upon the degree of relationships between the various objectives and the level of abstraction used to hold the topics within the common frame of reference. For example, a respondent's opinion on three topics such as antivivisection, the United States' role in the United Nations, and parent-child relations in the United States might be conceived as three separate, non-related topics. However, if the objectives of the interview include discovering the respondent's personality characteristics and relating them to his opinions on selected public issues, then these three topics become merely three selected public issues and are subtopics more related to each other than to a battery of questions regarding the respondent's personality traits. This example illustrates that what might be a whole interview in one case is a topic within an interview in another case; it could also be a subtopic within a topic of another interview. Regardless of how finely we slice the total subject matter of the interview into topics, we are faced with the problem of deciding how the specific questions must be grouped into topics or subtopics and what their chronological order will be.

Chronological order of topics and subtopics

Although it is impossible to provide specific rules for determining the chronological order of subtopics within an interview, it is possible to indicate some of the most important questions that must be considered when determining the order of topics. However, these questions can be answered specifically only within the context of a particular interview problem. Too frequently, the interviewer tends to arrange the order in a purely logical fashion in order to simplify the coding and analysis of the data, or to arrange questions in a sequence that seems natural to him. Although both of these criteria are important, the criterion which has precedence over either of these is the effect upon the respondent's willingness and ability to give the relevant information. If the order which maximizes the flow of valid, relevant information is also the logical order which will minimize the problems of analyzing the data, this is fortunate. But it is not always the case.

Let us look at some examples in which the order of topics has an effect upon the flow of information.

Ego threat. Frequently one sequence of topics is more ego threatening than an alternate sequence of the same topics. If we wish to discover the relationship between a person's premarital sex behavior and his subsequent marital adjustment, the interview obviously contains a minimum of two separate topics. In this case, we might have to do several exploratory interviews to determine which of these topics seems to threaten the respondent the least. Is he more likely to withhold the details of his premarital sex behavior after discussing his marital adjustment, or vice versa?

To give another example, suppose we want to discover the relationship between the respondent's opinion on foreign aid and his religious participation. Foreign aid is an opinion topic while his religious participation (such as what his church affiliation is, how many times a year he attends, whether he participates in action projects sponsored by the church) is not. In this case, it is highly probable that the interview should first discuss the respondent's opinions on foreign aid before reminding him of his religious connections. If the procedure were reversed, there would probably be a greater tendency for the respondent to present his opinions on foreign aid as being more harmonious with his professed religious principles.

In other instances the respondent's ego is threatened by the fact that the sequence of topics is structured in a logical fashion that makes him aware that his arguments are not logical, and contain some threatening inconsistencies. For example, an interview might contain five subtopics represented by the following questions:

(1) Do you believe that the United States has sufficient military power to destroy the Russian industrial civilization?

(2) Do you think that Russia has enough military power to destroy the United States industrial civilization?

(3) Do you think that either Russia or the United States has an efficient system of defense which would prevent the other from destroying its industrial civilization in the event of an all-out atomic war?

(4) Do you think that Russia feels that the present military power of the United States is sufficient to crush her industrial civilization in the event of an all-out atomic war?

(5) Do you feel that the United States should continue to put an increasing proportion of her national wealth into augmenting her military power?

It is highly probable that the respondent who feels that the United States should continue increasing its military power would feel threatened in stating this opinion if the question were preceded by the other four as suggested above. It is possible that such a respondent would find himself in the position of saying that the purpose of armaments and military power from the point of view of the United States is to deter Russia from attacking. He may also feel that we have enough military power to destroy the Russian industrial civilization and that Russians believe that we have such power. Furthermore, he may feel that there is no way for either Russia or the United States to defend themselves against an all-out atomic attack of the other. In view of these premises, he might find it quite difficult to justify his feeling that we should continue to increase the military power of the United States.

Stimulating the memory. It is often possible for the sequence of topics to have an effect upon the respondent's recall of relevant detail, and subsequently upon the possibility of chronological or inferential confusion clouding his reports.

There are several remedies for this. For example, the respondent might be asked to give the most easily recalled facts first. These may be more easily recalled because they happened more recently or because they were more ego-involved for the respondent. In an interview to determine the relationship between student adjustment to a field of study and the factors which influenced him to pursue this field, it might be preferable to begin by discussing his adjustment to the field in which he is presently engaged. After this has been developed sufficiently, an abrupt transition could be made to the question of how he decided to enter the field. (Reasons for using either abrupt or smooth transitions from one topic to another will be discussed later in the chapter.)

In this case, it is clear that discussing the person's adjustment in his field of endeavor is inevitably going to bring about certain associations with how he got into the field and how things actually were in the field compared to his expectations. When shifting to the second topic of how he decided to go into the field, every effort must be made by the interviewer to help the respondent overcome chronological confusion by distinguishing between his reasons for preferring the field now that he is in it and his initial reasons which involved preliminary perceptions and expectations.

It is also possible to minimize the problem of inferential confusion in an interview having two distinctly different kinds of topics, one which asks the person for specific factual details about certain events or a certain period of time and another topic which asks the person for his judgments, opinions, or overall perspectives on these events or period of time. In this case, it is highly probable that a more accurate account of the person's overall feelings and views can be obtained if we first develop the detailed facts of the events. In this way, the respondent is allowed to review in detail with the help of the interviewer the specific factual events which have to be considered in order to make a valid overall judgment of the situation.

Maximizing facilitators. If we wish to get off to a good start in the interview and build rapport, it is often helpful to begin with a particular subtopic that maximizes the amount of recognition to be given to the respondent or which gives him a chance to obtain sympathetic understanding or catharsis, or to begin with a topic that stimulates his need for meaning and raises questions that arouse his interest.

In some complex interviews, there may be three or four topics that would have great natural interest for the respondent and another three or four that would be quite boring or inconsequential for him. Sometimes it is helpful to alternate between one type of topic and another.

Varying the sequence of topics with the respondent. In some cases, it is quite clear that one sequence of topics is better for maximizing the flow of information and maintaining optimum interpersonal relations than another and that this optimum sequence would be the same for all respondents. In other cases, it may be apparent that the optimum sequence varies from respondent to respondent, depending upon the nature of each respondent's particular relationship to the topic or his particular experience. It may be necessary to do exploratory interviews to know whether we can use a fixed sequence of topics or whether we should allow it to vary to fit the needs of a particular respondent.

There are several ways in which the interviewer can allow the respondent to select his own sequence. The first way is simply to begin the interview with a broad question covering all the topics and subtopics and then allow the respondent to begin where he chooses. Once he finishes the subtopic with which he began, the same general question or another slightly narrowed may be asked, allowing him to pursue any of the remaining subtopics. For example, in interviewing disaster victims, we needed to know what the person actually *observed* during the crisis period, what he *did* during the crisis period both to protect himself and to help others, what he thought about what was going on, and numerous subtopics covering the later phase of relief and rehabilitation which may have lasted for days or weeks. The subtopics of the crisis period could be introduced by the general question, "Tell me what happened to you in the storm." The subtopics related to the relief and rehabilitation period could be introduced by the broad question, "Tell me about some of the relief work that went on after the storm was all over."

Another means of giving the respondent the choice of topic sequence is to simply announce at the beginning that you are going to cover three or four topics and give the respondent his choice as to where he should begin, as in this example:

Metropolitan Studies is interested in your opinion on three issues which are being discussed on the local scene. The first is the antivivisection issue; the second is the issue of metropolitan government; and the third is the juvenile delinquency wave. With which of these would you like to begin?

A third general tactic for allowing the respondent to discuss topics in his own sequence is to use a pivot question to introduce a new topic area. This method is discussed in detail in the following section.

Introducing each topic

Once we have decided whether or not we can predetermine the order of topics and if so how, we need to consider how each new topic or subtopic can best be introduced.

Using lead-in questions.   A lead-in question is one that is not directly relevant to the objectives of the interview but which has the function of effectively leading the respondent to a relevant question area in a way that prepares him to give more accurate and valid information. In some cases, where none of the questions seems to be of any great interest to the respondent, it is helpful to ask a preliminary question that is interesting to him and also related to the topics which follow. This we might call the interest lead-in question.

For example, in a study of the differences in the amount of interaction between the child, his family and the school in high and low delinquency areas of a large city, the opening question was, "Do you think this neighborhood is a good or a bad place to raise kids?" This question seemed to appeal to heads of households in both types of areas and gave the interviewer an opportunity to build rapport by showing his interest in the problems of child-rearing in the area. This easily led to questions about the amount and type of interaction between child and parents, then between parents and the school.

Another type of lead-in question is the chronological lead-in. This is a question regarding a point or period in time which precedes the period relevant to the objectives of the interview. This type of warm-up question gives the respondent a chance to get in a reminiscent mood which stimulates recall of a particular period of time. It also prevents chronological confusion by having the respondent looking forward in his mind to a bit of the past rather than looking back at it from the perspective of the present. For example, if we are interested in an employee's view of management's handling of an educational meeting for the employees, it might be well to introduce the topic with a question such as, "When did you first know there was going to be a special meeting for the employees?" This question might be followed by other lead-in questions such as, "Where was the meeting held?" "Who did you go to the meeting with?" These questions all establish a specific, concrete feeling of the past and lead the respondent up to the point of evaluating the meeting itself.

Another function of the lead-in question is to establish an appropriate atmosphere by allowing the interviewer to display the proper attitudes toward the respondent and toward a subject matter closely related to the relevant information. For example, if the purpose of the interview is to discover problems North American students have adjusting to their Colombian host families, the interview with the Colombian *señora* could begin with a lead-in question or lead-in topic about problems *other señoras* have had with their North American guests.

All types of lead-in questions (or statements that imply a question) share one characteristic. The information sought by the lead-in question is not going to be used in the analysis of the data because it is not directly relevant to the objectives of the interview.

Using pivot questions. A pivot question acts as a turning point in the line of questioning by determining which of two or more possible new topics would apply to the particular respondent. The pivot question is sometimes called a "filter question," particularly when used in a questionnaire. Whenever we introduce a new topic for discussion in an interview, we usually make certain assumptions regarding the appropriateness of the new line of questioning. We assume that the respondent has had the appropriate experiences (*a*) to understand the question and (*b*) to have some relevant information. The pivot question is an attempt to test these assumptions before proceeding with the next topic.

We cannot always anticipate the need for pivot questions in advance simply because we are not aware of the assumptions we are making regarding the experiences of the respondent. It is often necessary, therefore, to do some exploratory non-scheduled interviews to determine the type and location of needed pivot questions. In this phase, the interviewer instead of using predetermined pivot questions must be constantly alert for unanticipated pivot *responses* which indicate a need for a change in the line of questioning.

For example, in the study of academic freedom mentioned previously, it was assumed that restrictions of academic freedom would center about controversial issues in economics and politics, particularly as they related to Communism. It was discovered that in a small minority of colleges, political issues had neither arisen nor been repressed. Instead, the main issues involved conflicts between fundamentalistic religious beliefs and the findings of the biological and social sciences. A professor might be threatened with dismissal if he insisted upon discussing Darwin's theory of evolution in a biology course. Only in interviewing a professor at such a college did it become apparent that the study of academic freedom had been based upon the assumption that such controversies between science and religion were no longer live issues on college campuses.

Similarly, in interviewing respondents living in disaster stricken communities, the interviewer would often assume that because the respondent was a resident of the community he would be able to give information on the disaster's effects on the community. In some cases, this was proved incorrect because (*a*) the respondent was out of town the day the disaster struck, (*b*) he was immediately rendered unconscious before he was aware of any approaching crisis, or (*c*) he completely withdrew from the situation and made no attempt to discover what had happened or to help any one. The respondent was usually willing to give information regarding (*a*) or (*b*) but would sometimes attempt to prevent the interviewer from discovering (*c*). In this situation, much confusion could be avoided if the interviewer would ask, "Where were you when the storm stuck Judsonia?" If the respondent had been in Judsonia at the time, another pivot question could follow: "Were you injured in any way?" If the respondent had been in Judsonia and was not injured, then a series of questions on his participation in the immediate rescue operations became relevant. The interviewer might have these specific pivot questions in mind and obtain the answers without directly asking each question. In any case, it was helpful for the interviewer to know whether he was talking to a rescuer or to one of the rescued.

Although a small number of exploratory interviews might discover all of the pivot questions that are needed, it is often impossible or impractical to do the amount of exploratory interviews needed in order to completely eliminate any surprises regarding the assumptions made. Therefore, in any interview that is complicated by several topics and subtopics, the interviewer will need to be alert for clues indicating that some lines of questioning are not applicable to a particular respondent. The preplanning of pivot questions is even less feasible when interviewing only one or two persons from each category of special respondents.

Providing transitions. Once we have decided upon the order of topics or subtopics and have located the points where pivot questions can determine the appropriateness of a new topic or subtopic, our next problem is to determine whether it is necessary to provide specific material to act as a bridge from one topic to another. There are at least three reasons for providing a special transition:

a) It may be needed to show the respondent the relationship between the old and the new topic in order to help him maximize any advantages in the particular sequence of topics.

b) It may relate the new topic to the basic objectives of the interview so that the respondent may not become confused or suspicious that the "real purpose" of the interview was not stated in the original explanation.

c) It may be needed to emphasize a change in frame of reference, perspective, or mood so that the respondent will not carry over an inappropriate context from a previous topic.

Let us give an example of transitions fulfilling each of these three functions.

In a study of the effects of foreign travel, we included the following five topics in the order indicated:

1) The respondent's specific experiences abroad within the past two years.

2) The effects of these experiences in *changing* his views of the foreign country.

3) The effects of these experiences in *changing* his views of his own country.

4) Courses taken in college that influenced the meaningfulness of the foreign experience.

5) Certain personality traits that might affect the respondent's adjustment to the foreign culture.

In the first few exploratory interviews it was discovered that the respondent usually did not make the correct connection between topics (1) and (2). His tendency was often to merely talk about interesting experiences he had abroad under the first topic and then forget to make any connection between these experiences and specific *changes* in his views of the foreign country. It was found helpful to provide the following transition:

You have told me about many of your experiences abroad which you found outstanding. Now that you have had a chance to think about your experiences in Germany, let us move on to a more difficult topic. I would like to know how any of these experiences you have mentioned or any others you might recall changed your views on Germany, the German people, or their culture. It is sometimes helpful to think of those things which surprised you because they were not what you expected or those which seemed to give you a more positive or negative feeling toward the country. Which of your experiences seemed to change your views on Germany?

Even with this transition aimed at making a connection between specific experiences and changes in beliefs or attitudes, there was still a tendency for the respondent to begin discussing his current views on the foreign country without stating whether these were new views gained by his recent experience or whether they were old views held before going abroad. The interviewer had to be constantly alert to establish which views represented *changes* and which specific experiences were associated with these changes. Needless to say, the respondent often found it difficult to link a particular change to a particular experience. In any case, providing the transition made it easier for the respondent to see the second topic in its proper perspective and reduced the number of times the interviewer had to redirect the respondent toward the objectives of the interview.

The second function of the transition as described in (*b*) above can also be illustrated with this same interview. Most interviewers discovered in the first exploratory interview that a transition was needed between topics (4) and (5). Since the first four topics had all obviously dealt with effects of foreign travel, specific questions under the fifth topic seemed out of place to the respondent. For example, questions like the following needed some transition:

In a group discussion do you usually tend to be one of the listeners or one who does much of the talking?

Do you enjoy making introductions at a party when you discover that some of the people aren't acquainted with each other?

Without some special attention to topic transition, these questions may seem so out of context to the respondent that he becomes suspicious that the whole interview "is really an indirect attempt to psychoanalyze me." As one respondent put it, "I thought you said you were interested in the affects of foreign experience, but now it looks like you forgot to bring your couch along." This suspicion can be avoided by a transitional statement such as the one that follows:

It is claimed by some people interested in this problem that the same foreign experience would have very different effects upon two people with different basic personality traits. I am going to ask you 10 simple straightforward questions about the type of person you think you are.

This transitional statement proved helpful in allaying suspicion about the relevance of the final 10 questions and also signaled to the respondent that the questions were not intended to be deep or devious.

The third function of the transitional statement described in (*c*) above is perhaps the most frequent. When two consecutive topics involve different but related frames of reference which might become confused in the respondent's mind, it is necessary to make a complete break between the two topics so that the old frame of reference is not unconsciously retained in the new topic. For example, in a study of factors influencing college students' choice of a vocation, college seniors were interviewed to determine: (*a*) the occupational field they had chosen and the extent to which they were sure of their choice; (*b*) their conception of the ideal way of making a living; and (*c*) the compromises with reality students made in selecting an occupation. In the exploratory interviews it was discovered that the respondents found it difficult to shift from the realistic frame of reference in the first topic (*a*) to the "ideal" frame of reference called for by the second topic (*b*). There was a tendency for the students not to want anything obviously beyond their reach. In some cases, it might have been a bit ego threatening to be reminded of the differences between one's realistic plans and one's ideal. The following transitional statement, however, helped encourage the respondent to relinquish his realism and to more enthusiastically discuss the idealistic conceptions called for in the second topic.

You have given me a clear idea of what you want to do vocationally after you graduate, and I get the feeling that you are very realistic and clear in your plans. Now I would like you to just let yourself go, throw realism to the winds and talk about what you see as the *ideal* way of making a living. By ideal, I simply mean that you are to consider only what you would *enjoy* doing for a living. Assume that there would be no question of your having the ability or talent needed, no problems in obtaining the necessary training, the job paid well and had high status in the world. The only taint of reality which I want you to retain is in limiting yourself to choosing some type of job which really exists. So take your pick, what type of job would you enjoy most assuming that you could obtain such a job and were capable of holding it?

This preliminary statement helped the respondent make a transition into the mood needed to encourage such unrealistic talk. Once the respondent caught the spirit and realized that the interviewer was not going to judge him for his lack of realism, it was not difficult for him to relinquish the realism of the previous topic. After the second topic was carefully explored, the respondent was brought back to reality by being asked what real limitations prevented him from aspiring to his ideal job.

In the above examples we have emphasized those situations where special care must be taken in making a transition either to maintain a connection between two topics, to show the relevance of a new topic, or to abruptly sever the connection between one topic and the next to prevent carrying over an inappropriate frame of reference. In some cases, however, the flow of the topics is such that no particular care must be taken in making the transitions because all of the topics obviously fall within the interview objectives, the relationship of each topic is obvious to the respondent, and each topic happily provides an appropriate background or frame of reference for the subsequent one. This lack of any need for special transitional statements is sometimes referred to as the "smooth" or the "natural" transition that can be achieved by merely arranging the topics in the correct order.

Preparing an interview guide

To clarify the meaning of "interview guide," let us compare it with two related instruments, the interview schedule and the questionnaire. Theoretically, the *questionnaire* has built-in all of the techniques and tactics of gathering the relevant information, so that nothing is left for the interviewer to do. The questionnaire may be either mailed to the respondent or handed to him in person, and it is supposed to be completely sufficient in specifying what information is relevant and in motivating the respondent to write in the information.

An *interview schedule,* as the questionnaire, specifies the questions to be asked, fixes their wording, supplies contexts where the need is anticipated, and determines the degree of answer structure to be supplied by the interviewer. Here, the interviewer is still necessary. He is needed from time to time (1) to clarify the intent of the question, (2) to probe for any clarification or elaboration of the responses so as to meet the objectives of the interview, and (3) to motivate the respondent by demonstrating appropriate attitudes toward the interviewing task, the information received, or the respondent himself.

An *interview guide* is used in the non-scheduled interview. In contrast to the interview schedule, which emphasizes the means of obtaining information, the interview guide emphasizes the *goals* of the interview in terms of the topics to be explored and the criteria of a relevant and adequate response. The interview guide is like the interview schedule in that it provides the framework for recording the responses or for keeping a running inventory of which objectives have been met and which ones have not. Thus the interview guide provides the interviewer with a conceptual map of the areas to be covered and a convenient way of recording the progress of the interview.

In actual practice, plans made by the interviewer may fall at some point between the interview guide, which provides only the *goals,* and the interview schedule, which provides the *complete means* to the objectives of the interview. To give a typical example, an interview guide might contain not only the list of topics to be covered but also a tentative sequence for covering them, alternative wordings of some specific questions, notes indicating where contexts and transitions should be supplied, and possible sequences of detailed questions within topics which may or may not be needed in each interview.

It is advisable, even in an apparently simple interview topic, to prepare an interview guide before approaching the first respondent. This is fruitful even though it may be necessary to change the guide or to structure it in greater detail as a result of experience. In some cases, it is possible and desirable for the interviewer to memorize the interview guide. In other cases, the guide might be memorized except for an answer sheet upon which the respondent's open-ended answers are coded during the interview.

Thus far, we have examined some of the tactical problems in determining the optimum sequence of topics within an interview and of introducing new topics with lead-ins, pivot questions, and transitional statements. Let us now examine the tactical problems of guiding and motivating the respondent toward the objectives of a particular topic. Here we will spell out some of the basic question patterns which can be used to develop a topic.

GENERAL PATTERNS OF QUESTIONS FOR DEVELOPING A TOPIC

It is usually not sufficient for the interviewer simply to have an interview guide listing the general objectives and subtopics of an interview, and then to ask only one question per topic. The interviewer must be constantly alert to guide the respondent toward the objectives of each topic by supplying any additional statements or questions to obtain further clarification or elaboration needed to meet the objectives of the interview. These additional questions, which are not specified in advance for all respondents but which the interviewer sees are needed to obtain more exact information, are usually referred to as "probes."

In this section we will deal with some of the basic patterns of questions that can often be employed in developing a topic to minimize the necessity for probing, and in the next section we will discuss several patterns of probing, showing their strengths and weaknesses.

The two general patterns of questions to be dealt with here are the "funnel sequence" and the "inverted funnel sequence." Each is useful under certain specified conditions that may usually be determined in advance of a particular interview. Both of these sequences are patterns of question-scope described as a technique in the preceding chapter.

The funnel sequence

In the funnel sequence each successive question has a narrower *scope* than the previous one and is either included within or related to the previous question. This type of sequence may characterize the whole interview as a unit, but it is more likely to occur within particular topics or subtopics of the interview.

For example, if we were interested in discovering how people's views of social problems are related to the magazines they read, we might want to know what sorts of things the respondent thinks of as social problems, the relative seriousness of each, the amount of information he has on the subject, the sources of his information, and whether certain magazines have influenced his thinking on the problem. If we were to ask the following questions, the sequence given below would be a funnel sequence.

(1) What do you think are some of the most important social problems in the world today, and why?

(2) Of all the problems you have just mentioned, which one do you think is the most important one to solve?

(3) Where have you gotten most of your information about problem X?

(4) Do you read *U.S. News and World Report?*

The above example might be more accurately described as two funnel sequences, since the scope of question (2) is clearly within that of question (1), and the scope of question (4) falls within question (3), but it is not clear that the scope of question (3) falls within that of question (2).

There are several situations in which the funnel sequence will avoid tactical problems and minimize the need for probing. We will discuss the four most important ones.

a) When the objective of the interview is to obtain a detailed description of an event or situation and when the respondent is motivated to give a spontaneous account of his experiences in that situation, then introducing the topic with the broadest question will often eliminate the need for asking myriad, detailed questions.

Under the above conditions it is more efficient if we can avoid asking every detailed question, also it is often more conducive to good interpersonal relations, since the interviewer interrupts the respondent less and is apparently interested in whatever is important to the respondent. Of course, there is always the danger of the broad question allowing the respondent to roam too far afield, but the alert interviewer can prevent this with fewer interruptions than if he had to ask every minute question.

For example, if we wish to know hundreds of details regarding a person's experience when his town was struck by a tornado, we could either begin by asking detailed questions such as, "Were you home when the tornado struck?" "Did you see the black funnel approaching before it struck?" "What did it do to your house?" "Are you married?" "Do you have any children?" "Were any of your immediate family injured?" "Were you injured?" "Did anyone help you after the tornado passed?" "Did you help anyone else?" "Were you able to take anyone to the hospital?" This approach would be much less efficient and much less likely to give the respondent an opportunity for recognition, sympathetic understanding, and catharsis, or to fulfill his need for meaning than if the interviewer had simply asked, "What happened to you in the storm?" This question is not only broad, it puts the spotlight on the respondent's experiences and allows him to tell his own story in his own way. It shows that the interviewer is interested in the respondent and his experiences rather than in countless details.

b) Under the conditions specified in (*a*) above, the funnel approach helps the respondent to recall details more efficiently since he is allowed to report them by following his own paths of association.

By giving the respondent greater freedom at the beginning, it is not necessary to interrupt his train of thought constantly to ask hundreds of specific details in an order which might be meaningless or disorganized from the respondent's point of view.

c) By asking the broadest questions first, the interviewer can avoid imposing a perspective or frame of reference upon the discussion before obtaining the respondent's perspective.

Once the respondent's perspective is discovered, the specific questions can be asked within this framework. Then the detailed questions could be worded to conform to the respondent's universe of discourse. Or it could be used where the broader question would allow the respondent to show the sequence in which he had certain experiences; the more detailed questions would then deal with each experience in order.

d) When the objectives of the interview are both to *discover* unanticipated responses and to *measure* the frequency of responses to certain anticipated categories, then the discovery function achieved by the broader question should be pursued first.

For example, we might wish to discover the variety of reasons people have for wanting to go abroad, regardless of where they would like to go. If we also wanted to measure the relative frequency of people's preferences for Mexico, Germany, and France as a place to go, then the questions should be dealt with in that order. In this case, the funnel would consist in the sequence of the two objectives or subtopics, rather than in a sequence of specific questions. The first objective would probably have to be pursued with many questions and probes before moving on to the second which could be achieved with one well-worded question.

The inverted funnel sequence

Under the heading, "Scope of the question," the preceding chapter discussed the conditions under which the narrow question is preferable to the broad question. That discussion considered only the isolated question. Here we will restrict the discussion to cases where a *pattern* of narrower questions followed by broader ones should be used. The phrase "inverted funnel" is borrowed from Kahn and Cannell.[1]

There are at least two kinds of situations in which detailed questions should be followed by broader questions.

a) When the topic of the interview is one which does not strongly motivate the respondent to speak spontaneously either because the relevant experiences are not important to him or not recent enough to be vivid in his memory, it is often helpful to begin with the narrower questions and reserve the broader ones until later.

It seems that the more specific questions are easier to answer than the more general ones when the respondent does not have strong positive motivation to speak on the topic. Often a respondent's feeling of inadequacy can be dispelled if he starts successfully with the simpler tasks and receives praise.

This inverted funnel often motivates the respondent to take an interest in the topic if the initial, specific questions stimulate his need for meaning. This form of intellectual seduction is most successful when the specific questions can be readily answered but where the answers themselves are either contradictory, inconsistent, or unsatisfactory to the respondent for some reason. The logic of his answers may violate his value system. These initial disturbances of his mental equilibrium may rouse the respondent from his complacency and stimulate him to respond more wholeheartedly to broader and more profound questions.

The second situation calling for the inverted funnel deals with the problem of avoiding inferential confusion.

b) If the objective of the interview is to obtain a generalization in the form of a judgment regarding some concrete situation, and if the facts of the situation are unknown to the interviewer but are known to the respondent, then the narrower questions aimed at establishing specific facts should precede the request for an overall judgment.

Two kinds of situations require the inverted funnel tactic to avoid inferential confusion. The first, mentioned by Kahn and Cannell, is the case where the respondent has no strong feeling regarding the topic or does not have a previously formulated judgment of the type sought in the interview. The interviewer's task is to help the respond-

1/ Robert L. Kahn and Charles F. Cannell, *The Dynamics of Interviewing* (New York: John Wiley & Sons, 1957), p. 160.

ent formulate a generalization by making inferences from specific facts.

In the second type of case, the respondent may have very definite feelings on the topic and a previously formulated judgment based upon prejudice rather than the facts of the case. Here, the interviewer aims at preventing the respondent from stating his prejudicial judgment before reviewing the facts of the case. Once the respondent has stated his position to the interviewer, any attempt to change it constitutes an ego threat. By first reviewing the facts in detail, the respondent is allowed an opportunity to change his position without appearing to have been influenced by the interviewer.

The latter type of problem was encountered in attempts to obtain a respondent's judgment regarding the effectiveness of the rescue operations during a disaster. There was a prejudice that became strongly fixed two or three days after a major disaster that made people say that the rescue operations were carried out with miraculous speed and effectiveness. This was particularly true in communities where no organized agency involving outsiders was participating in the rescue operation. In this case, it was better to deal with the specifics first, later asking for the generalization:

1) How many people were killed in the tornado?

2) How many do you suppose were injured so seriously that they had to go to the hospital?

3) Was there a need for blood transfusions at the hospital the next morning?

4) How do you think that most of the people died (electrocution, internal injuries, brain concussions, bleeding, asphyxia, or what other cause)?

5) How long was it before most of the injured got to the hospital?

6) Did you see anyone administer first aid by giving artificial respiration or stopping bleeding? Who was it?

7) Did you have an opportunity to give any first aid yourself? If so, what kind?

8) In general, how well do you think the first aid and rescue operations were carried out?

If this eighth question were asked first, the respondent had a tendency to base the generalization on wishful thinking. He was glad to be alive, and began to feel that it was miraculous that only 50 people were killed in a town of 3,000 where 90 percent of the buildings had been demolished. With this context in mind, his response was that the first aid and rescue operation was something close to a miracle.

However, if the general question were preceded by the seven more specific questions, the respondent's account of the rescue operation would show that people were dug out of the rubble, and the seriously injured laid in rows beside the road waiting for it to be cleared so a truck or ambulance could get through. Once a victim was lined up for the ambulance, the rescuers would go back to dig someone else out. It was rainy and cold; there was often a lapse of one or two hours before a person could be taken to the hospital, and in the meantime the respondent had neither seen nor heard of anyone stopping bleeding or giving other first aid. When this picture began to emerge, the respondent became acutely aware that many people must have bled to death or died of shock while lying in the rain.

In this case, the inverted funnel sequence had the effect of making the respondent able to give a more realistic assessment of the situation, but the ego threat involved in the awful conclusion based upon the evidence the respondent himself had given would often reduce his willingness to verbalize what he had on his mind and subject the respondent to an unnecessary shock. In this case, since the objective was not to have the respondent himself assess the factual evidence, the evidence given by the respondent could be assessed by the interviewer and the last general question omitted. In order to further protect the respondent's ego and avoid a possible breakdown in the rapport, the first five questions in the series could be asked of the hospital officials who would not blame themselves for not having given artificial respiration or having stopped bleeding in the few minutes after the disaster struck. This example illustrates how a specific tactical pattern may be technically effective, but in certain situations have an unfortunate side effect when tested in the field.

We have shown some of the conditions under which the use of the funnel or the inverted funnel pattern can solve certain tactical problems. Regardless of the way the relative scope of questions is arranged in the interview, there still remains a certain amount of probing to be done to adequately meet the objectives. The next section will deal with types of probes according to their tactical relationship to information previously given by the respondent.

272   *Interviewing: strategy, techniques, and tactics*

PROBING TO MEET THE OBJECTIVES OF THE INTERVIEW

Even though the interviewer makes an appropriate transition to a new topic, asks a well-chosen question introducing the topic, and has planned a pattern of subsequent questions to cover the topic, there is often a need to elicit further clarification or elaboration on the first question before moving on to the next. This is particularly true at the beginning of a funnel sequence where the first question is broad in scope. Once the interviewer has developed understanding of the objectives of the interview and is critically evaluating the responses in terms of these objectives, he becomes aware of the inadequacies of many responses. His perception of the discrepancy between the content of the response and the information needed urges him to probe the respondent for further elaboration and clarification. *Most of the tactical problems of interviewing center around the problem of using the right type of probe at the right time.*

The neophyte interviewer will often ask relevant questions and dutifully record the respondent's reply but his most common weakness is in not realizing that the response is inadequate for the purposes of the interview, or in not knowing how to obtain further information. In the first case, he may move from question to question with ritualistic calm, ignorant of his failure. In the second case, he may move on in panic, not knowing what else to do, or in his attempt to elicit further information, he may actually suggest responses.

To avoid the meager results of the innocent ritualistic plodding or of the panicky flight through the interview, the interviewer must not only be intimately acquainted with the specific objectives of the interview, but also must be able to use skillfully a variety of probing tools when the initial response does not meet the objectives of the question.

The concept of probing is usually used to refer to those attempts of the interviewer to obtain a more relevant, complete or clear answer to the immediately preceding question. This means that the probing must be done at the discretion of the interviewer; it depends upon his judgment whether the response was adequate to meet the objectives or not. If not, he must decide on the nature of the inadequacy and then probe to obtain more relevant information in a way which will make sense in view of what the respondent has already said and elicit more relevant information without suggesting any specific response.

In the fixed-schedule interview, probing is usually restricted to those attempts of the interviewer to obtain a more relevant, complete or clear answer to the immediately preceding question.

To illustrate probing within the scheduled interview the example below shows the relationship between the objective of a question, the actual wording of the question, probing instructions, and some inadequate responses that would require probing to meet the objectives.

Objectives (Specified in the instructions to the interviewer)
> Question 7: Since the shooting of Senator Robert F. Kennedy there have been various attempts to legislate restrictions on the sale and possession of firearms to private citizens. We want to know how people now feel on this topic six months after the assassination without being reminded by the interviewer of the use of guns to assassinate public figures. We are interested in discovering *what* the respondent thinks *should* be done in this controversial area. We are not interested in what he thinks *others* want to have done, nor in *why* he feels something should be done, nor in *how* he thinks it could be done.

The question (The seventh question in the interview schedule)
> 7. What do you think should be done, if anything, to regulate the sale of guns and rifles and other firearms to private citizens?

Possible probing instructions (Immediately following the question)
> *a*) Probe (for what respondent thinks should be done)
> *b*) Probe if needed
> What do *you*, personally, think should be done?
> Should anything be done or not?
> What, for example, should be done?
> Should anything else be done?

Some inadequate responses which need to be probed
> *a*) I really think it is time to do something about it!
> *b*) There has been a lot of talk about that lately.
> *c*) I agree, something should be done quickly!
> *d*) I hope something will be done but I doubt if it can.
> *e*) The gun manufacturers aren't going to like any change.
> *f*) The NRA (National Rifle Association) would object.
> *g*) I personally feel the federal government should do something.
> *h*) I haven't the foggiest notion what can be done.

An examination of this small sample of inadequate responses shows that it is impossible to specify the exact probes to meet every possible form of inadequate answer. Instead, the interviewer must have the objectives clearly in mind, carefully listen to evaluate the relevance and adequacy of the response, then probe to help the respondent provide more relevant information without restricting, distorting or suggesting answers.

Topic control

When the objectives are more exploratory and the schedule less fixed, the interviewer has a broader responsibility in probing.[2] In this case he is free to decide whether he should probe to clarify the response to a particular question before going on to the next or to take a probe note at the time and wait until later to probe to avoid inhibiting the respondent's momentum or interrupting his chain of associations. In the less structured interview, then, the probe may concern the immediately preceding response or any of the preceding responses. The following situation is one in which the interview is not scheduled. It illustrates the need for a wider range of probing tools. This full range of probing we call "topic control."

A lawyer is questioning in his office a possible witness to an accident in which his client has been involved. He is trying to reconstruct the scene and assess the evidence for guilt.[3]

I: I need your help in getting a clearer picture of the accident. Could you tell me in your own words what happened? (1)

R: Well, actually I didn't see much. (3) I just came out of Kronsky's pool hall when I heard some brakes screeching, and the cars plowed into each other at the corner.

At this point the interviewer can do a variety of things. The choices are endless, and the progress of the interview will depend upon the alternative chosen by the interviewer at this point. Among the many possible forms of probes are the following:

I: *a*) Whose fault was it?
　　 b) Where is Kronsky's exactly?
　　 c) Just what did you see of the accident?
　　 d) Tell me a little more about it.
　　 e) Pause for three or four seconds

Here, the range of probes varies. The most topic control is (*a*) where

---

2/ Barbara Snell Dohrenwend and Stephen A. Richardson, "Directiveness and Non-Directiveness in Research Interviewing: A Reformulation of the Problem," *Psychological Bulletin,* Vol. 63 No. 5 (1963), pp. 475-85. This is a useful step forward in the conceptualization of the idea of directiveness in interviewing.

3/ The numbers in parentheses indicate the number of seconds of silence.

the focus of the discussion is shifted from "what happened" to "whose fault it was." This probe also demands a *specific* answer to what might be a highly complex question. The lowest degree of topic control is (*e*) which is a "silent probe." The success of this silence depends upon whether the respondent is actually intending to continue his story without waiting for a specific question and upon the interviewer's ability to show an interested, expectant attitude. It should be noted that the silent probe, if successful, allows the respondent to continue in the same trend of thought, to elaborate some previous response in greater detail, or to change the topic completely.

Probe (*b*) does not shift the focus outside the scope of the previous response, but narrows it to a specific detail, the location of Kronsky's pool hall. Probe (*c*) controls the topic less than (*b*) because it refers to the general area the respondent is already talking about and allows him to select the particular details he wants to mention. Probe (*d*) exercises even less topic control than (*c*) because it does not narrow the boundaries of the discussion to what the respondent *saw;* thus, probe (*d*) would allow him to continue his story, regardless of whether it dealt with what he had or had not seen, felt, heard, or inferred.

The examples of the opinion-poll interviewer and the lawyer illustrate how the variety of probing tactics the interviewer is allowed to use is greater as the interview is less structured by a fixed schedule. Of the seven types of topic control defined below, the first four can be used in both fixed-schedule and unscheduled interviews; the remaining three can be used only in less structured interviews.

Types of topic control. At this point we are not yet concerned with which of the possible probes would be the most productive, but are merely illustrating what is meant by degrees of topic control. In order to be able to discuss this aspect of interviewing technique, we list the following categories of topic control ranked in order of the degree of control with (1) representing the least control. This rank order usually, but not always, holds true since it sometimes depends upon the *context* in which the probe occurs. The interviewer should learn to recognize and to manage his own tendency to control either too strongly or weakly.

1. *Silent probe.* The silent probe is a very useful technique which will allow the respondent to proceed in whatever direction is most interesting and meaningful to him. In a sense, it is the most neutral of all possible probes because it neither designates the area of the discussion nor structures the answer in any

way. The interviewer must learn to distinguish between the "permissive pause," which is often very productive and the "embarrassing silence," which can be damaging to rapport.

2. *Encouragement.* This category includes all remarks, non-verbal noises, and gestures which indicate that the interviewer accepts what has been said and wishes the respondent to continue speaking without in any way specifying *what* the respondent should talk about. This includes such things as: "uh huh," "really," "I see," "hmmm," "is that so!" a nod of the head, or an expectant facial expression.

3. *Immediate elaboration.* The interviewer may go beyond encouraging the respondent to continue speaking by indicating that he would like the respondent to elaborate upon the topic at hand, whatever that topic may be. A request for elaboration may take several forms. First, elaboration might imply a need for continuing the "story" or finishing the trend of thought. This would include such probes as, ". . . and then?" "Then what happened?" "What happened next?" Note that the interviewer is not asking for anything specific. Second, the elaboration might not imply a "moving on" with the story, but merely requests the respondent to say more about the topic at hand. For example: "Tell me more." "Tell me more about that." "Would you like to tell me a little more about that?" "What else could you say about that?" "Is there anything you would like to add?" "Could you spell that out a little more?" "Would you please elaborate on that?"

4. *Immediate clarification.* The clarification probe not only asks for more information on the topic under discussion, but it also specifies the kind of additional information that is needed. A request for clarification may take many specific forms of two general types. First, the interviewer might request that the respondent give a more detailed *sequence* of events, beginning at a certain point in the action described in the immediately preceding response. For example: "What happened right after you opened the door?" "Where were you just before the lights went out?" "What happened that night after you got home?" Second, the interviewer might probe for more detailed information on some specific aspect, rather than some particular period of time. This would include such probes as: *"When* did that happen?" *"How* did you find out about that?" "How did you *feel* when you saw the building collapse?" *"Why* do you suppose they did that?"

5. *Retrospective elaboration.* In this type of probe, the interviewer indicates a general interest in a topic that has been mentioned by the respondent some time previous to the immediately preceding response, but he does not specify *what* he wants to know about that topic. For example: "A while ago you said that your mother didn't want you to go out with girls when you were 15 years old. Could you tell me more about that?" "Let's go back to the point where you had the argument with your high school chemistry teacher; tell me more about that." Note that the form of these probes is in essence the same as those under

(3) above. The difference is that the topic referred to is *not* contained in the immediately preceding response but was further back in the interview.

6. *Retrospective clarification.* This type of probe specifies what additional information is needed as in type (4) above. The difference is that the area to be clarified was not contained in the immediately preceding response. Here, the topic is changed to one which has been mentioned by the respondent before the immediately preceding response, and the interviewer specifies what he wants to know about this topic. For example: "You told me how you looked out the window and saw this big black funnel and realized it was a tornado; what was the first thing you *did* when you saw the funnel?" "What did you say to your mother that first time she waited up for you and you got in late?" Note that here clarification has the same meaning as in type (4) above, but the *retrospective* clarification refers the respondent to a *previous* topic of discussion.

7. *Mutation.*[4] This type of probe introduces a new topic that cannot be construed to be an elaboration or clarification of any preceding response. The interviewer takes the initiative in introducing the new topic, rather than waiting for the respondent to lead into it naturally. Sometimes the interviewer softens the abruptness of the transition by bridging it with some specific topic which has already been discussed or by showing how the new topic fits into the overall purpose of the interview. For example: "So far, you have given me a very good picture of how you and the rest of your family got along during the disaster, but I need to know something about what other people in the community were doing meanwhile; could you help me with that?"

The author's analysis of many interviews done by beginners shows the two most "natural" types of topic control are types (4) and (7). The other five types are relatively rare in the neophyte's interviews but are used more frequently once he becomes aware of their value. Usually the beginning interviewer is simply not aware of the wide range of topic control which is possible and so cannot consider the value of the various possibilities.

Using topic control

We cannot assume that the interviewer must always exercise strong topic control to attain the objectives of the interview efficiently. In some types of interviews, strong topic control may lower the respondent's motivation; it may also degenerate the interview into a "battle of wits" or into a rigid question-answer session in which the

---

4/ This term was borrowed from Merton and is used in the same general way as in Robert K. Merton, "The Focused Interview," *American Journal of Sociology,* Vol. 51 (May, 1946).

respondent plays a passive role; or it may prevent the interviewer's obtaining the respondent's own frame of reference on the topic, or tend to bias the response by suggesting certain contexts or answer categories.

In other interviews, it may be appropriate to exercise strong topic control because a low level of respondent motivation is already present, or because the respondent's task is simply to give a few salient facts such as his name, address, and occupation. Or the topic may be such that if the respondent were given great freedom he would tend to give much irrelevant information.

It must be remembered that even though low topic control may be useful in building rapport, it also may fail to obtain all the relevant information. In some cases, low topic control may make the respondent feel insecure because he is not sure what information is wanted. This insecurity can grow into hostility when the respondent feels that the interviewer has no clear objectives and is merely wasting time in chit-chat. As we consider some of the values and dangers of each type of topic control, it will become apparent that most interviews call for a wide range of topic control.

Values of the silent probe. The silent probe, rarely used by the beginner, has several legitimate functions. Since it exercises absolutely no topic control, it allows the respondent to follow his own path of associations. This is useful when discovering associations is a purpose of the interview, or when the respondent needs to refresh his memory by telling the story his own way. The liberal use of silence also helps to establish a slower pace and a more thoughtful mood. Then, too, the only sure way to know that we are not interrupting the respondent is to use a silent probe before trying a verbal probe. Using the silent probe also gives the interviewer time to think of the most appropriate verbal probe (which is often not needed because the silent probe itself is successful).

Of course, there is a danger in using too much silence at the wrong point in the interview. For example, if the respondent has nothing he is eager to say, does not know exactly what the interviewer expects, and feels a need for some support and direction from the interviewer, then the pregnant pause becomes an embarrassing silence.

Values of neutral probes. The term "neutral probe" refers to two types of topic control, the encouragement probe and the elaboration probe. Both are neutral in the sense that their wording does not tell the respondent what information is desired. They merely imply that the interviewer understands and accepts what has been said, and that he wants to hear more.

When the respondent actually has more information to give, the neutral probe has several advantages. Like the silent probe, the neutral verbal probes give the respondent freedom in following his own paths of association. The neutral probes also imply a strong interest in what the respondent is saying. Unlike the silent probe, they give the interviewer more opportunity to communicate positive attitudes through the tone of voice used. The interviewer can give the respondent recognition, show sympathetic understanding, and allow the respondent to obtain catharsis when the need is there.

Perhaps the most important value of neutral probes is realized when they are used to follow up a broad question. When the broad-scope question is more appropriate than a series of narrow and specific questions, we need some way of motivating the respondent to continue speaking on the broad topic without having to suggest specific subquestions. As explained earlier, the value of the broad question lies (*a*) in its ability to obtain specific bits of information without pointing out any ego threatening relationships between them, and (*b*) in allowing the respondent to provide his own context, frame of reference, or perspective on these specifics without a barrage of detailed questions interrupting his trend of thought. The interviewer needs a tactic which motivates the respondent to elaborate further but does not control the path he takes. This is the unique value of the neutral probe.

Another important tactical function of the neutral probe is to give the interviewer time to formulate a more specific probe which is appropriate. Often, tactical errors are made when the interviewer is caught by surprise and blurts out some specific question that is inappropriate. A great deal of concentration is demanded of the interviewer; he must show an interest in the respondent as a person, listen carefully to what is being said at the moment, evaluate the relevance of the information, and constantly reformulate probes that might be needed in case the respondent stops talking. Needless to say, there are times when the respondent stops talking at an inopportune moment when the interviewer is not clear on what to probe. In this case, the ability to use a spontaneous neutral probe that fits the context of the interview is a great boon. It relieves the interviewer of the fear that he may be caught unprepared and inadvertently bias the response or damage rapport. Of course, the interviewer's non-verbal communication must not indicate that he is caught unprepared or is using a time-stalling tactic. This tactic should not be used so frequently that topic control becomes weak when it should be strong. In most cases, even if the neutral probe does not succeed in eliciting the desired information, neither does it interrupt the respondent's trend of thought. Furthermore, it allows the interviewer time to organize his own thoughts. This function of the neutral probe can only be fully appreciated by those with experience in non-scheduled interviewing.

Of the two types of neutral probes (encouragement and elaboration), it will be noted that elaboration probes exert more topic control than encouragement probes. The former must at least indicate to the respondent whether he is expected to "move on" with the story or to elaborate the current theme, while the encouragement probe merely indicates that the respondent should keep talking. It is possible, however, that neither one of these neutral probes will furnish the respondent with the guidance and support he needs. The interviewer must be sensitive to the respondent's reaction to low topic control and not allow him to develop a feeling of insecurity or hostility toward the interviewer.

It should be recognized that when encouragement takes the form of praising the respondent for a specific response by saying, "Good!" for example, we are exerting considerable topic control regardless of whether or not the respondent feels that these comments influence his answers. We should distinguish between encouragement by showing an interest in the respondent's efforts and in whatever he may say and showing interest by praising specific comments of the respondent which may bias the results as shown in an experiment by Hildum and Brown.[5]

Elaboration versus clarification. It is obvious that the clarification probe exerts more topic control than the elaboration probe because the latter merely indicates that the respondent should continue on the current theme while the former singles out some particular aspect of the previous response for clarification.

The elaboration probe is most useful in cases where the objective of the interview is to obtain detailed descriptions of objective situations or of subjective reactions and orientations. It is also helpful where the respondent is willing and able to elaborate without undue

5/ D. C. Hildum and R. W. Brown, "Verbal Reinforcement and Interviewer Bias," *Journal of Abnormal and Social Psychologyy,* Vol. 52 (July, 1956), pp. 100-111.

strain or without resorting to fabrication in order to fill the vacuum. Under these conditions the elaboration probe has two distinct advantages over the clarification probe: (*a*) it allows the interviewer to obtain specific details he might never think to ask for, and (*b*) it often elicits the answer to several detailed questions without the interviewer's having to ask them. Clarification probes, both immediate and retrospective, will be needed after the elaboration probes reach a point where they are not producing much relevant information.

There are conditions where the clarification probes should be used without first trying elaboration probes. If the objectives of the interview call for only a few isolated facts, not related in the respondent's mind to a particular topic, period of time, or event, then the tactic of using specific questions followed by clarification probes where needed is more efficient and less threatening to the respondent's ego.

Immediate versus retrospective probes. The distinction between an *immediate* and a *retrospective* elaboration or clarification might seem arbitrary in that the immediate probe is related to the immediately preceding response while the retrospective probe is related to *any* of the responses before the immediately preceding one. Even though the range of choice in formulating retrospective probes is much greater than it is with immediate probes, in actual practice the distinction between the two seems to be more important than differences within either category. From the respondent's point of view, any probe regarding the current theme exerts less topic control than reverting to some previously mentioned topic. This, in turn, exerts less topic control than a mutation—changing the subject to some new topic not yet mentioned by the respondent.

An important tactical decision must be made repeatedly. Should each elaboration or clarification be obtained immediately, before the respondent can move on to other topics? Or should it be delayed until the respondent's momentum wanes or the topic has been covered as completely as possible with the use of only silent and encouraging probes? When the interviewer decides to wait until later to return to the theme at hand, he is exchanging less topic control early in the interview for more topic control later.

The question then becomes, when should the interviewer postpone his probing until later in the interview and when should he probe immediately for elaboration or clarification? In making this tactical judgment the interviewer should probably postpone the probe until later, if

1) the objectives of the interview call for a wealth of detail, including some "unanticipated" information which the interviewer would not think to ask for specifically;

2) topics, subtopics or questions are so interrelated that there are opportunities for the respondent to give several needed specifics in response to subsequent general questions;

3) the topic is one in which the respondent can be motivated to talk fairly spontaneously in response to broad questions; or

4) there is a danger that too many interruptions for needed clarifications might inhibit the respondent's spontaneity, as is often the case early in an interview.

Conditions (1) and (2) depend mainly upon the nature of the problem and are, therefore, more constant throughout the whole interview. Conditions (3) and (4) tend to fluctuate from moment to moment and therefore require the interviewer to vary the amount of topic control he uses.

Whether using an immediate or a retrospective probe, the following precautions should be observed:

1) Do not interrupt the respondent in order to probe; wait until you are sure he has finished his current thought. If you intend to use an immediate elaboration probe, it might be well to first use a silent probe in case it will accomplish the same purpose.

2) Be careful that your probe doesn't give the impression that you have failed to hear something the respondent has said.

3) Use the respondent's own words whenever possible in referring to something he has said.

The following illustrates the difference between a good and a bad probe for immediate clarification.

Example of good clarification probe:[6]

R: In general, I got along fine with both of my parents. We lived out in the country and I went to high school on the bus, so none of the kids came to my house. Of course, we had a little skirmish now and then, but basically I liked my parents and they liked me, even when I was a wild teenager.

I: I see. (3) Tell me a little about some of the skirmishes you had now and then. What were they about?

R: Well, there weren't too many of them. (3) I remember one when I wanted to use the car to go to a basketball game and Dad wanted to go to a Grange

6/ The numbers in parentheses equal seconds of silence.

meeting. We finally compromised and he took me to the game and I went home with someone else so he could go to the Grange meeting.

Example of bad clarification probe:

R: By the time I was a senior in high school I guess I gave my folks a rough time now and then. I don't know who I thought I was kidding, because I always came out second best and usually cut off my nose to spite my face.

I: Why do you suppose you usually lost the battle?

R: I wouldn't say I lost the battle because there wasn't really any open fight. I was just stubborn and wouldn't do things just because I thought my folks wanted me to.

Although using the right tactic does not always guarantee complete success, these two excerpts are typical of the tactics and the results obtained by two different interviewers working on the same study of parent-child conflict in families with teenage children. Note that both interviewers are trying to obtain more specific description of some concrete conflict situation. The first interviewer actually has two probes in one in that he first gives an encouraging "I see" followed by a three-second silent probe. He then makes it clear that he has been listening and is interested by using the respondent's own key word, "skirmishes," in phrasing the probe. In return, the respondent gives some detail regarding a concrete instance of conflict with his father.

The second interviewer has precisely the same problem as the first, in that the previous response was general, vague, and unclear. However, his attempt to clarify is unsuccessful for several possible reasons. First, he interrupts the respondent to ask the question (since he allowed no silence before probing); second, he does not use the respondent's own words in phrasing the probe. Instead of asking, "How did you give your folks a rough time?" he attempts to paraphrase what he thinks is the central ideal of the response. This paraphrase is perceived as inaccurate by the respondent who, instead of giving any concrete information, defensively denies that there was a "battle."

The interviewer must take particular care to prevent giving the impression that he has not heard or remembered pertinent information when using retrospective probes. It is also probably more important to use the words of the respondent so that he can immediately recognize the exact point the interviewer is probing. Sometimes it is helpful to preface the retrospective probe with a contextual statement which provides a clearer orientation to the past point being probed and which gives the respondent recognition for information already given on the particular point. For example:

I: Very good! Now let's go back to the point where you had the first disagreement with your parents over dating. You mentioned that you wanted to take this girl to the strawberry festival and your mother objected. Tell me a little more about that situation.

This is infinitely better than the following probe which indicates a certain degree of insensitivity to the problem from the respondent's point of view:

I: Now tell me something about any disagreements you had with your parents over dating!

This probe does not show the respondent that the interviewer heard, remembered, and appreciated information already given, nor does it provide a concrete "handle" for the respondent's memory to grasp.

The recapitulation probe.   The recapitulation probe is a special form of the retrospective elaboration probe which takes the respondent back to the *beginning* of the time period covered by the interview. This return to the beginning of the story is a tactic which has many advantages when used correctly under appropriate conditions.

The recapitulation probe is subject to all the same conditions and precautions as any retrospective probe, plus one additional condition. The topic must be one which the respondent tends to elaborate as a chronologically organized story. There are many types of topics in which the respondent tends to relate events in chronological order, particularly when encouraged by the interviewer to do so. A person's life history or any aspect of it such as his marital relations, his car-buying habits, his experiences in a crisis, his account of an accident he has witnessed, his views of the changes in the social structure of his community, or his political behavior—all may be elicited in story form.

The following three examples of recapitulation probes are taken respectively from interviews on human behavior in disasters, car-buying motivations, and development of delinquency behavior. After each of these interviews had been underway from 20 to 45 minutes, these recapitulation probes proved particularly useful:

You said that the sky turned sort of yellow-green and you looked out the kitchen window and saw this black funnel coming toward you. Can you tell me more about that moment?

You mentioned that the first time you drove a car was when you learned to drive a jeep in the army in Colorado. You said it gave you a good feeling. Tell me more about how you felt about driving the jeep.

Now the first time you remember ever "lifting" anything was when you were about 11 years old and used to steal candy bars and pocket knives from Schmidt's Drugstore. Could you tell me more about the gang of kids you ran around with then?

Where there is a tendency for the respondent to relate his experiences in story form, he will usually add new detail to the story the second time through. In order to help the respondent cover the whole time period again, it is usually necessary for the interviewer to follow the recapitulation probe with a series of silent probes and neutral probes designed to keep the respondent moving forward in his story. Thus, if the respondent has once covered the relevant period of time but omitted thirty needed details, the interviewer could either ask 30 specific questions or use one recapitulation tactic which might obtain 15 to 25 of the needed details.

This natural tendency of the respondent to give further elaboration in the second telling of the story gives several important advantages to the recapitulation probe. It is often an efficient method of obtaining information since it reduces the number of interruptions of the respondent's thoughts and cuts down on the number of detailed probes needed. This also encourages spontaneity and aids the respondent's memory by giving him freedom to associate events in his own way.

Another advantage is that this tactic provides an indirect way of obtaining material where a direct question would constitute an ego threat. For example, if the interviewer were to ask directly, "Did you remember to take the children with you when you ran from the burning building?" and if the respondent had been so panicky that he ran out without them, the ego threat might cause him to falsify the report by simply answering "Yes." If the interviewer, instead, has the respondent give a detailed chronological account beginning with, "What happened when you first realized that the apartment was on fire?" and then follows with recapitulation probes, it may be obvious that the respondent did not actually think about his children until he saw a neighbor woman leading them out of the burning building.

The recapitulation probe is also an effective exploratory tactic which will maximize unanticipated responses by eliciting relevant information which the interviewer would never think to ask for.

A final and obvious advantage of the recapitulation probe is in obtaining a chronological picture of the respondent's covert or overt behavior. A series of recapitulation probes will often provide a cross-check on the chronological order of specific events.

The reflective probe. We use the term "reflective" in slightly broader sense than defined by Rogers[7] who emphasizes the reflection of the respondent's *feelings.* Here, a reflective probe is any attempt by the interviewer to elicit additional information by repeating the respondent's implicit or explicit statement without including a direct question. In the following excerpt, the first, the third, and the last probes are all reflective.

R: The main reason I came to Antioch College was because of the combination of high academic standards and the work program. It appealed to me a lot.

I: It appealed to you a lot?

R: That's right.

I: Could you tell me a little more exactly why it had this appeal for you?

R: I don't know—it was just that the place sounded less stuffy and straight-laced than a lot of places with just as good an academic program.

I: You don't like places that are stuffy and straight-laced?

R: You can say that again. A lot of places spend most of their time trying to work out a way of controlling the students, assuming that they are completely incapable of self-control. They have a housemother in every dorm, require class attendance becauses classes are so dull that no one would come if there wasn't a cut system, and they require chaperones at every party . . . that sort of thing.

I: Why do you suppose Antioch has less supervision by the administration?

R: Well it is part of the educational philosophy, and it would be ridiculous to send students all over the United States on jobs—New York, Los Angeles, Cabbage Key, and even Paris—where they are on their own and trusted to act like adults with no one to tell them when to go to bed, what to eat, and how to behave with the opposite sex, and then to treat them like children when they get back to campus.

I: Let me see if I have grasped the whole picture—you like a school with high academic standards, but which is not too straight-laced and operates on the assumption that college students can exercise self-control if they are not treated like children. These are the things you like about Antioch?

R: That hits it on the head. People go away to college because they want a chance to grow, to be autonomous as an adult should. I think this is a vital part of a liberal education.

Note that there is considerable variation in the form and function of the three reflective probes. Within our definition there are three subtypes of reflective probes which can be distinguished:

7/ Carl R. Rogers, "The Non-directive Method as a Technique for Social Research," *American Journal of Sociology,* Vol. 51 (1945), p. 143.

a) the *echo* probe, which simply repeats certain words from the previous response;

b) the *interpretive* probe, which does not literally repeat the respondent's words but attempts to reflect the meaning or feeling behind the words in the previous response, and

c) the *summary* probe, which might combine selected elements from a long previous response or from several previous responses.

It is possible to combine types (*b*) and (*c*) in the same probe as the interviewer has done in his last comments above. His first remark, "It appealed to you a lot?" is an example of the echo probe and his comment, "You don't like places that are stuffy and straight-laced?" is an example of an interpretive probe where the interpretation is limited to explicitly stating implied feelings.

Under what conditions is each type of reflective probe likely to be useful in achieving the objectives of an interview? In our experience we have found the simple echo probe to be relatively useless if the interviewer repeats the immediately preceding phrase which happens to have little emotional content for the respondent. The most typical response is, "That's right," "Yes," "Uh huh," "That's what I said," or something to that effect. If the interviewer repeatedly uses the echo probe with purely factual details that happen to occur at the end of a response, the respondent may feel that the interviewer is not listening closely or that he is being very mechanical. Regardless of whether the echo is in the form of a statement or whether it is given an upward inflection to imply a request for elaboration or clarification, the result is about the same. However, if the echoed phrase contains material of great emotional implications for the respondent, it is enough to start him elaborating the topic, probably because the respondent feels that the interviewer is aware of the importance of the particular phrase.

Similarly, when the reflective probe is one which interprets what is meant by a statement or what feeling is implied by the statement, the respondent feels that the interviewer is interested in what is being said, and responds empathically to the feelings behind what is being said. It is more important to note that the attitude expressed by the interviewer in interpreting the respondent's feelings must be nonjudgmental or sympathetic. If the tone is even slightly accusing or rejecting, it would be better if the feelings were left unreflected.

There are times when the *correct* interpretation and reflection of the respondent's feelings may damage rapport. This is true when the feeling is socially unacceptable (for example, hating one's mother) and the respondent is not yet ready to accept this feeling as his own. His repression of the feeling is complete enough to hide the feeling from himself, and he sincerely believes that the interviewer either has not been listening carefully or is projecting some of his own distorted ideas.

There is also always a danger that the interviewer may incorrectly reflect the respondent's words or implied feelings. This danger is probably greater in the interpretive-summary probe where the number of opportunities to make an error is greater. Richardson[8] found in one experiment that only one out of 43 times did the respondent correct the interviewer who made an incorrect summary of what had been said. These uncorrected, distorted summaries lead to inaccurate information and, in some cases, a lowered rapport with the respondent, who feels that the interviewer does not understand what is being said.

There are other conditions under which the distorted summary would stimulate a voluminous and spontaneous response that would clarify and enrich the information obtained. On rare occasions, we have found that a summary intentionally distorted to convey an incorrect picture which is less socially acceptable than the respondent's actual behavior may lead the respondent to elaborate upon his actual behavior to correct the interviewer's "misunderstanding." The conditions of success are very similar to those described in the earlier discussion of leading questions.

Mutations. Although a "mutation" is certainly a type and degree of topic control, it cannot properly be called a probe, since it is actually a general question introducing a new topic not yet discussed in the interview.

If a series of topics in an interview are interrelated in the respondent's mind, it is often possible for the interviewer to avoid using mutations to introduce the next topic or subtopic by allowing the respondent to take the lead in moving into the new topic. Whether or not such a smooth transition is desirable has already been discussed earlier in this chapter under the topic of transitions.

In general, the neophyte interviewer tends to use mutations too soon, before exhausting the relevant information on the current topic. Frequently, the beginner actually interrupts the respondent, who is still giving information relevant to the current topic, and

8/ Stephen A. Richardson, "Training in Field Relations Skills," *Journal of Social Issues,* Vol. 8, No. 3 (1952).

rushes on to the next topic only to discover, when analyzing the interview data, that the first topic had been sketchily discussed.

It is helpful for the interviewer to get in the habit of asking himself whether the current topic is covered adequately before going on to a new one. Sometimes, if the current topic is complex, several precautions can be taken to avoid leaving it prematurely. First, the interviewer can obtain time to check his interview guide and his probe notes (which are described in the next section) by simply saying to the respondent, "Excuse me for a moment while I check to see if you have given me all the information I need. Meanwhile you might think of something else you would like to add on this topic before we move on." Or, if the interviewer is sure that all of the anticipated information has been obtained and he wants to give the respondent one more chance to give some relevant but anticipated type of information, he can simply give a summary of what the respondent has said and ask if there is anything he would like to change, revise, or add. Before going on to a mutation, the interviewer should always use a silent probe to be sure the respondent has nothing more to add.

There is one situation where it is appropriate to change the topic of discussion before exhausting the current one. This would be advisable when for some reason the respondent needs to be jolted out of some undesirable rut in the current topic by leaving it temporarily. For example, the respondent may have become defensive about the topic or may be fabricating information in an attempt to be consistent with a previous, incorrect statement or to meet what he thinks are the etiquette requirements or the interviewer's expectations. If the interviewer suspects this, it may be useful to act as though the topic has been covered satisfactorily and go on to some unrelated topic. Later, after he has had an opportunity to establish a more sympathetic atmosphere and to show his interest in critically analyzing the information, the interviewer can then approach the old topic from a new angle so that the respondent will not revert to his defensive mood.

Taking probe notes

Taking notes in an interview has two general functions. First, note taking is a method of storing relevant information; and second, the notes are a tactical aid to remind the interviewer which areas have been adequately covered, what points need further elaboration or clarification and what words the respondent used in talking about points that need further probing. We refer to notes serving the second purpose as "probe notes."

The distinction becomes clear in a non-scheduled interview in which the whole conversation is tape recorded. Obviously, notes are not needed to store the information, since it is on the tape in complete and accurate form. Nevertheless, the experienced interviewer takes probe notes if the interview is complex enough to warrant the use of a tape recorder. The less scheduled the interview, the less topic control used, and the more complex the interview, the greater the need for probe notes.

Assuming that the nature of the interview calls for taking probe notes, there are several points of techniques to be observed if the notes are to be of maximum value:

1) The notes should not be voluminous, but should include only key words or phrases to remind the interviewer of what the respondent has said.

2) These key phrases should be in the respondent's own words so that if the interviewer wishes to probe, he can use the respondent's own words.

3) The key phrases may either be written as a continuous story in the order given by the respondent, or may be recorded under appropriate categories provided by the interview guide. In this case, the guide should provide ample space for notes under each category.

4) If certain ideas need further elaboration or clarification, the interviewer can underline or circle the key phrase as a reminder.

5) As these points are elaborated and clarified, with or without probing, the key phrases which had been underlined can be crossed out to indicate that a probe is no longer needed.

6) If the interview is not tape recorded and the notes must, therefore, also act as a means of storing the information, it is helpful to take triple-spaced notes. The extra space allows the interviewer to fill in omitted words and phrases immediately after the interview.

This system of note taking can be expanded, contracted, or modified, depending upon the complexity of the interview, the degree to which the interviewer is familiar with its objectives, and the amount of topic control called for.

Even when a tape recorder is used, the interviewer often finds it useful to make notes of all the main relevant ideas rather than trying to note only the points that need probing. There are two reasons for this. First, the interviewer is not always immediately aware that a particular idea needs probing; it may become problematical later when it apparently conflicts with subsequent information. Second, it is often easier to record all relevant key phrases than to decide which ones to omit or include.

Considerable experience is required before an interviewer can gauge the appropriate amount of note taking in various types of interviews and before he prevents its distracting him from listening carefully to the respondent. The skill lies in selecting only key phrases and words. In training interviewers, the author has found that the use of probe notes in tape recorded interviews vastly decreases the amount of missing or ambiguous information in the nonscheduled interview.

DEALING WITH SYMPTOMS OF RESISTANCE

In describing some of the typical forms of resistance by the respondent and in offering suggestions for countering such resistance, we make no promise that the solution will always be effective. No studies have been done of a large enough number of these tactical attempts to show precisely which conditions in the situation account for their success or failure, and the reader may think of a specific circumstance in which some of the following suggestions would not apply. They are offered as possible solutions when nothing obviously better occurs to the interviewer. Each form of resistance will be dealt with, insofar as possible, in the order in which it is most likely to occur in the interview.

"I'm too busy now!"

In situations where the interviewer contacts the respondent without a previous appointment, there is the possibility that the respondent will be too busy at the moment to cooperate or he will use this excuse when the real source of his resistance may be lethargy, ego threat, or dislike of talking to strangers.

The tactics that are possible at this point depend, among other things, on whether (*a*) the respondent must be included in a sample or whether a substitution can be made, and (*b*) whether it is possible for the interviewer to return at another time.

In some cases, the interviewer suspects the respondent is making an excuse, but it is necessary to interview this particular respondent. If it is possible for the interviewer to return, the following tactic may be effective in avoiding a return trip.

I: How do you do? I am Mr. Gregg. I'm helping with a study of the community which is being done by Metropolitan Studies, Inc. You have probably read in the Dayton Daily Times about how this study is going to help plan improvements in traffic, parking, and shopping problems.

R: I think I have heard something about it, but right now I am too busy to talk about it.

I: I see. I realize that you didn't expect me at this time. Since it is so important to talk to a wide sample of people, I will be willing to come back at any time you say—this week or next week, it doesn't matter.

R: Well, I don't know—let's see . . .

I: The interview doesn't take much time, we just want to know something about your shopping habits, where your children go to school and that sort of thing.

R: Both of my children go to high school, and I don't even go downtown to shop any more since the new shopping center went in.

I: You have already answered two of the things I wanted to know. There are just a few more questions like that.

R: Well, if it won't take long, you might as well come in and let's get it over with and you won't have to come back.

I: Thank you very much.

When this tactic is used, the person who is really too busy but would be willing to talk will usually not hesitate to make an appointment. If the respondent actually has the time at the moment, but is hoping to turn the interviewer away, he realizes that this will not work since the interviewer will return again. Also, in this case, once the respondent knew the nature of the questions, she felt less threatened and decided to "get it over with."

In some cases, the interviewer has overcome resistance at this point by explaining how short the interview is, the importance of the project, that the respondent need not stop his work while answering the questions, that Mrs. X (a friend of the respondent's) warned that she would probably be very busy, but she would be able to give the needed information, or that it is very important to get the opinions of busy people rather than the leisure class.

Often, such a situation can be prevented if the interviewer is able to launch immediately into an initial question which rouses the respondent's interest, appeals to his ego, and shows that the interview is not difficult. This can sometimes be done even before a full explanation of the purpose of the study is given. The explanation can be given in installments where it is directly relevant to the information requested.

In rare cases in which the respondent is very fearful of the interview, he may make an appointment and then be out when the interviewer returns. This evasive tactic was found several times in a study of marital success[9] when making appointments with a few of the people who felt that their marriage had been a failure and did not want the interviewer to discover it. In these cases, the interviewer learned to arrive for an appointment about 15 minutes early. In some instances, he encountered the couple leaving their apartment house 10 minutes before the appointment time.

When the respondent feels the pressure of competing time demands, persuading him to submit to the interview is sometimes of little value. He may feel tense and apprehensive throughout the interview if he is neglecting his own work. In these cases, the interviewer might suggest that he return to finish the interview at another time.

"I don't know anything about that!"

The interviewer who meets this phrase from the respondent just as he has finished his explanation of the purpose of the interview or has asked the first question may become a bit panicky. For example:

I: How do you do? I am Mrs. Karen. I am working with the Community Service in doing a study of people's opinions on antivivisection. Do you know what antivivisection means?

R: Oh yes, it has something to do with cutting animals that are alive. But I don't know a thing about it. Why don't you talk to my next door neighbor? Her husband works at the drugstore and he knows all about that sort of thing. I just couldn't help you a bit.

I: But it's not necessary to know all about it. I just want to find out what people do know.

R: That's easy! I know nothing.

I: Oh, I'm sure you have something to say. You have probably seen it mentioned lately in the paper because there has been a big controversy over it.

R: I said I knew nothing about the subject . . . I think you should interview someone else. (slams door)

Compare the interviewer's performance above with the episode which follows:

9/ E. W. Burgess and Paul Wallin, *Engagement and Marriage* (Philadelphia: Lippincott, 1953).

I: How do you do? I'm Mrs. Gerhardt. I am working with the Community Service in doing a study of people's opinions on antivivisection. Do you know what antivivisection means?

R: Yes, vaguely. It deals with operating on live animals, but I don't know any more about it than that.

I: I see. Why do you suppose this is done?

R: I don't know. I suppose it is done to give medical students practice so that they won't have to practice on people.

I: Is there any other reason that anyone might operate on a live animal?

R: Well, of course, veterinarians operate on dogs when they are sick or to keep them from having puppies.

The contrast between these two episodes demonstrates a basic principle which emerged from experience with a wide variety of interviews: the interviewer should avoid challenging the respondent or even persuading him to cooperate. In a sense, the first interviewer is almost demanding a declaration of surrender from the respondent before he will formally launch the interview. The second interviewer simply accepts the idea that the respondent knows very little about the topic, but proceeds immediately with a relevant question without formally declaring the interview started and without seemingly trying to persuade the respondent to surrender.

If possible, the interviewer should focus the attention immediately on the respondent as in the following example:

I: How do you do? I am Mr. Black with the National Opinion Research Center. We are doing a study of how people manage in disasters in order to be of some help in planning for future disasters during either peace or war.

R: Well, I can't help you none because I wasn't even in Judsonia when the tornado struck.

I: I see. Where were you at the time?

R: I was all the way over in Searcy when I saw the big clouds over Judsonia way.

I: What did you think it was when you saw the clouds?

R: I was afraid to my bones that it was a twister. And I knowed that some of my family was here and I didn't know what was happening to them.

I: Then what did you do?

R: I got in the pickup truck and high-tailed it for home as fast as I could git. It seemed like a hundred miles because I was in a hurry and the road was full of all kinds of trees, telephone poles, and everything. I had to go off the road several times, but still couldn't get through with a car. I had to walk the last mile and a half. I just couldn't believe my eyes. With all the houses and the water tower blown away, I could hardly find the way to my house, or I should say the place where my house used to be . . .

As it was, the respondent was well on the way without having formally consented to the interview. The interviewer was able to put the spotlight on the respondent by asking, "Where were *you* at the time?" Instead of this, the interviewer could have gone into a long explanation of why he had to obtain a random sample, what a random sample was, and why the respondents who were not in the town at the moment the storm struck still had useful information. All of this would be more time-consuming and more likely to cause resistance in the respondent.

In the type of study where there is no need for a random sample and where we want to locate key respondents who can give an objective report of specific facts and events, we often should not attempt to persuade a reluctant respondent to cooperate by being interviewed. Instead the interviewer should ask him for advice on who might have the kind of information he is seeking.

"I don't want to be on tape!"

On rare occasions, respondents will consent to being interviewed but will object to having the interview tape recorded. If after an explanation the respondent still objects, the interviewer's next move depends upon whether a tape recording is essential or merely convenient, and whether the respondent also objects to the interviewer's taking notes. If the former is not essential and the latter is permissible, then written notes are the solution.

It is sometimes helpful for the interviewer to clarify the nature of the respondent's objections so that they can be met. The interviewer can simply ask, "Would you mind telling me why you would prefer not to have the interview tape recorded?" This question followed by some appropriate probes put in a sympathetic spirit has elicited responses such as the following:

a) I have heard some of these tape recorded interviews with newspaper reporters on TV newscasts and they sound silly!

b) I don't want everybody hearing what I have to say. I don't mind telling you, but I don't know who else might hear it!

c) My voice sounds bad and I don't see any reason to preserve it for posterity.

d) I might say something that is not correct, or that I don't really mean, and there it is on the record forever.

The first response, if it is the genuine reason for the objection, can easily be overcome by explaining the difference between the purpose of the interviewer and of a news reporter. The second response and its variations can be dealt with by giving any of the following explanations when they are true: that no one but the interviewer will hear the tape; that the tape will be used over again after relevant information is taken off; that the transcribing will be done by people who are far away and do not know anyone interviewed in the study; that no exact quotes will be used; or that if quotes are used, the respondents will not be identified.

The third response can sometimes be overcome by reassuring the respondent that the tape does not sound like the real person since it is not high-fidelity. Or the interviewer might demonstrate how he sounds on the recorder, then ask the respondent whether he thinks it sounds like the real thing. The interviewer might record the response to this question and play it back to show the respondent that having one's voice recorded is not a painful experience. If the respondent's initial resistance seems to be giving way to his curiosity, the interviewer might propose that they try recording the first two or three minutes, and then if it still seems to cause "stage-fright" it can be turned off.

The last response is closely related to the first two, but is more concerned with the apparent permanence of the responses when recorded or with the fact that the tape records precisely what the respondent says rather than what he really means. It could also indicate a fear that the interviewer might pressure the respondent into saying something he does not mean, or not give time for the respondent to carefully consider or to correct his own responses. In this case, several tactics have been found useful. The interviewer can suggest that the tape recorder be used and that if at the end of the interview the respondent still feels the tape recording does not represent his views accurately he can either have the recording erased on the spot or suggest any corrections or additions after listening to it. In such a case, the respondent usually discovers in the progress of the interview that the interviewer is genuinely concerned with helping him express his views as accurately as possible without high pressure tactics, and he loses any desire to eliminate the tape recording.

In this type of situation the interviewer might need to check any possible inhibiting effects of the presence of the tape recorder by using an informal post-interview which is explained later.

"Why are you taking notes?"

Even though the need for note-taking might have been explained at the outset of the interview, sometimes the respondent seems to become suddenly aware of the fact that the interviewer is taking notes. He may ask directly why notes are being taken, or he may merely show non-verbally or indirectly that he is concerned. His concern may be only with the interviewer's recording a particular statement or with note taking in general. If the interview is being tape recorded, he might merely be curious about what the interviewer chooses to write down and what he omits.

The sensitive interviewer who detects the respondent's concern can discover what is bothering him and give the appropriate explanation. Often, the respondent is satisfied by the interviewer's offer to show him the notes. This offer should not be made if the interviewer cannot follow through without endangering rapport. If the notes are in the respondent's own words and do not involve any interpretation or evaluation, there is little danger in showing them. Any suggestions the respondent might have should be accepted gracefully. Interviewers have discovered repeatedly that the main problem lies in being sensitive to symptoms of the need for an explanation of the note taking. Once the explanation is given, the respondent is usually satisfied.

"I don't remember, I don't know!"

Often after the interview is well underway, the immediate response to a specific question is "I don't know" or "I don't remember." Usually, this is not a form of resistance by the respondent but merely expression of modesty, tentativeness, or cautiousness with which many people preface an answer. Systematic analysis of tape recorded interviews has shown that only rarely does the respondent literally mean that he does not know. It would be safer in many cases to translate this as "give me a moment to think." Apparently, the most successful tactic in this situation is to allow a moment's silence and show by your expression that you are assuming that the respondent is thinking. If this does not bring results, the interviewer can say something to the effect, "I realize that the question might be difficult to answer without some careful thought." Also, the interviewer can supply some cues in an attempt to aid the respondent's memory.

All of this will be unsuccessful if (*a*) the respondent never had the information, (*b*) it is deeply repressed or completely forgotten, or (*c*) if the respondent has the information but does not want to give it because of ego threat, trauma, or etiquette. In the latter two situations, it is well to avoid directly pressing for the information and wait for recapitulation probes to either stimulate recall or allow time for a more permissive relationship to be built up.

There are two general types of questions that will often obtain the "I don't know" response because the respondent feels that he cannot give a precise enough answer. One of these types is the question dealing with the future such as, "Is your daughter going to college next year?" or "Do you think that prices will be higher or lower six months from now?" If the objective of the interview is to obtain the respondent's best estimate, then the interviewer will have to encourage the respondent to do the best he can. If the respondent says "I don't know," the interviewer can say, "Well, of course, nobody knows for sure, but the way it looks now, what do you think?" Another type is the question which asks for some factual or quantitative information such as, "About how many hours per week do you watch television?" To encourage the respondent, the interviewer can say, for example, "I don't have to know exactly. What is your best guess?"

In some cases, "I don't know" represents a case of incipient resistance. Here it is better to avoid pressing for an answer and to merely accept the response at face value while continuing the discussion. For example, a Colombian interviewer is speaking to a Colombian housewife about the North American student who lived in her home for six months:

I: Was your North American guest the tidy type or not?

R: I don't know.

I: I see . . . you just didn't have an opportunity to observe!

R: Well, not exactly . . . I just don't know how to put it. Because I noticed a lot of things about her behavior in my house, but they are not consistent!

I: What do you mean by "not consistent"?

R: She was very neat in the way she dressed, but she always left the bathroom a mess in the morning. Also, she would make her bed very well, but would leave her shoes and slippers on the floor. She never put her books and papers away, but left them on the desk in her room.

In this case, the interviewer skillfully led the respondent into giving the answer without the dangers involved in not accepting the response by saying, for example, "Surely, you had some impression of her since she lived in your house for six months!"

"What do you think about that?"

There are several reasons why the respondent might ask the interviewer this question after the interview has been in progress for some time. He might have already expressed his own opinion on the matter and feel uneasy about expressing himself so freely without knowing the interviewer's opinion. This is most likely to happen when discussing controversial issues. At other times, the question merely represents the natural desire to seek some responsiveness from the interviewer. It is also possible that the respondent is simply curious about the interviewer's position on the subject.

The basic problem is to find a way to satisfy the respondent so he will not feel rejected or feel that the interviewer is secretive, and yet avoid offering information which will inhibit or bias subsequent responses. If the respondent's question is in response to a straightforward fact question from the interviewer, and if it is clear that the respondent does not know the answer, the only danger in answering is that it might change the respondent's frame of reference. This is undesirable when the objectives of the interview include discovering the frame of reference used by the respondent. There is also the danger that the respondent might feel inferior or that he is being "tested" by someone who already knows all the answers.

In many circumstances it would be better for the interviewer to say something like, "I'm not sure about that, but even if I knew I'm not allowed to give my opinions. It is your opinion that counts." Or he could say, "I'm not allowed to try to influence you by giving my opinions. My job is to understand and respect your opinion." If the respondents in the study are not in communication with each other, if the interviewer has already used statements similar to those above more than once in the interview, and if there seems to be a danger of the rapport breaking down because of the interviewer's refusal to reciprocate, then the interviewer could say, "I'm not trying to keep any secret from you, but I'm not allowed to say anything to influence your answers. But I will be very glad to answer any questions you have as soon as I get your opinions. I would enjoy that."

There are times when it is in the best tactic for the interviewer to tell the respondent how he feels about the issue being discussed.

However, this should be done only if (*a*) the interviewer is sure of the respondent's point of view on a particular issue, (*b*) if the interviewer agrees with some aspect of the respondent's point of view, (*c*) if the respondent exhibits a need for some support from the interviewer, and (*d*) if the interviewer agrees spontaneously and naturally. There is always the danger that the interviewer might miscalculate the respondent's point of view and thus unintentionally disagree with the respondent. This tactic should be used only when there is no danger that one respondent will communicate the interviewer's point of view to a future respondent. This condition often exists in studies of a random sample of people in a large metropolitan area.

"What do you mean by that?"

When the respondent asks this question in response to the interviewer's question, it may be a symptom of mild resistance in which the respondent is attempting to shift the attention from himself to the interviewer. It may also be a way for the respondent to stall for time while he thinks of the answer or finds a way to avoid giving the answer. Perhaps the most common meaning is simply that the respondent is not sure what the interviewer's question means.

Regardless of the meaning behind the question, the interviewer must treat it as a simple request for clarification. The problem is to communicate the meaning of the question without suggesting an answer and without changing the meaning so that different representative respondents are asked different questions.

If the object of the interview is to discover the respondent's frame of reference for interpreting the question, the interviewer must avoid providing an interpretation. One tactic often used is to say that the question should be answered according to what it means to him and then repeat the question in exactly the same words.

This tactic is of little value if the purpose of the question is to communicate a particular frame of reference for its interpretation, but the respondent does not understand it. In this situation it is sometimes helpful for the interviewer to ask, "Could you tell me what it is about the question that you are not sure about?" Often the respondent will then say, "I don't know whether you mean X or Y." If the clarification of these alternatives does not interfere with the purposes of the interview, the interviewer can say, "I mean X in this case." Or, the respondent may point to a specific phrase which is not clear to him in the context of the question. In this case, the question may be reworded or a more complete context provided so that the respondent understands how the information is to be related to other parts of the discussion. For example:

I: What attracted you to your present location in Ohio?

R: What do you mean, to the neighborhood where we live, or the plant where my husband works or the school where the kids go?

I: That's right—you live here in Wright View and your husband works in Dayton, and the kids go to school in Fairborn. Take the whole situation; what did you hear about it while you were still in Harlan County that made you decide to leave Kentucky and come to Ohio?

R: That's easy! It was the job. My husband had some friends working in Dayton and they promised they could get him a steady job, and that's something he didn't have in Kentucky. He had worked only 5½ months last year and the pay was bad. We had a little patch of land for vegetables and raised chickens or we wouldn't have kept body and soul together.

It was fortunate that the respondent did not understand the first question above since it did not supply the clear context needed to be sure the respondent would answer the question in terms of what she knew about the Ohio situation *before* coming from Kentucky. It would have been easy for her to list a lot of specific things she liked about the neighborhood, the city of Dayton, her husband's work, and the children's school. Most of these would be irrelevant to the question of why the family left Kentucky and came to Ohio, since the details would have been learned *after* living in Ohio.

Sometimes the respondent does not understand a particular word in the question. In this case, the interviewer must be careful to reword the question so that it carries the original meaning. In the following excerpt, a representative of the Z Telephone Company is interviewing a subscriber regarding his attitude toward the service he is receiving and toward a possible rate increase. The interviewer rewords the question to avoid the word "subscriber";

I: How do you feel most subscribers feel about the kind of service they get from Z Telephone?

R: What's that got to do with telephones?

I: I should have said, how do you think most of the people who have telephones feel about the kind of service they get from Z Telephone?

R: As far as I know they have no kicks about it, and it is improving all the time.

The interviewer had assumed that the subscriber would be familiar with the word in connection with the telephone company since much of the literature included with the monthly bills had a salutation to the "subscriber."

It is often useful to give examples to clarify a question. Although they often save time and make the respondent feel secure, there is a danger that the illustrations might suggest an answer to the respondent or unintentionally narrow the scope of the question to the area suggested by the specific example. The following is a flagrant instance of such a biasing effect:

I: How do the officers show unnecessary superiority over the men?

R: What do you mean?

I: Well, for example, officers not introducing anyone but officers to girls at a public dance, or officers not going to a certain dance hall because too many enlisted men come.

R: Yes, that's right. They do just that!

It is sometimes safer to either give examples of what is *not* intended by the question or to supply the full range of abstract categories of behavior which would be considered relevant to the question. The following example combines both:

I: How do the officers show unnecessary superiority over the men?

R: I'm not sure what you mean!

I: I assume that for purely military reasons there must be difference in rank and authority to keep order under battle conditions. I wouldn't call that *unnecessary* display of superiority, but in other areas of peacetime military ritual, religious functions, social and recreational situations, housing arrangements for families, and that sort of thing.

R: Oh, I see. Let me think . . . in the social area there are a lot of distinctions which I feel are unnecessary.

I: Uh huh. Can you think of a specific case?

Regardless of the particular tactic used to clarify the meaning of a question, the interviewer should be alert to judge by the response whether the revised question has carried the intended meaning to the respondent. Sometimes several attempts at clarification are necessary before the respondent accurately grasps the question. This problem usually arises more frequently in the early exploratory stages of interviewing on a particular topic where many of the same questions are asked of different types of special respondents to obtain their differences in perspective. In this case a particular question may be very clear to one type of respondent and unclear to another.

The interviewer must also be alert for symptoms of the respondent's misunderstanding when the respondent himself is not aware of his confusion and, therefore, does not ask for a clarification.

Again, we would like to caution that our suggestions for dealing with active resistance by the respondent do not specify all the conditions for their success. However, sharing our experiences will sensitize an interviewer to the problem of resistance and show some of the tactics that have been successful for us and other interviewers in this situation.

Dealing with falsification

Falsification by the respondent is usually a symptom of ego threat or the etiquette barrier. Much potential falsification can be *prevented* if certain precautions are taken. First, if there is a possibility that the respondent may lie to hide certain facts that the interviewer already knows, it is often good to let the respondent know immediately that the interviewer has the information and makes no judgment concerning it. This often avoids the embarrassing situation where the respondent is forced to spin out an increasingly complicated fiction in order to be consistent with certain falsifications laid down early in the interview.

A second preventative tactic is useful when the interviewer has information the respondent would be tempted to hide, but rapport would be damaged if the respondent realized this. In this case, the interviewer needs to obtain a "voluntary" admission from the respondent. If this information is the subject for the remainder of the interview, then the admission must be obtained early in the interview. This is a point where the leading question strongly loaded in the direction of the least socially acceptable answer is often useful. This was the tactic used by Kinsey, as discussed earlier.

A third general preventative tactic is to leave those questions judged in advance to be potentially ego threatening until the latter part of the interview so that the interviewer will have more time to build up the non-judgmental atmosphere.

In spite of precautions aimed at preventing falsification, there are instances when the respondent still fabricates his report. This is particularly likely when the interviewer was unable to predict the potential ego threat in a question. For example, the apparently innocuous question, "Where were you when the tornado struck your house?" did not ordinarily constitute an ego threat, but in the following excerpt the interviewer correctly suspects that it does. He wisely *retreats* from the point before the respondent makes a point of denying his actual whereabouts.

I: Where were you when the tornado struck your house? Were you home?
R: No.

I: What time do you get off work at the box factory?

R: Four thirty. (The respondent begins to appear very uneasy for the first time in the interview.)

I: How did you find out that the tornado struck your house?

Here the interviewer's natural tendency was to ask, "Where were you between 4:30 when you got off work and 6:30 when the storm struck your house?" Instead he guessed by the respondent's reaction that he did not want to divulge where he was during that two-hour period. The interviewer tactfully skipped the topic and an hour later in the interview the respondent volunteered that he had stopped by the Oasis Tavern for a drink with some of the boys. The tavern was demolished by the same tornado that struck the respondent's home and injured his wife and child. The respondent's need for catharsis led him to admit his guilt feelings for having been flirting with "one of the girls that hangs out at the tavern" when he should have been home helping his wife and child during the storm.

In rare cases, the interviewer may directly *challenge* the respondent he suspects of lying. For example, he might say, "I'm amazed that such a thing could happen! I think you are trying to kid me." or "You don't have to give that old line because I don't expect it." or "I find that very difficult to believe; it doesn't jibe with the rest of the picture." or "This is not consistent with what you said earlier; which is correct?"

These are very strong tactics and always carry the potential of completely inhibiting the flow of information. For this reason, such tactics should be used only as a last resort and, if possible, postponed until all of the other relevant information has been gathered. Also, the attitude with which the interviewer "challenges" the respondent is important. It can be done without hostility or condescension but in a spirit of equality as if to say, "You don't have to hide things from me; we both know better." Further, the direct challenge can be followed by a qualifying phrase such as, "If what you say is literally true, then you will have to explain to me how it fits in with the fact that . . ."

If all of the usually appropriate techniques and tactics are tried and the respondent still persists in fabricating, then the interviewer usually has nothing to lose by challenging the respondent as a last resort. The one danger is that even though the challenge is successful the respondent might become hostile and retaliate by contacting potential respondents to warn them of the "third degree" tactics used by the interviewer. This possibility can be minimized by following the formal portion of the interview with a short, informal post-interview.

THE INFORMAL POST-INTERVIEW

The informal post-interview is a "chat" which takes place after the interview is formally closed and that is not defined as part of the interview by the respondent.

The informal post-interview has two tactical functions. First, it can be used as an ego-building period designed to leave the respondent in a good mood so that he will not spread negative attitudes to potential respondents. In addition to giving sincere praise to the respondent at crucial points throughout the interview, it is sometimes especially important to spend a few minutes after the formal information gathering is finished to build up the respondent's ego and give him a chance to express any anxieties about his performance and to regain his composure. This is particularly important where the nature of the subject matter and the objectives of the interview lead the respondent to give information which is difficult to recall, ego threatening, or traumatic. Even though the interview may have been very successful in the amount and quality of the information obtained, it may leave the respondent disturbed. If the nature of the study calls for many interviews in the same community where one respondent knows and communicates with another, it becomes crucially important not to leave a respondent with an unpleasant feeling about the interview. He might prevent others from cooperating by referring to the "third degree" or to "psychoanalysis," and similar comments. Five minutes added to the regular formal interview for ego-building may be well invested.

A second function of the informal post-interview is to detect any possible inhibiting effects of certain aspects of the formal portion of the interview. There are times when the interviewer feels that the respondent generally has been withholding information throughout the interview. For some reason, the interviewer senses a lack of the proper spontaneity. His hunch might be correct, or it might simply be a characteristic of the respondent's personality or his lack of information on the subject of the interview. If the respondent has actually resisted, some of the reasons could be verified in an informal post-interview. For example, the respondent might be uneasy about the interviewer's using a tape recorder or his taking notes. He might feel that even though the interviewer himself is to be trusted, the sponsor is not worthy. Or the formality of the situation might give him the impression that he is going "on record" even though he has been told that his responses will be kept anonymous. However, if the respondent feels threatened by the interviewer himself for any reason, the informal post-interview will show no better results.

The informal post-interview takes place after the interview is formally closed. The end of the formal interview can be indicated in a variety of ways. If it is being tape recorded, turning off the recorder marks the end; if the interviewer is taking notes, he ceases to do so. The interviewer might bring the interview to a formal close by saying, "Now the last question I have to ask is . . ." or he can thank the respondent for his cooperation and launch into an informal conversation.

Launching into the informal post-interview can usually be done with little effort. For example, the casual remark, "Are you glad that's over?" will often start the respondent talking about his reactions to the interview. Sometimes the respondent will ask questions about the purpose of the interview, the nature of the study, or whether he can see its results. This offers a springboard for the interviewer to branch off into exploration of the respondent's feeling about the interview itself. In some cases, the interviewer may have to ask a direct question such as, "Did you enjoy it in general?" "What were some of the things that made it difficult in spots?" "Do you have some suggestions on how I could make it easier for people I will interview from now on?" "What do you think might stop some people from giving information of this type?" "Do you think everyone would be willing to give me this information?" "If some people were a little reluctant or cautious, why do you think this might be?"

Interviewers who have experimented with the informal post-interview in a variety of situations agree that there is usually nothing to be lost except a few minutes of time, and often much to be gained. Some report, for example, that what they had interpreted to be a fear of the tape recorder was actually nothing but personal peculiarity of the respondent, still apparent after the tape recorder was turned off. In other cases, the respondent would confess that he had fabricated certain portions of the interview because of his perception of the possible audience. In the words of one respondent, "I didn't want to insult anybody, particularly when they had done their best and their intentions were good." Sometimes the interviewer trying this tactic was shocked to find that much of his introductory explanation of the purposes, sponsorship, and anonymity of the interview had been quickly forgotten by the respondent.

The interviewer may actually try to obtain some of the information that was not forthcoming in the formal interview, or he may only attempt to evaluate the respondent's attitude toward the interview in order to estimate the completeness and validity of the information given. If he discovers that the respondent has withheld vital information, he may attempt to relieve the respondent's suspicions or fears, leaving the door open for another interview under better conditions.

SUMMARY

In this discussion of tactics the emphasis has been upon the relationship between a particular question or probe and the whole interview up to that point. Thus, we were not interested in the form or mode of delivery of a particular question or probe in isolation from the interview as whole but in the *patterns* of relationships between questions and responses as the interview progresses. *Tactics should be tentatively planned in advance of the interview.*

To the extent that the sequence of topics and the mode of introducing each can be anticipated, they should be built into an interview guide. This guide should be used flexibly to remind the interviewer of the specific objectives of the interview, suggest possible tactics for achieving these objectives, and provide a convenient means of keeping track of what has been covered in the interview.

The more successful the interviewer is in arranging the topics and the questions within each topic in the best possible order, the more efficient the flow of communication will be. The information will be more valid, and less probing will be necessary within a topic.

Within each topic or subtopic of an interview, questions can be arranged in a funnel or an inverted sequence, depending upon the objectives, and the types of inhibitors and facilitators which each sequence brings into play. Use of the funnel sequence may reduce the number of specific questions it is necessary to ask. These two patterns of question scope should also be planned in advance.

Regardless of how successfully the interviewer has anticipated the optimum arrangement of the questions, there will always be some need, particularly at the exploratory phase, for additional probing within each topic or question to obtain information sufficiently relevant, clear and complete to meet the objectives of the interview. Probes cannot be planned in advance. Each of the seven types of topic control are valuable under certain conditions and the interviewer must be prepared to vary his initiative in expanding, contracting, or shifting the focus of the discussion.

Both techniques and tactics are means to the same end of gathering valid information. They differ from each other in the same way that the parts of a machine differ from the whole. The specific parts (techniques) may or may not function successfully, depending upon the way in which they are assembled (tactics). Thus, the specific wording of a question or structuring of the answer may or may not be successful depending upon where in the interview sequence it appears. The effectiveness of a particular question depends upon the larger context in which it is used.

Once the interview has begun, the interviewer's skills in both techniques and tactics are brought into play. The interviewer's tactical skills are placed under the greatest strain when respondent is skillfully evading or resisting giving the information. The parry and thrust of the verbal duel and the admiration for the skills involved should not obscure the fact that most of the success in an interview depends upon *pre-planning.*

7
Developing skills
in interviewing

Once the interviewer is conscious of the basic tasks of interviewing, has a theoretical framework to guide him in anticipating inhibitors and facilitators of communication, and is familiar with a wide range of strategy, technique and tactical tools, he will become acutely aware of the need to increase his skill in the interview situation. In order to avoid becoming paralyzed by the awesome multiplicity of specific tasks and tools, the interviewer must concentrate upon a few basic processes or activities.

BASIC INTERVIEWER TASKS DURING THE INTERVIEW

Let us review some of the specific skills related to the interviewer's tasks: maximizing the flow of relevant information and maintaining optimal interpersonal relations with the respondent. In order to accomplish this, during the interview the interviewer must focus his attention upon (a) accurately receiving verbal and non-verbal communication from the respondent, (b) critically evaluating the information received in terms of the objectives of the interview and as indicators of the state of interpersonal relations between interviewer and (c) regulating his own verbal and non-verbal behavior.

Accurately receiving information

The task of accurately receiving information can be broken down into several specific skills. It involves (*a*) accurately *hearing* what the respondent has said, (*b*) *observing* the respondent's non-symbolic behavior, and (*c*) *remembering* information received. Let us examine each skill separately to see why it is important and to note some of the factors which interfere with its accurate performance.

Accurately hearing the respondent. It is important to hear accurately what the respondent has said even though every word is being recorded on tape. The interviewer must hear to be able to probe for elaboration or clarification. Also, if the interviewer shows that he has not accurately heard the respondent, it is likely to damage *rapport* or bias future questions and responses.

In discussing tape recorded interviews with the interviewers themselves, the writer discovered several common conditions that interfere with an accurate perception of the respondent's words. Certain reasons were given repeatedly for situations in which the interviewer had overlooked a significant comment by the respondent that needed to be probed for further elaboration and clarification.

Often the interviewer was too absorbed in the process of *taking notes* to concentrate fully on the respondent's statements. This can be overcome by limiting the amount of writing to key phrases and not looking at the paper, by using a tape recorder to reduce the amount of note taking needed, and simply by practicing.

Another distraction was a certain amount of *anxiety* in the interviewer who worried over what and how to probe or over the interpersonal relations in the interview. Inexperienced interviewers would sometimes report that their minds "went blank" because of insecurity, anxiety, or tension.

A third frequently reported cause for inaccurate perception was the *loss of interest* either in the topic of the interview or in the respondent as a person. This source of inaccuracy was increasingly frequent as the interviewer had done more interviews on the same topic. The interviewer would begin with a natural curiosity which was soon satisfied, and he would neglect to probe relevant clues because he had not realized what the respondent was saying.

A fourth cause closely related to the boredom factor is simple *fatigue.* The result of fatigue has been quantitatively observed by the author while supervising the work of interviewers in the field. For example, in a field study where 30 interviewers worked for 12 days doing approximately 600 tape recorded interviews one to two hours in length, it was discovered that the second interview of each day was always shorter than the first one by approximately five written pages. The first interview averaged almost 30 pages, and the second only 25 pages. The effect of the combination of fatigue and boredom could be seen in the fact that the length of the first interview of each day became shorter over the 12-day period.[1]

A fifth common cause of inaccurate perception of information lies in the interviewer's *expectations* of what the respondent is going to say and his interpretation of the meaning of the response in accord with these expectations. Instead of probing to obtain a more precise clarification, the interviewer merely assumes that the respondent means what the interviewer expected him to say.[2]

This difficulty arises when the interviewer has done several interviews on the same topic and begins to anticipate what all respondents or certain types of respondents are going to say. When the response is vague, the interviewer projects his expectations into his interpretation of the response. This difficulty often arises when the interviewer is a friend or acquaintance of the respondent or when the respondent is a stranger strongly stereotyped by the interviewer. In the first case, the interviewer assumes that he knows how his friend feels because "he feels the same way I do; that's why we are friends." In the second case, an expectation that the respondent will behave "true to type" is so strong that it blinds the interviewer to any responses that do not fit.

A sixth cause of failure to hear the respondent correctly can be distractions in the interview setting. The room temperature may be uncomfortable or the air stuffy. There may be noise or disturbing visual stimuli. Of course, the distraction is greater if it involves persons with some relationship with the interviewer or respondent. It requires diplomacy to remove a wandering visitor from the interview, particularly if that person ordinarily has access to the space being used, as in the case of the interrupting child in the home or the fellow worker in the office. All of these can distract the interviewer as well as the respondent from the central task and should be considered in the selection of a time and place for the interview.

1/ Raymond L. Gorden, *An Interaction Analysis of the Depth-Interview,* unpublished Ph.D. dissertation, Department of Sociology, University of Chicago, 1954, p. 122.

2/ H. L. Smith and Herbert Hyman, "The Biasing Effects of Interviewer Expectations on Survey Results," *Public Opinion Quarterly,* Vol. 14 (Fall, 1950), pp. 491-506. This experiment shows that the interviewers often recorded the answer they expected rather than the answer actually given.

Language barriers can also interfere with hearing the respondent. The barrier may be only a local accent, or the interviewer or the respondent may be using a second language that they understand fairly well, but which at times causes them to lose some of the subtleties of the conversation. This problem can be dealt with at the strategy level in selecting bilingual interviewers, or at the tactical level by asking the respondent to speak more slowly or to repeat. Of course, if the objectives of the interview require a spontaneous flow of associations from the respondent, the language barriers must be removed by linguistic matching of interviewer and respondent.

Accurately observing the respondent. It is important to observe the non-verbal accompaniment to the flow of verbal information both to interpret the meaning of the words and to assess the possible effect on inhibitors and facilitators of communication.

It has been demonstrated that trained observers can agree on the attitude of the respondent in an interview with a high level of reliability. Furthermore, this does not depend upon agreement between the observers on specific "operational" clues to each attitude. Oldfield[3] shows that the observers could agree on the respondent's attitude even though they did not use the same clues. Some would listen to the respondent's tone of voice, others would watch his hands, others would take special note of the respondent's posture, and so on.

Studies have shown how body motion is an indicator of a person's attitudes, and Birdwhistle[4] has shown how observation of the eye and hand movements of the respondent can be used by the interviewer.

Some of the common types of non-verbal behavior noted by interviewers are laughing or giggling nervously, using the "formal tone" as if speaking to an audience, looking about apprehensively as if someone might be listening, trailing off into a whisper or mumble, losing flexibility in pitch or pace, watching the tape recorder or the note taking, halting abruptly in the middle of sentences, sighing, fidgeting, fingernail biting, doodling with a pencil, perspiring, grinding teeth, refusing to look at the interviewer, or playing with a handkerchief or other object.

All of the conditions which were previously mentioned as interfering with the interviewer's ability to accurately hear what the re-

3/ R. C. Oldfield, "The Display and Perception of Attitudes," *The Psychology of the Interview* (London: Methuen, 1947).
4/ R. Birdwhistle, "Body Motion Research and Interviewing," *Human Organization* (Spring, 1952), p. 37.

spondent is saying also interfere with his observation of what the respondent is doing. There is an additional factor which interferes with observing the nonsymbolic behavior of the respondent which can be called *over-rapport*. In this case, the interviewer is so spontaneously responsive to the respondent's non-verbal behavior that he reacts to it without consciously observing it. The interviewer must retain a higher degree of detachment and objectivity than he would when chatting with his friends, otherwise the respondent will control the situation. The problem for the interviewer is to make conscious the observation upon which his reaction depends.

Remembering what the respondent has said. Skill in remembering information received is particularly important in the non-scheduled interview for at least three reasons. It is necessary if the interviewer is to probe for clarification and elaboration where needed. It allows the interviewer to see inconsistencies and contradictions even though they occur at widely separated points. In studies involving repeated interviewing of the same person over a long period of time, it becomes increasingly important to recognize inconsistencies, contradictions and changes in point of view. It is important that the interviewer does not arouse resentment in the respondent by showing that he has forgotten information received.

Of course, the skillful use of probe notes will be a great aid in remembering what has been said. However, if the interviewer is to give the necessary attention to the respondent, he must often take very sketchy notes giving cues to the interviewer's recall but not substituting for it. The more acute the interviewer's memory, the fewer notes he must take, the more skillfully he can use them, and the less his note taking will interfere with his other functions.

All of the same factors that interfere with the interviewer's ability to listen accurately to the respondent also interfere with his ability to remember what the respondent has said. There are some additional factors which interviewers report. First, if the interviewer is unfamiliar with the topic of the interview and all its specific objectives, he has difficulty remembering parts of the responses that are relatively meaningless to him.

Another common complaint is that when two interviews are done in rapid succession, there is sometimes a tendency for the interviewer to confuse information given in the first interview with information given in the second. The same confusion also applies to questions asked. The best solution for this is skillful use of probe notes.

Another source of memory distortion not reported by interviewers but demonstrated experimentally by Fisher[5] is the tendency for the interviewer to remember statements that agree with his own point of view and to forget those that disagree. This principle applies to relatively inexperienced interviewers asking questions on a controversial issue.

Assuming that the interviewer has accurately received the information due to his careful listening to the verbal message, his thoughtful observation of its non-verbal accompaniment, his clear memory of the past responses, and his accurate recording of the key phrases, then his next task is critically evaluating the information received.

Critically evaluating the information

The non-scheduled interviewer must be able to do an instantaneous evaluation of information received. He must be able to keep a running inventory of the relevance and adequacy of the information with respect to the objectives of the interviewer and with respect to the state of the interpersonal relations between interviewer and respondent. Without this constant vigilance there is little hope that the interviewer will be able to use his array of techniques and tactics successfully.

The interviewer's critical evaluation of the information depends upon two kinds of skills: (*a*) his ability to recognize information that is relevant or irrelevant, adequate or inadequate in terms of the objectives of the interview, and (*b*) his ability to evaluate empathically the presence of potential inhibitors and facilitators of communication.

The first skill, assuming that the conditions for accurate reception of information prevail, depends upon the interviewer's familiarity with the objectives of the interview. This familiarity must be intimate and precise; otherwise the interviewer may obtain large quantities of information applicable to the general topic of the interview but only vaguely related to its specific objectives.

The second skill, assuming that the conditions for accurate reception of information prevail, depends upon the interviewer's ability to empathize with the particular respondent. Many of the conditions for successful empathy are determined at the strategy level in selecting the particular combination of interviewer and respondent. Insofar as we are concerned with increasing the interviewer's skill in em-

5/ Herbert Fisher, "Interviewer Bias in the Recording Operation," *International Journal of Opinion and Attitude Research,* Vol. 4 (1950), p. 393.

pathizing with the respondent, we must concentrate on creating conditions allowing the interviewer to utilize fully his empathic potential.

Appropriately regulating the interviewer's behavior

Once the interviewer has accurately received the information and has critically evaluated it, he must then move from the diagnostic phase into the action phase. At this point he must regulate his own behavior in a manner appropriate to the objectives of the interview and the present state of interpersonal relations.

Before the interviewer can be successful in appropriately regulating his own behavior to fit the needs of the situation, he must have sufficient facility in using the full range of techniques and tactics so that he does not feel uneasy, stiff, or mechanical. If the interviewer does not feel natural, there is a strong possibility that he may sound insincere to the respondent.

In order to regulate his own behavior, the interviewer must also learn to *observe himself* much more objectively than he would in ordinary circumstances. Most interviewers find it more difficult to be constantly aware of their own non-verbal behavior than of their verbal techniques or tactics. An interviewer can be totally unaware of the fact that he sounds bored, unsympathetic, anxious, rushed, flippant, condescending, or unsure of himself. The pacing, tone of voice, posture and other non-verbal cues can sometimes neutralize the positive effects of good verbal techniques and tactics. It is quite common for a neophyte interviewer who is anxious about the situation to report sincerely that all of his respondents seem to be uneasy and unspontaneous. This may be either because he unwittingly communicates his own anxiety to the respondent, or because his own feelings are so strong that he projects them into his observation and interpretation of the respondent's behavior.

The interviewer must have the *self-discipline* actually to *do* what the situation calls for without wandering from the course. The lack of this self-discipline shows very quickly when the interviewer is fatigued. He will find himself rationalizing that he need not probe any further; he may escape into a sociable chat on the pretext of building rapport; he may be distracted by the temptation to pursue therapeutic bypaths; or he may succumb to morbid curiosity or his desire to be a detective. Methods for increasing skill in the use of techniques and tactics, for improving one's self-observation and self-discipline are suggested in the following section.

A PROCEDURE FOR IMPROVING INTERVIEWING SKILLS

Improving interviewing fundamentals depends upon more than simply putting in time interviewing. The effect of the practice depends upon the degree of self-consciousness with which it is done. The degree of self-consciousness of the practice depends as much upon what the interviewer does *before* and *after* the interview as during it. Therefore, the description of the learning procedure begins with preparation for the interview and ends with the analysis of the results. We will indicate the steps of the procedure in chronological order and point out what can be done at each step to maximize the learning of skills.

Preparing for the interview

Becoming familiar with the objectives. There is no possibility of success in a non-scheduled interview unless the interviewer is intimately familiar with the objectives of the study. Only if the objectives are thoroughly understood can the interviewer reduce them to specific questions to be asked, anticipate and plan for potential inhibitors and facilitators of communication, have criteria for critically evaluating information, and know what points need further probing to meet specifications.

This preparatory step of becoming familiar with the objectives contributes in several ways to skillful performance in the interview.

a) The interviewer can receive information more accurately because he can concentrate his attention on making distinctions relevant to the objectives of the interview.

b) Familiarity with its complexities often increases his interest in the problem. This increased interest contributes to a more skillful performance of all the tasks in the interview.

c) A thorough understanding of the interview objectives supplies the criteria for critical evaluation of the information and guides the interviewer in his probing.

d) This increased intellectual appreciation of the interview goals reduces the danger of *over-rapport* that interferes with objective observation of the respondent and oneself in the interview.

e) This understanding facilitates note taking by allowing a faster and more accurate selection of relevant material.

Regardless of whether the objectives of the interview have been determined by the interviewer himself or have been assigned to him by someone else, the interviewer must so sensitize himself to the specifications that the interview becomes "his problem." This is perhaps more difficult when the problem is assigned to the interviewer.

In studying and analyzing the objectives of the interview, there are several questions that the interviewer should ask himself. First, he should ask: What is the central purpose of the interview? The purpose can be viewed in terms of the central focus of the *information* and in terms of the actual *purpose* for which the information is to be used. If the purpose of the information is to test theory, then the interviewer must be intimately familiar with the theory he is testing. If the purpose is to gather information as a basis for social action, the interviewer should know to what extent the alternative actions are predetermined and to what extent the purpose of the interview is to discover categories of possible action perceived by the respondents. If the alternatives are predetermined, then the interviewer should be familiar with what the alternatives are and their relationship to the specific objectives of the interview.

Second, he should ask: What categories and subcategories of information are needed to fulfill the central purpose of the interview? How are the categories defined? Do these definitions articulate with the central purpose of the interview? Can the categories be broken down into subcategories for increased clarity or to assist the respondent in more completely covering the topic? What specific questions are needed to obtain information relevant to each category? How are the categories and subcategories of information related? What level of abstractness or concreteness is required by the objectives?

Third, the interviewer should try to anticipate the potential range of relevant responses and even some of the apparently related but irrelevant responses. How abstract or concrete must the answer be to fulfill the purposes of the interview?

Interviewers often fail to appreciate the meaning of the need for *concrete examples.* To be truly concrete, an example of an object, event, or situation must be located in a *unique time and place,* and therefore involve a unique scene, objects, actors, and plots.

Potential dangers in being familiar with the objectives. In discussing the need for the interviewer to be intimately familiar with the objectives of the interview, we have neglected to point out that there are potential, but not inescapable, dangers in having knowledge of the theoretical or practical objectives of a study.

Knowledge of the hypotheses being tested or of the social-action implication of the findings may tend to bias the interviewer's behavior in gross or subtle ways which distort the responses themselves or the interviewer's interpretation or recording of the responses. One of the best general collection of studies of experimenter effects is presented by Rosenthal.[6] He reports many experimental studies of the effects of the sciences. We have already mentioned the classical study by Rice[7] in which he had 12 skilled interviewers talk individually with a sample of 2,000 applicants for charity. The interviewers were to diagnose the cause of their dependency status. One of the interviewers, who was a staunch prohibitionist, found three times as many persons blaming alcohol as did another interviewer with socialist views who, in contrast, found many more responses blaming industrial factors. Rice interpreted these results to mean that the *responses* had actually been different. But more recent studies would suggest that much of the bias was in the interpretation and recording of the responses. Since the interviews were not tape recorded, there is no way of testing the truth of these alternative hypotheses.

Just as the respondent tends to give answers that he feels the interviewer wants or expects, so may the interviewer tend to produce results which he thinks the study director, the theory, the hypotheses or the sponsoring organization may desire. One of the many experiments reported by Hyman[8] shows that under some circumstances the interviewer will consciously fabricate answers to questions they never asked and force ambiguous answers into the categories supplied by the interview schedule when they obviously do not fit. In this experimental study, "planted" respondents carefully rehearsed answers especially designed to be ambiguous, equivocal or contradictory in order not to fit the categories provided.

More subtle effects, not involving intentional fabrication, were demonstrated by Wyatt and Campbell[9] in an experimental study of

6/ Robert Rosenthal, *Experimenter Effects in Behavioral Research* (New York: Appleton, Century, Crofts, 1966).

7/ Stuart A. Rice, "Contagious Bias in the Interview: A Methodological Note," *American Journal of Sociology,* Vol. 35 (1929), pp. 420-23.

8/ Herbert H. Hyman *et al., Interviewing in Social Research* (Chicago: University of Chicago Press, 1954).

9/ D. F. Wyatt and D. T. Campbell, "A Study of Interviewer Bias as Related to Interviewers' Expectations and Own Opinions," *International Journal of Opinion and Attitude Research,* Vol. 4 (1950), pp. 77-83.

the effects of the interviewer's expectations on a survey regarding the 1948 presidential election. They found that the interviewers who expected more of the respondents to have discussed the campaign with others tended to obtain responses that bore out this expectancy.

Several different solutions have been practiced to prevent the interviewer's knowledge of the purposes of the study from biasing the results.

Using highly structured interview schedules. This is perhaps the most commonly used method in large scale opinion and attitude surveys. It is assumed that by not allowing the interviewer any freedom of selection of techniques and tactics we will at least standardize the questions so that they will not be unwittingly loaded to bias the responses in any systematic way. This is true to a great extent, but has three clear limitations. First, it does not control all of the *paralinguistic* communication which can bias the response by either changing the meaning of the question or by showing the interviewer's attitude toward the question. Second, this procedure does not eliminate the problem but merely shifts the responsibility for its solution from the interviewer to the person designing the interview schedule. This may be an improvement, however, if it shifts the responsibility to a more highly trained and qualified person. But in those cases where the interview objectives cannot be attained with a highly structured interview schedule, the responsibility must be shifted back to the interviewer. Third, even though by controlling and standardizing the stimulus question we can avoid biasing the actual response, this does not prevent misinterpretation or inaccurate recording of the response even when the answer categories are pre-structured. As we have seen, this is particularly true when the responses are vague, ambiguous or contradictory.

Using a tape recorder. The tape recorder may be used to train the interviewer by allowing him to hear his own verbal and non-verbal techniques and detect possible biasing effects. The recorder is also invaluable in allowing more than one person to hear precisely the same interview and to interpret, record and categorize the responses to do a test of the reliability of the data.

Reducing the interviewer's presence. The interviewer can in some instances be entirely removed from the scene by using a mailed questionnaire instead of an interview. A partial removal of the interviewer is achieved by tape recording questions which have been tested and standardized in advance to avoid any bias in wording or tone of voice. Also, all of the possible bias of the visual cues is automatically eliminated since the interviewer is now invisible. Both of these methods have their legitimate application, but cannot be used where the respondent needs active help in interpreting the question or where he must be motivated to supply a relevant and valid answer. The warmth of the human contact has been shown experimentally to be a strong motivational factor in many kinds of performances of subjects in experiments as well as respondents in interviews. For example, Ware, Kowal, and Baker[10] found that, regardless of the various conditions of environmental stimulation occurring during the signal detection task, those subjects who had been contacted by warmer acting experimenters detected signals significantly better than those who had been contacted by the cooler acting experimenters. Also, the experiment by Reece and Whitman[11] shows the same motivational effect of the warm experimenter and has the added advantages of clearly and operationally defining warm versus cool behavior. In the "warm" behavior, the experimenter leaned toward the subject, looked directly at him, smiled, and kept his hands still. In the "cool" behavior, the experimenter leaned away from the subject, looked around the room, did not smile, and was drumming his fingers.

Counterbalancing the bias. It is actually possible under certain conditions to obtain the same result from one study where all of the interviewers are unbiased and another study in which half of the interviewers are biased in one direction and half in the other. If we do not know the direction or strength of the bias of any of the interviewers, it is sometimes proposed that we simply select several interviewers at random who in turn select a large sample of respondents at random. In this way it might be assumed that we not only cancel out the biases of the interviewers but also of the combination of interviewer and respondent. However, this is not necessarily the happy result of opposing biases. In their analysis of an opinion survey, Stember and Hyman[12] demonstrated that interviewers holding the more popular opinion tended to report data that inflated the number of respondents with the same opinion as their own. But the

10/ J. R. Ware, B. Kowal, and R. A. Baker, *The Role of Experimenter Attitude and Contingent Reinforcement in a Vigilance Task,* unpublished paper, U.S. Army Armor Human Research Unit, Fort Knox, Kentucky, 1963.

11/ M. M. Reece and R. N. Whitman, "Expressive Movements, Warmth and Verbal Reinforcement," *Journal of Abnormal and Social Psychology,* Vol. 64 (1962), pp. 234-36.

12/ C. H. Stember and H. H. Hyman, "How Interviewer Effects Operate Through Question Form," *International Journal of Opinion and Attitude Research,* Vol. 3 (1949), pp. 493-512.

interviewers holding the less popular opinion did not simply inflate the opposite answer, but inflated the "don't know" category instead. In this case, rather than cancelling out the distortion by one interviewer's bias counteracting the other's, the error was cumulative. This strongly suggests that it is much more desirable to correct error at its source than to depend upon statistical randomization or purposive selection of interviewers with opposing biases.

All of the above solutions to the possible biasing effects of the interviewer's knowledge about, and attitude toward, the purposes of the study, place external restraints upon the interviewer or depend upon counterbalancing the error after it occurs. Both solutions work under limited conditions, but become less appropriate (*a*) when the major purpose of the interview is discovery, (*b*) when there is no highly structured interview schedule, (*c*) when more flexibility is needed to communicate the question to different kinds of respondents and (*d*) when more interviewer activity is needed to motivate the respondent to give relevant and valid information.

Under these conditions, the only solution is to select and train interviewers to know when active flexibility must be exercised and how to use the freedom to motivate the respondent to give valid information rather than to bias his response. The interviewer must learn to replace external restraints by internal ones which allow more creative activity.

Anticipating potential inhibitors and facilitators. In attempting to anticipate potential inhibitors and facilitators of communication, the interviewer should keep in mind that the inhibitor or facilitator is *potentially* present, depending on the type of information the prospective respondent has to give. Whether or not the potentiality becomes actuality depends upon the nature of the interviewer-respondent relationship as seen by the respondent in the larger context of the interview situation.

Unfortunately, the interviewer does not know in advance the type of information the prospective respondent has to give; therefore in anticipating potential inhibitors he must consider the possible range of answers to the specific questions he intends to ask. If some of the possible answers to the question would tend to be inhibited by the respondent, then the question should be treated as a potential communication inhibitor, and appropriate strategy, techniques, and tactics should be used to minimize the inhibiting effect.

Each topic, subtopic, and question that is planned in advance of the first interview should be earmarked to show which main inhibitor or facilitator might be involved. Subsequent experiences might prove these anticipations incorrect in some instances. Nevertheless, the attempt to anticipate will be generally useful and contribute to a more skillful performance.

Planning the strategy of the approach. Now that the interviewer is clear on the precise objectives of the interview and has considered some of the potential inhibitors and facilitators of communication, he is ready to consider the means of obtaining the information. Usually, it is well to consider the strategy problems first. If we assume that the problem is within the interviewer's ability and role repertory, the next strategy decisions are selecting the appropriate role for the interviewer, choosing a respondent most willing and able to give the required information, setting an appropriate time and place for the interview and, finally, deciding how to structure the interview situation.

Structuring the interview situation includes introducing oneself to the respondent, explaining the sponsorship of the study, explaining the purpose of the interview, explaining how the respondent has been selected, providing anonymity, and planning the method of recording the interview. All of these facets of the situation are relevant only insofar as they relate to the respondent's ability or willingness to give relevant information. Usually, it is a good rule to say that if a problem can be anticipated and solved at the strategy level this should be done rather than depending upon techniques and tactics. Usually enough problems will remain which can be solved only on the spot, in the interview situation.

Preparing an interview guide. The interview guide has two basic functions. It not only helps guide the interviewer through the interview, but also furnishes a method of recording what has been covered. To provide a method of recording, the guide may include a list of specific topics, subtopics, specific questions or categories of answers that may be checked off after they have been covered adequately. Or, the guide might provide space under each topic or subtopic for probe notes to remind the interviewer what should be clarified or elaborated to meet the specifications of that topic. In some cases when a tape recorder is not used, enough space is provided under each topic to take notes on all the relevant information received. Various combinations of these three formats can be used.

The interview guide, particularly before the first interview has been done, should be viewed as a flexible aid rather than a fixed outline that prevents the interviewer from using any technique or tactic that might prove to be appropriate on the spur of the moment. The degree to which specific techniques and tactics can be planned in advance depends upon the nature of the subject matter and the number of interviews that have gone into the reformulation of the interview guide.

In preparing the interview guide, the interviewer must translate the objectives of the interview into (*a*) subtopics, (*b*) questions which need to be answered that may or may not have to be asked directly, (*c*) possible probes to use, and (*d*) in some cases, categories of relevant answers that might be expected. Wording of questions should be planned carefully considering the vocabulary, context, scope, answer structure, and the possibility of using intentionally leading questions. The usual two criteria should be used in selecting among various possible techniques: (*a*) their relevance to the information objectives of the interview, and (*b*) their probable effect upon minimizing potential inhibitors and maximizing potential facilitators of relevant information.

In addition to planning the verbal techniques that to some extent can be built into the interview guide, the interviewer should also do an introspective analysis of his own attitude toward the topic of the interview, toward the interviewing task, and toward the type of respondent to be interviewed. In this way he may be able to anticipate certain points at which he must exert special effort to withhold expression of negative attitudes and to express positive attitudes.

Once the objectives of the interview have been reduced to specific subtopics and questions, tentative plans can be made for the sequence in which subtopics will be discussed, how they will be introduced, what transitions or pivot questions might be needed, where funnel or inverted funnel sequences might be needed to develop a topic, how much topic control to use in probing each topic, and how any symptoms of resistance in the respondent might be treated.

The pre-planning of strategy, techniques, and tactics suggested above may not be followed in every detail during the interview; nevertheless, careful pre-planning will help the interviewer to improve his interviewing skill. In the first place, it makes the interviewer aware of the differences between what he expects and what actually happens in the interview and lays the foundation for the post-interview analysis where he attempts to account for these discrepancies. And second, since much of the pre-planning is successful, it reduces the amount of confusion in the interview, allowing the interviewer to concentrate on the types of tactical problems which cannot be anticipated.

Of course, the process of becoming familiar with the objectives and anticipating potential inhibitors and facilitators is necessary before any of the pre-planning can be done. Both are also necessary for skillful probing in the interview.

Doing the interview for self-improvement

Pre-testing the situation. Regardless of how much experience an interviewer might have, he should always pre-test the specific interview situation associated with a series of interviews on a new topic. This is particularly vital for the person aiming to improve his skills. By "pre-testing the situation" we mean that the interviewer should become accustomed to the concrete details of the setting and the instruments to be used in the interview before doing the first interview. This would include such things as becoming familiar with the place where the interview is to be done, insofar as possible making the physical arrangements conducive to communication, becoming familiar with the use of the tape recorder in the specific setting, practicing taking probe notes and using the interview guide in the particular physical setting, and perhaps role-playing some practice introductions by which the situation is structured for the respondent.

Without these precautions it is improbable that even the best plans and sophisticated theory could be skillfully implemented because of some unanticipated, ridiculously obvious practical problem. The following are typical examples of such practical problems found by interviewers: there may be too much noise in the area, the room may be so small that it soon becomes stuffy, there may not be the right type of electrical outlet for the tape recorder, the interviewer may not know how to operate the particular tape recording machine that is available, the machine may be out of order, there may be no available surface for writing probe notes. Most of these problems can be avoided by pre-testing the situation and arriving in advance of the interview to check the setting and equipment. There is nothing more embarrassing for the interviewer than to find that neither he nor the respondent has a pencil or that some simple mechanical error in the use of the tape recorder has resulted in a blank tape. Familiarity with the interview setting eases the interviewer's mind and makes it easier for him to concentrate on the task of helping the respondent relax.

Using a tape recorder. In order to make the most of each interview for the purpose of improving basic skills, the interview should be electronically recorded. This is particularly important in learning non-scheduled interviewing because it frees the interviewer from the burden of trying to record all of the relevant details and allows him to devote more attention to the respondent and to regulating his own techniques and tactics. Since he is able to use tactics and techniques more self-consciously he is more likely to learn from the experience. In addition, the tape recording allows the interviewer to re-live the experience by listening to it later when he is freer to observe his own and the respondent's behavior.

Using the interview guide. An interview guide is usually a necessity when the interview is even slightly complex, when the interviewer has not had experience with many interviews on the same topic, and particularly when the interviewer is attempting to improve his interviewing skills. Since the guide is a reminder of the specific interview objectives, it should alert the interviewer to any inadequacies of information *during* the interview in time to test various techniques and tactics for obtaining the information vis-à-vis the respondent.

Taking probe notes. The taking of probe notes in conjunction with the use of an interview guide helps the interviewer keep a running account of what has been covered. Probe notes also provide vital clues to what needs to be probed further and supplies some of the vocabulary to be used in probing. This, in turn, makes the interviewer more secure and less likely to panic, which frees his energies for tactical problems. This increased attention to the important problems during the interview maximizes the learning value of the experience. Taking probe notes during the interview also lays the basis for a more meaningful post-interview analysis.

Focusing on the basic tasks. Once all the pre-planning is done, the situation has been pre-tested, and the objective procedures of using a tape recorder, taking probe notes, and using an interview guide are previewed, the problem during the interview is to *concentrate* on a few major tasks. The interviewer should not spend interview time in taking an inventory of all the specific techniques and tactics possible concerned or in worrying about his performance and how it might appear to the respondent.

He should constantly be asking himself: What is the respondent saying? What portion of it is relevant? Is it adequate or does it need clarification or elaboration? What question or probe should be used next to meet the objectives of the interview? What are the verbal and non-verbal clues to the state of the interpersonal relations between the respondent and myself? How might these affect the informational objectives of the interview?

In sensitizing himself to the respondent's non-verbal behavior, it is often helpful for the interviewer to concentrate his attention on *changes* in the non-verbal communication whether these be changes in tempo, tone of voice, posture, hand movements, facial expression, eye movements, or forcefulness of speech. It is important to focus upon changes in the respondent's behavior rather than attempting a direct comparison of one respondent's manner with another's because of general personality and cultural differences between respondents. For example, we cannot always assume that a deliberate, measured pacing with frequent pauses indicates that the respondent is being cautious about the information he is divulging. If the person's normal speech pattern is rapid and fluent and at some point becomes halting and monotonous, the interviewer should note this change and in the context of the total situation judge whether anything can or should be done about the tension which is indicated.

Analysis of the interview for self-improvement

The interviewer can improve his skill more rapidly in a series of interviews if he carefully analyzes each one *before* attempting another in the series. The interviewer must not be so disappointed with the results of his first attempt in an interview series that he is sure that he can improve without bothering to analyze his experience. It is tempting to assume that it was mainly the respondent's peculiarities which were to blame for the inadequacies in the information and believe that the next interview is destined to be better. Or, the interviewer may be extremely lucky in one interview and not realize how much of the relevant information was obtained *despite* rather than because of the methods he used. If this is the case he may be shocked by the difficulties encountered in later interviews.

In order to make solid progress in interviewing skills the interviewer must resist any tendency to abandon impatiently a calm analysis of each interview in favor of rushing into feverish activity of "learning by doing."

The analysis of the results of each interview should be translated into improved plans for the next interview. In doing this it is important for the interviewer to avoid assuming that any technique or tactic which did not succeed in one interview should be abandoned in future interviews. It might simply be that the particular respondent did not actually have the information or that certain inhibitors of communication were operating because of the role relationship between interviewer and respondent. In either case, the specific techniques or tactic should not be blamed.

Let us now examine some of the specific steps in analyzing the results of an interview as a means to improving skills.

Analysis of strategy. In view of his experience in the first interview of a series, the interviewer is often aware of some improvements which can be made in his selection of and approach to the respondent. The interviewer should make a checklist of all the strategy problems that might be involved and then indicate which ones were dealt with in the strategy plans, which of these were apparently adequate in actual practice, and which problems had not been anticipated. It is also probable that some of the strategy plans were not actually needed. Any suggested improvements in strategy can be incorporated in the plans for approaching the next respondent.

Analysis of non-verbal responses. Before becoming involved in the detailed analysis of the information obtained or the methods used to obtain the information, it is often helpful for the interviewer to listen to the tape recorded interview to note the non-verbal responses. At this time the interviewer is freer to concentrate fully on the respondent since he does not have to take probe notes or plan the next question. Of course, the tape does not preserve the visual non-verbal responses but it is helpful in showing changes in tone of voice, pacing, pitch, hesitations, nervous giggling, self-interruptions, and interruptions by the respondent. As was previously suggested, it is best to concentrate upon *changes* in the quality of the non-verbal communication.

When such changes are noted, the interviewer can raise the question of whether any of the inhibitors or facilitators of communication which he had anticipated might underlie the fluctuations in the non-verbal communication. If the interviewer is able to diagnose any difficulty, he can plan to meet it better in future interviews on the same topic. The interviewer should ask himself whether he had noticed all of the non-verbal messages while actually doing the interview. If some were not noted, perhaps the interviewer can discover why. If the respondent's non-verbal behavior shows symptoms of either inability or unwillingness to give information, then the interviewer should note what he either did or neglected to do about it.

Analysis of adequacy of information. By listening to the tape a second time the interviewer can analyze the information obtained. This should be done by using either the interview guide or a special coding system to categorize all of the information that is relevant to the objectives of the interview.[13]

This content analysis can be more meaningful if done by both the interviewer and another person. If two people independently analyze the results and then discuss any disagreements they have, both will increase their sensitivity to inadequate responses and the need for probing to obtain clear and complete information. Disagreements between the interviewer and the other coder about the relevance of a particular item of information are often due to the tendency of the interviewer to assume hopefully that the respondent meant more than he said. Another possibility is that one of the coders or both do not understand the precise specifications of the information sought.

Any time there is a disagreement between coders as to the meaning, relevance, or completeness of the information, they should discuss what type of probe would have helped to clarify any ambiguity or to supply any incomplete information. It might also be necessary to discuss the criteria of relevance by clarifying the definitions of the categories of information. Either type of discussion will clarify the objectives and sensitize the interviewer to means of reaching these objectives.

Of course there will be many occasions when both coders agree that certain information which was accepted as relevant and adequate during the interview breaks down under cold analysis into a meaningless confusion. In this case, it becomes clear that the interviewer either neglected to pursue the objectives or was unsuccessful in his attempt. It has been found that in the early stages of learning non-scheduled interviewing, most interviewers do not obtain all the relevant information. Either they lack a precise understanding of the objectives of the interview or they fail to recognize the inadequacy of the information until they begin to analyze the results. A novice rarely tries to probe persistently for clarification and elaboration to

13/ Lester Guest, "A New Training Method for Opinion Interviewers," *Public Opinion Quarterly*, Vol. 18 (Fall, 1954), pp. 287-99. The author shows that the interviewer's error was reduced more when coding (interview analysis) was included in the training program than when practice interviews were included.

discover whether the respondent is unable or unwilling to give the information.

Once the interviewer has become acutely aware of the adequacies and inadequacies of the information, he is in a better position to analyze the techniques and tactics he used.

Analysis of techniques and tactics. By listening to the tape recording a third time the interviewer can hear the techniques and tactics he used. He should become aware of how much of the specific information was obtained by careful questioning, how much was obtained without any special effort, how much was missed because of his failure to probe, and how much was missed in spite of his attempts to probe.

The interviewer should critically examine his every probe and question and decide whether there might have been a more appropriate one at that point. In doing this, the interviewer must consider the type of information sought and the potential inhibitors and facilitators to be dealt with. He should be sensitive to any failure to communicate the question clearly and the need to re-word it, provide contexts, or change its scope. He might also discover misused leading questions or neglected opportunities for using leading questions advantageously.

In listening to the tape the interviewer should try to evaluate his own attitudes as demonstrated in the interview. Does he manifest positive attitudes toward the interviewing task? Does he show a non-judgmental attitude toward the information he receives? Does he evince a vital interest in the information and indicate that he does not accept everything uncritically? Does he show positive attitudes toward the respondent as a person? Are there opportunities where the respondent could be praised for his effort or performance? Does the interviewer give such praise? Does the interviewer sound afraid, unsure, or confused? All of these questions can be answered by listening carefully to both the verbal and non-verbal behavior of the interviewer.

There are some symptoms of confusion and tension which the interviewer should learn to detect in himself. Three of these symptoms found most frequently are (*a*) the tendency to re-word questions for no defensible reason, (*b*) the tendency to use multiple questions, and (*c*) the tendency to mechanically use the echo probe. Let us examine some typical examples.

Re-wording the question. The frequent recurrence of this form of verbal behavior often indicates that the interviewer is tense and fears that the respondent will not understand the question. Sometimes it indicates that the interviewer has a low opinion of the respondent's ability. Even though this is not true, there is the danger of the respondent's so interpreting the behavior. The general compulsion to re-word questions must not be confused with the occasional self-correction or clarification. The following are typical examples of compulsive rewording.

I: When was the first time you ever owned or drove a car? When did you become an owner or learn to drive any type of automobile?

I: Have you had any disagreements with your parents in the last year? Have you had any squabbles, arguments, or verbal battles with them recently? Either one of them?

Regardless of the interviewer's reason for re-wording the question, a failure to pause between each successive re-wording tends to give the impression that the interviewer is impatient and wants to accelerate the pace of the interview.

Multiple questions. A related habit shared by many neophyte non-scheduled interviewers is the tendency to add one question to another before the respondent has an opportunity to answer the first. For example:

I: What is your general philosophy of raising children? Do you feel that modern psychology is of any value or not? Would you be more in agreement with psychoanalytic approaches or not?

This example is typical in that multiple questions are often in the form of a funnel sequence becoming increasingly specific without allowing the respondent to answer them in turn. This defeats the purpose of a funnel sequence and gives the respondent the impression that the interviewer is impatient or confused.

Sometimes such behavior is prompted by the fear that the respondent will not be able or willing to answer the broader question. Usually such a fear is groundless and is actually a projection of the interviewer's general insecurity in the situation.

Echo probes. The reader will recall that the echo probe is generally the least fruitful of the three types of reflective probes. It is usually effective only if the words which are echoed happen to be emotionally charged for the respondent. When this is not true, as in the example below, the echo probe is useless.

R: When I heard the first explosion, I thought it was the city blasting for the new water main. But then when I heard a bigger explosion next door I knew something had gone wrong. I think that was about 12:30 when I heard the second blast!

   I: About 12:30?

Generally, such a probe merely elicits a "that's right" from the respondent. If the same type of echo probe is used too frequently, it may give the respondent the impression that the interviewer does not hear well or is not paying attention. For some interviewers the echo probe is unconsciously developed as a stopgap measure in cases where they do not know what else to do.

It is often worthwhile to pay special attention to the use of silence as it affects the general pace and mood of the interview. The interviewer should note the extent to which he adjusts to the respondent's pace or vice versa. He should check whether the pacing is monotonous and mechanical or flexible and meaningful in the context of the interview, and he should look for interruptions of the respondent whether intentional or not.

In critically listening to his own tactics, the interviewer should first be aware of any deviations from the tactical pre-planning and ask whether the deviation was intentional and whether it was an improvement over the original plans. Was the original arrangement of topics and subtopics followed? Were there some questions which should have been introduced by lead-in questions, pivot questions, or transitional statements? If so, what should they have been? When was the funnel or inverted funnel sequence of questions used? When should it have been used?

The interviewer should listen carefully to his on the spot probing to detect tendencies to under-control or over-control. Awareness of one's natural tendency in probing can help the interviewer become more flexible and use a wider range of topic control when it is appropriate.

Although the basic skills in which we are interested are associated with the phases of the interviewer's activity *during* an interview, the general procedure for learning these skills emphasizes the learner's activity *before* and *after* the interview. The ultimate goals are to receive information from the respondent more accurately, evaluate this information more critically, and to exert more control over one's own behavior during the interview. However, these goals can be reached more rapidly by thoughtful preparation before and careful analysis after each interview before rushing on to the next.

Up to this point we have only talked about how to develop the full range of one's interviewing skills. The next logical step would seem to be to stop talking and get on with the doing. However, it will be profitable to precede this action phase with the experiences of thinking through all of the dimensions of a real data-gathering problem.

In the following problem the reader can observe the type of thinking which generated a research problem, see one approach to solving the problem, share the author's critique of this approach, and evaluate the author's proposed solution to the problem. This vicarious experience provides some insights into the complexities of both the planning phase and the analysis phase which are so essential for converting the act of interviewing into a learning experience.

It will be more useful to the reader if he sketchily writes his own critique and solutions *before* reading the author's critique and suggested alternatives.

A DATA-GATHERING PROBLEM

Up to this point we have focused on one methodological aspect at a time. But in an actual data-gathering project several aspects are intertwined as the following example illustrates. After studying the purposes of the project, criticize the methods used in collecting the information. Assuming that the original formulation of the problem, the selection of respondents, and the field conditions are unaltered, what might be an alternative strategy (including any pre-structuring of techniques and tactics) which might obtain better results?

Description of the study

A group of physical, biological, and social scientists were discussing the attitudes of laymen toward science. There was general agreement that college freshmen had a blind faith in the physical sciences and a highly skeptical attitude toward the application of scientific method to the study of human behavior even though they were equally ignorant of both fields. For example, as one physicist put it,

When I show the freshman a model of a molecule or a diagram of an atom, he hasn't the slightest doubt of their existence, even though he has never seen either. But if I discuss such concepts as the subconscious mind, he shows great skepticism. Yet if I were called upon to give a classroom demonstration showing direct evidence of the existence of either an atom or the subconscious mind, I think the latter would be easier. It would require no more than a demonstration of post-hypnotic suggestion. I suppose this is because no one has constructed a theoretical model of the subconscious mind as a pedagogical device to help the freshman focus his attention.

There was an agreement among scientists in all three fields that the accumulation of systematic scientific generalizations had proceeded further in the physical and biological sciences than in the social sciences but that the layman was not aware of the progress which had been made in the social sciences and was more skeptical of the fruitfulness of the social sciences than of the physical or biological sciences.

After some discussion the following chain of hunches was constructed to provide a very tentative explanation of the phenomenon of the differential awareness of physical and social sciences.

First, the layman's conception of science is mainly composed of the *products* of science, and he is mostly aware of the practical products as opposed to the theoretical products such as a principle, law, hypothesis or theory.

Second, the type of practical products he is most aware of are those which are frequently mentioned in the mass media of communication such as TV, radio, newspapers, movies, and magazines. Here the word "science" is most frequently heard in an advertisement of some consumer product or in connection with national interests in the cold war.

Third, since the products of the social sciences (for example, unidimensional attitude scales, I.Q. tests, random sample surveys, sociometric analysis, and so on) are rarely saleable to individual consumers on a mass basis, they are rarely mentioned in advertising. Neither is this type of product as adaptable to visual presentation as are physical gadgets. Even biological processes such as a headache or a stomach-ache must be represented on TV as a series of mechanical gadgets operating within the human body.

Fourth, the omnipresence of physical science and the absence of social science products in the context of mass media leads the layman to assume that physical science is more potent than it is and that social science is less potent than it is. Perhaps this lack of faith in social sciences is accompanied by the layman's fear that social sciences aim to reduce human behavior to a mechanical formula and, therefore, human freedom to zero. This fear flows quite naturally from applying the imagery of physical sciences to the social sciences. The "reasoning" would be somewhat as follows: "The more that is known about the laws of physics, the more man makes a slave of the physical world; therefore, the more that is known about the laws of human behavior, the more man will make a slave of himself."

Fifth, this combination of lack of faith in the possibility of developing social sciences and the fear that they might become too developed constitutes a barrier to the progress of the social sciences at a time when they are most sorely needed to solve many of the social problems resulting from the advance of physical science and technology and to seek ways of resolving international conflicts without resort to war before man destroys himself with his new physical and biological inventions.

In order to try to bring this armchair speculation to an empirical test, the scope of the problem was considerably narrowed to conduct a small-scale pilot study of a small segment of laymen and narrow the problem to test a few crude hypotheses. On the basis of this pilot a followup study could be done with more precision and larger numbers of people. The small segment of laymen chosen for study was all the freshmen at one small liberal arts college.

The hypotheses do not cover all the points in the speculation mentioned above but were considered some of the most easily tested points of departure. The hypotheses were

1) Most freshmen tend to think of "science" as strictly physical to the exclusion of biological and social sciences.

2) Most freshmen are more concerned with the practical results or applications of sciences and have very little awareness of the methods by which they are attained or with the aims of pure theoretical science.

3) Those freshmen who show some awareness of and interest in the means used by the scientists to solve their problems will be more aware of specific techniques and instruments which can be easily represented visually than with general scientific methods as applied in all fields.

4) Most of the freshmen's knowledge of the results of science will be the type which is supplied by the mass media of communication, particularly in advertising consumer products and headline news items.

5) Freshmen will have little awareness of inventions or discoveries in the biological or social fields.

6) Most freshmen will have a definition, often unconscious, of inventions and discoveries that prevents them from including biological and social inventions.

7) Most freshmen will assume that the physical sciences can accomplish feats which physical scientists themselves feel impossible according to their own theory, and they will assume that the social sciences cannot perform feats which have already been accomplished.

This last hypothesis was considered of crucial importance because it distinguishes between a simple lack of awareness of social sciences due to their lesser accomplishments and a form of prejudice against the latest immigrant into the scientific world.

It was decided that 250 freshmen (all at the one college) would be included in the study.

Since this was an exploratory study, it was decided to proceed in such a way as to discover aspects of science that were important to the respondents other than those included in each hypothesis. For example, in connection with the second hypothesis there might be other aspects of science with which the freshmen are concerned other than practical results, theoretical aims, and methods or techniques. Also, in the third hypothesis, for example, it would be desirable to discover what other possible sources of influence affect the respondent's image of science.

Campus situation. At this college all of the freshmen live in double rooms in college dormitories. The freshmen are not mixed with older students but have their own dormitories. All freshmen were taking a general education course in social sciences, biological sciences, physical sciences, and English. The college is coeducational, private, and nondenominational. It has a general liberal arts program.

Method used. The study was done under the auspices of social science departments who reached all freshmen by making the following announcement in the four introductory social science classes during the ninth week of the 12-week spring quarter.

As you all know, there is a growing concern with improving science programs throughout the country. The upgrading of training and of the quality of people recruited is a concern of the physical, social, and biological fields. We are beginning a study of some of the important aspects of the problem. We need your cooperation. You will be contacted by student interviewers from the psychology and sociology departments beginning next Monday.

We are telling you about this now for two reasons: first, so that you will understand the general nature of the problem and, second, you will have some time to think about it between now and then so that you will be able to give more relevant information in a short time to the interviewer.

The interviewer will talk with you about your ideas of science, where you got these ideas, your definitions of invention, what you perceive to be scientific method, and differences in your perception of the physical, biological, and social sciences. They are not interested so much in any specific knowledge but only in your general ideas and opinions. The interview will not take much of your time, perhaps only half an hour, and you will find it an interesting experience. We will appreciate your help.

This explanation was given on Thursday, and the interviewers began interviewing the freshmen in the dormitory rooms on the following Monday. The approach used by the interviewer was as follows:

I am John Jacobs. I am working on the study of attitudes toward science which was announced in class last Thursday. I have just nine questions I would like to ask. Do you have any questions you would like to ask before we begin?

(Here the interviewer was instructed to answer any questions the respondent might have to ease his mind before proceeding. Usually there were no questions, and the interviewer went ahead with the first question.)

The interview schedule is presented in the following section. In the questions with structured answers, the interviewer merely checked the most appropriate response, or if the respondent had an answer not provided for by the categories, the interviewer would write it in. In the open-ended questions (eight and nine), the interviewer was instructed to write everything the respondent said. If the respondent spoke too rapidly, the interviewer was to take sketchy notes and fill them in immediately after the interview. The interviewer was instructed to follow the order of the interview schedule shown.

INTERVIEW GUIDE

Freshman's name ——————————

Major field ——————————

(if chosen)

1. When you hear the word, "science," which do you think of? (*Hand the respondent the card with the following categories.*)
   a) —— The physical sciences only.
   b) —— Physical and biological sciences.
   c) —— Physical, biological, and social sciences.
   d) —— Biological and social sciences only.
   e) —— Biological sciences only.
   f) —— Social sciences only.

2. When you think of science, which aspect comes to your mind mainly? (*Hand the respondent the card with the following categories.*)
   a) —— A general method of solving problems of cause and effect.
   b) —— Specific techniques used in a certain field of science.
   c) —— Practical results or applications of science.

d) ____ Theoretical aims or results of science.

e) ____ Something else (if so, what?).

3. Where do you get most of your ideas about science? (*Do not give answer categories to respondent, but classify his responses by checking all the sources he mentions.*)

    a) ____ From a course in high school.

    b) ____ From courses now being taken in college.

    c) ____ From family.

    d) ____ From friends.

    e) ____ From TV, radio, movies, newspapers, or magazines.

    f) ____ From own independent study of scientific books.

    g) ____ From other source (if so, what?).

4. Now you have mentioned getting ideas from _____ . Which of these has had the most influence for you?

5. Most of us have some degree of blind faith in something. Would you say that you tended to have the most blind faith in which of the following:

    a) ____ The ability of physical science to solve physical problems.

    b) ____ The ability of social sciences to solve social problems.

    c) ____ The ability of biological sciences to solve biological problems.

    d) ____ None of these.

6. Which of the following ideas do you think should be included in a definition of a "scientific discovery"? (*Hand respondent the card.*)

    a) ____ Can be something found accidentally.

    b) ____ Must be intentionally sought.

    c) ____ Must have theoretical importance.

    d) ____ Must have practical importance (immediate application).

    e) ____ Can be a physical (non-living) tangible object.

    f) ____ Can be a living object.

    g) ____ Can be a principle, law, or theory.

    h) ____ Can include social phenomena.

    i) ____ Other _____

7. Which of the following ideas do you think should be included in the definition of invention? (invention as a noun.) (*Hand card to respondent.*)

    a) ____ Must be a result of intentional human effort.

    b) ____ Must solve some human problem.

    c) ____ Must be of practical value.

    d) ____ Must be a physical object of some kind.

    e) ____ Can include a living object.

    f) ____ Can include a process by which a result is achieved.

    g) ____ Other _____

8. I will give you one minute to name as many results of science as you can. By results I mean discoveries or inventions.

9. What sort of picture comes into your mind when you think of a scientist? (Areas to be covered in probing: What is he doing? Location of work. Type of problem he is working on. For whom is he working? What kind of person is he? How is he dressed? What does he do when he is not working? What kind of social life does he have?)

A SAMPLE INTERVIEW[14]

I-1: Hello, I'm Jerry Levi. I am working on the study of attitudes toward science which was explained in class last Thursday. I have been assigned to interview everybody in this dorm. I would like to ask you about nine questions. Do you have any questions you would like to ask me before we start?

R-1: Yes, what's the first question on this test? (smiling)

I-2: Good (smiling back), here it is. When you hear the word "science" which of these do you think of? (*Hands card to respondent.*)

R-2: Hmmm, let's see. Well, I think of all of them. Then the answer would be *c*. Who would only think of social sciences!

I-3: When you think of science, which aspect comes to your mind mainly? (*Hands respondent the card.*)

R-3: I'd say that all of these would be included.

I-4: Which would be the main one?

R-4: Well, of course everyone is interested in results, but you can't get any results unless you know the methods and techniques. Detailed techniques are interesting, even the cyclotron is a technique, but the broadest, (3) and I'd say the most important, aspects would be the general method because it is something that is applied in all fields of science.

I-5: I see, that's a good way of putting it. Where do you get most of your ideas about science?

R-5: You see, I've always been interested in science. I think my high school chemistry teacher was the first one to make science interesting for me. And of course now I'm taking the course called the Physical Science World-Picture. I find that very interesting. It is a lot different from the high school course.

I-6: Any other sources of ideas about science?

R-6: I have done some reading on my own because I am interested in it. I have even read some science fiction just for kicks.

I-7: Anything else?

R-7: No, that's all I can think of.

I-8: Now you mentioned that your ideas came from the high school chemistry course, your college course called the Physical Science World-Picture and your own independent reading of books. Which one of these sources do you feel had the most influence on your general idea of science and the feeling you have toward it?

R-8: I think that it depends mostly on my own reading. After all I have

14/ The numbers in parentheses indicate seconds of silence.

been in college only six months and I have been reading on my own since before that.

I-9: Most of us have some degree of blind faith in certain things. In which one of the following would you tend to have the most blind faith? The ability of physical science to solve physical problems, the ability of the biological sciences to solve biological problems, the ability of the social sciences to solve social problems, or none of these?

R-9: I'd say "none of these" if you are talking about *blind* faith, because that's one thing a scientist should not have is blind faith. He has to have faith in human intelligence, but that is well founded on the past history of man's successful efforts to solve all kinds of problems. Physics, for example, has demonstrated that it can get results to fulfill anything man is capable of imagining. I'd go so far as to say that I have faith in the physical sciences, but I wouldn't call it blind. Yes, I'd say I have *blind* faith in none of these!

I-10: Which of the following ideas do you think should be included in a definition of a scientific discovery? (*Hands card to respondent.*)

R-10: It doesn't have to be found intentionally. A lot of discoveries were accidental. Wasn't the way of curing rubber discovered accidentally? Many times a scientist is looking for one thing, but finds another. I'd call it a discovery if it had either theoretical or practical use. In either case it is of some value to man. Also it can be a tangible object, either living or non-living, or some principle or law. It would also have to include any practical or theoretical finding about social phenomena. I can't think of anything else that should be included.

I-11: That's fine. Now which of the following ideas do you think should be included in the definition of invention? Here we are using "invention" as a noun. (*Hands card to respondent.*)

R-11: That's right—the invention is a result of intentional human effort. You just can't make inventions accidentally like you can discoveries. And it must solve some sort of human problem—using the term broadly—you know, building a better mouse trap and all that. A mouse trap is an invention that solves a problem. Practical value—well, yes. If it solves a problem, it's practical. Yes, I suppose an invention is always a physical object. It cannot be a living object because then it is not man-made. No, the process is not the invention, but the product of the process might be an invention. Also an invention is something that people usually patent and sell.

I-12: I will give you just one minute to name as many results of science as you can. I'll tell you when to start and when your minute is up. By "results of science" I mean any discoveries or inventions you can think of. All right, start now.

R-12: Airplane, penicillin, radio, cotton gin, telephone, internal combustion engine, atomic energy, television, polio vaccine, sputnik, ICBM, transistor, vacuum tube, electric light bulb, electricity, washing machine (4).

I-13: Your time's up. That was very good.

R-13: Gosh, I got stuck and couldn't think of another thing. I'll probably think of a million things later.

I-14: What sort of picture comes to your mind when you think of a scientist?

R-14: A scientist . . . the easiest thing to conjure up is a man in a white coat over a gurgling retort or watching the dials on some electronic machine.

I-15: What kind of problem is he working on?

R-15: I don't know . . . he is trying to invent some sort of wonder drug or working with radioactive isotopes. There is a lot going on in that field now—trying to use atomic physics in combating cancer. Or maybe he would be figuring a way to simplify the new breeder reactor; you know that's the machine which allows one atomic fuel to be converted into another type of atomic fuel. It sounds like it defies the law of conservation and energy.

I-16: Where is he working?

R-16: In some laboratory—gosh, I don't know!

I-17: Well, who is he working for?

R-17: I don't know exactly. He might be working for the government or some big industry or some university. It depends on the project.

I-18: I see. Now tell me a little about what kind of person he is.

R-18: First of all he is devoted to science. He lives to make discoveries. He has learned to discipline himself so that he is not distracted by the routine events that most of us spend so much time with. Sort of like Madame Curie. You know, that's funny, sometimes when you say scientist, I think of a bald-headed neatly shaven man in a white coat. Other times I think of a man with sloppy long hair and an old wrinkled sweatshirt like Einstein. I guess that is the philosopher or mathematician. The man with the technical know-how is neat.

I-19: What kind of social life does the scientist have?

R-19: Social life? He has no social life—except when they have a party to celebrate some accomplishment. He has just a small circle of trusted friends who don't make too many demands on him. They have a simple life with little or no publicity unless he makes a breakthrough on some problem.

The answers the interviewer recorded on his code sheet for the first seven questions, which have structured answers, are as follows: (1) *c,* (2) *a,* (3) *a, b, f,* (4) *f,* (5) *d,* (6) *a, e, g, h,* (7) *a, b, c.* (*At this point the reader should record his own criticisms of the strategy, techniques, and tactics used and his own suggestions for alternative solutions.*)

Author's critique and alternative solutions

We will indicate errors in strategy, tactics, and techniques, explaining as we go our reasons for classifying them as errors and finally suggesting an alternative strategy, which we consider superior, for obtaining the same information. As much as possible we will follow the same format suggested under "analysis of the interview for self-improvement."

In giving suggestions the writer has a distinct advantage in that he has the hindsight resulting from having done such a study. There is no claim that the approach suggested is flawless, but it is better in many ways than the one which the reader has been asked to criticize.

Strategy errors. These may be classified into the following six categories.

Sponsorship. The first error is in announcing the study in the social science classes. In the eyes of the students, this might mean that the project is sponsored by the social science departments. Since the main objective of the study is to determine the extent to which social sciences are thought of in connection with "science," this sponsorship would probably bring the etiquette barrier into play for the student who does not want to disillusion the social science departments by demonstrating that he still does not consider the social sciences to be "real science." There might be a suspicion that his view of social science might enter into the evaluation of his work in the social science course he is currently taking. There would have been bias in the other direction if the study had been announced in either the physical or biological science classes. The solution to this problem is shown later.

Interviewer's role. There is some danger in announcing that the interviewers would be psychology students. This might add to the bias of the etiquette barrier, and respondents might tend to emphasize the importance of psychology.

Advance warning. It was probably a mistake to inform the students in advance of the arrival of the interviewers for two reasons. First, if we want to know what a freshman is ordinarily thinking regarding science, we should not warn him so that he can "bone up" on information he feels will please the interviewers. Second, there is some danger that the respondents will get together and talk about the topic as preparation for the interview. This is particularly probable in this case since all the freshmen on campus live together in special dormitories. Although most of the talk might be only between roommates or friends in the same hall, there is the additional possibility that rumors about the "real" purposes of the study might create a resistance and group solidarity that the interviewers would find difficult to counteract.

Timing the launching of the study. The ninth week of a 12-week quarter is an inopportune time to interview the freshmen whose study habits usually allow a backlog of work to accumulate, making it necessary to "cram" for the last two or three weeks. This time pressure would tend to produce short interviews or the desire to avoid the interview if possible.

Place of the interview. Interviewing students in their rooms presents a problem when they have roommates. The value of the interview could be seriously impaired with another person present, particularly if the respondent knows that the other person disagrees with him.

Anonymity. None of the information given to the respondents explained that the individual was going to be anonymous, nor did it explain how the information was to be used and reported. Neither did it promise that the respondent would be able to see the report. In this vacuum, the respondent might conjure up all kinds of anxieties about the use of the information, or at least he might fail to be highly motivated because he was not considered important enough to merit an explanation.

Errors in the structure of the interview schedule. Considering the exploratory objectives of these interviews, it is clear that the interview schedule is much too structured, limiting the range of responses.

Degree of structuring suggests answers. Structuring in this case tends to suggest answers which the respondent might not have thought of otherwise. For example, question 1 requires the interviewer to hand the respondent the card containing acceptable categories of responses. Since students in liberal arts colleges like to show themselves as broadminded and interdisciplinary, they would tend to select answer *"c"* more frequently when reminded of the social sciences, but would omit it if asked the open-ended question alone. This possibility is illustrated in the sample interview where it can be noted that, even though the respondent includes social sciences in his answer to question 1, *all* of the subsequent references are to physical and biological sciences. In effect forgetting to include the social sciences in the larger area of science would be an ego threat for a freshman who perceives himself as a budding intellectual. The same objection to structuring the answer applies to questions 2, 3, 6, and 7. These highly structured answers tend to put the respondent in a passive role thus preventing the degree of spontaneity needed for an exploratory study.

Directness of the approach. In general the questions ask directly for the information needed rather than helping the respondent to *recall* specific experiences, feelings, and images to be classified by the interviewer.

Question 2 uses the word "aspect," which might be meaningless to the respondent unless he is furnished with categories of aspects, something which would not be done since it would lead the respondent.

It is highly improbable that the objectives of question 3 could be attained in such a simple and direct manner since most people either forget where they obtained many of their ideas or are not even conscious of assimilating these ideas. A person's image of "science" is built up over a period of years. Certainly one's family has some influence in this, but it is rarely reported as having any effect unless considerable time is spent skillfully probing. Similarly, freshmen do not quickly report any effect of the mass media of communication. It is necessary to first discover the specific salient images the respondent has in his mind before tracing them to their source. The difference is great between the difficulty of discovering what a person knows or feels at a given moment and discovering the source of that knowledge or attitude.

Question 5 seems to be a rather naive strategy for obtaining this information because college freshmen with their newly acquired intellectual skepticism are reluctant to admit *blind* faith in anything. It is an ego-threat to admit to anything but "reasoned conviction." The wording of the question attempts to overcome this difficulty by conveying a non-judgmental attitude toward blind faith, but this is not enough. People with blind faith do not know that they have it. Its power lies in the feeling that the conclusion is "obvious." Some other strategy must be used to obtain valid evidence of one's blind faith.

Also we should note that the question as it stands does not accurately fit hypothesis 5, which it is supposedly testing. Without being guilty of blind faith, it is possible to give evidence that physical science has solved more physical problems than social science has social problems. On the other hand, knowing that physical science has solved more problems might be the basis for a prejudice of the type mentioned in hypothesis 7. This might be the case if a person judges something to be insoluble not on the basis of any direct knowledge of the particular problem but on the *a priori* basis that it falls into the category of social problems. Evidence of any "blind faith" could be better obtained by an indirect strategy which will be described later.

Sequence of questions. Some of the errors of sequence are built into the interview schedule. The interview schedule unfortunately moves from highly structured questions to open-ended varieties. This is an error on two counts. First, the respondent is led to expect a highly structured interview in which he can play a rather passive role, and then in the last two questions suddenly he is expected to be more active and autonomous. Second, and more serious in this case, the first open-ended question is one which could be strongly influenced by the context and answer structure that has preceded it. For example, after question 1 the respondent is more likely to feel obligated to include a social scientist among his "portraits" of the scientist. After questions 2, 6, and 7 the respondent might be more inclined to think of general scientific methods and theoretical goals in the activities of the scientist dealt with in question 8.

After the suggestions furnished in previous questions, the probability is great that we would find the answer to question 8, the first open-ended question, quite different from the answer obtained if we had asked the open-ended question at the beginning of the interview.

Errors in the interview's techniques and tactics. In addition to the built-in error in sequence, the interviewer himself makes several tactical mistakes. He actually interrupts the respondent with every question except I:13, where he waits four seconds before probing.

In (I:2) the interviewer does not notice that the respondent has called this a "test." Instead of immediately rushing into the first question, he should have dispelled the respondent's feeling that this was a test situation by saying in a surprised tone, "Did you think this was going to be a test? We are only interested in a few opinions; there are no wrong or right answers."

The technique used in two probes (I:6 and I:7) is not appropriate for the situation. In view of the memory barrier involved in reporting the *sources* of one's ideas, the respondent needs more help in stimulating his recall. These probes lead the respondent to feel that the interviewer expects him to simply list, in an off the cuff manner, the sources of his ideas. This demands more than the respondent is ready to give within the first 90 seconds of an interview. There is danger in the respondent's giving just a partial picture of only what he can recall at the moment, or in listing some abstract sources that he assumes might have had an influence but which are not connected to any *concrete* experience in his own life. In some cases the respondent might fabricate material to fill in the gap between what is expected of him and what he is able to recall.

In I:15, after hearing the respondent picture a scientist, the interviewer uses too much topic control. Now that he is free of the highly structured interview schedule and is trying to encourage the respondent to associate freely about "scientists," he should not rush on to the next question. The respondent may not yet be ready to say what problem the scientist is working on. A more neutral probe should be used such as: Pause, nod head thoughtfully, "That's interesting, can you give me more of that picture?" Instead, the interviewer (in I:15, I:16, and I:17) rushed ahead in a way that discourages a reflective mood and full elaboration by the respondent. Also (in I:16), the interviewer accepts the respondent's "I don't know" at face value and goes on to the next question. Neither the respondent nor the interviewer is adjusting to the shift from the highly structured to the open-ended portion of the interview. Care should be taken in making this transition. In his next probes (I:18 and I:19), the interviewer again neglects to provide any transition to the new topic.

Coding errors. It should be noted that the interviewer incorrectly coded the answers to questions 5, 6 and 7. The answers should have been coded as follows:

5.) *a*
6.) *a, e, f, g, h, i* (can have practical use, must be of value to man)
7.) *a, b, c, d, g* (usually patent and sell inventions)

In his answer to question 5, the respondent is trying to give the impression that he is not *blind* in his faith but his actual statements about the physical sciences show that he has a strong tendency toward such a blind faith in that one area. In coding the answers to questions 6 and 7, the interviewer overlooked several of the answers and omitted the "other" category in both cases.

Let us now suggest an approach that avoids most of the strategy errors mentioned above and which would obtain better results even though the interviewer has more freedom to make errors in techniques and tactics.

An alternative strategy design

Instead of announcing the study in the social science class where the sponsorship might bias the results, the following procedure was used. All freshmen, upon arriving in English class, were given the following assignment to do immediately in class.

Today we will do an exercise in class to develop your impromptu writing skill. We have purposely not announced the topic before so that you would have no time to prepare. You will be given 20 minutes to write on a topic of broad and general interest in the modern world.

Your work will be evaluated according to two criteria: (*a*) the spontaneity and naturalness of your expression, and (*b*) the number of ideas or amount of elaboration of ideas. In other words, we are not interested in whether you make mechanical errors in spelling, punctuation, and grammar, since this obviously must be a rough draft. It need not be organized in any particular way. It can be a flowing, free association of ideas which would ordinarily have to be reorganized to make a finished paper. The whole idea is to let the ideas flow and not be inhibited by any technical considerations. On the other hand, we do not want you to fictionalize but to paint your personal image and feelings on the subject.

If you all have paper and pencil ready, I will announce the topic and let you know when 20 minutes have passed. ARE THERE ANY QUESTIONS BEFORE I ANNOUNCE THE TOPIC?

The topic is simply "SCIENCE"—whatever comes into your mind on the subject. Let's go!

At the end of 20 minutes, the following announcement was made:

The 20 minutes are up. Please be sure your names are on the papers and pass them in immediately. Don't worry if you are in the middle of a paragraph.

After the papers had been collected, the following announcement was made:

Now that you are all in a spontaneous mood, we have one more topic I would like to have you treat in the same manner in the next 20 minutes. Are there any questions? The second topic is entitled "A Comparison of Physical, Biological, and Social Sciences." Don't worry about the relationship between this essay and the one you just completed. They will be evaluated independently.

After the second topic was completed, the instructor added the following explanation:

You might be interested to know that the topic of science and people's ideas about it has become the object of research lately. Although these papers will all be used for the purpose we have stated, the college is doing a study of students' perceptions of science, and the testing office will do a statistical analysis of the frequency of appearance of certain images, ideas or themes. This will be just one phase of a larger study, and the results will be reported next year. Naturally, all individuals will remain anonymous in reporting the results.

Next Monday I will report on some of the common characteristics and some of the individual differences in these impromptu essays and talk about how this form of "brainstorming" fits into the larger process of good writing.

This procedure accomplished several things. First, it prevented pressuring the students to include social science out of consideration for the social science instructors. An English class is neutral ground. Second, the surprise element prevented any preparation and the goal of the impromptu essay provided an acceptable reason for being surprised. This also gave no respondent the excuse that he did not have time since it was done as part of the regular classroom activities. Also this setting made the motivation relatively high. The "impromptu aim" and the insistence that in this case the evaluation did not depend upon mechanical perfection or even organization put the emphasis upon the *ideas* and *images* the respondent had with regard to science. Third, this approach prevented any collusion between the students and did not allow time for negative rumors to interfere. And finally, in using the testing office as the agent for the content analysis, there was still no hint that any particular discipline was sponsoring the study.

The content analysis provided the basis for a more realistic guide for a non-scheduled interview to be done with a random sample of freshmen. Although it was recognized that the two 20-minute essays might not represent a respondent's complete thinking on the subject, it was clear that collectively, the 250 freshmen essays would cover a wider range of ideas, images, and attitudes than could be obtained in an equal amount of staff time devoted to interviewing. In effect, this cut down the time needed for exploration so that the study could be completed before the freshmen left campus.

A random sample of 50 freshmen was selected for intensive interviewing. In order to avoid the time pressure which might make it difficult to obtain high quality interviews from the complete sample, the essays were written during the second week of the quarter and the follow-up interviews were completed in the third and fourth weeks.

Ten students who were majors in journalism, business, pre-med, history, sociology, anthropology, and psychology were used as interviewers. They had all had a course in interviewing in which they were instructed to give the following explanation to the respondents in the sample.

Hello! Are you John Wingut? I am Peter Pagus. I am helping the testing office with the study of students' perception of science. You probably remember the anouncement in English class last Friday when you did the impromptu essay on science. They said the testing office was also using the essays as part of a larger study. Your name happens to be one of the 50 in a random sample to be interviewed. We are doing all the interviewing in the small conference room in the student union building. When would you have time to talk to me for a little over an hour? I can do it almost any time that is convenient for you.

After the appointment was made, the interviewer carefully pointed out the following:

Incidentally, this is not a test of any kind, but a sample opinion poll. The testing office is doing it because they happen to have the facilities and staff to analyze the results. Also they are known for their ability to keep results anonymous.

The small conference room in the Student Union Building was selected because it provided privacy and was centrally located for all students since it was near student mail boxes and the cafeteria.

When the students arrived to keep their appointments, the interviewer gave the following explanation:

Hello John! Are you all ready to go? Well, here's the way this interview works. I won't ask any specific questions but just introduce about four areas of discussion about science. You just let your ideas flow freely, and I might occasionally interrupt to clarify certain points. We use a tape recorder so that we can get all your ideas accurately. I listen to it later and type up all the relevant material and then use the tape over again for another interview. I'll also take a few notes from time to time to remind me of points I might want to clarify later. Do you have any questions?

After answering any questions the respondent might have, the interviewer asks the opening question from the following Interview Guide.

INTERVIEW GUIDE

Opener: (To warm up the respondent and to allow the interviewer to show a non-judgmental attitude.)

"What do you think comes to most people's minds when they think of science?" (Probes: "That's interesting, what other ideas would they think of?" "Tell me more about that idea." etc.)

Areas and aspects of science: (To test hypotheses 1, 2, and 3.)

1. "What do *you* think of when you think about science?" (Use the following types of probes to explore the areas of science indicated in the chart on the last page. "Could you tell me more about that? What do you mean by _____? Could you tell me more about the aims of science?")

During the first phase of exploring this area the interviewer should not suggest any of the specific aspects or sub-areas of "science" but should merely follow the respondent's lead and encourage him to enlarge upon his free associations.

After this tactic has reached a point of diminishing returns, the interviewer may then directly suggest any of the sub-areas that have not yet been discussed.

Probes for the initial phase: "That's interesting, tell me more about that." "What do you mean by that?" "Could you tell me more about the aims of science?" "You mentioned some of the results of biological sciences, what else could you add along that line?" etc.

Probes for the second phase: "You gave me some good material on your ideas about the aims of the physical sciences and the biological sciences. Now what about the aims of the *social* sciences?" "You haven't had a chance to say anything about the results of biological sciences, what sorts of results come to your mind?" and so on.

Inventions: (To test hypotheses 4, 5, and 6)

2. "In general what would you say are the results of science?"

3. "Tell me about as many scientific discoveries and inventions as you can think of now.

4. "What are some inventions or discoveries in the biological sciences?"

5. "What are some inventions or discoveries in the social sciences?"

If the respondent cannot think of any inventions or discoveries in the biological or social sciences, ask him why he cannot think of any and encourage him to talk about the nature of inventions and discoveries to discover whether he has a definition of each that rules out their occurrence in either the biological or social realm.

"Why are there so few discoveries in the biological (or social) sciences?" "Why are there so few inventions in the biological (or social) sciences?" "Are there any other kinds of results of scientific work in these areas?" "If so, what?" "If there are no results, why is this?"

Faith in different fields: (Hypothesis 7)

6. "What are some of the main differences between physical, biological, and social sciences?" (Probe for details)

7. "In which of the three areas can scientific method be most fruitfully applied?" "What has been the case in the past?" "Why?" "What about the future?" "Why?"

8. "What are some of the kinds of problems which will probably be solved in the future by the physical sciences?" "The biological sciences?" "The social sciences?"

9. "What kinds of problems do you think will never be solved by the physical sciences in the future?" "Biological sciences in the future?" "Social sciences in the future?"

Sources of ideas: (Hypothesis 4)

10. "You have given me a lot of ideas about science. Where do you think most of your ideas came from?" (for physical science, biological sciences, and social sciences)

11. "For example, you mentioned ⎯⎯⎯⎯⎯⎯; where did you get that idea (image, feeling, etc.)?"

PROBE-NOTE GUIDE FOR QUESTION 1					
	AIMS		METHODS		RESULTS	
Areas	Practical	Scientific	Technique	General	Practical	Scientific
PHYS.	(1)	(2)	(3)	(4)	(5)	(6)
BIOL.	(7)	(8)	(9)	(10)	(11)	(12)
SOC.	(13)	(14)	(15)	(16)	(17)	(18)
GEN.	(19)	(20)	(21)	(22)	(23)	(24)

This non-scheduled interview is considered as the second of a three-phase study. The questions and answers are based upon information obtained in the two essays on science but dig more deeply into relevant areas to provide either quantitative tests of some of the hypotheses or qualitative data to be used in designing a more structured data-gathering instrument to follow.

Thus, this interview is a link between an even more exploratory approach and a more quantitative approach. For example, the *Probe-Note Guide for Question 1* (shown above) contains the same categories on both dimensions that were found useful and reliable in coding the results of the first essay on "Science." The interview allows us to probe more deeply and uniformly for the respondent's images and ideas in each area of science and to obtain quantitative results for question 1 to test hypotheses 1, 2, and 3. Questions 2 through 5 provide a quantitative test also of hypotheses 4 and 5. Question 5, with the ensuing discussion, is not expected to render quantitative data to test hypothesis 6, but it will allow us to discover some of the elements in the layman's definition of "invention" and "discovery" that he actually applies in making judgments. This would serve as the basis for a more refined test of the sixth hypothesis with either a more structured questionnaire or interview. Similarly, questions 6 through 9 will render some meaningful qualitative data (recurring themes, vocabulary, categories, conclusions and underlying assumptions) that could be used to construct a valid and reliable quantitative data-collection instrument. Questions 10 and 11 provide data related to hypothesis 4 (that the major source of information on the results of science is mass media advertising), but they are not conclusive in themselves, since the student is reporting only what he feels to be the sources of information. For example, if in questions 2 through 5 the student gives only images presented in mass media advertising, then questions 10 and 11 can detect the degree to which he is aware of this fact, or they can provide information on other possible sources of the same images. In any case, these two sets of questions afford a broader, more valid basis for developing a more structured approach in the third phase of the study.

Not only did the initial analysis of essays yield ideas regarding substantive questions and answer categories, but it also provided clues to the appropriate organization of the interview.

The "opener" was included not because it dealt directly with any of the hypotheses to be tested but because it allowed the respondent to give what he thought others thought or to give his own ideas in disguise if he wished. In any case, it provides an opportunity for the interviewer to demonstrate a non-judgmental attitude and establish the thoughtful mood required.

Most of the time was spent discussing question 1, which provides data to test the first three hypotheses. The Probe-Note Guide provides a reminder for the interviewer of the possible areas to cover and the numbers in each box are used as code numbers to classify the material after it has been transcribed. This allows a quantification of the content. In many of the interviews, certain cells would be blank. In order to know that this was not simply because the interviewer neglected to probe in this area, each interviewer made a few probe notes in each cell to indicate that certain things needed to be probed further. When he was satisfied that the area had been covered adequately, he put a diagonal line through that cell.

The areas of discussion are arranged in what was discovered, after a few interviews, to be the best sequence. It is important not to ask questions 10 and 11 until after the others have been adequately covered, because we found that if we asked about the source of each idea as we came to it, the respondent became aware that few of his ideas came from the "right source." He would therefore begin to inhibit the popular science or science-fiction approach and mention only more recently acquired academic material.

Furthermore, if questions 6 through 9, which deal with the student's faith, are posed after the first five questions there is always a good chance that some useful lead will develop allowing the interviewer to move smoothly into this sensitive area.

The specific wording of all the questions is only suggestive. Often it is not necessary to ask all the questions directly because the natural flow of the respondent's associations on the topic will supply the information.

SUMMARY

A person may independently acquire or improve interviewing skills over the full range of strategies, techniques, and tactics. First, it is important to have a clear understanding of the objectives of the interview. These objectives can then be converted into subproblems or topics. Then a tentative form of the questions should be developed along with a tentative sequence of topics and the necessary contextual materials introduced at appropriate points.

All of this planning is done in an attempt to minimize the barriers and maximize the facilitators of communication. The success of an interview for either training or data gathering depends upon this pre-planning more than upon a brilliant impromptu performance.

It is important to do a thoughtful post-analysis of the interview before going on to do another. Without this objective analysis of effort, the interviewer merely is engaging in activity rather than in learning. Without pre-planning, interviewing, and reflective analysis in this sequence, years of interviewing experience can simply harden some initial misconceptions of the nature of interviewing into a mechanical set of reflexes often inappropriate for the task at hand.

8
Epilogue

After dealing with the complexities of interviewing methods and the procedures for learning to interview, it is time to reaffirm the essential spirit and purpose of this book and renew its perspectives. We will specify some of the book's underlying assumptions, review the high points of interviewing methodology, and make some general observations about the subjective experience of learning to interview.

AIMS AND ASSUMPTIONS

The direct empirical study of human behavior includes interviewing, empathy, participation, and observation. Each of these approaches could be dealt with at length separately, but interviewing involves certain aspects of the other three general methods.

Interviewing, unlike any of the basic methods in the physical sciences, depends upon an empathic relationship between the observer and the observed. There is nothing to be gained by lamenting or ignoring the fact that there are dangers of mis-empathizing or over-empathizing, since empathy is a necessary element in human communication.

On the contrary, one of the advantages the social sciences have over the physical sciences is the fact that under certain conditions the human observer may successfully empathize with the object of his observation. The study of human behavior not only depends upon but also helps to develop empathy. Thus, we assume a complementary rather than an antithetical relationship between empathy as a common human characteristic and social science as a specialized, abstract, objective analysis of human behavior. Qualitatively valid observations must always precede any quantitative observation or analysis. This complementary relationship is further emphasized in the fact that the application of the results of any social science study depends upon an empathic relationship between the social engineer and the people in the community where the results are to be applied.

Thus, the whole social science enterprise may be viewed as a systematic extension of the range and quality of human empathy. The ability of man to invent and build the social structures needed to support cooperation over ever-widening circles, from familial and tribal to national and international, depends upon this progressive extension of empathy.

The foregoing assumptions may at first glance seem to have little connection with learning to interview. Actually, these ideas regarding the relationship between human empathy, social science, and the general welfare of society have been some of the silent assumptions underlying this particular approach to interviewing. Instead of perceiving empathy and objectivity as antithetical, we see the problem as being one of developing an "informed empathy" that gives the observer of human phenomena an advantage over, for example, the psychologist studying the motivation of rats.

The successful application of the theoretical framework of inhibitors and facilitators of communication rests upon the interviewer's ability to empathize in the planning, execution, and analysis phases of the interviewing enterprise. This is not to say that we blindly trust empathy but that, since we cannot avoid using it, we must try to use its positive aspects and avoid its pitfalls. Methods of analyzing both the interviewing process and the resulting data can help correct empathic error.

The writer has been considering interviewing as including the total process of planning, executing, and analyzing the interview, rather than taking the narrower view that interviewing properly includes only that portion of the process which is performed vis-à-vis the respondent.

This perspective does not conceal the vital interdependence between the strategy planning and the methods used by the interviewer when he faces the respondent. If the strategy is designed without benefit of exploratory participation, observation or interviewing in the field, there is the grave danger that the conceptualization of the problem may be inappropriate, the questions may be beside the point, or the contexts, wording, and sequence of questions may all work to inhibit rather than facilitate communication. Only in rare cases can the skilled interviewer completely overcome the initial disadvantages of a poorly planned strategy or an ill-conceived interview guide.

The selection from among the many tools of strategy, techniques, and tactics is the essence of the creative process of interviewing, and like all creative processes it is not a fixed mechanical sequence. For this reason no set of "do's" or "don'ts" can realistically be offered as a guide to successful interviewing. Instead, we can learn to use tools, concepts, and principles.

REVIEW OF CONCEPTS AND TOOLS

Interviewing as maximizing communication

The basic tasks of the interviewer include accurately communicating the question to the respondent; maximizing the respondent's ability and willingness to answer the question; listening actively to determine what is relevant; and probing to increase the validity, clarity, and completeness of the responses. All of the strategies, techniques, and tactics of interviewing must contribute in some way to accomplishing these central tasks.

The interviewer must proceed in a way that will maximize the flow of relevant information while maintaining optimum interpersonal relations with the respondent. The flow of relevant information depends on the interviewer's maximizing the facilitators of communication and minimizing the inhibitors. The writer has found the inhibitors and facilitators of communication to be a practical sensitizing framework for people who plan, do, or evaluate interviewing. The eight inhibitors (competing time demands, ego threat, etiquette, trauma, forgetting, chronological confusion, inferential confusion, and unconscious behavior) and eight facilitators (fulfilling expectations, giving recognition, providing altruistic appeals, supplying sympathetic understanding, giving new experiences, fulfilling the need for meaning, facilitating catharsis, and supplying extrinsic rewards) of communication are not proposed as an elegant theoretical model fitting neatly within one discipline. The variables are related to several disciplines bearing upon human behavior. Two values of this eclectic frame of reference are that each concept clearly represents a real factor found in face-to-face communication situations; also, each concept is relatable to basic theory and empirical findings in the social sciences.

We have not undertaken a systematic presentation of the evidence from empirical studies or of the basic theories of the social sciences in order to keep closer to the task of learning to interview. However, we have pointed out some results of experiments dealing specifically with interviewing.

To use this sensitizing framework effectively, we conceive of the inhibitors as potential forces that are activated only under certain circumstances. Thus, it is not necessary to know that the potential has been activated in the specific case at hand, nor do we have to be sure that the remedies (in terms of certain strategies, tactics, or techniques) are actually needed before we apply them. Generally, a preventative approach can be used without damage to the communication process.

Similarly, it is not necessary for the interviewer to wait until it is clear that certain facilitators are needed before applying them. Nor can he expect magical stimulus-response reactions to his attempts to maximize the facilitators in a particular interview. What we can expect is that statistically we will be much more successful in establishing a fruitful relationship with the respondent if we make the effort to nourish these facilitating social-psychological forces.

Strategies of interviewing

Strategy includes all those decisions regarding the approach and setting made before a particular interview is underway. Initially, someone must decide whether interviewing is the most valid and efficient way to obtain the information needed. Sometimes it is a grave error to assume that interviewing should be used instead of public records, census data, diaries, letters, or essays written by the respondents for the occasion. Only after it is clear that interviewing is needed must we then decide who should be interviewed, who should do the interviewing, what would be the most appropriate role to be used by the interviewer, when and where the interview should be done, how to define the interview situation for the respondent, and how to record the interview.

All of this planning should be considered tentative, to be modified after the first field experiences. To be fruitful, the strategy planning must begin with the broadest view of the total situation. There is a danger of beginning a field study with a bundle of restrictive assumptions, often unconscious, regarding the range of strategies to be considered. Often, these assumptions are built upon previous experience, direct or vicarious, with strategies for collecting data in a particular situation. Even the professional researcher may be caught in the net of habit and try to solve a new problem with only old formulas. For example, a person accustomed to doing public opinion polls or census-type surveys may unintentionally cripple a study of the local community power structure by assuming that all of the respondents should be randomly selected. This strategy of selecting respondents would make it impossible to trace the informal chain of command or to cross-check one witness' account with that of another person participating in the same situation.

One American accustomed to studying pre-literate people in exotic cultures assumed that, in order to study the role conflicts experienced by Latin American professional women, he must first have a series of informal visits with each potential respondent in order to build up rapport before doing any formal interviewing. This was soon seen as a waste of valuable time for both the interviewer and the respondent who might say during the first visit, "I'm fascinated with your study of the roles of professional women. Are you going to use non-directive interviewing or do you have a questionnaire?"

Some of the basic dimensions of the field situation that determine or limit appropriate strategies are whether the interviewer is operating (*a*) in friendly or hostile territory, (*b*) in open or closed communities, and (*c*) whether he is making single or multiple contacts with each respondent.

Once we are aware of the actual and potential field situation in which a study has to operate in view of the type of information to be sought, we can then decide what types of key informants, special respondents, or representative respondents are needed and in what order they should be approached. Once we know the different types of respondents needed, we can then deal with the selection of the most appropriate interviewers.

In selecting the interviewers we must try to assess the probable effects of the individual's overt characteristics (such as age, sex, race, accent, mode of dress and grooming) upon the inhibitors and facilitators of communication in view of the information sought and the characteristics of the respondent.

Also, we must consider which roles the interviewer is capable of assuming and which would be most appropriate under the specific circumstances. General dimensions of role relationships, such as the in-group—out-group or the subordinate-superordinate, have demonstrable effects on the types of information which will be communicated in the interview situation. Always the interviewer has the central role of interviewer. This role may be clearly defined to him, but it may be vague to the respondent. In this case, the interviewer's auxiliary role assumes more importance, and he must choose carefully the ones he wishes to bring to the foreground of the interview situation.

Once the plot (the interview purpose) is clearly specified and the actors (the respondents and interviewers) are chosen, then we can consider the scene (time, place, and definition of the situation) in which the "minidrama" called the interview will take place. Time and place are not to be considered as physical aspects relevant only to the logistical efficiency and convenience of the field study; they must be evaluated in terms of their symbolic value in the communication of the particular information needed. Thus, time and space must be seen in relationship to both the nature of the information sought and to the interaction between interviewer and respondent.

Important aspects of the scene other than time and place include the psychological props which establish a certain definition of the situation for both interviewer and respondent. The way the interviewer is introduced, the way the sponsorship, purpose of the interview and selection of the respondent are explained, and the method of recording all bear upon the potential communication of a particular type of information.

Once the interviewer has begun with his opening question, much has already been done to influence the outcome of the interview. Yet much of the outcome still depends upon the skillful use of techniques and tactics during the interview.

Techniques in interviewing

Techniques are specific forms of verbal and non-verbal behavior used during the interview to communicate a particular question and motivate the respondent to answer it. Silence is an important interviewing technique. Its successful use depends upon the interviewer's sensitivity to the respondent's behavior and upon the interviewer's ability to control his own impulses to a degree not customary in ordinary sociable conversation.

There is a tendency for interviewers to be unaware of the need to supply a context for the interpretation of questions. Often, it is necessary to do some exploratory interviewing to detect several possible interpretations of a question by the respondents. These varying interpretations may surprise the interviewer who has carefully used clear and unambiguous wording. Differences in interpretation may spring from different subculture backgrounds of the respondents, multiple frames of reference possessed by a particular respondent, or changes in frames of reference due to recent personal experiences or current public events. Often, the interview schedule can avoid having over-complicated questions by providing an introductory context, meaningful to a range of respondents, which will help them all arrive at the interpretation intended by the interviewer.

These verbal contexts may help to clarify and standardize the meaning of a question by defining terms, providing the appropriate time perspective, building a special perspective, furnishing criteria for judgment, or supplying needed facts. In addition to clarifying the meaning of the question, a verbal context may motivate the respondent to give the answer; it may arouse interest, give recognition to the respondent for his special qualifications, help prevent falsification, reduce the etiquette barrier, stimulate memory, reduce chronological confusion, or help the respondent probe his own unconscious experience.

Assuming that the essential meaning of a particular question can be clearly communicated, the interviewer designing the questions must decide the extent to which the scope of the question should be made broad or narrow, the extent to which the answer should be left open or structured, and finally whether or not a leading question should be used to suggest a particular answer. All of the different combinations of question scope and answer structures have a valid use. Each type is likely to obtain accurate and complete information under certain conditions. Each form of question must be evaluated in terms of the probable effect upon the flow of specific types of information under certain interviewing conditions.

Techniques also include the non-verbal expression of attitudes. These attitudes are as essential in their effect as are the verbal techniques; yet they cannot be mechanically structured or turned on and off at will. The interviewer who thinks that he can produce the appropriate attitude on cue probably is merely deceiving himself, but he is likely to be less successful in deceiving the respondent.

How then can we use expressions of attitude as a technique? In some cases, we must select interviewers who already have the needed positive attitudes toward the interviewing task in general, toward the specific kinds of information sought, and toward the type of respondent to be interviewed.

An interviewer can avoid the expression of negative attitudes by concentrating on the positive attitudes which he already has. Also, many of the needed positive attitudes are strengthened with actual practice in interviewing a variety of people on many subjects.

The most important attitude needed in many types of interview is a non-judgmental attitude toward the respondent as a type of person and toward any behavior which he reports. This is not a mere attitudinal vacuum; it consists of showing interest in the information, appreciation for the respondent's efforts in giving it, interest in the respondent as a person, and critical assessment of the relevance of the information.

All this does not mean that the interviewer must have no values or beliefs contrary to those of the respondent. He does not need to be a socio-psychological chameleon, but he must perceive that in his role as interviewer his task is to see the world through the eyes of the respondent, not to approve or disapprove of what he sees. In his role as citizen he is free to judge whether or not the purposes of the particular proposed study are in agreement with his own values. If they are not, he should not participate in the study. Maintaining an operational distinction between his role as interviewer and as citizen is one of the disciplines a successful interviewer must learn.

We may describe techniques in a particular interview in terms of the verbal forms of each specific question and its underlying non-verbal attitudinal accompaniment. However, a new dimension of interviewing must be introduced to take into consideration how these discrete questions are interconnected in the on-going flow of the interview as a whole.

Interviewing tactics

Tactics are those *sequential patterns* of techniques which facilitate the flow of relevant information and which maintain optimum interpersonal relations. Part of this sequential dimension can be built into the interview schedule in advance, but some aspects may have to be improvised in the give-and-take of the interview.

Building tactics into the interview schedule. Several dimensions of tactics may be tentatively planned in advance for the first trial interview. Some of the sequential patterns may be revised on the basis of the pre-test interviews. The pre-testing may also show that other sequences have to be left for the interviewer to determine in each interview. A tentative initial plan should specify the sequence of topics and the sequence of questions within each topic.

After the tentative order of the topics is decided, we can think in terms of the types of contexts needed to launch the first topic, to connect one topic with another, or to determine which topics or questions are pertinent for a particular respondent. The use of lead-in questions, pivot questions, and transitional contexts varies greatly from one general subject matter to another and from the very simple interviews to the very complex ones.

Even though it is often possible to freeze the sequence of topics and the questions within a topic on the basis of careful pre-testing, we cannot predict the precise probes needed to obtain a relevant response.

Probing to meet the objectives of a topic. Even though the interviewer gives an appropriate introduction or transition to a topic and asks a well-worded question, there is often a need to probe to obtain further clarification or elaboration of the response. Generally, probing is needed more frequently with open-ended questions of broad scope, but it is also needed to clarify the response to a question that has a completely structured answer in order to be sure that the coding of the response is valid and reliable.

Usually, the interviewer probes to complete and clarify the response to one question before going on to another. This is not always the best way to maximize the flow of relevant information. Sometimes it is better to wait until the respondent spontaneously covers several questions and begins to lose momentum before interrupting with a probe of any kind.

Seven types of probes represent varying degrees of topic control: silent probe, encouragement, immediate elaboration, immediate clarification, retrospective elaboration, retrospective clarification, and mutation. Each of these types has unique values under different conditions. The interviewer must learn to use the full range of topic control rather than following the habits acquired in sociable conversation. Only after mastering the mechanics of the full range of probe types, can the interviewer begin to develop a sense of when each is appropriate. For example, the interviewer who is unaware of the possibilities of the silent probe, the encouragement probe, or the recapitulation probe will never find an occasion to use them.

Not only does the interviewer have to be constantly alert for the need to probe, but he must also have an emergency kit of tactical tools to deal with a respondent's possible resistance to giving relevant information.

Dealing with symptoms of resistance. We cannot know in advance when the respondent is going to resist the efforts of the interviewer by saying, "I'm too busy now," "I don't know anything about that," "I can't remember," or "What do *you* think about that?" If the interviewer is unprepared for such respondent action, he may become flustered, damage the rapport in his efforts to respond, or be thrown into a state of panic. We have discussed some of the general ways of dealing with these potential hindrances which can induce panic in the inexperienced.

The informal post-interview. The informal post-interview is that sociable chat between interviewer and respondent which takes place after the formal interview is over. The end of the formal interview can be signaled by a verbal statement, by putting away notebook and pencil, by turning off the tape recorder, or any of several other ways. In this post-interview period the situation is redefined and the relationship between interviewer and respondent is changed.

There are two basic functions of the post-interview period. First, it may provide an opportunity to build the respondent's morale and confidence so that he will have a better feeling toward the interviewer as a person and toward the study which he is doing. This is particularly important in field studies where one disgruntled respondent might infect potential respondents with a negative attitude toward being interviewed. Second, it gives the interviewer an opportunity to detect any change in behavior that would indicate that some aspect of the formal interview had been inhibiting the respondent. In this case, it might be possible to glean some of the missing information during the informal period, to re-interview the respondent at a later date under different conditions, or to change the strategy, tactics, and techniques in future interviews.

Developing skills in interviewing

There is a considerable distance between having an intellectual understanding of interviewing and being able to do excellent interviewing. For this reason we have suggested a three-phase procedure for improving interviewing skills which includes thoughtful planning, self-conscious interviewing, and critical evaluation of the performance. We have given a demonstration example of this procedure to launch a self-directed program of improving interviewing. Even those interviewers with years of experience find this self-improvement procedure not only effective in improving skills but also in rejuvenating their interest in the whole interviewing process.

SUBJECTIVE ASPECTS OF LEARNING TO INTERVIEW

In training interviewers with widely differing backgrounds, the writer has encountered many subjective reactions to learning to interview. Often these are curiously parallel to the culture shock felt when one must change his linguistic and other habit patterns to adjust to a new way of life. Of course, this jolt is not so keenly felt when we simply read *about* an exotic culture or *about* interviewing. The experience is more profound when we must learn to *act* in a new way, when old habit patterns are no longer appropriate under the new circumstances, when we have an opportunity to see ourselves in a new perspective. In the cross-cultural experience, this new perspective is attained when we are able to communicate with the foreigner well enough to understand that his perception of us does not agree with our own image of ourselves. In learning to interview we can more quickly attain this new perspective by hearing ourselves interviewing on tape.

The shock of self-recognition can be both depressing and refreshing at different phases of the learning process. The writer has observed a tendency for an initial euphoria to develop as the person plays with some of the new concepts, sees a broader horizon before him, and accepts the challenge to expand his repertoire of basic skills. Then comes a phase in which the learner's morale may drop as he increases his awareness of the complexities of the task, of the type and amount of skill needed, and of some of his own shortcomings in controlling his own behavior in accordance with his intellectual understanding of the problem.

In this curiously contradictory situation his self-esteem as an interviewer may drop as his actual performance is making dramatic improvement. For example, in cases where the learner does a tape recorded interview at the beginning and at the end of a training period and is asked to discuss each interview with the instructor immediately after each recording session, there is a clear tendency for the learner to be much more critical of his performance in the post-test interview than he was of his pre-test interview earlier. Yet, the post-test interview is usually far superior to the pre-test. The remedy for this drop in morale was simple and dramatic. When the learner was allowed to hear a portion of both his pre-test and post-test in the same session, he was impressed and often surprised by his substantial improvement. Often, however, in order to demonstrate his increased awareness of the problems and solutions in interviewing, he would use the more modest approach of remarking about how gullible or insensitive he was in the pre-test, rather than directly saying how perceptive and sensitive he was in the post-test.

The learner must avoid allowing his desirably increased appreciation of the tasks of interviewing and his greater ability to criticize his own behavior to dampen his appreciation of the progress he has made or his faith in continued improvement.

Also, to avoid being overwhelmed by the intellectual complexity of the interviewing task, the reader should remember that, although we have illustrated many interviewing problems in a relatively short space, only a small proportion of them would normally occur in any series of interviews in a particular field study. The sheer number of strategies, techniques, and tactics need not lead to despair since only a few of them may be legitimately used in any one study. Furthermore, it is not necessary to retain the whole inventory of interviewing tools in one's mind since most of these decisions are made in the planning and evaluation stage in which we can use references. Although some of these interviewing tools may be rarely used, it is important to be familiar with them because we cannot predict when the situation will arise in which they are sorely needed.

The areas which the interviewer must master as his own are the performance skills of listening, manifesting positive attitudes, critically evaluating the information received, probing for elaboration and clarification of the responses, taking notes, and dealing with symptoms of resistance in the respondent. This is enough for anyone to concentrate on at one time!

One way the neophyte can convert his early euphoria into depression is to jump into a practice interview unprepared and expect inspiration to guide him to success. This is not to say an interviewer should never go into an interview unprepared; it might help jolt him out of his old habits and leave him free to experiment. It is more likely, however, to show him the need for advance planning.

In the early stages of learning to interview, it is best to avoid attempting long and highly complex interviews with many topics and subtopics. The basic skills can be developed just as well in a short, simple interview. Fatigue and confusion do not enhance the learning value of the experience for the beginner. He can build endurance later.

The person learning to interview should not select a friend or acquaintance as the respondent. This creates a confusion of roles in which both the interviewer and the respondent may be tense, confused or amused by the sudden change in his friend's behavior. This creates an artificial relationship incompatible with both friendship and interviewing. For the initial experience, it is easier and more fruitful to interview a stranger, but he should be someone in the same social class and subculture as the interviewer to avoid possible communication problems that could unnecessarily complicate the interview.

It is sometimes essential to morale for the interviewer to realize that the best of strategies, techniques, and tactics will sometimes be relatively unproductive for reasons that are not his fault. For example, the respondent may simply not have the relevant information. In this case, good interviewing may appear to be unproductive since no useful information is obtained. Actually, this is a positive rather than a negative outcome since the insensitive interviewer with a "bull in the china shop" approach might obtain a large quantity of fiction worse than useless. Also, a respondent who has relevant information may be fatigued, irritable, or sick. Sometimes the physical environment may be uncomfortable or lack privacy. It is even possible in rare cases that a personal characteristic of the interviewer may have some special meaning to the respondent who simply "can't talk to that type of person." These idiosyncratic circumstances do not arise often and should not be allowed to lower the interviewer's morale. The experienced interviewer will quickly diagnose such an interview situation as impossible and simply find a graceful way out.

The intelligent interviewer realizes that interviewing can never be a magical process by which the "truth, the whole truth, and nothing but the truth" can be efficiently extracted from any respondent. All of the present-day knowledge combined with the most intelligent and skillful application will not completely avoid some distortion or incompleteness in the information obtained from some respondents. But when we consider the contrast between the conditions and methods that can be used in much social science interviewing with the conditions and methods of communication between a prosecuting lawyer and a hostile witness, between an employer and potential employee, or between an applicant for admission to a university and the admission officer of that university, we see that many serious decisions are based upon information received under conditions not nearly so favorable to obtaining truth as can usually be attained in the social science interview.

If the reader will consider the ideas in this book as something to act upon, to verify and modify in active interviewing practice, the rewards will be much greater than if he views the book merely as a collection of theoretical concepts seasoned with interesting illustrative cases. It is hoped that this book will not be accepted on faith as gospel nor rejected because some of the ideas do not form an elegant theoretical or literary model that pleases the esthetic senses.

The book should be accepted for what it is. It is the writer's sincere attempt to organize his insights, based upon his own and others' experiences in interviewing and upon ideas assimilated from systematic studies of the interviewing process, into a meaningful progression of conceptual and experiential steps. The writer has attempted to share his discoveries in a way designed to launch the interviewer into a period of self-sustained development rather than to limit his potential growth by presenting a set of rules on interviewing. Insofar as the writer has been able to share this voyage of discovery, the reader will have a broader grasp of the nature of the interviewing task, an expanded repertory of interviewing tools, and crescent insight into the appropriate use of these tools in a variety of interviewing settings. The continued development of interviewing skills will depend upon practice that combines thoughtful planning and disciplined interviewing with a critical evaluation of one's own performance and of the concepts presented here.

Bibliography

Abelsar, Herbert. "A Role-Rehearsal Technique for Exploratory Interviewing," *Public Opinion Quarterly,* Vol. 30, No. 2 (1966), pp. 302-5.

Abrams, Mark. "Possibilities and Problems of Group Interviewing," *Public Opinion Quarterly,* Vol. 13 (1949), pp. 502-6.

Adams, J. S. *Interviewing Procedures: A Manual for Survey Interviews.* Chapel Hill: University of North Carolina Press, 1958.

Adams, Richard N. *Human Organization Research.* Homewood, Ill.: Dorsey Press, 1960.

Anderson, Nels. *The Hobo: The Sociology of the Homeless Man.* Chicago: University of Chicago Press, 1923.

Armstrong, Fred G. *An Experimental Study of a Structured Interview for Determining Vocational Interests.* Thesis, Temple University, 1957. University of Michigan Microfilm 746.

Athey, K. R.; Coleman, J. E.; Reitman, A. P.; and Tang, J. "Two Experiments Showing the Effect of the Interviewer's Racial Background on Responses to Questionnaires Concerning Racial Issues," *Journal of Applied Psychology* (1960), pp. 244-46.

Axelrod, Morris, and Cannell, Charles F. "A Research Note on an Attempt to Predict Interviewer Effectiveness," *Public Opinion Quarterly,* Vol. 234 (Winter, 1959), pp. 571-76.

Babchuk, Nicholas, and Gordon, C. Wayne. "The Child as a Prototype of the Naive Informant in the Interview Situation," *American Sociological Review,* Vol. 23, No. 2 (April, 1958), pp. 196-98.

Back, Kurt W., and Stycos, J. Mayone. *The Survey under Unusual Conditions:*

Methodological Facets of the Jamaica Human Fertility Investigation, Society for Applied Anthropology, Monograph No. 1 (1959).

Backstrom, Charles H., and Dursh, Gerald D. *Survey Research.* Evanston, Ill.: Northwestern University Press, 1963.

Bain, Robert K. "The Researcher's Role: A Case Study," *Human Organization,* Vol. 9 (Spring, 1950), pp. 23-28.

Balinsky, Benjamin. *The Executive Interview: A Bridge to People.* New York: Harper & Row, 1959.

Balinsky, Benjamin, and Dispenzierei, A. "An Evaluation of the Lecture and Role Playing Methods in the Development of Interviewing Skills," *Personnel Guidance Journal,* Vol. 39 (1961), pp. 583-85.

Basset, Glenn A. *Practical Interviewing, A Handbook for Managers.* New York: American Management Association, 1965.

Becker, Howard S. "A Note on Interviewing Tactics," *Human Organization* (Winter, 1954), pp. 31-32.

Becker, Howard S. "Becoming a Marijuana User," *American Journal of Sociology,* Vol. 59 (July, 1953-May, 1954), pp. 235-42.

Becker, Howard S. "Problems of Inference and Proof in Participant Observation," *American Sociological Review,* Vol. 23 (December, 1958), pp. 652-60.

Becker, Howard S. *The Professional Dance Musician in Chicago.* Thesis, University of Chicago, 1949.

Belson, William, and Bell, C. R. *A Bibliography of Papers Bearing on the Adequacy of Techniques Used in Survey Research.* London: Oakwood Press, 1960.

Benney, M.; Riesman, D.; and Star, S. A. "Age and Sex in the Interview," *American Journal of Sociology,* Vol. 62 (September, 1956), pp. 143-52.

Benson, L. "Studies in Secret Ballot Technique," *Public Opinion Quarterly,* Vol. 5 (1941), p. 79.

Berdie, Ralph. "Psychological Processes in Interviewing," *Journal of Social Psychology,* Vol. 43 (August, 1943), pp. 3-31.

Berelson, Bernard. "The Verbal Report," *Human Behavior: An Inventory of Scientific Findings.* New York: Harcourt, Brace and World, Inc., 1964, pp. 29-33.

Berent, Paul. "The Depth Interview," *Journal of Advertising Research,* Vol. VI, No. 2 (June, 1966), pp. 32-39.

Bermosk, Loretta L., and Mordan, Mary I. *Interviewing in Nursing.* New York: The Macmillan Company, 1964.

Bessie, J. "The Effect of Praise on Respondent's Answers in a Public Opinion Poll," *American Psychologist,* Vol. 13 (1950), p. 629.

Bevis, J. C. "Interviewing with Tape Recorder," *Public Opinion Quarterly,* Vol. 13 (Winter, 1949), pp. 629-34.

Bindman, Aaron. "Interviewing in the Search for TRUTH," *Social Quarterly*, Vol. 6, No. 3 (Summer, 1965), pp. 281-88.

Bingham, W. V. D.; Moore, B. V.; and Gustad, J. W. *How to Interview*, 4th ed. New York: Harper & Bros., 1959.

Birdwhistle, R. "Body Motions Research and Interviewing," *Human Organization* (Spring, 1952), p. 37.

Blanc, H. "Multilingual Interviewing in Israel," *American Journal of Sociology*, Vol. 62 (September, 1956), pp. 205-9.

Blankenship, A. "The Effect of the Interviewer upon Response in a Public Opinion Poll," *Journal of Consulting Psychology*, Vol. 4 (1940), p. 134.

Blau, Peter M. *Exchange and Power in Social Life*. New York: John Wiley & Sons, Inc., 1964.

Blum, Fred H. "Getting Individuals to Give Information to the Outsider," *Journal of Social Issues*, Vol. 8 (1952), p. 35.

Blumer, Herbert. "Collective Behavior," in Robert S. Park (ed.). *An Outline of the Principles of Sociology*. New York: Barnes & Noble, 1946.

Booker, H. S., and David, S. T. "Differences in Results Obtained by Experienced and Inexperienced Interviewers," *Journal of the Royal Statistical Society*, Vol. 115, Part 2 (1952), pp. 232-57.

Boyd, H. W., Jr., and Westfall, R. "Interviewers as a Source of Error in Surveys," *Journal of Marketing*, Vol. 19 (April, 1955), pp. 311-24.

Bucher, Rue; Fritz, Charles E.; and Quarantelli, E. L. "Tape Recorded Interviews in Social Research," *American Sociological Review*, Vol. 21, No. 3 (June, 1956).

Burgess, E. W., and Wallin, Paul. *Engagement and Marriage*. Philadelphia: J. B. Lippincott Co., 1953.

Cady, H. M. "On the Psychology of Testimony," *American Journal of Psychology*, Vol. 35 (1924), pp. 110-12.

Cahalan, D.; Tamulonis, V.; and Verner, H. W. "Interviewer Bias Involved in Certain Types of Opinion Survey Questions," *International Journal of Opinion and Attitude Research*, Vol. 1 (March, 1947), pp. 63-77.

Cannell, C. F., and Axelrod, M. "The Respondent Reports on the Interview," *American Journal of Sociology*, Vol. 62 (September, 1956), pp. 177-81.

Cantril, Hadley. "Experiments in the Wording of Questions," *Public Opinion Quarterly*, Vol. 4 (1940), p. 330.

Cantril, Hadley. *The Psychology of Social Movements*. New York: John Wiley & Sons, Inc., 1941, pp. 53-77.

Caplow, T. "The Dynamics of Information Interviewing," *American Journal of Sociology*, Vol. 62 (September, 1956), pp. 165-71.

Chandler, Margaret. "An Evaluation of the Group Interview," *Human Organization*, Vol. 13, No. 2 (Summer, 1954), pp. 26-28.

Clark, John P., and Tifft, Larry L. "Polygraph and Interview Validation of Self-Reported Deviant Behavior," *American Sociological Review,* Vol. 31 (1966), pp. 516-23.

Clive, Victor B. "Ability to Judge Personality Assessed with a Stress Interview and Sound Film Technique," *Journal of Abnormal and Social Psychology,* Vol. 50, No. 2 (March, 1955), pp. 183-87.

Colcord, Joanna C. "A Study of the Techniques of the Social Case Work Interview," *Social Forces,* Vol. 7 (1929), pp. 519-27.

Corey, S. "Professed Attitudes and Actual Behavior," *Journal of Educational Psychology,* Vol. 28 (1937), p. 271.

Crespi, L. P. "The Interview Effect in Polling," *Public Opinion Quarterly,* Vol. 12 (Spring, 1948), pp. 99-111.

Crutchfield, R. S., and Gordon, D. A. "Variations in Respondents' Interpretations of an Opinion-Poll Question," *International Journal of Opinion and Attitude Research,* Vol. 1 (September, 1947), pp. 1-12.

Davies, Martin. "Interviewing Techniques," *New Society,* Vol. 3 (1964).

Dean, J. "Participant Observation and Interviewing," in J. T. Doby (ed.). *An Introduction to Social Research.* Harrisburg, Pa.: The Stackpole Co., 1954.

Dean, Lois R. "Interaction, Reported and Observed," *Human Organization,* Vol. 3 (Fall, 1958), p. 36.

De Graer, Albert. "L'Art de Guerir Chez les Asande," *Congo,* Vol. X, pt. 1, pp. 220-21.

Deschin, C. S. "Research Interviewing in Sensitive Subject Areas: III. Some Further Applications and Suggested Principles," *Social Work,* Vol. 8, No. 2 (1963), pp. 14-18.

Dexter, Lewis A. "Good Will of Important People: More on the Jeopardy of the Interview," *Public Opinion Quarterly,* Vol. 28, No. 4 (Winter, 1964), pp. 556-63.

Dexter, Lewis A. "Role Relationships and Conception of Neutrality in Interviewing," *American Journal of Sociology,* Vol. 62 (September, 1956), pp. 153-57.

Dohrenwend, Barbara Snell, and Richardson, S. A. "Analysis of the Interviewer's Behavior," *Human Organization,* Vol. 15 (Summer, 1956), pp. 29-32.

Dohrenwend, Barbara Snell, and Richardson, S. A. "A Use for Leading Questions in Research Interviewing," *Human Organization,* Vol. 23 (1964), pp. 76-77.

Dohrenwend, Barbara Snell, and Richardson, S. A. "Directiveness and Nondirectiveness in Research Interviewing: A Reformulation of the Problem," *Psychology Bulletin,* Vol. 63, No. 5 (1965), pp. 475-85.

Dorner, K. "Interview and Exploration," *der Newvenarzt,* Vol. 37, No. 1 (1966), pp. 18-25.

Dotson, Floyd. "Intensive Interviewing in Community Research," *Journal of Educational Sociology*, Vol. 27, No. 5 (January, 1954), pp. 225-30.

Drake, Frances. *Manual of Employment Interviewing*. New York: American Management Association, 1946.

Durbin, J., and Stuart, A. "Differences in Response Rates of Experienced and Inexperienced Interviewers," *Journal of the Royal Statistical Society*, Vol. 114, part 2 (1951), pp. 163-95.

Dvorak, B. J.; Fox, F. C.; and Meigh, C. "Tests for Field Survey Interviewers," *Journal of Marketing*, Vol. 16 (January, 1952), pp. 301-6.

Edsall, R. L. "Getting 'Not-at-Homes' to Interview Themselves," *Journal of Marketing*, Vol. 23 (October, 1958), pp. 184-85.

Ekman, Paul. "Body Position, Facial Expression, and Verbal Behavior during Interviews," *Journal of Abnormal and Social Psychology*, Vol. 68, No. 3 (1964), pp. 295-301.

Elkind, David. "Piaget's Semi-clinical Interview and the Study of Spontaneous Religion," *Journal of the Society for the Study of Religions* (1965).

Engel, J. F. "Tape Recorders in Consumer Research," *Journal of Marketing*, Vol. 26 (April, 1962), pp. 73-74.

Fearing, F. "The Appraisal Interview," in MacNemar, Q., and Merrill, M. (eds.). *Studies in Personality*. New York: McGraw-Hill Book Co., 1942.

Feldman, Jacob J.; Hyman, Herbert; and Hart, C. W. "A Field Study of Interviewer Effects on the Quality of Survey Data," *Public Opinion Quarterly* (Winter, 1951-1952).

Fenlason, Anne; Beals, G.; and Abrahamson, A. *Essentials in Interviewing*. Rev. ed. New York: Harper & Row, 1962.

Ferber, Robert. "On the Reliability of Responses Secured in Sample Surveys," *Journal of the American Statistical Association*, Vol. 50 (September, 1955), pp. 788-811.

Ferber, Robert, and Wales, H. G. "Detection and Correction of Interviewer Bias," *Public Opinion Quarterly*, Vol. 16 (Spring, 1952), pp. 107-27.

Festinger, Leon. *A Theory of Cognitive Dissonance*, Evanston, Ill.: Row-Peterson, 1957.

Festinger, Leon, and Katz, Daniel. *Research Methods in the Social Sciences*. New York: Dryden Press, 1953.

Field, Joan B. "The Effect of Praise in a Public Opinion Poll," *Public Opinion Quarterly* (1955), pp. 85-90.

Fields, Harold. "An Analysis of the Use of the Group Oral Interview," *Personnel*, Vol. 27, No. 6 (1951), pp. 480-86.

Finesinger, Jacob E. "Psychiatric Interviewing," *American Journal of Orthopsychiatry*, Vol. 105, No. 3 (September, 1948), pp. 197-204.

Fink, Raymond. "The Retrospective Question," *Public Opinion Quarterly*, Vol. 24, No. 1 (Spring, 1960), pp. 143-48.

Fisher, Herbert. "Interviewer Bias in the Recording Operation," *International Journal of Opinion and Attitude Research,* Vol. 4 (1950), p. 393.

Franzen, R., and Williams, R. J. "A Method for Measuring Error Due to Variance among Interviewers," *Public Opinion Quarterly,* Vol. 20 (Fall, 1956), pp. 587-92.

Freeman, G. L. *et al.* "The Stress Interview," *Journal of Abnormal and Social Psychology,* Vol. 37 (1942), pp. 427- 47.

Frenkel-Brunswik, E. "Dynamic and Cognitive Categorization of Qualitative Material," *Journal of Psychology,* Vol. 25 (1948), pp. 261-77.

Freud, Anna. *Introduction to the Technique of Child Analysis.* New York: Nervous and Mental Disease Publishing Co., 1928.

Garber, C. W., Jr. "Play Techniques for Interviewing on Durable Goods," *Public Opinion Quarterly,* Vol. 15 (Spring, 1951), pp. 139-40.

Gardner, Burleigh B., and Whyte, William F. "Methods for the Study of Human Relations in Industry," *American Sociological Review,* Vol. 11 (1946), p. 509.

Garfinkel, Harold. *Studies In Ethnomethodology.* Englewood Cliffs, N.J.: Prentice-Hall, Inc., 1967.

Garfinkel, Harold. "Studies of the Routine Grounds of Everyday Activities," *Social Problems,* Vol. 11, No. 2 (Winter, 1964), pp. 225-50.

Garrett, A. *Interviewing: Its Principles and Methods.* Family Welfare Association of America, 1942.

Geismar, Ludwig L., and La Sorte, Michael A. "Research Interviewing with Low-Income Families," *Social Work,* Vol. 8, No. 2 (April, 1963), pp. 10-13.

Gill, Merton N.; Newman, Richard; and Redlich, Frederick. *The Initial Interview in Psychiatric Practice.* New York: International Universities Press, 1954.

Goffman, Erving. *The Presentation of Self in Everyday Life.* Edinburgh: University of Edinburgh Social Science Center, 1956.

Goldman, Alfred E. "The Group Depth Interview," *Journal of Marketing,* Vol. 26, No. 3 (July, 1962), pp. 61-68.

Gorden, Raymond L. *An Interaction Analysis of the Depth Interview.* Thesis, University of Chicago, 1954.

Gorden, Raymond L. "Interaction Between Attitude and the Definition of the Situation in the Expression of Opinion," *American Sociological Review,* Vol. 17, No. 1 (1952), pp. 50-58.

Griaule, Marcel. "L'Enquette Orale en Ethologie," *Revue Philosophique de la France,* Vol. 142 (October, 1952), pp. 537-53.

Gross, N., and Mason, W. "Some Methodological Problems of Eight-Hour Interviews," *American Journal of Sociology,* Vol. 59, No. 3 (November, 1953), pp. 197-204.

Guest, Lester. "A New Training Method for Opinion Interviewers," *Public Opinion Quarterly,* Vol. 18 (Fall, 1954), pp. 287-99.

Guest, Lester, and Nuckols, R. "A Laboratory Experiment in Recording in Public Opinion Interviewing," *International Journal of Opinion and Attitude Research,* Vol. 4 (Fall, 1950), pp. 336-52.

Gusfield, Joseph R. "Field Work Reciprocities in Studying a Social Movement," *Human Organization,* Vol. 14, No. 3 (Fall, 1955), pp. 29-33.

Haberman, Paul W., and Sheinbergh, Jill. "Education Reported in Interviews: An Aspect of Survey Content Error," *Public Opinion Quarterly,* Vol. 30, No. 2 (Summer, 1966), pp. 259-301.

Hall, Edward T. *The Silent Language.* New York: Doubleday Co., Inc., 1959.

Hammond, Phillip E. (ed.). *Sociologists at Work: Essays on the Craft of Social Research.* New York: Basic Books, 1964.

Hamovitch, Maurice B. "Research Interviewing in Terminal Illness," *Social Work,* Vol. 8, No. 2 (April, 1963), pp. 4-9.

Hanson, Robert H., and Marks, Eli S. "Influence of the Interviewer on the Accuracy of Survey Results," *Journal of the American Statistical Association,* Vol. 53 (September, 1958), pp. 635-55.

Hare, Paul A. "Interview Responses: Personality or Conformity?" *Public Opinion Quarterly,* Vol. 24, No. 4 (Winter, 1960), pp. 679-85.

Hare, Paul A., and Davie, James S. "The Group Interview," *Sociology and Social Research,* Vol. 29, No. 2 (November-December, 1954), pp. 81-87.

Harral, Stewart. *Keys to Successful Interviewing.* Norman: University of Oklahoma Press, 1954.

Hart, Clyde. "Bias in Interviewing," *American Philosophical Society Proceedings,* Vol. 92, No. 5 (1948), p. 399.

Heath, Clark W. "An Interview Method for Obtaining Personal Histories," *New England Journal of Medicine,* Vol. 234 (1946), pp. 251-57.

Heyns, Roger W., and Lippitt, Ronald. "Systematic Observation Techniques," in Gardner Lindzey (ed.). *Handbook of Social Psychology,* Vol. I. Reading, Mass.: Addison-Wesley Publishing Co., 1954.

Hildum, D. C., and Brown, R. W. "Verbal Reinforcement and Interviewer Bias," *Journal of Abnormal and Social Psychology,* Vol. 52 (July, 1956), pp. 100-111.

Homans, George C. *Social Behavior: Its Elementary Forms.* New York: Harcourt, Brace and World, Inc., 1961.

Hyman, Herbert H. "Do They Tell the Truth?" *Public Opinion Quarterly,* Vol. 8 (1944), pp. 557-59.

Hyman, Herbert H. *et al. Interviewing in Social Research.* Chicago: University of Chicago Press, 1954.

Janes, Robert W. "A Note on Phases of the Community Role of the Participant-Observer," *American Sociological Review,* Vol. 26, No. 3 (June, 1961), pp. 446-50.

Jonsson, Erland. "On the Formulation of Questions in Medico-Hygienic Interview Investigations," *Acta Sociologica,* 1963.

Kahn, Robert L., and Cannell, Charles F. *The Dynamics of Interviewing.* New York: John Wiley and Sons, Inc., 1957.

Katz, Daniel. "Do Interviewers Bias Poll Results?" *Public Opinion Quarterly,* Vol. 6 (Summer, 1942), pp. 248-68.

Kemsley, W. F. F. "Interviewer Variability and a Budget Survey," *Applied Statistics,* Vol. 9, No. 2 (June, 1960), pp. 122-28.

Kephart, Newell C. *The Employment Interview in Industry.* New York: McGraw-Hill Book Co., 1952.

Kincaid, H. V., and Bright, M. "Interviewing the Business Elite," *American Journal of Sociology,* Vol. 63 (November, 1957), pp. 304-11.

Kincaid, H. V., and Bright, M. "The Tandem Interview: A Trial of the Two-Interviewer Team," *Public Opinion Quarterly,* Vol. 21 (Summer, 1957), pp. 304-12.

Kinsey, Alfred C. *et al.* "Interviewing," *Sexual Behavior in the Human Male.* Philadelphia: W. B. Saunders Co., 1948.

Kish, Leslie. "Studies of Interviewer Variance for Attitudinal Variables," *Journal of the American Statistical Association,* Vol. 57 (March, 1962), pp. 92-115.

Klare, G. "Understandability and Indefinite Answers," *International Journal of Opinion and Attitude Research,* Vol. 4 (1950), p. 91.

Krause, Louise. *Personal Adjustment in Old Age.* Thesis, University of Chicago, 1950.

Krugman, Herbert E. "Interviewing Ex-Communists in the United States," *Public Opinion Quarterly,* Vol. 20, No. 2 (Summer, 1956), pp. 473-77.

Langdon, Grace. *Teacher-Parent Interviews.* New York: Prentice-Hall, 1954.

Lasswell, Harold. "The Contribution of Freud's Insight Interview to the Social Sciences," *American Journal of Sociology,* Vol. 45 (1939), p. 375.

Lazarsfeld, Paul. "The Controversy over Detailed Interviews—an Offer for Negotiation," *Public Opinion Quarterly,* Vol. 8 (Spring, 1944).

Leighton, Alexander. *The Governing of Men.* Princeton: Princeton University Press, 1945.

Lennings, Mary J. "Explorations of the Personalistic Approach in Interviews with Mexican Entrants to the United States," *Civilizations,* Vol. 14, No. 4 (1964), pp. 289-313.

Lenski, Gerhard E., and Leggett, John C. "Caste, Class and Deference in the Research Interview," *American Journal of Sociology,* Vol. 65 (1960), pp. 463-67.

Lerner, Daniel. "Interviewing Frenchmen," *American Journal of Sociology,* Vol. 62, No. 2 (September, 1956), pp. 184-87.

Lewis, Oscar. *Life in a Mexican Village: Tepoztlan Restudied.* Urbana: University of Illinois Press, 1951.

Lindzey, Gardner. "A Note on Interviewer Bias," *Journal of Applied Psychology,* Vol. 35 (June, 1951), pp. 182-84.

Litwak, Eugene. "A Classification of Biased Questions," *American Journal of Sociology,* Vol. 62, No. 2 (September, 1956), pp. 182-88.

Maas, James B. "Patterned Scaled Expectation Interview: Reliability Studies on a New Technique," *Journal of Applied Psychology,* Vol. 49, No. 6 (1963), pp. 413-33.

Maccoby, Eleanor E., and Maccoby, Nathan. "The Interview: A Tool of Social Science," in Gardner Lindzey (ed.). *Handbook of Social Psychology,* Vol. 1, chap. 12. Reading, Mass.: Addison-Wesley Publishing Co., Inc., 1954.

Maier, Norman R. F. *The Appraisal Interview: Objectives, Methods and Skills.* New York: John Wiley and Sons, Inc., 1958.

Maier, Norman R. F.; Hoffman, L. Richard; and Lansky, Leonard M. "Human Relations Training as Manifested in an Interview Situation," *Personnel Psychology,* Vol. 13 (1960), pp. 11-30.

Manniche, E., and Hayes, D. P. "Respondent Anonymity and Data Matching," *Public Opinion Quarterly,* Vol. 21 (Fall, 1957), pp. 384-88.

Matarazzo, Joseph D., and Wiens, Arthur N. "Interviewer Effects on Interviewee's Speech and Silence Durations," *Proceedings of the 74th Annual Convention of the American Psychological Association* (1966).

Mauldin, W. P., and Marks, E. S. "Problems of Response in Enumerative Surveys," *American Sociological Review,* Vol. 15 (October, 1950), pp. 649-57.

McGinnis, Robert. "Scaling Interview Data," *American Sociological Review,* Vol. 18 (October, 1953).

Menzel, H., and Katz, E. "Social Relations and Innovation in the Medical Profession: The Epidemiology of a New Drug," *Public Opinion Quarterly,* Vol. 19 (1956), pp. 337-52.

Merton, Robert K. *The Focused Interview: A Manual of Problems and Procedures.* New York: The Free Press, 1956.

Miller, S. M. "The Participant-Observer and 'Over-Rapport,' " *American Sociological Review,* Vol. 17 (1952), pp. 97-99.

Mills, C. Wright. "Situated Action and the Vocabulary of Motives," *American Sociological Review,* Vol. 6 (December, 1940), pp. 904-13.

Moore, B. V. "The Interview in Industrial Research," *Social Forces,* Vol. 7 (1929), pp. 445-52.

Moore, Mary Rowena. *The Effects of Two Interviewing Techniques on Academic Achievement and Certain Non-intellectual Factors Affecting Academic*

Success. Thesis, Indiana University, 1958. University of Michigan Microfilm 1916.

Moos, Rudolf H., and Porter, Langley. "The Retention and Generalization of Operant Conditioning Effects in an Interview Situation," *Journal of Abnormal and Social Psychology,* Vol. 66, No. 1 (January, 1963), pp. 52-58.

Morrison, Denton E. "A Boxing System for Interview Schedules," *American Sociological Review,* Vol. 23, No. 1 (February, 1958), pp. 83-84.

Moscovici, S. "Attitudes and Opinions," *Annual Review of Psychology,* Vol. 14 (1963), pp. 231-60.

Murray, Henry A. "Dyadic Creations," in Warren G. Bennis *et al. Interpersonal Dynamics.* Homewood, Ill.: Dorsey Press, 1964.

Muscio, B. "On the Influence of the Form of a Question," *British Journal of Psychology,* Vol. 8, pp. 351-89.

Namias, Jean. "Measuring Variation in Interviewer Performance," *Journal of Advertising Research,* Vol. 6, No. 1 (March, 1966), pp. 8-12.

National Opinion Research Center. *Interviewing for NORC.* Denver, 1947.

Newstetter, W. I. "Social Psychological Problems in Relation to Social Work Practice and Theory," in Sherif, Muzafer, and Wilson, M. O. (eds.). *Emerging Problems in Social Psychology Series III.* Norman, Okla.: The University Book Exchange, 1957.

Oldfield, R. C. "The Display and Perception of Attitudes," in *The Psychology of the Interview.* London: Methuen, 1947.

Parker, C. A.; Wright, E. W.; and Clark, S. G. "Questions Concerning the Interview as a Research Technique," *Journal of Educational Research,* Vol. 51 (November, 1957), pp. 215-21.

Parsons, Talcott, and Bales, Robert F. *Family, Socialization and Interaction Process.* New York: The Free Press, 1955.

Paul, B. D. "Interview Techniques and Field Relationships," in A. L. Kroeber (ed.). *Anthropology Today.* Chicago: The University of Chicago Press, 1953.

Payne, S. L. *The Art of Asking Questions.* Princeton: Princeton University Press, 1951.

Phillips, Bernard S. *Social Research, Strategy and Tactics.* New York: Macmillan Co., 1966.

Podell, Lawrence. "An Interviewing Problem in Values Research," *Sociology and Social Research,* Vol. 41, No. 2 (November-December, 1956), pp. 121-26.

Redl, Fritz. "Strategy and Techniques of the Life Space Interview," *American Journal of Orthopsychiatry,* Vol. XXIX, No. 1 (January, 1959).

Reece, M. M., and Whitman, R. N. "Expressive Movements, Warmth and Verbal Reinforcements," *Journal of Abnormal and Social Psychology,* Vol. 64 (1962), pp. 234-36.

Rice, Stuart A. "Contagious Bias in the Interview: A Methodological Note," *American Journal of Sociology,* Vol. 35 (1929), pp. 420-23.

Richardson, Stephen A. "Training in Field Relations Skills," *Journal of Social Issues,* Vol. 8, No. 3 (1953).

Richardson, Stephen A. "The Use of Leading Questions in Non-schedule Interviews," *Human Organization,* Vol. 19, No. 2 (1960), pp. 86-89.

Richardson, Stephen A.; Dohrenwend, Barbara Snell; and Klein, David. *Interviewing, Its Forms and Functions.* New York: Basic Books, Inc., 1965.

Riesman, David. "Orbits of Tolerance, Interviewer, and Elites," *Public Opinion Quarterly,* Vol. 20, No. 1 (Spring, 1956), pp. 49-73.

Riesman, David, and Benney, Mark. "Asking and Answering," *Journal of Business,* Vol. 29 (October, 1956), pp. 225-36.

Riesman, David, and Glazer, Nathan. "An Experiment in the Interpretation of an Interview," *International Journal of Opinion and Attitude Research,* Vol. 4 (Winter, 1950-51), pp. 515-40; Vol. 5 (Spring, 1951), pp. 53-78.

Roethlisberger, F. J., and Dickson, W. J. "Interviewing Methods," in *Management and the Worker.* Cambridge, Mass.: Harvard University Press, 1946.

Rogers, Carl R. "The Characteristics of a Helping Relationship," in *On Becoming a Person.* Boston: Houghton Mifflin, 1961.

Rogers, Carl R. "The Non-directive Method as a Technique for Social Research," *American Journal of Sociology,* Vol. 51 (1945), p. 143.

Rogers, Carl R., and Roethlisberger, F. J. "Barriers and Gateways to Communication," *Harvard Business Review,* Vol. 30, No. 4 (July-August, 1952), pp. 46-52.

Rose, Arnold. *Human Behavior and Social Processes.* Boston: Houghton Mifflin Co., 1962.

Rose, Arnold. "Interviewing to Test for Validity and Reliability," *International Journal of Opinion and Attitude Research,* Vol. I (1947), p. 100.

Rose, Arnold M. "A Researcher Note on Experimentation in Interviewing," *American Journal of Sociology,* Vol. 51 (1945), pp. 143-44.

Rosenthal, Robert. *Experimenter Effects in Behavioral Research.* New York: Appleton, Century, Crofts, 1966.

Roth, Julius A. *Timetables: Structuring the Passage of Time in Hospital Treatment and Other Careers.* Indianapolis: The Bobbs-Merrill Company, 1963.

Ruch, F. L. "Effects of Repeated Interviewing on the Respondent's Answers," *Journal of Consulting Psychology,* Vol. 5 (July-August, 1941), pp. 179-82.

Salzinger, K., and Pisoni, Stephanie. "Reinforcement of Verbal Affect Responses of Normal Subjects during an Interview," *Journal of Abnormal and Social Psychology,* Vol. 60 (1960), pp. 127-30.

Sapir, Edward. "The Unconscious Patterning of Behavior in Society," in E. S.

Dummer (ed.). *The Unconscious: A Symposium.* New York: A. A. Knopf, 1927.

Schatzman, Leonard, and Strauss, Anselm. "Social Class and Mode of Communication," *American Journal of Sociology,* Vol. 60, No. 4 (1955), pp. 329-38.

Schutz, Alfred. *Collected Papers.* Maurice Natanson (ed.). The Hague: Martinus Nijhoff, 1962.

Schwartz, Morris S., and Schwartz, Charlotte Green. "Problems in Participant Observation," *American Journal of Sociology* (January, 1955), pp. 343-53.

Scott, Marvin B., and Stanford, Lyman M. "Accounts," *American Sociological Review,* Vol. 33, No. 1 (February, 1968), pp. 46-62.

Sears, Robert R. "Comparison of Interviews with Questionnaires for Measuring Mothers' Attitudes towards Sex and Aggression," *Journal of Personality and Social Psychology,* Vol. 2, No. 1 (July, 1965), pp. 37-44.

Sewell, William H. "Field Techniques in Social Psychological Study in a Rural Community," *American Sociological Review,* Vol. 14 (1949), pp. 718-26.

Shapiro, S., and Eberhart, J. "Interviewer Differences in an Intensive Survey," *International Journal of Opinion and Attitude Research,* Vol. 1, No. 2 (1947), p. 1.

Shaw, Clifford R. *Brothers in Crime.* Chicago: University of Chicago Press, 1938.

Sheatsley, P. B. "An Analysis of Interviewer Characteristics and Their Relationship to Performance," *International Journal of Opinion and Attitude Research,* Vol. 4 (Winter, 1950-51), pp. 473-98; Vol. 5 (Spring, 1951), pp. 79-94; Vol. 5 (Summer, 1951), pp. 101-220.

Sheatsley, P. B. "Closed Questions Are Sometimes More Valid than Open End," *Public Opinion Quarterly,* Vol. 12 (1948), p. 12.

Sidney, Elizabeth, and Brown, Margaret. *The Skills of Interviewing.* London: Tavistock Publishing Co., 1961.

Sjoberg, G. "The Interviewer as a Marginal Man," *The South-Western Social Science Quarterly,* Vol. 38 (September, 1957), pp. 125-32.

Smigel, E. O. "Interviewing a Legal Elite: The Wall Street Lawyer," *American Journal of Sociology,* Vol. 64 (September, 1958), pp. 159-64.

Smith, H. L., and Hyman, Herbert. "The Biasing Effect of Interviewer Expectations on Survey Results," *Public Opinion Quarterly,* Vol. 14 (Fall, 1950), pp. 491-506.

Star, Shirley A. "Obtaining Household Opinions from a Single Respondent," *Public Opinion Quarterly,* Vol. 17 (Fall, 1953), pp. 386-91.

Stember, C. H., and Hyman, H. H. "How Interviewer Effects Operate Through Question Form," *International Journal of Opinion and Attitude Research,* Vol. 3 (1949), pp. 493-512.

Stember, Herbert. "Which Respondents are Reliable?" *International Journal of Opinion and Attitude Research,* Vol. 5 (Winter, 1951-52), pp. 475-79.

Stember, Herbert, and Hyman, Herbert. "Interviewer Effects in the Classification of Responses," *Public Opinion Quarterly,* Vol. 13 (Winter, 1949), pp. 669-82.

Stephan, F. F. "Public Relations and Research Interviewing," *Public Opinion Quarterly,* Vol. 28 (1964), p. 118.

Stock, J. S., and Hochstim, J. R. "A Method of Measuring Interviewer Variability," *Public Opinion Quarterly,* Vol. 15 (Summer, 1951), pp. 322-34.

Stycos, J. M. "Interviewer Training in Another Culture," *Public Opinion Quarterly,* Vol. 16 (Summer, 1952), pp. 236-46.

Sudman, Seymour. "Time Allocation in Survey Interviewing and in Other Field Occupations," *Public Opinion Quarterly,* Vol. 29 (1965), pp. 638-48.

Sullivan, Harry S. *The Psychiatric Interview.* New York: W. W. Norton and Co., Inc., 1954.

Sutherland, E. H. *The Professional Thief.* Chicago: University of Chicago Press, 1937.

Symonds, P. M., and Dietrich, D. H. "The Effect of Variations in the Time Interval Between an Interview and Its Recording," *Journal of Abnormal and Social Psychology,* Vol. 36 (1941), pp. 346-53.

Taietz, Philip. "Conflicting Group Norms and the Third Person in the Interview," *American Journal of Sociology,* Vol. 68, No. 1 (July, 1962), pp. 97-104.

Thomas, Dorothy S., and Nishimoto, R. S. *The Spoilage.* Berkeley: University of California Press, 1946.

Thumin, F. J. "Watch for Those Unseen Variables," *Journal of Marketing,* Vol. 26 (July, 1962), pp. 58-60.

Toman, W. "Pause Analysis as a Short Interviewing Technique," *Journal of Consulting Psychology,* Vol. 17, No. 1 (1953), pp. 1-7.

Vaughn, C. L., and Reynolds, W. A. "Reliability of Personal Interview Data," *Journal of Applied Psychology,* Vol. 35 (February, 1951), pp. 61-63.

Vidich, A., and Bensman, J. "The Validity of Field Data," *Human Organization,* Vol. 13, No. 1 (Spring, 1954), pp. 20-27.

Vidich, A., and Shapiro, A. "Comparison of Participant Observation and Survey Data," *American Sociological Review,* Vol. 20, No. 1 (February, 1955), pp. 28-33.

Volkart, Edmund H. (ed.). *Social Behavior and Personality.* New York: Social Science Research Council, 1951.

Wales, Hugh G., and Ferber, Robert. *A Basic Bibliography on Marketing Research.* 2d ed. Chicago: American Marketing Association, 1963.

Wallen, R. "Ego Involvement as a Determinant of Selective Forgetting," *Journal of Abnormal and Social Psychology,* Vol. 37 (1942), pp. 20-39.

Wallin, Paul. "An Appraisal of Some Methodological Aspects of the Kinsey Report," *American Sociological Review,* Vol. 14 (1949), pp. 197-210.

Walsh, Bruce W. "Validity of Self-Report," *Journal of Counseling Psychology,* Vol. 14, No. 1 (1967), pp. 18-23.

Ware, Caroline F. *Greenwich Village 1920 to 1930.* Boston: Houghton Mifflin Co., 1935.

Ware, J. R.; Kowal, B.; and Baker, R. A. *The Role of Experimenter Attitude and Contingent Reinforcement in a Vigilance Task.* Unpublished paper, U.S. Army Armor Human Research Unit, Fort Knox, Kentucky, 1963.

Warner, William Lloyd, and Lunt, P. S. "Field Techniques," in *Social Life of a Modern Community.* New Haven: Yale University Press, 1941.

Wax, M., and Shapiro, L. J. "Repeated Interviewing," *American Journal of Sociology,* Vol. 62 (September, 1956), pp. 215-17.

Weinland, James D., and Gross, Margaret V. *Personnel Interviewing.* New York: The Ronald Press Company, 1952.

Weiss, D. J., and Davis, R. V. "An Objective Validation of Factual Interview Data," *Journal of Applied Psychology,* Vol. 44 (December, 1960), pp. 381-85.

Whyte, William F. "Interviewing for Organizational Research," *Human Organization,* Vol. 12, No. 3 (Summer, 1953), pp. 15-22.

Whyte, William F. *Street Corner Society: The Social Structure of an Italian Slum.* Chicago: University of Chicago Press, 1943.

Wilkie, Charlotte H. "A Study of Distortions in Recording Interviews," *Social Work,* Vol. 8, No. 3 (July, 1963), pp. 31-36.

Willingham, W. W., and Jones, M. B. "On the Identification of Halo through Analysis of Variance," *Educational and Psychological Measurement,* Vol. 18 (Summer, 1958), pp. 403-7.

Wilson, Elmo C., and Armstrong, Lincoln. "Interviewers and Interviewing in India," *International Social Science Journal,* Vol. 15, No. 1 (1963), pp. 48-58.

Womer, S., and Boyd, H. W., Jr. "The Use of a Voice Recorder in the Selection and Training of Field Workers," *Public Opinion Quarterly,* Vol. 15 (Summer, 1951), pp. 358-63.

Wyatt, D. F., and Campbell, D. T. "A Study of Interviewer Bias as Related to Interviewers' Expectations and Own Opinions," *International Journal of Opinion and Attitude Research,* Vol. 4 (1950), pp. 77-83.

Young, Pauline V. *Interviewing in Social Work.* New York: McGraw-Hill Book Co., 1935.

Zygmunt, Joseph F. *The Role and Interrelationship of Symbolic and Structural Processes in the Development of a Sectarian Movement.* Thesis, University of Chicago, 1960.

Index

*This book has been set in 11 and 10 point Press
Roman, leaded 2 points. Chapter numbers and
titles are 16 point Helvetica Bold. The size of
the type page is 27 by 46 picas.*